A POPULAR

HISTORY OF ENGLAND,

FROM THE EARLIEST TIMES

TO THE ACCESSION OF QUEEN VICTORIA

BY

FRANÇOIS PIERRE GUILLAUME GUIZOT, LL.D.,

MEMBER OF THE FRENCH ACADEMY, THE ROYAL SOCIETY (LONDON), THE SOCIETY
OF ANTIQUARIES (LONDON); AMBASSADOR AT THE COURT OF
ST. JAMES; PRIME MINISTER OF FRANCE
UNDER LOUIS PHILIPPE, ETC.

ESTES AND LAURIAT'S

LIBRARY OF STANDARD HISTORY.

GUIZOT'S POPULAR HISTORY OF ENGLAND,

FROM THE EARLIEST TIMES TO THE ACCESSION OF VICTORIA.

Four Vols., Royal Octavo.

GUIZOT'S POPULAR HISTORY OF FRANCE,

FROM THE EARLIEST TIMES TO THE FIRST REVOLUTION.

Six Vols., Royal Octavo.

HENRI MARTIN'S POPULAR HISTORY OF FRANCE,

FROM THE FIRST REVOLUTION TO THE PRESENT TIME.

Three Vols., Royal Octavo.

ALFRED RAMBAUD'S POPULAR HISTORY OF RUSSIA,

FROM THE EARLIEST TIMES TO 1880.

Three Vols., Royal Octavo.

Each of the above works are issued in uniform style. They are illustrated with wood and steel plates, by the best artists, are printed in the best manner, on superfine paper.

PRICE PER VOLUME:

Cloth, Bevelled, ...	$5.50
Library Sheep, Marbled Edge, ...	6.50
Half Calf, Extra, " "	7.50
Half Mor., " " "	7.50
Full Morocco, or Tree Calf, Gilt, ...	10.00

IN PREPARATION:

A POPULAR HISTORY OF GERMANY,

FROM THE EARLIEST TO THE PRESENT TIME.

G. Staal del. Massard sc.

ELISABETH.

Estes and Lauriat, Boston

A POPULAR

HISTORY OF ENGLAND,

FROM THE

EARLIEST TIMES TO THE ACCESSION OF VICTORIA.

By M. GUIZOT,

AUTHOR OF "A POPULAR HISTORY OF FRANCE," "THE HISTORY OF CIVILIZATION," "HISTORY OF THE REVOLUTION IN ENGLAND," ETC.

TRANSLATED BY

M. M. RIPLEY.

Fully Illustrated with Wood and Steel Plates,

FROM DRAWINGS BY THE MOST CELEBRATED ARTISTS, AMONG WHOM ARE A. DE NEUVILLE, SIR JOHN GILBERT, P. LEYENDECKER, G. STAAL, EMILE BAYARD, T. WEBER.

Vol. II.

BOSTON:

DANA ESTES AND CHARLES E. LAURIAT,

301 Washington Street.

ELECTROTYPED
AT THE BOSTON STEREOTYPE FOUNDRY,
19 SPRING LANE.

Printed at the University Press, Cambridge.

TABLE OF CONTENTS.

VOLUME II.

LIST OF PLATES AND ILLUSTRATIONS.

VOLUME II.

A POPULAR

HISTORY OF ENGLAND

FROM THE EARLIEST TIMES.

CHAPTER XIV.

HENRY VI. 1422–1461.

NO life in its brevity had been more active than that of Henry V., and no monarch was more bitterly lamented; he was so even in France, for the people saw themselves thrown back into the horrors of internal dissensions; he was mourned for in England, with sincere and profound grief. After the magnificent ceremonies performed in France, the body was brought to England, and solemnly interred at Westminster, beside the shrine of Edward the Confessor. King James of Scotland was chief mourner, while the Duke of Bedford, profoundly sad, seized in France the ill-secured power which his dying brother had confided to him, and endeavored to secure the two crowns upon the head of the child destined to lose them both.

The religious ceremonies had been prolonged in France. Queen Catherine was embarking in the month of October, accompanying her husband's body, when her father, King Charles VI., died of quartan ague. Notwithstanding his thirty years of madness, and the evils which they had suffered under his reign, the French had remained attached to their unhappy monarch, and the populace thronged the hall of the Hôtel St. Paul, where his remains lay in state. "Ah! dear prince!" it was said, amid tears, "never shall we have one as good as you; you have gone to your rest; we remain in tribulation and grief, and seem made to fall into the distress in which were the children of Israel during the Babylonish captivity." The Duke of Burgundy was bitterly reproached for not having visited the king during his sickness, and for not having followed his funeral; the Duke of Bedford was chief mourner, and on the 10th of November, 1422, in England and in France, at Westminster and at Saint-Denis, the obsequies of King Henry V. and those of King Charles VI. were solemnly performed. The royal remains being lowered into the grave, the heralds broke their wands, and cried, "God grant long life to Henry, by the grace of God King of France and of England, our sovereign Lord." And the people shouted, "Long live the king!" The hand which was to bear this weighty inheritance was not yet one year old.

The Duke of Bedford had taken the reins of government in France without opposition; in England, the lords of the Parliament had contested the right of the deceased king to designate the regent of the kingdom, and had given to the Duke of Gloucester the title of Protector of the State and of the Church, which was to remind him, it was said, of his duties. Henry Beaufort, Bishop of Winchester, King Henry IV.'s half-brother, was appointed to second the Earl of Warwick in the education of the little king. Parliament voted the necessary subsidies, and the war in France continued.

The death of Charles VI. had rallied a few adherents around the Dauphin, proclaimed King of France at Mehun-sur-Yèvres, in Berry, under the name of Charles VII. Shortly afterwards he caused himself to be crowned at Poitiers, Rheims being in the power of the English. Right was upon the side of Charles, dispossessed as he was; the memory of the kings his ancestors, the natural aversion to foreigners, increased by eighty years of war, fought in his favor; even the noblemen who did not rally around him were less eager to serve the Duke of Bedford than they had been to second Henry V., and already it had been necessary to stifle, at Poissy, a trifling insurrection in favor of the Dauphin.

Meanwhile, the Duke of Bedford had caused all the large towns and constituent bodies in France to swear fidelity to his nephew, and in order to strengthen that intimacy with the Duke of Burgundy which had preoccupied King Henry even upon his deathbed, he had married Anne of Burgundy, the Duke's sister. Madame de Guienne, the widow of the first Dauphin, shortly afterwards gave her hand to the Count of Richemont, brother of the Duke of Brittany, and a solemn treaty of friendship united the three dukes to each other. Brittany and Burgundy, at the same time, concluded a private alliance unknown to the Duke of Bedford.

The Regent was returning from Troyes, where his marriage had been celebrated, and was fighting upon the way, when he learned that the Earl of Buchan was attacking his fortress of Crevant-sur-Yonne, endeavoring to open a communication between the northern territories, which recognized the authority of Charles VII., and the southern provinces, where his cause had made great progress. The Earls of Salisbury and Suffolk were immediately dispatched to relieve Crevant; a troop of Burgundians joined them. The Duke of Bedford's orders were precise: the archers had carried their stakes, and the battle was to be fought on foot, as at Agincourt, giving no quarter to the enemy. The army of King Charles VII. was, it was said, superior in numbers to that of the English.

On arriving before Crevant, the assailants found themselves arrested by the river Yonne, and remained two days in sight of the enemy; when the English had at length forced a passage, they attacked the Scots, leaving the French troops to the Burgundians. "There is no other antidote for the English than the Scots," said Pope Martin V. after the battle of Baugé; but at Crevant the Scots were defeated. The French had promptly yielded, only the bravest knights had supported their allies; Lord Buchan and the Count of Ventadour had each lost an eye, and were carried prisoners as well as Saintrailles, a famous Armagnac knight, when the English returned to Paris in triumph. But Scotland was not exhausted of knights in search of adventure. Archibald Douglas had just landed at La Rochelle with five thousand men, and King Charles VII., in his gratitude, conferred upon him the title of Duke of Touraine; he loaded with honors the other Scottish noblemen, of whom several finally became naturalized in France; the barons began to complain of the favors which the king lavished upon his foreign allies; the Duke of Milan had sent him a large reinforcement of Italians.

The Duke of Bedford was made uneasy by the relief which continually arrived from Scotland to his adversaries, and he hoped to dry up the source of it by sending back King James into his dominions. Negotiations had been set on foot; the marriage of the captive prince with Jane Beaufort, daughter of the Earl of Somerset, and niece of the Bishop of Winchester, had been celebrated; the ransom was arranged, and James I. returned to Scotland after nineteen years of captivity, there to govern with an honest firmness to which his people had not been accustomed. But the tide of emigration towards France, slightly slackened, had not however ceased. The justice of the king was rigorously exercised upon the old enemies of his family, and a considerable number of Scottish knights, flying from his anger, took refuge in the army of Charles VII. It was with their assistance that the royalist noblemen marched, in the month of August, against Ivry, in Normandy, which the Duke of Bedford was attacking. But the position of the English was strong; discord reigned in the French army, deprived of its head by the indolence of Charles VII. Douglas and Buchan wished to make an attack; the Count of Alençon and the Count of Aumale refused their consent to it, and drew the army with them. In withdrawing they surprised Verneuil; the town was important, and the Duke of Bedford followed the French thither. A tumultuous council resolved to repulse him in the open plain; the royalists, all on foot, quitted Verneuil; the Milanese alone remained on horseback. The English awaited the attack from behind the stakes of their archers. "Let us allow them to come," said Douglas; but the French noblemen despised the adventurers, as they called their valiant allies, and themselves made the attack. The combat was terrible; at one moment, La Hire and Saintrailles, at the head of the Milanese, broke the reserve of the archers; but reinforcements from the main army repulsed them, and they were completely routed. Douglas was slain, as well as his son. Lord Buchan lay upon the field of battle with the Counts of Narbonne, Tonnerre, and Ventadour; the Count of Alençon and the Marshal de la Fayette were prisoners. On his side, the Duke of Bedford had suffered, but the army of King Charles VII. was destroyed; the town of Verneuil surrendered immediately, and the Duke of Bedford caused to be beheaded those of the prisoners who, having sworn allegiance to his nephew, had not kept their oaths.

Bedford conducted affairs in France with firmness and prudence, but he was thwarted in his policy by the thoughtless and passionate acts of his brother, the Duke of Gloucester. The latter had become smitten with Jacqueline of Hainault, the daughter and heiress of the Count of Hainault, and married, in the first instance, to the second Dauphin, John, poisoned at Compiègne. Still young at the death of that prince, she had married the Duke of Brabant; but she had soon conceived a horror of her husband, who had, she said, the taste for favorites of low degree, and abandoning him after three years of union, she had taken refuge in England, where King Henry IV. had received her with great honors. He had, however, opposed his brother's matrimonial project, and upon his deathbed had recommended him to renounce it. The Pope, Martin V., had refused to annul the marriage of Jacqueline of Hainault with the Duke of Brabant; but she pleaded the degree of relationship, and addressed herself to the anti-Pope, Benedict XIII., who had refused to submit to the decision of the Council of Constance to cause the termination of the schism. Too happy to perform pontifical functions, Benedict pronounced the nullity of the marriage, and the Duke of Gloucester espoused Jacqueline of Hainault. The remonstrances of the Duke of Burgundy became more urgent; he had, from the first moment, defended the rights of his cousin, the Duke of Brabant, proposing to refer the case to the arbitration of the Duke of Bedford. "I am content," said he, "that we should take as judge my very dear and beloved cousin and also your brother, the regent, Duke of Bedford, for he is such a prince, that I know that to you and to me and to all others, he would be an upright judge." The Duke of Gloucester had listened to no remonstrance, and the dangerous disaffection of Duke Philip was secretly becoming graver, when, shortly after the battle of Verneuil, Gloucester and Jacqueline landed at Calais with a body of English soldiers, notwithstanding the entreaties of their uncle Beaufort, in England, and those of the Duke of Bedford in France; they traversed the dominions of the Duke of Burgundy, and attacked the Duke of Brabant in Hainault; they had already taken possession of Mons, when the Duke of Burgundy, in a state of fury, wrote to Gloucester, to challenge him to single combat. At the same time he sent considerable assistance to the Duke of Brabant, accepting for that object the service of his former enemies; Saintrailles was among the number of the knights who went to fight against the English in the Low Countries. The bonds which united the House of Burgundy to England were beginning to be weakened, and the Pope was already working secretly in concert with the Duke of Savoy to negotiate an agreement with Charles VII. The Duke of Gloucester had returned to England; fearing the influence of his uncle Beaufort, he had left with Jacqueline the task of defending her inheritance. Scarcely had he departed, when the majority of the towns opened their gates to the Duke of Burgundy; and Jacqueline, at first shut up in Mons, then led a captive to Ghent, escaped with great difficulty and took refuge in Holland.

So much imprudence and self-seeking on the part of his nephew had irritated the Bishop of Winchester so far as to bring about an open quarrel. The Duke of Bedford was compelled to repair to England towards the end of the year 1425 to prevent bloodshed between the two parties. He had some trouble in effecting a reconciliation, sincere on the part of the Duke of Gloucester, whose character was as frank as it was impetuous; doubtful in the case of the priest, more implacable than the warrior. The Bishop of Winchester resigned the seals, and finding himself elevated by Martin V. to the dignity of the Cardinalate, he quitted England with the Duke of Bedford. The latter had been recalled to France by the defection of the Duke of Brittany, who had recently declared himself in favor of King Charles VII. at the instigation of his brother, the Count of Richemont, who had some time before returned to his allegiance, and whom the king had made Constable. Scarcely had Bedford set foot upon French soil, when he sent an army into Brittany; the country was devastated, the Duke of Brittany was shut up within Rennes and so closely pressed that he found himself compelled to sever his alliance with the King of France; he swore for the second time to the treaty of Troyes, and did homage to the little king Henry VI.

The Pope, Martin V., had solemnly declared the nullity of the marriage of Jacqueline of Hainault with the Duke of Gloucester, and the latter had consoled himself for this by espousing Eleanor Cobham, formerly a lady of his wife's household. The Countess Jacqueline still held out bravely in Holland. The Duke of Brabant had recently died; his brother, who had succeeded him, had no claim upon Jacqueline or upon her dominions. She would have been free if the enemy whom she had raised up had not been too powerful and too greedy to relinquish an affair so well under way. From town to town, from territory to territory, the Duke of Burgundy prosecuted his conquest, and Jacqueline, abandoned by nearly all her vassals, defeated by sea and land, at length consented, in the summer of 1428, to recognize Duke Philip as her heir, and to intrust to him immediately the government of her dominions. The duke, satisfied with the English, who had not hindered him in this last act of his ambition, promised troops for the great expedition which was in preparation against the country beyond the Loire, now almost entirely loyal to King Charles VII.

The war had languished since the battle of Verneuil; the King of France was poor, indolent, and delivered up to favorites. The Sire de Giac and the Sire de Beaulieu had given place to the Sire de la Trémoille, more adventurous and more dangerous than the two others; he counteracted with the king the influence of the Constable de Richemont and of the true friends of France. The Duke of Bedford, for a long time paralyzed by the Duke of Gloucester's quarrels, had recently received reinforcements from England, under the orders of the Earl of Salisbury. The latter resolved to undertake the siege of Orleans. On the 12th of October, 1428, he appeared before the city, commencing his siege preparations according to the most scientific rules of the time, but disregarding the fact that he had given time for the place to furnish itself with men and victuals, to repair its fortifications, and to place itself in a state of defence; the best knights of the King of France had shut themselves up in Orleans.

The assaults had failed, the citizens of Orleans valiantly supporting the garrison. The Bastard of Orleans, Count of Dunois, had brought reinforcements; Salisbury was thinking of changing the siege into a blockade, when, observing the city from the Tournelles fort, which he had taken at the outset, he was struck in the face by a stone, shot from a falconet, which rebounded against the embrasure of the window and killed his esquire beside him. The general was dying; it was found necessary to carry him to Ferté-sur-Meung, where he died in a few days, to the great joy of the people of Orleans. The Earl of Suffolk arrived to take the command, and the siege continued. The English army, badly lodged in log huts, suffered with cold and often with hunger; the surrounding country was hostile and devastated. The Duke of Bedford resolved, in the month of February, to send provisions to him from Paris. It was during Lent, and the convoy, which was intrusted to Sir John Fastolf, consisted especially of herrings, when, on the 12th of February, he was attacked by the French near the village of Rouvray, between Graville and Orleans. As usual, the Scotch and the

French quarrelled among themselves; the former wishing to fight on foot, the latter to remain on horseback; they were within bowshot, and the English archers began the attack; the rout was not long delayed, and Sir John Fastolf arrived triumphantly at the camp with the herrings which gave their name to his victory.

This defeat threw discouragement into Orleans; hunger began to make itself felt; the citizens spoke of surrendering their city, not to the English, but to the Duke of Burgundy. The latter came to Paris to consult about it with the Regent. "No," said Bedford; "it is just that those who have had the trouble should have the honor." Philip did not remonstrate; disquieting rumors were beginning to circulate among the Burgundians: it was said that the Duke of Bedford had declared that the Duke of Burgundy would finally proceed to England to drink more beer than would quench his thirst. The duke quitted the court, dissatisfied and gloomy. The King of France was at Chinon; his affairs appeared desperate; many noblemen had abandoned him, and he would have willingly retired to the south, abandoning to their fate Orleans and the banks of the Loire, but for the efforts of his wife, Mary of Anjou, and the anger of Dunois. La Trémoille had caused the Constable to be sent away.

Deliverance was approaching by the weakest instrument which it has ever pleased God to employ for the accomplishment of His designs. A young girl was growing up in the village of Domrémy, upon the borders of Lorraine and Burgundy; she was named Joan of Arc; she was eighteen years of age, she was gentle and pious. For a long while already—from the age of thirteen years—she had begun to have visions, to hear voices, Saint Michael, Saint Catherine, and Saint Margaret commanding her to go to France, to the assistance of the king: as she grew older the voices became more urgent.

JOAN OF ARC RECOGNIZING THE KING.

People began to talk in the village of Joan's strange enthusiasm. The Sire de Baudricourt, in command at Vaucouleurs, wished to see her; but he sent her back ridiculing her. Being urged, however, by others, he resolved to send her to the king. "I must go to the king before Mid-Lent," said Joan, "even should I have to wear my legs to the knees to reach him, for nobody in the world, neither king nor duke, nor daughter of the King of Scotland, can deliver the kingdom of France. I should prefer to remain and spin with my poor mother, for this is not my work; but I must go, because my Lord wills it." "Who is your lord?" it was asked. "It is God," said Joan; and the noblemen who had charge of her were struck with admiration on seeing her pass the night kneeling in the churches, and fasting on bread and water.

When she arrived at Chinon, the king refused for several days to see her, saying that she was a mad woman; but the rumor of her journey had already spread. Dunois and the besieged in Orleans had caused inquiry to be made as to who this young girl was that was to deliver them. Joan was admitted into the great hall, full of noblemen richly dressed; no one of them detached himself from the groups; she went straight towards Charles VII. and knelt before him. "I am not the king, Joan," he said, and he pointed out to her one of his courtiers. "By my God, gentle Prince," she said, "it is you and no other. Most noble Lord Dauphin, the King of Heaven sends a message to you through me, that you shall be consecrated and crowned in the city of Rheims, and that you shall be His Lieutenant in the kingdom of France." Charles was won over; he drew Joan into a corner, and asked her a thousand questions. Confidence began to spread in the army; the soldiers asked that Joan should be placed at their head, to go and deliver Orleans. The doctors and the bishops caused her to undergo interrogations; after having said that she was mad, they feared that she might be a sorceress, but neither examinations nor questioning shook her simplicity and resolution. "The sign which I am to give is to raise the siege of Orleans," she said. "But if God wishes to deliver France, He has no need of armed men," insisted the doctors. "Ah!" she replied, "the soldiers will fight, and God will give the victory."

At length it was resolved to make the venture; and Joan, as if she had been a military leader, set out from Blois at the head of a considerable convoy, led by the best captains of the French army. She wished to attack Orleans from the right bank, saying that her Voices had commanded her to do it: but the captains were of a contrary opinion; they deceived Joan, and came up the left bank. Dunois came out in a little boat to meet the convoy. "Are you the Bastard of Orleans?" she said to him. "Yes; and very much pleased at your arrival." "You gave advice that we should come by the Sologne," she said, "and not by the Beauce, across the dominion of the English: in this you did not agree with my Lord. I bring you the best succor that ever knight or city received; it is the succor of the King of Heaven." And everybody was surprised on hearing her speak so well. The convoy entered Orleans without striking a blow; the soldiers went back to Blois, but Joan wished to remain in the city. The besieged crowded round her, already reassured and encouraged by her presence. Anxiety prevailed in the English camp; the leaders declared that Joan was mad; the soldiers feared that she might be a sorceress. She had written to the Earl of Suffolk and to Talbot, inviting them to retire. As they would not listen to her, and loaded her with insults, she became very angry, and demanded that they should be attacked immediately. A second convoy had entered the city; Joan was sleeping; suddenly she awoke. "Ah! Lord," she said, "the blood of our people is flowing; why was I not summoned sooner? My arms! My horse!" and she ran towards the fortress of Saint-Loup. She had not been deceived: a few soldiers had attempted a sally against the fortress occupied by the English; they were beginning to waver when Joan arrived; many soldiers had followed her; the English were repulsed, and the fortress recaptured. Joan had fought like a knight, and every one had admired her; but she was sad; many men had died without confessing. "I have compassion for their souls," she said. Terror spread among the English. "She performs miracles," it was said at Orleans. "She is a sorceress," said the enemy's archers; but they began to fear her.

From fort to fort, from rampart to rampart, all that the English had gained was by degrees taken from them; the Tournelles fort had been recently taken; the citizens of Orleans were rejoicing; the Earl of Suffolk and his lieutenants had resolved to retire. However, they did not wish to escape ignominiously. The camp had been fired, and, arrayed in battle order, the English appeared to await an attack. It was on the 8th of May, 1429. "Do not assail them first," said Joan; "for the love and honor of the blessed Sunday, let them be allowed to depart if they wish to go: if they should attack you, defend yourselves boldly, and you shall be masters." The English did not make an attack, and retreated without a struggle; Joan could not prevent the soldiers from throwing themselves upon the rear of the English army and gaining a large quantity of booty. Plunder, like disorder of all kinds, agitated and saddened her: she asked pardon of God in the churches for all the evil which she had not been able to prevent.

Great satisfaction prevailed at the court of King Charles, who was causing festivities in honor of Joan; but she took no pleasure in the amusements; she wished the king to go and be consecrated at Rheims. "*They* urge me strongly to conduct you thither," she said. "I shall last but one year or scarcely more; I must therefore employ it well." And as she was questioned about the voices, "I was in prayer," she said; "I was lamenting that you would not believe what I say; thereupon the Voice came and said, 'Go! go! my child, I will help you; go!' and it made me very joyful; I could wish that it might last for ever." On the 11th of June the French army was before Jargeau, where the Earl of Suffolk had shut himself up. At the head of the attacking party was the Duke of Alençon, recently withdrawn from captivity. "Forward, gentle Duke, to the assault!" cried Joan; and as he delayed, "Ah! gentle Duke, are you afraid?" said she; "you well know that I have promised to your wife to return you safe." A large stone overthrew Joan; they thought her dead, but she immediately arose. "Come! come! at the English!" she cried; "my Lord has condemned them; they are ours." Jargeau was carried by storm; the Earl of Suffolk and his brother, John de la Pole, were made prisoners; several fortresses fell into the hands of the French, and the English retreated towards La Beauce, under the orders of Talbot.

The Constable had recently rejoined the army; it was resolved to follow the enemy. "Ah! my God!" said Joan, "we must fight them; were they even hung in the clouds, we should have them, for God has sent us to punish them. The gentle Dauphin will to-day gain the greatest victory which he has yet had; my Counsel has told me that they are ours."

The English had halted in the open, in the environs of Patay; Sir John Fastolf and many others were inclined not to fight. The soldiers were discouraged by their recent defeats, they said, and the spells of Joan had taken away all their courage. But Talbot was ashamed of having retreated so far; he began to make his arrangements for the fight; and the archers were driving in their stakes, when the advanced guard of the French army fell upon them with that inconsiderate ardor so sadly rewarded at Crécy and at Poitiers. But this time the English were still in disorder; the soldiers who had remained on horseback fled; the rout was complete, and Sir John Fastolf galloped to Paris, where the Duke of Bedford, in a great rage, wished to send him the Garter. Lord Talbot and a large number of knights were made prisoners. "Well, Messire Talbot," said the Duke of Alençon, "you did not expect this, this morning?" "It is the fortune of war," replied the Englishman, without emotion. Joan no longer spoke of anything but the visit to Rheims.

The counsellors of King Charles still hesitated; the Sire de la Trémoille feared lest he might be supplanted in his master's favor; he contrived once more to remove the Constable; at length the persistence of Joan prevailed, and the king started with his little army. Auxerre, summoned to surrender, promised to open its gates if Troyes and Rheims would do likewise. The Burgundian garrison of Troyes resisted, and the French were short of provisions. They began to murmur against Joan; she urged the king to make the assault. "You will enter Troyes within two days, by love or by force, and the treacherous Burgundians will be completely dismayed." "Whoever should be certain of obtaining possession of it in six days, could well wait, Joan," said the chancellor, Archbishop of Rheims. "Yes," she persisted, "you shall have it to-morrow." On the morrow the entry into Troyes was made; Friar Richard, a famous preacher, came to meet Joan, and besprinkled her with holy water, to assure himself that she was not a sorceress; Joan smiled. On the 15th of July, 1429, Rheims opened its gates, and on the 7th the king was at length crowned in the cathedral. Joan stood beside him, holding her white standard, with these two words: "Jesus, Maria." When the king had received his consecration, she threw herself at his feet, in tears. "Gentle King," she said, "now is fulfilled the good pleasure of God, who willed it that you should come to Rheims to receive your worthy consecration, to show that you are king, and he to whom the kingdom of right belongs." And, from that day, she talked only of returning to her village. "I have accomplished that which my Lord commanded me," she repeated, "which was to raise the siege of Orleans and to cause the gentle king to be crowned; I wish he would now send me back to my father and mother, who would be so pleased to see me again. I should keep their sheep and cattle, as I was wont to do."

Meanwhile, the Duke of Bedford was collecting reinforcements; the dissensions which continued in the English council between the Duke of Gloucester and Cardinal Beaufort impeded the sending over of men and money; the Regent had even been compelled to weaken his garrisons in Normandy in order to assemble an army in the neighborhood of Paris, when his uncle, the cardinal, sent him a corps of two or three thousand men, whom he had raised with the object of making war in Bohemia, against the partisans of John Huss, excommunicated in a body by the Pope. The cardinal had already furnished heavy sums to carry on the war in France, and this fresh succor enabled the Duke of Bedford to make an expedition into Normandy, for the purpose of stifling the insurrections which had attracted the Constable. The noblemen favorable to the French were restrained and the Constable repulsed; but meanwhile Charles VII., led by

Engraved by W. Wellstood & Co 46 Beekman St. N.Y.

JOAN OF ARC.

Joan of Arc, whom he had retained with him, made an attempt upon Paris. Soissons, Senlis, Beauvais, had opened their gates to him, but the soldiers marched unwillingly towards the capital. The captains did not agree; the assault was lightly made, and Joan was wounded. The troops were furious. "You told us that we should be in Paris this evening," they said to Joan. "And so should we have been if you had fought well," she replied. The king, discouraged, retired to Bourges, to spend the winter.

While the King of France was going away from his good city of Paris, the Duke of Burgundy arrived there, still hesitating between the two parties, notwithstanding the efforts of his sister, the Duchess of Bedford, to cement anew his former friendship with the English regent. By degrees the influence of national feeling began to reawaken in the soul of Duke Philip, as his thirst for vengeance was appeased; the French promised him every conceivable reparation for the assassination of John the Fearless, and it was necessary, in order to retain him in the camp of the English, for the Duke of Bedford to offer him the command of the allied forces, thus abdicating in his favor. The Regent retired to Normandy, where he preserved his full authority. Joan was waging war upon the banks of the Loire; she had taken the castle of Pierre-le-Montoir, but she had been repulsed before La Charité. When the king at length took the field in the spring of 1430, Joan accepted the task of delivering Compiègne, besieged by the Duke Philip in person, and she had succeeded in entering the town. The fatal moment was approaching.

On the 25th of May the garrison of Compiègne had made a sally. Joan led the troops, and she had attacked an important position occupied by the Burgundians, when an overwhelming force made her fall back. She was covering and directing the retreat: at the moment when she was about to re-enter the town, the drawbridge was raised, and, whether by mistake or by treason, Joan found herself almost alone outside the walls. She rallied a few soldiers around her, and was endeavoring to escape into the country; but she had been recognized; she was surrounded and thrown from her horse. She was still upon the ground when she surrendered to the Bastard of Vendôme, who conducted her to the quarters of John of Luxembourg.

The rejoicing was great in the English and Burgundian camp; the Duke of Bedford caused the *Te Deum* to be sung. But the French did not concern themselves about the heroine who had delivered them; her task was accomplished; she had restored courage to the soldiers and hope to the captains; her enthusiasm had drawn along the most distrustful. Now she was a prisoner. Her enemies were negotiating among themselves to possess her; but those whom she had saved by the help of God did not raise a sword in her defence, and did not find a farthing for her ransom.

The Duke of Burgundy had returned to his dominion of Flanders, agitated by several insurrections, when the Bishop of Beauvais, Peter Cauchon, at the instigation of the English, claimed Joan from John of Luxembourg. "The sorceress had been captured in his diocese," he said, "and should be tried by the Church." The count resisted for a long time, but they finally gave him ten thousand livres, and he sold Joan. She was led in the first place to Arras, then to Crotoy; at length she was taken to Rouen, where the little king, Henry VI., had recently arrived. The French arms continued to make fresh progress; every day the English lost some towns. Duke Philip, lieutenant-general of the kingdom, who had recently become master of Brabant by the death of the young duke, was now held to the English alliance by such slight bonds that one more disaster might suddenly break them; the anger and shame of the English willingly attributed all their misfortunes to Joan: when she appeared they were at the height of success; since then everything had failed with them. Perhaps her death might bring a return of luck. The most enlightened among the English captains looked upon her as a sorceress. "She is an agent of Satan," the Duke of Bedford had written to the Council of England. Hatred always finds cowards to serve her; Peter Cauchon had been driven from Beauvais by his flock, as English, when the town had surrendered to Charles VII.; he had been proposed to the Pope by the Duke of Bedford for the archbishopric of Rouen; his vengeance and ambition impelled him to ruin Joan. The English, however, had not sufficient confidence in him to place her in his hands. Joan was kept in the large tower of the castle, in the custody of the Earl of Warwick.

The noblest hearts, the firmest minds of the Middle Ages appeared to lose all generosity and all justice when they found themselves confronted with an unhappy wretch accused of sorcery. The brave Warwick concealed himself to hear what the prisoner said to the treacherous confessor who had been brought. She was conducted before the Council of Inquisition, presided over by the Bishop of Beauvais. Neither violence nor malice could confuse her: nothing disconcerted this poor country girl, who knew only her prayers. "Are you in the grace of God?" she was asked suddenly. "It is a great thing," she replied, "to answer such a question." "Yes," said one of the magistrates, "and the accused is not obliged to answer." "You would do better to hold your tongue," exclaimed the bishop angrily. "If I am not," replied Joan, "may God receive me into it; and if I am, may God preserve me in it." "What virtue do you attribute to your banner?" asked the bishop. "None at all; I said, 'Enter boldly among the English,' and I entered myself." "Why, then, did you hold it beside the altar at Rheims?" "It had been in all the trouble," said Joan, smiling, "therefore it was quite right that it should witness the honor."

In vain was she interrogated upon her visions; she always replied that St. Catherine and St. Margaret visited her and encouraged her in her prison; it was by their advice that she refused to discard man's attire, which had been made a crime against her. She was urged to submit herself to the Church, but she did not understand what was asked of her, and seeing before her priests hostile to her cause and to her king, she implored that there might be among the judges some men of her party.

At last the sentence was pronounced: the Church rejected Joan as an impure member, and delivered her up to secular justice. The justice was the vengeance of the English. The unhappy prisoner was conducted to the public square, where two scaffolds were erected; Joan was placed upon one of these, the preacher who was to expound the sentence to the people was upon the other, the multitude were crowded together below.

So long as the Doctor of the Sorbonne dwelt upon her misdeeds and the deceptions by which she had deluded the poor people of France, Joan listened in silence; but when he exclaimed, "Charles, who proclaimest thyself her king and governor, thou hast adhered like a heretic as thou art to the words and acts of a woman defamed and without honor," the loyal heart of Joan was unable to contain its emotion. "Speak of me," she exclaimed, "but not of the king; he is a good Christian, and I dare say and swear under pain of death that he is the noblest among the Christians who best love their faith and their Church." "Silence her," cried the Bishop of Beauvais.

They wished to make her sign her abjuration. "What is abjuration?" she said. "It is that your judges have judged well." She refused. "What I did, I did well to do," she repeated. At length she yielded. "I submit to the Universal Church," she said, "and since the clergy say that my visions are not credible I will no longer maintain them." "Sign, or you will perish by the fire," said the preacher. She made a cross at the foot of the paper which was presented to her, and was taken back into her prison. Her submission pledged her to resume woman's clothing.

The English murmured, not understanding the manœuvres of the bishop. "All goes ill, because Joan escapes," said the Earl of Warwick. The priests smiled. Two days after her abjuration, Joan, on awaking, found only in her chamber a man's dress: she resisted for a long time. "You know that I have promised not to wear it," she said; she was obliged to rise, however. The jailers went and informed the bishop. "She is taken!" said the Earl of Warwick. "You have fallen back into your illusions," said Cauchon to the prisoner; "you have heard your voices." "Yes," said Joan resolutely, "and they have told me that it was a great pity to have signed your abjuration in order to save my life. I only signed through fear of the fire. Give me a comfortable prison, and I will do what the Church may wish."

The stake awaited her. "Farewell," cried Cauchon to the Earl of Warwick, on going out of the prison. The poor child tore her hair when she learned the sentence passed upon her. "I had seven times rather that they should behead me," she repeated. She was on her way to execution, when she perceived the Bishop of Beauvais. "Bishop, I die through you," she said. Eight hundred Englishmen accompanied the cart. She prayed aloud with so much fervor that all the French wept as they heard her; several of the magistrates who had taken part in the prosecution had not the strength to follow her to her punishment. The public square was reached. "Ah! Rouen! Rouen!" she said, "is it here that I am to die?" The preacher had reproached her with her relapse; she listened to him with calmness, redoubling her prayers. The Bishop of Noyon descended from the scaffold, being unable to bear this spectacle; the Bishop of Winchester wept; Joan was embracing the parish cross, which had been brought to her. The executioner seized her. Above the stake were written these words: "RELAPSED HERETIC, APOSTATE, IDOLATER." Joan's new confessor, a good monk who did not betray her, had mounted upon the stake with her; he was still there when the fire was lighted. "Descend quickly," said Joan, "but stay near enough for me to see the cross. Ah! Rouen! Rouen! I greatly fear that you may suffer for my death." The flame enveloped her; she was still heard praying; at length a last cry — "Jesus!" — and all was ended. The English themselves were touched. "It is a fine end," said the soldiers; "we are very happy to have seen her, for she was a good woman." "She has died a martyr, and for her true Lord," said the French. The executioner went to confession on the same evening, fearing never to obtain the forgiveness of God. Cardinal Beaufort caused the remains of the funeral pile to be cast into the Seine, fearing that they might be made into relics; and the King of England addressed to all the princes of Christendom a letter recounting the proceedings, and how the victim herself had acknowledged that evil and lying spirits had deluded her. The process of rehabilitation, afterwards made at the court of Rome, at the request of Charles VII., the only token of remembrance which he gave to the unhappy Joan, established in its real light the historical truth; but public opinion had already done her justice. "She was a marvellous girl, valiant in war," it was said in Flanders, as well as in Burgundy and in France; the English have wickedly caused her death, and through revenge." Peter Cauchon was never Archbishop of Rouen; he became Bishop of Lisieux, where he was interred in the wall of St. James's church, as though he did not feel himself worthy to repose in the sacred place.

In burning Joan the English had hoped to regain their former good fortune: no such result followed. Every day a fresh town opened its gates to the French. However indolent Charles VII. still might be, national sentiment now fought for him. The Duke of Bedford wished to satisfy the taste of the Parisians for festivals, and at the same time to give religious sanction to his nephew's claims upon France: on the 17th of December, 1431, therefore, the little King Henry VI., nine years of age, was solemnly crowned at Notre Dame. The ceremony was magnificent; wine and milk flowed in the streets; but the French noblemen were few, the Duke of Burgundy had not arrived, and Cardinal Beaufort himself placed the crown upon the head of Henry VI.: it was the English coronation of an English prince. The young sovereign set out shortly afterwards for England, leaving to all those who had approached him a sad impression of feebleness and melancholy.

Meanwhile the war languished: men and money were lacking to the English, and the quarrels of the favorites with the great French noblemen continued around King Charles VII.; but the Duke of Burgundy detached himself more and more from England. The Duchess of Bedford died without children in the month of November, 1432, and six months after her death the duke married Jacquette of Luxembourg, daughter of the Count of Saint Pol. The Duke of Burgundy considered himself offended by the shortness of the mourning, and by the union contracted without his authority with one of his vassals. He was seeking a pretext for a quarrel; his treaty with King Charles was almost concluded; the blood which had inundated France for fourteen years sufficed, it was thought, to appease the shade of Duke John. The counsellors of the king urged the duke towards peace; but he made much of his scruples in respect to the oaths which bound him to the English. Appeal was made to Pope Eugenius IV., and through his efforts a great congress assembled at Arras, in 1435. The Duke of Burgundy summoned all his nobility; King Charles sent twenty-nine noblemen, the Constable at their head. Cardinal Beaufort, with twenty-six barons, half English and half French, represented the interests of England. Duke Philip displayed, for receiving such great company, all his wonted magnificence; festivals succeeded festivals, and jousts followed tournaments; but negotiations meanwhile went on, and so manifestly inclined to the advantage of the French, that Cardinal Beaufort shortly retired in disgust, denying the authority of the congress. Affairs proceeded more rapidly after his departure; Duke Philip caused his forgiveness and his alliance to be dearly purchased; but at length the treaty was concluded, and on the 26th of September, 1435, the Duke of Burgundy, relieved of his oaths to the English, promised to live in peace and friendship with the King of France. All the noblemen swore likewise; when it came to the turn of the Sire de Lannoy, he cried, "I have already five times sworn with this hand to keep the peace during the war which has just ended, and my five oaths have been violated. By God's grace, I will keep this one."

The Duke of Bedford had not lived to see the conclusion

of a treaty which virtually took from England the conquests of King Henry V.; he had died at Rouen, on the 14th of September, exhausted by the struggle which he had sustained for thirteen years, with a courage, firmness, and prudence worthy of the confidence which had been manifested towards him by his dying brother. Three days after the signing of the peace, an unnatural mother, abandoned by all her children — Queen Isabel of Bavaria, died alone in Paris, in solitude and destitution, the just punishment of her crimes. The Duke of Burgundy now publicly declared war against the English, and in the month of April, 1436, at his instigation, the feeble English garrison which was stationed in Paris was overcome by the people, and found itself compelled to open the gates to the Marshal of Isle-Adam: the capital once more became French, the English were driven back into Normandy, where their authority remained complete. The Duke of York, for a moment regent of France, had been replaced by the Earl of Warwick, who established the seat of his government at Rouen, where he died. Two towns yet remained to the English near Paris — Meaux and Pontoise; these were taken by the troops of King Charles VII. For a moment, in 1436, the Duke of Burgundy even threatened Calais with a considerable army; but before the arrival of the Duke of Gloucester, who had challenged him to combat, and claimed to take possession of the dominions of his wife, Jacqueline, who had recently died, Duke Philip retreated precipitately into his dominions, impelled by his troops, who were disbanding. In 1444, through the efforts of Isabel of Portugal, wife of the Duke of Burgundy, added to the representations of the Duke of Orleans, recently snatched from the captivity which he had suffered since the battle of Agincourt, a truce of two years was concluded between the two nations; the horrors of the Hundred Years' War were at length reaching their end.

While the English were losing ground by degrees in France, England, impoverished by the necessities of the war, underwent the commotion of a continual struggle between the two chiefs of the government, the Duke of Gloucester and Cardinal Beaufort. Queen Catherine, the king's mother, had retained no influence, and three years after the death of Henry V. she had married a plain Welsh gentleman, Owen Tudor, by whom she had three sons, whom, at her death in 1437, she confided to the young King Henry VI. The Duchess of Bedford followed her example, by wedding Sir Richard Woodville, or Wydeville; but these misalliances had proved grave dangers to the ambitious men, elevated to a rank for which they had not been born: Tudor and Woodville were both thrown into prison, and the wife of the Duke of Gloucester, Eleanor Cobham, accused of sorcery, was condemned to do public penance and to be imprisoned for the remainder of her days. The young King Henry had assumed no authority over his kingdom. He was twenty-two years of age; he was tall and handsome, but languid, apathetic, timid, solely occupied with his books and his devotions. He might have become a holy monk, but he was destitute of the qualities necessary to a king in difficult and hard times. A wife was sought for him who might supply the defects of his character, and the choice of his advisers fell upon Margaret of Anjou, cousin of the Queen of France, and daughter of René of Anjou, King of Sicily and Jerusalem, Duke of Maine, Anjou, and Bar; but a king without kingdom, a duke without duchy, a chevalier and a poet, without other fortune than his harp and his sword. His daughter was purchased of him by restoring to him his two provinces of Anjou and Maine, which the French arms had not yet been able to break through. The English now held but Normandy and a few towns in Guienne. The marriage of the king concluded by the Earl of Suffolk and Cardinal Beaufort, against the advice of the Duke of Gloucester, had not been well received in England. There, much regret had been felt for the loss of the two provinces which once formed part of the territory of the Angevin kings, and which England had always regarded as her own. Queen Margaret, besides, with her beauty, her wit, and her energy, brought into her new country ideas of government which were little favorable to English independence. She had confidence in the worthy Suffolk, who had become a Marquis and soon afterwards a Duke; she shared his power, and treated with haughtiness those who approached her. She manifested, in particular, little liking for the Duke of Gloucester, whom she considered as her enemy. In the month of February, 1447, the Parliament was convoked at Bury St. Edmund's; the partisans of Suffolk were assembled in the neighborhood, when the Duke of Gloucester arrived on the day after the opening of the session. Being immediately arrested and accused of the crime of high-treason, he was found dead in his bed on the 28th of February, as had been formerly at Calais another Duke of Gloucester. A few of his servants were executed after his death, under pretext of a plot to release the Duchess Eleanor. Suffolk took possession of the property of the duke, whom the public voice accused him of having murdered. Cardinal Beaufort had recently died in his palace of Walvesey (on the 11th of April), leaving immense riches consecrated to the foundation of charitable institutions which still exist. Suffolk remained the sole master of the government. King Henry VI. was occupied in the creation of Eton College, and in the erection of King's College, at Cambridge, where the marvellous beauty of the chapel remains as a monument of the exquisite taste of the poor king, so little suited to the affairs of this world.

Meanwhile the truce with France, several times renewed,

had been violently broken by King Charles VII., under pretext of an infraction which well suited his wishes. France was recovering herself, and England was profoundly weakened by internal dissensions. The troops assembled in Maine entered Normandy; the Duke of Somerset, who commanded there, had few soldiers and no money. Dunois marched against Rouen, and notwithstanding the desperate resistance of Talbot, who was consigned as a hostage into the hands of the French, the citizens delivered up the city to him. Sir Thomas Kyriel, dispatched as a reinforcement to the Duke of Somerset, was defeated on the 13th of April, 1450, near Formigny, by the Constable and the Count of Clermont. Bayeux, Avranches, Caen yielded one after the other; Cherbourg was taken by storm, and by the 12th of August the English had lost the whole of Normandy. In the following year the towns which yet held out for them in Guienne surrendered without striking a blow. Henry VI. had now nothing left but Calais upon French soil. Charles VII., drawn at last from his elegant indolence, proposed negotiations. "My sword shall never return to its scabbard until I have retaken all that I have lost!" cried the poor King Henry VI., who had never drawn a sword in his life. France feared him no longer.

Internal difficulties sufficed to engross the efforts of the faithful servants of the English king. Parliament had at length risen against the Duke of Suffolk; he had been conducted to the Tower, protesting his innocence. The accusations brought forward against him were confused, ill-founded, and frivolous; the graver subjects of distrust had scarcely been touched upon. The duke threw himself upon his knees before the king, refused to shield himself with his privilege by demanding the judgment of his peers, and consigned himself to the justice of his master, who wished to save him. He was simply banished from England for five years. The Parliament accepted this compromise, not without a protest on the part of the lords in favor of the rights of their order.

The anger of the population of London was not so easy to disarm as the vengeance of Parliament. Suffolk had difficulty in retiring safe and sound to his estate; he had gathered around him his friends and partisans, swearing before them that he was innocent, when he embarked for the Continent on the 1st of May, 1430. He was sailing the next day between Dover and Calais, when a large war-ship, the *Nicholas of the Tower*, hailed his little vessel. The duke was summoned on board the ship. "Welcome, traitor!" said the captain, as he stepped upon the deck, and Suffolk was immediately placed under arrest. Two days elapsed; the duke had asked for a confessor; a little bark came up with the *Nicholas;* she bore an executioner and an axe. Suffolk was led upon deck and beheaded. None inquired whence had come the warrant; but the importance of the ships intrusted to arrest the banished man at sea, caused a supposition that the great personages of the kingdom had not remained strangers to the execution. The populace was satisfied, its vengeance was consummated. New events absorbed all minds.

Numerous insurrections had recently broken out in different parts of England. An adventurer, Jack Cade, an Irishman by origin, who had for a long while served in the English armies in France, placed himself at the head of the insurgents. He had assumed the name of Mortimer, and gave himself out as a relative of the Duke of York, who then commanded in Ireland. Thirty thousand men had soon gathered around Cade, nearly all from the county of Kent. It was said that the queen wished to avenge herself upon this county for the death of her favorite, whose decapitated body had been carried by the waves to the coast of Dover. Cade brought his forces to Blackheath, as Wat Tyler had formerly done, and the "complaints of the commons of Kent" were dispatched to the king at London. Among their other demands the insurgents begged Henry VI. to recall to his councils his blood-relatives, the Dukes of York, Exeter, Buckingham, and Norfolk, in order to punish the traitors who had caused the death of the Duke of Gloucester, and also of the holy father in God, Cardinal Beaufort, and had lost the dominions of Maine, Anjou, and Normandy. The reply of the court was the dispatch of an army against the rebels; but the first detachment was defeated: the soldiers murmured, saying that they did not like to fight against their countrymen, who claimed the liberties of the nation. Concessions were attempted; but the forces of Cade swelled every day, and on the 3d of July he entered London. Lord Say, one of the most unpopular ministers, was dragged from the Tower, whither he had been sent by the court in the hope of satisfying the insurgents; and, notwithstanding his protestations, he was executed after a mock trial. Some houses were pillaged, and on the morrow, when the rebels wished to re-enter London, after having been encamped at Blackheath, the citizens defended the bridge. Cade was compelled to retreat. Some vain concessions were made to him, and the promise of an amnesty; but he was soon afterwards pursued and killed in the struggle, and his head was planted upon London Bridge. The insurrection was stifled; but the name of the Duke of York had been put forward; it circulated from mouth to mouth, and many people began to ask whether the rights to the throne which he held through Anne Mortimer, his mother, did not supersede those of King Henry VI. Prince Richard, son of the Earl of Cambridge, had succeeded to the title of Duke of York, at the death of his paternal uncle; the successes which he had obtained in his government of Ireland had increased his popularity.

Suddenly, towards the end of August, 1451, the Duke of York appeared at the court without giving a reason for having quitted Ireland, and after a short visit to the king, withdrew to his castle of Fotheringay. Henry VI. endeavored to place in opposition to him the Duke of Somerset, the head of the younger branch of the House of Lancaster; but the duke was under suspicion, as a favorite of the queen, and too much ill feeling existed against him for the loss of Normandy, for it to be possible to counterbalance the influence of the Duke of York. In the Parliament, which opened in November, a proposal was made in the House of Commons to declare the Duke of York heir to the throne, as the king had no children. The author of this proposal was sent to the Tower, and projects menacing to the liberty of the Duke of York began to circulate. He retired into Shropshire, where he assembled together some troops, all the time protesting his fidelity towards the king. Whilst an army was marching against him, he advanced upon London; the gates of that city were closed to him, and it was at Dartford that he met the king. After some peaceful negotiations, York repaired alone to the royal tent; he was immediately arrested there. The Duke of Somerset was in favor of a summary trial and execution; but the king athwart his mental incapacity had a horror of blood: he sent the Duke of York to the Tower, whence he was soon released upon the rumor of the approach of his son, the Earl of March, at the head of an army. He then promised to be faithful to the king, and was left free to return to his castle at Wigmore. The Duke of Somerset remained at the head of the government.

A movement in favor of the English had manifested itself in Guienne. The brave Talbot was dispatched thither, notwithstanding his eighty years, at the head of a small army of picked men. Bordeaux surrendered easily, and the red cross of England reappeared in the greater number of the southern towns, when King Charles VII. entered the province with his troops. He had gathered a considerable force, and was laying siege to Castillon, when Talbot resolved to relieve the town; he made the attack on the 30th of July, 1453, and was about to carry the position, when the Count of Ponthieu fell upon him with reinforcements; the English retreated, and Talbot was slain. The French army presented itself before Bordeaux; the garrison held out bravely during two months; hunger compelled it to capitulate, and on the 10th of October, the English soldiers, accompanied by a great number of citizens of the place, embarked for England. Guienne was henceforth French, and the last fragment of the inheritance of Eleanor of Aquitaine had slipped from her descendants.

The mental derangement of King Henry VI. continued to increase, and Parliament had recalled the Duke of York to the council. A son had been born to Queen Margaret; she had, from that circumstance, assumed more pride and a more fixed determination to exercise royal authority at her pleasure. Meanwhile the Commons had obtained the impeachment of the Duke of Somerset, who had been sent to the Tower. The Parliament of 1454 was opened by the Duke of York, as the king's lieutenant. For some time past, efforts had in vain been made to ascertain the real state of King Henry; twelve peers, who had contrived to be admitted to him on the occasion of the death of the chancellor, found him incapable of understanding a word or of replying to their questions. Upon their report, the Parliament nominated Richard of York Protector and defender of the throne of England, with the condition that this dignity should be resigned in favor of the Prince of Wales, as soon as the latter should attain his majority. York protested his loyalty, and furnished

WARWICK CASTLE.

proof of it in the following year, when the king, having recovered his reason, reclaimed the royal power. The first use which he made of his recovered authority was to release the Duke of Somerset. The poor monarch endeavored to reconcile the two rival houses; but the Duke of York shortly afterwards affected to believe himself in danger, and again raised some troops. The king marched against him with Somerset; a battle began in the very streets of St. Alban's. The archers of the Duke of York were good marksmen: the Duke of Somerset, the Earl of Northumberland, Lord Clifford, fell beneath their arrows; the king himself was wounded. York, seeking him after the victory, found him in bed, in the house of a tanner, and both repaired together to the church, the victor treating with respect the vanquished king. The duke did not immediately take advantage of his success, and contented himself with appearing before the Parliament as the lieutenant of the king. But the Commons claimed for him the title of Protector, and they imposed their will upon the Lords. With the moderation which had always characterized his political conduct, York contented himself with consigning to trustworthy hands some important offices, intrusting the custody of Calais to his brother-in-law and faithful friend, the Earl of Warwick; but he did not wreak vengeance upon his enemies, and resigned the power to the king without objection at the beginning of 1456, when the monarch, again restored to health, wished to take back the authority. Soon, however, Queen Margaret everywhere replaced the friends of York by her favorites; the duke then retired to his estates, and the great men of his party did likewise, for the relatives of the noblemen slain at St. Alban's were talking loudly of vengeance.

Hopes were still entertained of arriving at some arrangement. In his intervals of reason, the king was gentle, charitable, and humane; he endeavored to re-establish peace around him. York and Warwick had again protested their fidelity towards him. Henry placed himself as arbitrator between the two parties, and decreed certain fines and reparations towards the families of the victims. The victors of St. Alban's accepted these conditions; the king, the queen, the Duke of York, and all the Yorkist and Lancastrian noblemen, solemnly repaired to St. Paul's Cathedral; the Duke of York offered his hand to the queen. The Earl of Warwick had remained at Calais.

Fresh quarrels soon brought about fresh insurrections. The two parties reciprocally felt too great a distrust ever to live in peace. In the month of September, 1459, the Earl of Salisbury, brother of Warwick, united his forces to those of the Duke of York, and, after a bloody combat in the environs of Drayton, in Shropshire, where the Lancastrians were defeated, the Earl of Warwick repaired to England with some troops which he had carefully drilled at Calais; but scarcely did his soldiers find themselves in the presence of the royal standard, when a loyal instinct carried them off into the ranks of the army of Henry VI. The strength of the Duke of York no longer allowed him to keep the field, and on the 20th of November the Parliament convoked by the queen at Coventry accused of high-treason the whole families of the Duke of York and the Earl of Salisbury. Warwick retired to Calais, taking with him his brother. When the governor sent by Queen Margaret to supplant him appeared before the town, he was repulsed, and the troops that he had brought went over to Warwick. At the end of June, 1460, the earl reappeared in England; the eldest son of the Duke of York marched at his side. The battle of Northampton placed the poor king in the hands of his enemies, and the queen was compelled to fly with her son into Scotland. A mass of great Lancastrian noblemen had remained upon the field of battle. In opposition to the great warriors of the preceding centuries, Warwick, the real chief of the Yorkist party, had for maxim to spare the common people, and to strike his enemies ruthlessly down, taking for his victims the men of distinction. Thanks to this practice, imitated by his adversaries, all the great families of England found themselves decimated during the Wars of the Roses.

A new Parliament had been convoked at Westminster. The throne was empty in the House of Lords, when the Duke of York came in. He advanced at first resolutely, placed his hand upon the cloth of gold which covered the royal seat, then fell back without mounting it. He had, however, firmly resolved to make good his rights. The Archbishop of Canterbury inquired of him whether he did not intend to pay a visit to the king, who was in the palace adjoining. "I know no one in this kingdom who should not pay me a visit first," replied the duke; and he established himself in the royal apartments, while Henry occupied those of the queen.

The peers had not responded to this indirect appeal, and on the 16th of October York dispatched a message to them, formally laying claim to the crown. The Lords replied that they could not give an opinion without the advice and the consent of the king. Now that he was separated from the queen, who had become more and more unpopular, public feeling began to be aroused in favor of Henry, who was regarded as a saint. But the Duke of York required an answer. When the peers repaired to the captive king, he reminded them that he had received, when but a child, a crown which had been borne with honor by his father and his grandfather; that it had rested for forty years upon his brow, and that those even who now wished to snatch it from him had on several occasions sworn fidelity to him. To these substantial reasons were added attacks against the hereditary rights of the Duke of York, imprudent and puerile conduct which so greatly embarrassed the peers that they called to their aid the judges, then the king's sergeants and attorneys, who knew not how to give their advice. On the 23d the Lords presented their objections, frivolous for the most part, with the exception of the oaths taken by all the peers to the House of Lancaster. A compromise was arrived at in the matter; Warwick and York used moderation, and the crown was assured to King Henry during his lifetime. After him it was to descend to Richard, Duke of York, and his heirs, to the exclusion of the son of Margaret of Anjou.

The negotiators of this curious treaty had reckoned without the queen. She had quitted Scotland, and was endeavoring to assemble all her partisans to defend the rights of her son. Already the hills and valleys bristled with lances. The Lancastrians were under the sons of the noblemen killed at St. Alban's; the Duke of Somerset, the Earl of Northumberland, Lord Clifford were there, thirsting for revenge, notwithstanding all the treaties of pacification. The Duke of York commanded his troops in person; he was as bold upon the field of battle as he was hesitating and prudent in the council. On the 30th of December, 1460, he attacked the enemy at Wakefield, in Yorkshire, with inferior forces, and was completely defeated. He was himself slain, and his friend, the Earl of Salisbury, who was made a prisoner in the flight, was beheaded the same day at Pontefract. The little Earl of Rutland, second son of the duke, was flying with his tutor, when he was arrested upon Wakefield Bridge by Lord Clifford. The child, speechless with terror, threw himself upon his knees. "It is the son of the Duke of York," cried the priest who accompanied him. "Thy father

ASSASSINATION OF THE EARL OF RUTLAND.

killed mine," said the fierce baron, "I will kill thee therefore, thee and thine." And plunging his dagger into the bosom of the young prince, he dispatched the chaplain to carry to his mother this fearful news. England was not yet accustomed to these scenes of slaughter, and a long cry of horror arose in the country when the news of the death of Rutland became known, and when above the gates of York was seen the disfigured head of the duke, surmounted by a paper crown. Margaret and her partisans had become intoxicated with the cup of revenge, without thinking of the terrible reprisals which awaited them.

Already the young Earl of March, the Duke of York's eldest son, had gained, on the 1st of February, at Mortimer's Cross, near Wigmore, a bloody victory, where a great number of royalists perished. All the prisoners of mark, among whom was Owen Tudor, father-in-law of King Henry VI., were beheaded after the battle, as though to appease the shades of the Yorkists who had fallen at Wakefield. This success counterbalanced the effect of a victory gained on the 17th of February, over Warwick, by Queen Margaret, between St. Alban's and Barnet. The earl was compelled to retreat so precipitately, that King Henry, forgotten in the tumult, was alone in his tent with his chamberlain, when his wife came to take possession of him before causing her prisoners to be executed. Five days later a proclamation of King Henry announced to his people that he had subscribed under constraint to the recent arrangements for the succession to the throne, and that he retracted them without reserve, declaring Edward, formerly Earl of March, a false traitor, "it being the duty of every subject of the king to hasten against him."

The Earl of March was in a position to hurl back on his enemies the title of traitor and to put a price upon their heads. He had joined the Earl of Warwick, and their united forces exceeded those of the queen. London was favorable to the change of dynasty, and the cruelties practised in the country by the troops that the queen had brought from the frontiers of Scotland, rallied the peasants around the Yorkists. Their forces went on increasing; and when, on the 25th of February, they approached St. Alban's, where Queen Margaret was with her army, she found herself compelled to retreat before them. Edward, Earl of March, had none of the scruples and hesitation of his father; he was resolved to seize immediately upon the throne. Traversing St. Alban's as a conqueror and a king, he advanced at once towards London, and entered there triumphantly, to the great joy of the people, "who came every day from all the country surrounding," says the chronicler, "to see this handsome and magnificent prince, the flower of chivalry, in whom they hoped for their joy and tranquillity."

A grand review had been announced in St. John's Fields; the crowd of citizens thronged to witness this warlike spectacle. Suddenly Lord Falconberg and the Bishop of Exeter, brother of the Earl of Warwick, addressed themselves to the crowd. "You know the incapacity of King Henry," they said, "the injustice of the usurpation which placed his family upon the throne, and to what extent you have been misgoverned and oppressed. Will you have this king to reign over you still?" "No! no!" cried the mob. The bishop began speaking again, depicting the valor, the talent, the activity of the Earl of March. "Will you have King Edward to reign over you, and serve, love, and honor him?" "Yes," replied the people; "long live King Edward!" On the morrow, the 2d of March, a great council of the Lords spiritual and temporal declared that Henry of Lancaster had failed in his engagements, by uniting himself to the forces of the queen, and by retracting his oath concerning the succession to the throne. By this conduct he had lost his rights to the crown, which belonged henceforth to the heir of the Duke of York, whose claims had been recognized as legitimate. The consent of the Commons, who were convoked later in Parliament, was dispensed with. On the 4th of March, Edward, followed by a royal retinue, repaired to Westminster, and immediately taking possession of that throne which his father had formerly touched with a hesitating hand, he himself explained to the assembly the rights of his house. Having been several times interrupted by plaudits, he repaired to church, where he made a similar address. A few hours later the heralds proclaimed King Edward IV. in all the public places of London, and the people responded with their cries of joy, "Long live King Edward!"

CHAPTER XV.

RED ROSE AND WHITE ROSE.

EDWARD IV. 1461–1483. — EDWARD V. 1483. — RICHARD III. 1483–1485.

IF the throne of Henry IV. had always appeared to him unsteady, from the morrow of a usurpation which had not caused a single drop of blood to be shed, that of Edward IV., based upon a transitory success of arms, was destined to cost much bloodshed and many tears to England. The coronation rejoicings were immediately followed by a renewal of hostilities. Scarcely had he been proclaimed when the new king left London. Queen Margaret and the Duke of Somerset had assembled their troops in the environs of York, and were preparing to march upon the capital. Edward, upon the advice of Warwick, did not allow them time for that purpose. The northern counties were in general favorably disposed towards the Red Rose, and the two armies were more considerable than ever, when they met on the 28th of March near Towton. The snow was falling in abundance, and blinded the combatants, but their fury knew no obstacle. The struggle lasted from nine o'clock in the morning until three, when the Lancastrians, broken up and disbanded, attempted to fly. The river Cock barred their way, and many of their number were drowned in it. The Earl of Northumberland and six barons were left dead upon the field of battle; the Earls of Devonshire and Wiltshire were captured and beheaded; their heads replaced those of Duke Richard and the Earl of Rutland upon the gates of York. Thirty-eight thousand combatants, it is said, perished on this fatal day: the Hundred Years' War had not cost as much blood to England as this single battle of the civil war. Queen Margaret, her husband, and her son, accompanied by the Dukes of Somerset and Exeter, took refuge in Scotland. Edward IV., triumphant, returned to London, there to conclude the ceremony of his coronation. Formally recognized by the Parliament, no allusion was made to the intellectual weakness of King Henry, or to the misgovernment of the queen and her favorites: all the arguments were confined to the legitimate rights to the throne asserted by the House of York in the person of King Edward. Henry and all his family were declared usurpers, and their partisans were all included in the same sentence: those of the Lancastrian barons who had not perished upon the field of battle were condemned to death; all their property was to be confiscated and their families degraded. Edward IV. was anxious to crush his enemies by a single blow.

Betrayed by the fortune of war and abandoned by her terrified partisans, Queen Margaret knew neither discouragement nor fatigue. Closely linked to the Scotch by an old alliance which she had sealed by ceding to them the town of Berwick, she essayed, with their assistance, two or three incursions into the northern counties of England; but her mediocre success decided her to seek help in her native country, France, where she had rendered many services and retained many friends. In the month of April, 1462, she embarked at Kircudbright, and landed in Brittany. The duke presented her with twelve thousand golden crowns, and she took the road to Chinon, where the court of France was situated. Charles VII. was dead, and Louis XI. had succeeded him. A cold politician, he was too shrewd to allow himself to be inveigled by the tears and the beauty of the queen into a disastrous war: he therefore at the outset refused all assistance; but when she spoke of ceding Calais as the price of his services, the monarch relaxed his sternness in a degree, gave some money to the queen, and permitted her to recruit soldiers in his kingdom. A distinguished knight, René de Brézé, seneschal of Normandy, ardently devoted to Margaret, placed himself at the head of the two thousand men that he had raised for her, partly at his own expense; a few vessels were equipped, and the queen returned to Scotland. The English exiles and a certain number of irregular border troops in a short time joined her, and three fortresses of Northumberland fell into her hands. But the Earl of Warwick was advancing with an army of twenty thousand men; the Lancastrians divided their forces in order to preserve their conquests; the queen returned to her vessels. The waves were as hostile to her as the land; the ships were destroyed in a storm; the queen and Brézé arrived at Berwick in a fishing-smack; five hundred French troops, which she had left behind her to defend Holy Island, were slaughtered to a man, and the three castles were compelled to surrender after a vigorous resistance. They had capitulated upon honorable terms. The Duke of Somerset and Sir Richard Percy made their submission to King Edward, who admitted them to mercy; while Margaret was wandering with the seneschal upon the frontiers of England, in vain endeavoring to rally her scattered and terrified adherents. It was in this winter campaign, one day in December, that the queen, accompanied only by her son and a feeble following, fell into the hands of a band of brigands. She had been stripped of everything, her attendants were killed or captured, and she was attempting to fly with her son, when another bandit encountered her. Margaret made no further effort to escape, but, taking the little

RICHMOND CROWNED UPON THE BATTLE-FIELD.

QUEEN MARGARET AND THE BRIGAND.

prince by the hand, advanced resolutely towards the outlaw. "Here is the son of your king," she said; "I confide him to you." All generous feeling had not been extinguished in the soul of the brigand: he extended his protection to the mother and the child, gave them the shelter of his hut for the night, and on the morrow conducted them to the outskirts of the forest. King Henry had been conveyed to Wales and placed in a fortress, while Queen Margaret recrossed the sea to seek fresh assistance on the Continent. She remained there for a long while. Louis XI. rarely supported the unfortunate; Duke Philip of Burgundy did not wish to set himself at variance with England, whose commerce was of importance to his dominions, and the poor princess, supported by a few secret gifts, royal alms which scarcely sufficed for her subsistence, took refuge in the duchy of Bar, which still belonged to her father. Here she was unceasing in her efforts to find enemies for King Edward and partisans for her husband and her son.

Meanwhile the war had recommenced, without her, in England, and struck the last blow to her hopes. The Duke of Somerset and Percy had again revolted, and in the month of April, 1464, King Henry, dragged from his peaceful retreat, was brought to the camp of his partisans. Lord Montague, the younger brother of the Earl of Warwick, assembled together the Yorkists, and on the 25th of April at Hedgely Moor, and on the 15th of May at Hexham, the two Lancastrian corps were defeated in succession. Percy died fighting; the Duke of Somerset, Lord de Roos, and Lord Hungerford were executed; Sir Ralph Grey, formerly a Yorkist, and since become a Lancastrian in consequence of a disappointment in ambition, was captured at Bamborough by the Earl of Warwick, and suffered the doom of traitors. Animosities and retaliations were accumulating for the future, but the present seemed to smile upon King Edward: King Henry had wandered during two months in Lancashire and Westmoreland, from castle to castle, from cottage to cottage, without any one dreaming of betraying him, without meeting a heart hard enough to refuse succor and protection to him. At length, in the month of July, he was seized, delivered up to his enemies, and conducted to the Tower. The war had become very cruel, and the troops had grown accustomed to many crimes, but none dared to lay a hand upon "the sacred head of the peaceful usurper," as Shakspeare calls him; the halo of his fervent piety protected him against all violence. He led a peaceful life in his prison, while Edward IV. was demolishing with his own hands the throne which he had conquered at the cost of so many sufferings. The Duchess of Bedford, Jacquetta of Luxembourg, had had several children by her marriage with Sir Richard Woodville. The eldest of her daughters, Elizabeth, married at an early age to Sir John Grey, who was killed at the second battle of St. Alban's in the ranks of the Lancastrians, begged of the king the restitution of her property. She was beautiful, skilful, ambitious: Edward IV. conceived an affection for her, and secretly married her on the 1st of May, 1464. It was not until the 29th of September that he dared to declare this union to his brothers, the Dukes of Clarence and Gloucester, and to his redoubtable ally, the Earl of Warwick, or the "Kingmaker," as he was called. Their dissatisfaction was great, but they knew how to restrain it. Elizabeth Woodville was solemnly recognized, in the month of December, at a great national council; and on the 25th of May following she was crowned at Westminster with the usual ceremonies. Her uncle, James of Luxembourg, had come to England upon this occasion in order to raise the family of the new queen a little. "Her father, Sir Richard, was but an esquire in our remembrance," it was said among the people. Future splendors were destined to efface the meanness of the origin. With Elizabeth his family ascended the throne: Sir Richard was made Earl of Rivers, and soon afterwards Lord High Constable; the queen married her sisters to the heirs of the noblest houses. Offices, honors poured down upon the Greys and Woodvilles; and the Nevils, formerly all-powerful by right of their services and their swords, saw their influence decrease day by day, the king no longer asked their advice, nor troubled himself as to their inclination. An annoying incident raised their anger to the highest pitch.

Warwick had for some time been engaged in negotiations for the marriage of the Princess Margaret of York, sister of Edward, with a prince of the royal house of France. The alliance of the princess was equally sought by the Count of Charolais, son of the Duke of Burgundy; but the "Great Earl" was opposed to this marriage, and, authorized by Edward, he repaired to France to conclude terms with King Louis XI. He resided at Rouen in the month of June, 1467, beside the royal palace, and the King of France saw him at all hours of the day and night, in great intimacy, negotiating with that air of mystery which he loved to wear everywhere. Warwick was on his return to London, in the month of July, accompanied by the ambassadors of France, empowered to conclude the royal alliance, when he learned that the Bastard of Burgundy had been at court for several days, under the pretext of a passage of arms, and that the marriage of Margaret of York with the Count of Charolais was almost decided upon. The last obstacle disappeared when Duke Philip died suddenly, on the 15th of July, leaving to his son vast dominions, a rich treasury, and a position in Europe superior to that of most crowned heads. The indignation of Warwick was not the less fiery; he complained of having been deceived, and retired to his castle of Middleham. King Edward feigned to be uneasy at the anger of the Earl: he doubled his guards, and a rumor was spread that Warwick had been won over to the House of Lancaster by King Louis XI. Warwick returned for a moment at the entreaty of his brother, the Archbishop of York; but the Woodvilles remained all-powerful, and the breach became wider every day. Edward with difficulty endured the haughty independence of the man who had made him king; he saw him now, supported by the Duke of Clarence, the heir presumptive to the throne (Elizabeth had had daughters only), who had recently married, at Calais, Lady Isabel, Warwick's eldest daughter. An insurrection broke out almost at the same moment in Yorkshire, directed especially against the relatives of Queen Elizabeth, who were accused of oppression. Lord Montague, who was present in the North, did not endeavor to oppose the movement, which spread with such rapidity that the king, having arrived at Newark, was compelled to retreat precipitately to Nottingham. He wrote with his own hand to Calais, begging the Duke of Clarence and the Earl of Warwick to come to his aid. But before their arrival the insurgents had defeated the Earl of Pembroke at Edgecote, on the 26th of July. Being captured in the pursuit, Earl Rivers and Sir John Woodville, the father and brother of the queen, as well as the Earl of Devon, had been beheaded. It was affirmed that the rebels were acting in concert with Warwick. When he at length landed in England, the king was almost alone at Olney, and the insurgents were advancing against him, but the presence of the Earl soon caused them to retreat. As they returned to their farms and heaths, Warwick conducted Edward IV. to Middleham, the prisoner of his deliverers. England had two kings, both captives.

Warwick did not yet think of changing the rose which he

wore upon his helmet: a fresh insurrection of the partisans of Henry VI. compelled him to march against them. But the army murmured at the captivity of the king: it was necessary to show him to the troops, and the Lancastrians being defeated, harmony appeared to be re-established between the king and the earl. Edward re-entered London: he had purchased his liberty by great gifts. The reconciliation was, however, only apparent: two or three fresh quarrels ended in a victory of the king over the insurgents of Lincolnshire, who were secretly abetted by Clarence and Warwick. Edward accused them publicly of high-treason. The earl did not feel himself powerful enough for an open struggle; he embarked for Calais; but the news of his rebellion had preceded him there; the cannon of the town were pointed against his vessels, and the lieutenant whom he had himself chosen denied him the entrance to the port. The Duchess of Clarence brought into the world her first-born son in her ship, before the town, and it was with great difficulty that a glass of wine was obtained to restore strength to her: "which was," says Commines, "great severity for a servant to show towards his lord."

Warwick sought refuge with King Louis XI. The friendly relations which he had contracted with the king had never been broken off. That astute monarch welcomed the fugitives and at first installed them at Valognes; he then received them at Tours and at Amboise, notwithstanding the anger of the Duke of Burgundy, several of whose vessels had been captured by Warwick. By way of reprisal, the French merchants who had repaired to the fair at Antwerp had been cast into prison by Charles the Bold. Louis XI. ridiculed this act and continued to shuffle the cards, hoping to secure the help of England against the duke, when the Kingmaker should have become once more all-powerful in his country.

It was at Amboise that Warwick and Queen Margaret met secretly, through the agency of the King of France. For fifteen years past the queen had attributed all her misfortunes to Warwick; the earl had not forgotten that she had sent to the scaffold his father, his brother, and his best friends; but a common and a more fervent hatred united them. Margaret consented to the marriage of Prince Edward, her son, with the second daughter of the earl, who thus assured the crown to his children, either in the event of his overthrowing Edward IV. in favor of the Lancastrians, or of his being induced to place Clarence upon the throne. Thanks to Louis XI. they contrived for the time being to amuse or to quiet the Duke of Clarence, notwithstanding all the efforts that the king his brother made to sever him from his allies, and Warwick shortly afterwards set sail, furnished with men and money. Charles of Burgundy had in vain placed in the Channel a fleet destined to arrest him; the earl landed on the 13th of September, 1470, upon the coast of Devonshire, and the entire population gathered under his banners. Sermons were preached in London in favor of King Henry, and Warwick turned his steps in the direction of the Trent. Edward IV. had been summoned to the North a short time before by a fresh insurrection; but the soldiers convoked under the banner of the White Rose did not respond to the appeal; those who hitherto had marched with Edward abandoned him. Warwick continued to advance; the position of King Edward became desperate. He was brave and resolute, but he took the course of flying. Two little Dutch vessels lay moored on the coast, at the mouth of the Wash: he threw himself into them with a few friends, without money and without resources, and crowded sail for the Low Countries, with great difficulty escaping the pirates who infested the seas. He landed near Alkmaar, and the governor "immediately sent tidings to the Duke of Burgundy, who would as well have liked to learn the death of the king," says Commines, "for he was in great apprehension of the Earl of Warwick, who was his enemy and had become all-powerful in England." In fact, everybody in London cried, "Long live King Henry!" Warwick had released from the Tower the poor monarch whom he himself had imprisoned there five years before. Queen Elizabeth Woodville had shut herself up in Westminster Abbey with her mother and her three daughters. It was there that she gave birth to a son, a new claimant to the throne, upon whom the Duke of Clarence looked with as much disfavor as upon the restoration of Henry VI. Louis XI. caused thanksgivings to be offered up to God in all the churches of France for the great victory gained by Henry of Lancaster, the legitimate King of England, over the usurping traitor, the Earl of March. The joy of the king was the more keen inasmuch as Warwick had already returned to him a portion of the money which he had borrowed. In reality, some pirates had seized the vessel and the gold which it carried, but the good intention of the earl was evident, and Louis XI. reckoned upon receiving back his advances, while assuring the power to the enemies of his good cousin of Burgundy; the politic monarch rubbed his hands.

Meanwhile affairs had already changed their aspect in England. As Louis XI. had assisted Warwick, the Duke of Burgundy assisted Edward: he gave him vessels and a small army corps, besides hiring for his service a certain number of pirates. It was with these feeble resources that Edward IV. disembarked on the 16th of March at Ravenspur, where Bolingbroke had landed seventy-two years before to dethrone King Richard II. The reception accorded by the people was not encouraging; none planted the White Rose. Edward no longer spoke of his rights to the throne; he wished only, he said, to reclaim his title of Duke of York. But when he had crossed the Trent he found himself surrounded by his partisans: every day his forces increased. The Marquis of Montague, brother of Warwick, had suffered him to pass. Before arriving at Coventry he had resumed all the royal insignia. The army of Warwick was coming to encounter him; but scarcely had the two parties found themselves face to face, when the Duke of Clarence went over, with all his troops, to the side of his brother. Thus weakened, Warwick was compelled to retreat without fighting. Edward marched upon London, where he was received by the acclamations of the populace. The sermons preached at St. Paul's Cross in favor of King Henry, and the open hospitality of the Earl of Warwick, had already been forgotten. A son had been born to King Edward, who had not yet seen him, and "the wealthy merchants, who had lent money to the king," says Commines, "hoped to be paid when he should have regained possession of the throne." The wives of the great citizens were accustomed to his acts of gallantry. London was merrymaking, but the Lancastrians were already in battle array on the plain of Barnet, within five leagues of the capital. Edward marched against them with the Duke of Clarence. The latter was troubled and uneasy: his wife was Warwick's daughter, and she had great influence over him; he offered his mediation to his father-in-law. "Tell your master," cried the earl, in indignation, "that Warwick is faithful to his oath, and is better than the treacherous and perfidious Clarence. He has referred this to the sword, which will decide the quarrel." It was on Easter-day: the morrow was awaited for the fight.

The struggle began on the 14th of April, at daybreak. Warwick always fought on horseback; but his brother, Lord

Montague, who had joined him, urged him to dismount. "Charge at the head of your men-at-arms," he said. Edward IV. was present in person among his partisans, sword in hand, doing good work. It was not long before both Warwick and his brother were killed; but the rout of the Lancastrians did not stay the slaughter. On returning from Flanders, King Edward had resolved no longer to spare, as formerly, the common people; he had conceived a great hatred of the peasants, so often favorable to his enemies. The field of battle was covered with corpses, when Edward IV. re-entered London, bringing with him the body of the King-maker, which was exposed during three days at Westminster, in order that all might assure themselves of his death. King Henry had been reconducted to the Tower.

Edward IV. had not yet triumphed over his most implacable adversary. Queen Margaret, who had been detained upon the coast of France by contrary winds, landed in England on the very day of the battle of Barnet. She soon learned that her friends had been beaten, that Warwick was killed, that King Henry was again a prisoner. She advanced, however, with her son and the auxiliaries whom she had brought from the Continent. The population was hostile to her; she found the fords and bridges of the Severn defended by her enemies, and was unable to join Lord Pembroke, who still held out in Wales. On the 4th of May, Margaret met King Edward near Tewkesbury. Her troops had skilfully intrenched themselves, but the Duke of Somerset wished to make the attack in the open: a small number of soldiers followed him, and when he attempted to fall back upon his ranks, the Duke of Gloucester had already broken through them. The queen and the prince were made prisoners. The young prince was conducted to Edward. "What brought you hither?" cried the king, angrily. "My right and my father's crown," said the son of Margaret proudly. Edward struck him upon the mouth with his iron gauntlet; the prince staggered, the servants of the king threw themselves upon him and slaughtered him. The great noblemen who accompanied Margaret had taken refuge in Tewkesbury church. The respect accorded to the sacred precincts had protected the wife and the children of King Edward while his enemies were all-powerful in London; but no consideration divine or human could stay him: he entered the church sword in hand. A priest, holding aloft the host, threw himself between the king and his victims: he succeeded in arresting him for a moment; an amnesty was even promised; but, two days later, all the Lancastrians who had taken refuge in Tewkesbury church were dragged forcibly therefrom, and were beheaded.

Queen Margaret had followed her conqueror; her haughty courage had resisted all defeats, all treacheries; she did not succumb beneath the last misfortune. She remained five years a prisoner, alone and poor, first at the Tower, then at Windsor, and finally at Wallingford. King Louis XI. at length obtained her liberty; she returned to France, there to live for several years more. She died in 1482. The king her husband had not survived the battle of Tewkesbury: on the morrow of the triumphal entry of Edward IV. into London, Henry VI. was found dead in the Tower; it was said that the Duke of Gloucester had stabbed him with his own hands. Remorse for this crime perhaps pursued him: when he was king, Richard III. caused the body of Henry VI. to be removed from the abbey of Chertsey, where it had been deposited; the bones of the holy king, it was said, accomplished miracles. When Henry VII. wished to bring them back to Westminster, they could not be found.

The White Rose triumphed everywhere. The great Lancastrian noblemen were dead or prisoners; the Earl of Pembroke and some others had succeeded in taking refuge upon the Continent; the little Prince of Wales had been declared heir to the throne by the great council of the peers; but the king and his brothers could not live in peace. Clarence and Gloucester were contending with each other for the inheritance of the Earl of Warwick. Gloucester had married the Princess Anne, widow of the young Edward assassinated at Tewkesbury. In vain had Clarence concealed her; Gloucester had pursued his prey even under the disguise of a servant, and King Edward had been compelled to divide between the two rivals the property of the "great earl," leaving his widow in veritable poverty; "for," says Commines, "among all the sovereignties in the world of which I have knowledge where public affairs are best managed, that in which there is the least violence towards the people, where there are no buildings cast down or demolished by war, is England; but misfortune and fate fall upon those who have caused the war." The House of the Nevilles was ruined; the enmity between the two brothers of the king was not less on that ground: it was to bring about fresh crimes.

The internal struggle appeared to be drawing to an end. King Edward began to return to foreign wars; the Duke of Burgundy urged him to lend him his co-operation against Louis XI. Edward crossed the sea with a small army and went to Calais; but "before he started from Dover," writes Commines, "he sent to the king our lord one of his heralds named Garter, who was a native of Normandy. He brought to the king a written challenge from the King of England, in beautiful language and in a beautiful style; and I think that never had Englishman put his hand to it." Edward publicly claimed the kingdom of France as his possession, "in order that he might restore the Church, the nobles, and the people to their former liberty," he said. The king read the letter to himself, then wisely retired to his closet, and caused the herald to be summoned thither. "Your king does not come here of his own accord," he said to Garter; "he is constrained by the Duke of Burgundy." And proceeding from this to make overtures of friendship to the King of England, "he privately gave to the said herald three hundred crowns, and promised him a thousand of them if the arrangement should be made, and publicly caused a beautiful piece of crimson velvet, consisting of thirty ells, to be given to him."

Garter, thus treated, advised King Louis XI. to enter into negotiations with Lord Howard or Lord Stanley, favorite ministers of Edward, who were not in favor of the war. The English forces which had recently arrived in Calais were more considerable than had at first been supposed in France. The King of England had concluded a truce with Scotland, and he had imposed on his vassals and the great citizens a new species of tax, under the form of free gifts, called "benevolences." Fifteen or eighteen thousand men were assembled at Calais; but the Duke of Burgundy had dissipated his resources elsewhere, and he presented himself at the place of meeting with a handful of soldiers. The discontent which this deception caused to King Edward inclined him to lend an ear to the proposals of Louis XI. The English army had been inactive before Péronne for two months, and the gold of the King of France circulated freely among the courtiers of Edward. Fifty thousand crowns had already been promised for the ransom of Queen Margaret, when the two sovereigns met at Pecquigny, on each side of a barrier, upon a bridge thrown across the Somme. "In the middle was a trellis, such as are made in the cages of lions, and the holes between the bars were no larger than to allow one's arm

INTERVIEW OF EDWARD IV. AND LOUIS XI.

to be put through with ease." King Louis arrived first, having taken the precaution, on that day, to cause Commines to be clad in the same manner as himself, "for he had long been accustomed to have somebody who dressed similarly to himself." The King of England entered, accompanied by his chamberlain, Lord Hastings. "He was a very handsome prince, and tall, but he began to grow fat, and I had formerly seen him more handsome; for I have no remembrance of ever having seen a more handsome man than he was when Lord Warwick made him fly from England. They embraced through the apertures; the King of England made a profound reverence, and the king began to speak, saying, 'My cousin, welcome; there is no man in the world whom I so much desire to see as you, and praised be God for that we are here assembled with such good intent.' The King of England replied upon this point in pretty good French."

King Louis had invited Edward IV. to come and see him in Paris, but he was rather uneasy lest his politeness should be accepted. "He is a very handsome king," he said to Commines: "he greatly loves the ladies; he might find one among them in Paris who would say so many fine words to him that she would make him wish to return. His predecessors have been too much in Paris and in Normandy. His company is worth nothing on this side of the sea; beyond it, I am very glad to have him for a good brother and friend." All the efforts of Louis XI. tended to conclude the treaty as soon as possible, in order to see the English return to their country; and for this purpose he lavished the treasures amassed with so much care. A pension of fifty thousand livres was assured to King Edward; the hand of the Dauphin was promised to Princess Elizabeth; the great noblemen of the English court had pensions and presents like their master, and a truce for seven years was signed.

The people murmured in England, for the extent of the preparations and the importance of the sums obtained by Edward had created hopes for the conquest of at least Anjou, Maine, Normandy, and Guienne. The French noblemen despised the policy of their king, who purchased the retreat of his enemies instead of repulsing them by arms; but Edward had recrossed the sea, and Louis XI. paid the pensions regularly; he even went so far as to demand a receipt, "and dispatched Maître Pierre Clairet to Lord Hastings, the great chamberlain, to remit two thousand gold crowns to him. And the said Clairet requested that he would deliver to him a letter of three lines, informing the king how he had received them, for the said nobleman was suspicious. But the chamberlain replied, 'My lord master, that which you say is very reasonable; but this gift comes of the good pleasure of the king your lord. If it please you that I take it, you will place it here in my sleeve and will have no letter or acknowledgment for it, for I will not have it said, "The great chamberlain of the King of England has been a pensioner of the King of France," or that my receipts should be found in his exchequer chamber.' With which the king was much incensed, but commended and esteemed the said chamberlain for it, and always paid him without a receipt."

Duke Charles the Bold had recently perished, at the battle of Nancy, in his campaign against Duke René of Lorraine (1477). His only daughter, Mary of Burgundy, inherited his vast dominions. The Duke of Clarence, a widower since the recent death of Warwick's daughter, at once claimed the hand of the young duchess. He was already out of favor at court, and this act of ambition excited the jealousy of the king his brother. Clarence was violent: he complained of the injustice used towards two of his servants, who had been accused of sorcery, condemned and executed. He protested so loudly that the king caused him to be arrested in his turn, and, accusing him of treason, ordered him to be imprisoned in the Tower. The prince appeared before the peers: being prosecuted by the king in person, no baron opened his mouth in his defence; but Clarence protested his innocence at each accusation of magic, rebellion, and conspiracy. Nevertheless the peers declared him guilty, and the House of Commons insisted shortly afterwards upon the carrying out of the sentence. The trial had been public; the execution was secret: on the 18th of February the report of the duke's death spread through London. None knew how he had died, but it was related among the people that the Duke of Gloucester had caused him to be drowned in a butt of Malmsey wine. The well-known tastes of the unhappy duke had no doubt brought about this supposition, for the most absolute mystery still rests over the fate of Clarence. Richard, Duke of Gloucester, maintained the best relations with the queen, and he received from the king a large portion of the estates confiscated from Clarence, while Edward continued to lead a life of feasting and debauchery, everywhere surrounded by ladies whom he entertained magnificently, causing silken tents to be set up for them "when he went to the hunting-field," says Commines; "for no man humored so much his inclination."

Meanwhile war had recommenced with Scotland. King James I. had fallen beneath the dagger of assassins in 1437. His son James II., whose long minority and bad government had thrown Scotland back into the disorder which his father had attempted to dispel, had died in 1460, through the explosion of a cannon which he was testing. James III., who had succeeded him while yet a child, was gentle and timid, little suited to impose his will upon his turbulent barons. Meanwhile the Duke of Gloucester, intrusted with the command of the army, had achieved no success; but the treason of the Duke of Albany, brother of James III., opened new hopes to England in 1482. Berwick had been delivered up to Gloucester, and the King of Scotland, having advanced to repulse the English, saw his favorite Cochrane carried off by the conspirators, who hung him upon Lauder Bridge and took James as their prisoner to Edinburgh. He was still detained in the castle, when the Duke of Gloucester entered the capital with the Duke of Albany. But the presence of an English army opened the eyes of the Scottish barons: they came to an understanding with Albany, who returned into favor with his brother. King James was restored to liberty, and the English retired, in consideration of the cession of the town of Berwick and a promise of certain sums of money. Gloucester re-entered London, where King Edward was meditating a fresh war.

The Princess Elizabeth was sixteen years of age: she had now been for ten years betrothed to the Dauphin, but King Louis did not claim his daughter-in-law. A rumor was even abroad that he had entered into negotiations with Maximilian of Austria, in order to obtain the hand of the Princess Margaret, the only daughter left to him by Mary of Burgundy, who had died in consequence of a fall from a horse in the month of February, 1482. While all the princes of Europe were contending against each other for the heiress of the Dukes of Burgundy, Louis XI. had stealthily taken possession of a portion of her dominions, and it was these conquests that he claimed to have recognized as dowry to "Margot, the gentle damsel," as Margaret of Austria was called. The little princess was but three years of age; but the towns of Flanders which held her in custody accepted the French alliance rejected by Maximilian, and consigned Margaret of Austria into the hands of Louis XI. During all these negotiations the King of France had contrived to amuse Edward IV., while purchasing the silence of Lord Howard, the ambassador at Paris; but when the marriage contract was solemnly celebrated at Paris, "with great festivals and solemnities, King Edward was much irritated therewith. Whoever had joy in this marriage, it displeased the King of England bitterly," says Commines, "for he held it as so great a shame and mockery, and conceived so great a grief for it, as soon as he learned the news of it, that he fell ill and died therefrom, although others say that it was a catarrh." King Edward IV. was not yet forty-one when he expired on the 9th of April, 1483, repenting, it was said, of all the wrong that he had done, and ordering his debts to be paid to all those of whom he had extorted money; but the treasury was empty, and the injured persons were obliged to content themselves with the repentance and the good intention of the dying sovereign. Cruel and suspicious, avaricious, prodigal, and debauched, King Edward IV. had no other virtue than the bravery which had placed him upon the throne; he left two sons, aged thirteen and eleven years, unhappy children, confided to an imprudent and frivolous mother, and to an uncle as ambitious as corrupt.

At the moment when King Edward was dying in London, his brother Richard, Duke of Gloucester, was upon the frontiers of Scotland, at the head of the army, and the Prince of Wales was at Ludlow Castle, the residence of his uncle, Lord Rivers. While the young king was returning slowly to the capital, accompanied by a small body of troops, the Duke of Gloucester, in full mourning, repaired to York with a numerous escort, caused the Church ceremonials to be solemnly performed in honor of the deceased monarch, made oath of fidelity to his nephew, caused all the noblemen of the environs to do likewise, and wrote to his sister-in-law, Elizabeth

Woodville, to assure her of his sentiments, and to place himself at her disposition. Already, however, notwithstanding the reconciliation which had taken place beside the deathbed of Edward IV., suspicions and discord reigned between the queen's party and the old favorites of her husband. Lord Hastings, High Chamberlain of England, wrote to the Duke of Gloucester; and the Duke of Buckingham, a prince of the royal house, a descendant of Thomas of Woodstock, the youngest son of Edward III., had received the emissaries of the crafty Richard. The young king and his uncle met on the 25th of April at Stoney-Stratford; on the preceding evening the Duke of Gloucester had received at Northampton the visit of the Lords Rivers and Grey, and had cordially welcomed them, as well as the Duke of Buckingham, who had arrived at his residence after them. But scarcely did Richard find himself in the presence of the little Edward V. and hold the child in his power, when he accused Lord Rivers of having endeavored to alienate the affections of his nephew from him; and he caused him to be arrested, as well as Lord Grey and several personages of the royal house. Gloucester and Buckingham bent their knees before the young king, saluting him as their sovereign; but the sovereign was a prisoner, and was taken to London, while his uncle and his servants were conducted to Pontefract Castle of lugubrious memory.

The rumor of these arrests had already reached the capital. Queen Elizabeth, alarmed, had retired into Westminster Abbey with her second son. Hastings, a traitor or a dupe, assured the population of the city that the two dukes were acting only in the interest of the public welfare. He set out to meet the young king, while the agents of Gloucester were spreading in London violent accusations against the queen, who had, it was said, plotted with her relatives for the death of the princes of the blood, in order to be able to govern the king at her pleasure. There were even shown the casks filled with arms, which she had, it was said, collected in order to destroy her enemies. The people began to declare that all these traitors must be hanged. The arrival of the little king was announced.

He made his entry into London on the 5th of June, magnificently dressed and mounted upon a beautiful horse. His uncle preceded him, bareheaded, with all the marks of the most affectionate respect. Edward V. at first took up his abode in the bishop's palace, then, upon the proposal which the Duke of Buckingham made to the council, he was transported to the Tower for greater security. The assembly of peers awarded to the Duke of Gloucester the title of Protector and Defender of the kingdom, and he installed himself in one of the royal palaces, where a crowd of courtiers thronged around him. A small number of noblemen, at the head of whom was Lord Hastings, met together at the Tower. "I know everything that goes forward at the duke's," said the high chamberlain of Edward IV. to Lord Stanley, who was becoming uneasy at the machinations of Richard. He was not aware, however, of the imminence of the danger that threatened him.

On the 12th of June Richard entered the council of the Tower with a serene countenance; he chatted gayly with the peers who surrounded him. "My lord," he said to the Bishop of Ely, "it is said that the strawberries of your garden in Holborn are excellent." "I will send and get some if it please your Highness," replied the prelate. While the strawberries were being gathered, the Protector had gone out; when he returned, his face had become overcast. "What do traitors who plot for my destruction deserve?" he exclaimed on entering. "Death!" replied Lord Hastings, without hesitating. "That sorceress, my brother's wife," replied Richard, "and that other sorceress who is always with her, Mistress Shore, have no other aim but to rid themselves of me; see how, with their enchantments, they have already destroyed and consumed my body!" And he raised his left sleeve, exposing his arm, emaciated and withered to the elbow. None uttered a word; all knew that the duke had been born with his arm thus deformed. He was tall like his brothers; his countenance was handsome, but he was hunchbacked and his features had never expressed a more bitter malignity than at the moment when, turning towards Hastings, he repeated his question. "I' faith they deserve death, my lord, if they have thus plotted against you." "*If!*" repeated the Protector; "why do you use *ifs* and *buts* to me? I will prove upon thy body the truth of that which I say, traitor that thou art!" and he struck a heavy blow upon the table angrily; at the same instant the door opened, and a band of armed men rushed into the council-chamber. "Traitor, I arrest you!" said Richard, taking Hastings by the collar. A soldier had raised his battle-axe against Lord Stanley, but the latter had taken refuge under the table; he was seized, however, and carried to prison, as well as the Archbishop of York and the Bishop of Ely. "As to my lord chamberlain," said Gloucester, "let him hasten to have himself absolved, for, by St. Paul, I will not sit down to table while he has his head upon his shoulders." A few moments later the unhappy Hastings, dragged by the soldiers into the courtyard of the chapel, was beheaded upon a log which happened to be there. On the same day, by order of Sir Richard Ratcliffe, who presented himself at Pontefract at the head of a body of troops, Lord Rivers, Lord Grey, Sir Thomas Vaughan, and Sir Thomas Hawse were executed before the castle, in public, but without being allowed to address a word to the crowd which thronged around the scaffold; for "Ratcliffe had long been in the confidence of the duke," says a chronicler, "and he was a man having experience of the world, of a crafty mind and a bold tongue, as far removed from all pity as he was from the fear of God."

Meanwhile the Protector had repaired to Westminster with the Archbishop of Canterbury and several peers and noblemen, demanding that Queen Elizabeth should at once consign to him the person of the Duke of York, whose company his brother wished for, and whose absence from the coronation would cause grievous and calumniatory rumors to be circulated against the Protector. The queen was defenceless; she had no party in the city, her relatives and friends were dead or prisoners; she yielded, tearfully embracing the son who yet remained to her, and who was now doubtless snatched away from her for his destruction. The little Duke of York went and joined his brother in the Tower.

Mistress Jane Shore, the favorite of Edward IV., had been condemned to do public penance for her bad conduct and sorcery; she had traversed the streets of London barefooted and in a sheet, with a taper in her hand, and had then taken refuge, deprived of all her riches, in a humble house where she was received in charity. It was on Sunday, the 22d of June, when a preacher, Dr. Shaw, drew a crowd at St. Paul's Cross, by loudly asserting that King Edward V. and his brother, the Duke of York, were not the legitimate children of Edward IV., who was already married when he espoused their mother. "Much more," he added, "who knows even whether King Edward IV. was the son of the Duke of York? All those who knew the illustrious Duke Richard, assert that the Earl of March bore no resemblance to him; on the contrary, see!" he cried, as the Duke of Gloucester appeared at a balcony near the pulpit, "judge yourselves whether the noble Protector is not, feature for feature, the image of the hero whom we mourn." The mob listened aghast; acclamations and a popular proclamation of King Richard had been hoped for; but the people preserved silence, the Protector knitted his brows, the preacher precipitately ended his sermon and disappeared in the serried ranks of auditors. It is asserted that he died of grief in consequence of this rebuff.

The ice was broken, however, and on the second day afterwards the cause was intrusted to a more illustrious advocate: the Duke of Buckingham presented himself at Guildhall, and, repeating to the citizens the arguments which the preacher had expounded before the populace, he asserted that the Duke Richard was the only legitimate descendant of the Duke of York, and that the noblemen, like the commons of the north, had vowed never to obey a bastard. The citizens still hesitated, no voice was raised from the crowd; the duke insisted upon having a reply; the poor people who thronged at the door threw their caps in the air, crying "Long live King Richard!" On the morrow the Duke of Buckingham had succeeded in gaining over a certain number of citizens, and he was accompanied both by the peers and the Lords of the Council when he presented himself at the Protector's. The latter at first affected to refuse to listen; the matter was urged, and the Duke of Buckingham, in the name of the Lords spiritual and temporal, as well as of the Commons of England, implored Richard, Duke of Gloucester, Protector and Defender of the kingdom, to relieve England from the misfortune of being governed by a bastard, by accepting the crown himself. The Protector hesitated, speaking of his affection for his nephews. "If you refuse," cried Buckingham, "the people of England will know well where to find a king who will accept without needing to be entreated." Richard no longer persisted. "It was his duty," he said, "to submit to

THE TOWER OF LONDON IN 1690.

the will of the nation, and, since it was required, he accepted the royal estate of the two noble kingdoms of England and France: the one, to govern and direct it from this day; the other, to conquer and regain it as soon as it should be possible." King Edward V. was dethroned before having reigned, and King Richard III. ascended the throne.

None protested, none objected in favor of the poor children confined in the Tower. The preparations begun for the coronation of the nephew served for the coronation of the uncle; Richard was consecrated at Westminster on the 6th of June, with his wife Anne, daughter of Warwick; Lord Howard was made Duke of Norfolk, the Archbishop of York was set at liberty, Lord Stanley was received into favor. The new king travelled from county to county, administering justice, listening to the complaints of his subjects, and repeated at York the coronation ceremony. Everywhere he was received with favor, and the disaffected did not show themselves.

In London, however, an agitation began to be stirred up in favor of the young princes; secret meetings had taken place, the health of the two children had been drunk, their partisans made overtures to Queen Elizabeth. The Duke of Buckingham himself, who had placed the crown upon the head of the usurper, and who had been richly rewarded for it, had doubtless conceived some misgivings as to the ulterior intentions of Richard towards him; for he suddenly altered his course and placed himself at the head of the confederates, who were working to create in the south of England a party for the restoration of Edward V. Appearances were favorable; already Queen Elizabeth was beginning to take courage, when suddenly the Abbey gates were found closed; it was forbidden to allow any one to enter or leave, and the unhappy mother learned at the same time that her cruel brother-in-law had been informed of the conspiracy, and that he had baffled it in advance; the two princes no longer existed.

Assassinations almost always remain enveloped in mystery: it is related that scarcely had Richard quitted London when he had sent back instructions to cause Sir Robert Brackenbury, the guardian of the Tower, to be corrupted. Finding him inflexible, he had simply deposed him for twenty-four hours, consigning his office into the hands of his master of the horse, Sir John Tyrrell. The latter had, it was said, entered the Tower in the evening, accompanied by two robbers, and during the night they had stifled under their pillows the young princes, lying in the same bed. Then they had been interred noiselessly at the foot of the staircase, and the murderers had gone back to King Richard to receive their reward.

Great were the consternation and horror among the conspirators, but they had gone too far to recede; they could expect no mercy. A claimant for the crown was sought: the Bishop of Ely proposed Henry, Earl of Richmond, grandson of Owen Tudor and Catherine of France, representing the House of Lancaster by the right of his mother, Margaret Beaufort, great-granddaughter of John of Gaunt. He lived in Brittany, exiled like all his race. He could, it was said, be made to wed Lady Elizabeth of York, eldest sister of the unfortunate Edward V., and thus unite the claims of the two royal Houses, whose strife had cost England so much blood. The project was immediately adopted; the Countess of Richmond, Henry's mother, had married, for her second husband, Lord Stanley, the secret enemy of Richard III. He entered with ardor into the conspiracy, which extended every day; but the secret was so well kept that the reply of the Earl of Richmond had arrived in England, and he was preparing to set out from Saint Malo, before

King Richard had learned the new danger which threatened him. At the first disclosure, he called together his army at Leicester; but he had not joined his troops when already the insurrection had broken out: the Marquis of Dorset had proclaimed Henry VII. at Exeter, the Bishop of Salisbury had declared himself in his favor in Wiltshire, the gentlemen of Kent and Berkshire had taken up arms, and the Duke of Buckingham displayed his banner at Brecknock.

The time was not yet ripe for the insurrection; the Earl of Richmond had been for a long time tossed about by contrary winds, and his forces were so insufficient when he approached the coast of Devonshire, that he did not venture to disembark. The Duke of Buckingham had found the rivers swollen in Wales: having arrived at the Severn, he had been compelled to retrace his steps; his soldiers had disbanded without striking a blow; the duke had disguised himself, endeavoring to escape, and had taken refuge in the hut of a peasant, who betrayed him. King Richard arrived at Salisbury as his former friend was being brought there; he refused to see him, and immediately caused him to be beheaded. The other insurgents had fled to the continent; those who were captured paid with their lives for their attempt; King Richard was everywhere triumphant, without having unsheathed his sword.

For the first time Richard had convoked a Parliament; he wished to have his usurpation and vengeance ratified. Trembling before him, the Peers and Commons of England declared that King Richard III. was the sole legitimate possessor of the throne, which belonged to his descendants forever, beginning with his son Edward, Prince of Wales. At the same time, and to punish the enemies of the new sovereign, the Parliament voted a bill of attainder, which deprived of their property and dignities all those who had been involved in the last conspiracy; the Countess of Richmond alone obtained mercy through the intercession of her husband, Lord Stanley, skilful in remaining on good terms with the two parties, and even in deceiving the perfidious and suspicious Richard.

Meanwhile the exiles had assembled in Brittany, where they enjoyed the favor of Duke Francis and the support of his minister, Pierre Landais. At the Christmas festivities, 1483, Henry of Richmond gathered his partisans around him, solemnly swore to wed Elizabeth of York as soon as he should have triumphed over the usurper, and received the homage of all present. But King Richard had not renounced his vengeance: Landais was gained over, and the protection of Duke Francis failing the exiles, they were about to be delivered up to their cruel enemy, when, warned in time, they escaped into France and found refuge and assistance at the court of King Charles VIII.

At the same time that Richard was pursuing with his hatred Henry of Richmond, he was laboring in England to deprive the earl of the support which alone could raise him to the throne. The Yorkists could not ally themselves with the Lancastrian prince, except in consideration of his marriage with Elizabeth of York; Richard resolved to sever from his alliance the queen and her daughter. He entered into correspondence with Elizabeth Woodville; she was weary of her voluntary prison, ambitious, and frivolous; she forgot all, the usurpation, the murder of her sons, of her brother, of her most faithful friends, and, after having obtained from the king a solemn oath to treat both herself and her daughters as good relatives, the queen quitted her retreat and appeared at court, where the Princess Elizabeth was loaded with honors. Her marriage with the Prince of Wales was already spoken of, although the latter was scarcely eleven years of age and the Princess Elizabeth was at least eighteen, when the boy died suddenly at Middleham Castle. For a moment Richard appeared to stagger under the blow, but he soon recovered himself; he had formed a new project. Queen Anne was ill, and at all the festivals the Princess Elizabeth appeared, wearing in advance the royal robes. "When will she come to an end, then?" said Elizabeth; "she is a long time dying!" The queen-dowager had written to her friends to abandon the Earl of Richmond, saying that she had found a better arrangement for the family. Anne died at length, but the friends of King Richard did not approve of his project: he was accused, they said, of having poisoned his wife. The support of the northern counties was due to their fidelity to the House of Warwick; the people considered this marriage with his brother's daughter as incestuous. Richard fell back before these objections; he felt his throne insecure. King Charles VIII. had furnished the Earl of Richmond with men and money, and the latter had recently embarked at Harfleur. The King of England was raising an army to defend himself; at the same time he was lavish of proclamations against "one Henry Tudor by name, of illegitimate descent on the side of his father as well as his mother, having no right to the crown of England, pledged to the King of France to abandon to him forever Normandy, Guienne, Anjou, Maine, and even Calais, and coming into England, followed by an army of foreigners, to whom he had promised the earldoms and bishoprics, the baronies and the fiefs of knights." He therefore summoned all his good subjects to defend their country like loyal Englishmen, by providing him with soldiers and money, and he promised to spare neither his property nor his person to protect them against the common enemy.

The last remains of Richard's popularity in London had disappeared before the forced loans which he had been obliged to make, and which the citizens called "malevolences." The royal banner had been raised at Nottingham, and a considerable army had rallied around the king; but the coasts were ill defended, and among the noblemen who had not replied to the appeal was Lord Stanley, ill, it was said, and detained in his bed. The king took possession of his son, Lord Strange, by way of hostage, and continued his march towards his rival; whose forces were not as yet very considerable. "There will not be one man in ten who will fight for Richard," asserted the Earl of Richmond, and he advanced resolutely as far as Atherston.

It is in the nature of tyrants and traitors to live in fear of treason. The House of York, so often stained with innocent blood, had never lacked courage. Richard III. had often exhibited the most brilliant valor. He was destined to give further proof of this on the morrow. It is, however, a touch of Shakspeare's incomparable genius to have assembled so many terrible visions around the pillow of Richard III. during the night before the battle, and to have caused all the victims of his perfidy to pass before him, like so many sinister heralds, announcing his doom. When daylight dawned, the king already felt himself condemned and conquered.

On the 22d of August, the two adversaries met in the plain of Bosworth: the invading army was small; King Richard surveyed it with disdain as he rode along his lines, the golden crown glittering upon his helmet. The combat began, "sharp and severe," says a chronicler, "and more severe would it have been if the party of the king had remained stanch to him; but some joined the enemy, and others waited to see to which side victory would turn." By degrees, the banners which just now waved in Richard's camp floated beside the Earl of Richmond; gaps were made in the royal ranks; Lord Stanley had just arrived with three thousand men, and was fighting for his son-in-law. King Richard hurried from group to group, now in the centre, then at the wings, encouraging, directing, urging the soldiers; the Duke of Norfolk and his retainers alone remained resolutely faithful to him; at length the king saw himself ruined. "A horse," Shakspeare makes him exclaim, "my kingdom for a horse!" He buried his spurs in the flanks of his steed. "Treason!" he cried, and he rushed into the midst of his enemies. He made his way towards Richmond, striking down to right and left those who resisted him; already he had overthrown the standard-bearer and aimed a blow at his rival, when the crowd of knights closed in around him; he fell, pierced with a hundred wounds. Lord Stanley picked up the crown, crushed by battle-axes and stained with the royal blood, and placed it upon the head of his son-in-law. "Long live King Henry VII.!" he cried. "Long live King Henry VII.!" responded the army, and the cry was repeated in the ranks of the enemy. The faithful partisans of Richard had perished like himself. The dead king was deprived of his arms, and was brought back to Leicester behind a herald; he was exposed for three days in the church, that the people might assure themselves of the death of the last prince of the House of York. When he was interred in the monastery of the Grey Friars, Henry Tudor, Earl of Richmond, was king under the name of Henry VII. The wars of the Two Roses had ended, and the era of the great reigns was about to begin for England.

CHAPTER XVI.

THE TUDORS.

RE-ESTABLISHMENT OF REGULAR GOVERNMENT. HENRY VII. 1485–1509.

THE new sovereign of England was destined to render her important services; he was not, however, a great man. Amid the general disorder, in view of the growing desire for order and peace, he was enabled to display, and did in fact display, a prudence and moderation which caused him to avoid the great faults, and preserved him from the terrible reverses which had attended his predecessors; but his character and his acts rarely excite our admiration and respect. His first care, on the morrow of the victory which had placed him upon the throne, was to transfer from the castle of Sheriffe-Sutton to the Tower of London, Edward Plantagenet, Earl of Warwick, son of the unfortunate Duke of Clarence, a boy of fifteen years, who had grown up in prison since his father's death, and who was destined there to pass the remainder of his life. He had recently had as a companion in his captivity, Princess Elizabeth, confined at Sheriffe-Sutton by her uncle, King Richard III., when he had been compelled to relinquish his scheme of marrying her. The young earl was now sent to the Tower, an abode fatal to the princes of his race. Lady Elizabeth was, on the contrary, loaded with honors and brought back, with a numerous retinue, to her mother, Queen Elizabeth Woodville, already

ROYAL MANOR AT RICHMOND.

HENRY VII. LAYING THE STANDARDS ON THE ALTAR.

willing to hail the new sovereign for and against whom she had plotted, and who at length promised her the satisfaction of her ambition.

These precautions being taken, Henry VII. made his entry into London, on the 27th of August, 1485, with much pomp, and laid upon the high altar of St. Paul's church the three standards under which he had marched to victory, — the figure of St. George, the Red Dragon, and — it is not known why — a brown cow. The people made merry in the streets, but already among the poor a distemper manifested itself, which soon spread into all classes of society, and made great ravages. It was a kind of sweating sickness, so called, which does not appear to have been known hitherto, and the attacks of which were, it is said, almost always mortal. It was necessary to wait for the amelioration of the public health before proceeding to the coronation of the new king. On the occasion of the ceremony, which took place on the 30th of October, by the hands of the Cardinal-Archbishop Bourchier, the same who, two years before, had proclaimed Richard III., the new sovereign raised his uncle, the Earl of Pembroke, to the rank of Duke of Bedford; his father-in-law, Lord Stanley, was created Earl of Derby, and Sir Edward Courtenay became Earl of Devonshire. The king at the same time took care to surround his person with a guard of robust archers; this innovation astonished and discontented the people, but Henry VII., nevertheless, kept his guard; he knew by experience the small value of moral guaranties in a time of disorder and corruption.

Parliament assembled at Westminster on the 7th of November. The accession of King Henry VII. to the throne was due to the discontent of the nation under the sanguinary yoke of Richard III. and to the hopes which were founded upon the projected union between the two rival Houses of

York and Lancaster. Henry himself attributed it to his valor upon the battlefield of Bosworth, from which event he always dated the commencement of his reign; but the national exhaustion and the royal conquest were not secure foundations upon which to build a throne, and in the speech of Henry VII. to the assembled Commons, he urged his hereditary rights, as well as the favor of the Most High, who had given the victory to his sword. This last clause excited some uneasiness among the great lords, who held all their titles and property from the fallen monarch. Henry hastened to reassure them, declaring that each should retain "his estates and inheritances, with the exception of the persons whom the present Parliament should think proper to punish for their offences." Scrupulous people for a moment were disquieted when they perceived that the majority of the members of the House of Commons had formerly been outlawed by the kings Edward IV. and Richard III.; the very sovereign who had convoked the Parliament found himself in the same position. Had the Houses the right to sit? The judges were consulted, and declared that the crown removes all disqualifications, and that the king, in ascending the throne, was by that fact alone relieved of all the sentences passed upon him; members of the House of Commons, who had been outlawed, were obliged to wait, before taking their seats, until a law should revoke their condemnation. The act was immediately passed, and the Lancastrians, excluded by the policy of the sovereigns of the House of York, re-entered Parliament; all were weary of the struggle, and the great noblemen easily obtained special ordinances which re-established them in all their rights and honors.

This was not, however, in all respects the king's wish; he was not bloodthirsty, and did not seek to avenge himself by the execution of his enemies; but he was greedy, he wanted money, and confiscations were an easy means of enriching himself without oppressing or exasperating the people. Henry VII. therefore presented to Parliament a law which antedated by a single day his accession to the throne, fixing it at the 21st of August, the eve of the battle of Bosworth, the new sovereign, who then in reality was but the Earl of Richmond, finding himself thus in a position to accuse of high treason all those who had fought against him, beginning with Richard III., whom he called the Duke of Gloucester, and of whom he enumerated with good reason all the tyrannies and crimes. Richard was dead, as well as the greater number of the partisans who had remained faithful to him; others had exiled themselves; but if the Duke of Norfolk had fallen at Bosworth, if Lord Lovel had taken refuge in a church, their visible property, the riches accumulated in their castles, had not disappeared with them, and the Act meekly voted by Parliament permitted the king to seize upon the lands and treasures. This he did not fail to do; no sanguinary vengeance sullied the beginning of the new reign; Henry VII. contented himself with filling his coffers.

It was still to Parliament, discredited as it was by the servility which it had for so many years manifested towards the rival sovereigns who had succeeded each other upon the throne, that belonged the right of constituting the new dynasty. The provident wisdom of King Henry VII. did not seek in this solemn act to find support in long genealogies, nor in the Divine favor manifested by the victory; he contented himself with causing the revocation of all the acts passed in the Yorkist parliaments against the House of Lancaster. Avoiding with care all allusion to the Princess Elizabeth and her family, he simply relieved her of the stain of illegitimacy, which Richard III. had inflicted upon her to justify his usurpation; Parliament contented itself with declaring that the inheritance and succession to the crown "should be, remain, and rest in the most royal person of our now sovereign Lord, King Henry VII., and of his legitimate descendants, forever, by the grace of God." The rights of the House of York to the throne were passed over in silence ; mention was not made of the projected union with the Princess Elizabeth ; Henry VII. was unwilling to have it said that he owed the crown to a woman.

The nation, however, had not forgotten its past misfortunes ; it hoped to enjoy a little peace only through the alliance of the two rival houses, and the king's delay in celebrating his marriage, the affectation which he made of not speaking of it, caused uneasiness, not only to his Yorkist enemies, but to the whole people. When the Commons came and solemnly offered to the king the duties upon ships and upon wools, now conceded for life, they accompanied their liberality by a peremptory request, asking him to take for his wife and spouse the Princess Elizabeth, "which marriage they hoped God would bless with a progeny of the race of kings." The Lords spiritual and temporal supported the petition of the Commons. Henry VII. understood that he had delayed enough, and on the 18th of January, 1486, the two Roses were at length united upon the same stem ; the hatreds and rivalries, which had cost so much blood to England, were definitively appeased by the marriage of King Henry VII., the descendant of the House of Lancaster through his ancestor, John of Gaunt, and the Princess Elizabeth, daughter of King Edward IV., the direct heiress of the rights and claims of the House of York. All the grants made by the sovereigns who had succeeded each other upon the throne of England since the thirty-fourth year of the reign of Henry VI., the period at which the war had begun to assume the character of a revolt, were revoked by Parliament; an amnesty was proclaimed for all those who were willing to submit to the royal clemency and take the oath of allegiance; the king reinstated in his property and honors the son of the Duke of Buckingham, the last victim of Richard III.'s cruelty; he loaded with favors the friends who had helped him to ascend the throne,—Chandos, Sir Giles Dunbury, Sir Robert Willoughby, the Marquis of Dorset, Sir John Bourchier; he caused his authority to be confirmed by a bull of Pope Innocent III., which proclaimed all the hereditary rights of the new sovereign, wisely omitted from the English Act of Parliament, granted to Henry VII. the necessary dispensation for his marriage with the Princess Elizabeth, of whom he was a relative, then confirmed the elevation of the king to the throne, freely interpreting the Act of Parliament, and declaring that in the event that the queen should die without children, or after having lost them, the crown should belong by right to the posterity of Henry VII. by a second marriage. All precautions being wisely taken, and his authority solidly established, the king pronounced the dissolution of his Parliament, and began a royal progress through the northern counties, in order to secure the good will of that portion of the kingdom still attached to the House of York.

Henry's customary prudence had failed him on one point. Jealous of the supreme power, he had kept in the shade the princess whom he had been compelled to wed, and had not taken her with him upon his journey through his kingdom; discontent was everywhere manifested upon this point in the north, but the pregnancy of the queen served as an excuse for her absence. The royal progress did not proceed, besides, without disquieting incidents. On the 17th of April the king was at Pontefract, when he learned that Lord Lovel had quitted the sanctuary at Colchester and barred his road with considerable forces. The lords and gentry of the counties through which Henry VII. had recently passed, assembled around him; he advanced against the rebels. Lord Lovel fled, concealed himself, and soon repaired to Flanders; his friends Humphrey, and Thomas Stafford, who had prepared an insurrection in Worcestershire, took refuge in Colesham Church, near Abington; they were dragged thence, and the elder Humphrey perished on the scaffold; the younger received his pardon; and the king, on the 26th of April, entered York, one of the rare spots in England where the memory of King Richard III. was affectionately preserved.

We have said that Henry VII. was greedy; but he knew how, on occasion, to relax his greed; he lavished gifts and honors, reduced the crown rents of the city of York, caused festivals to be celebrated, and thus conquered the favor of the people, who cried in the streets, "God save King Henry! God preserve that sweet and handsome countenance!" When he resumed his march towards the south-east, Henry VII. continued, from town to town, the practice which he had established at York. He attended regularly upon divine service; but after mass, every Sunday and holiday, one of the bishops who accompanied him read and expounded to the faithful the papal bull, threatening with eternal punishment all the enemies of the monarch, whose rights to the throne were therein so carefully set forth. The king had just reached London, in the month of June, when he received an embassy from James IV., King of Scotland, with whom he concluded a treaty of alliance, promising to cement it later by a union between the two families; peace and mutual good feeling were equally important to both kings, surrounded by enemies whom they dreaded to see take refuge in the neighboring kingdom. The little prince, whose hand Henry VII. had already promised, was born on the 20th of September, at Winchester, and was named Arthur, in memory of the hero of the old romances,

King Arthur of the Round Table, whose death tradition still denied.

Usurpations engender conspiracies; no reign was to be more constantly agitated by them than that of Henry VII.; he had occupied the throne for fifteen months only, when, in November, 1486, a priest and a youth of most charming countenance disembarked at Dublin. The priest announced that his young companion was no other than Edward Plantagenet, Earl of Warwick, escaped by a miracle from the Tower of London. By degrees, partisans gathered around the young man; he was handsome and intelligent, his manners were noble; he had been carefully instructed in his part, and experienced but little difficulty in deceiving minds prepossessed by an hereditary attachment to the father and grandfather of the Earl of Warwick, who had both succeeded in rendering themselves popular in their government of Ireland. Edward Plantagenet had even been born in that country, and thus possessed additional rights to the attachment of the nation. The great noblemen, who might have shown themselves more clear-sighted, were, in general, little in favor of the state of affairs recently established in England, and the Earl of Kildare, Lord Lieutenant of Ireland, received the pretended Warwick with open arms, presenting him to all his friends as the legitimate heir to the throne in the character of the only male descendant of Richard of York. On all sides the impostor was saluted with the title of king; messengers had already borne the news to Flanders, where the Dowager Duchess of Burgundy, sister of Edward IV., was holding her court, and receiving into her good graces all the enemies of the new King of England, when the latter learned, in London, the danger that threatened him. He immediately summoned his Council; discontent was general, the amnesty had been ill-observed, a mass of restrictions had hindered the application of it, and the real Earl of Warwick was not the only inhabitant of the prison of the Tower. The first care of the prudent king was to proclaim a fresh amnesty, more complete and sincere than the first, and, at the same time, to produce in public, in all parts of London, the real Edward Plantagenet, Earl of Warwick, who had not for a single instant left his prison. The third measure of the king appeared at variance with the clemency manifested by the amnesty; the Dowager Queen, Elizabeth Woodville, was arrested under the frivolous pretext that she had formerly broken faith with the Earl of Richmond, now King of England, since, after having promised him her daughter in marriage, she had given her into the hands of the usurper, Richard III., who wished to marry her. The real motive of the disfavor which suddenly attacked the intriguing widow of Edward IV. has never been known. It has been supposed that she was compromised in the conspiracy which had caused a new pretender to the throne to spring up in Ireland; it has been said that she alone could have instructed the young man or his tutor in the private details which he related about the royal family; but these assertions remain at least doubtful. What is certain is the confiscation of Elizabeth Woodville's property, and her imprisonment in a convent near Bermondsey.

Meanwhile the young pretender to the throne had received an unexpected support. The Earl of Lincoln, son of John de la Pole, Duke of Suffolk, and of Elizabeth, sister of Edward IV. and Richard III., who had formerly been designated by his uncle Richard to succeed him upon the throne, had quitted England and repaired to the residence of his aunt, the Duchess of Burgundy. She had furnished him with money and troops, and Lincoln had embarked for Ireland with Lord Lovel. He could not be deceived about the imposture; he knew the Earl of Warwick, but it suited his views to adopt

KENILWORTH CASTLE IN RUINS.

the cause of the pretender, and he caused him to be crowned in Dublin Cathedral. The golden crown from a statue of the Virgin was borrowed to represent the royal diadem, and the young man, being proclaimed under the name of Edward VI., was carried in triumph upon the shoulders of his new subjects, while King Henry VII. was raising troops and quietly riding about in his kingdom, selecting by preference for his visits the counties where the influence of the Earl of Lincoln was especially exercised.

The queen and the little prince were already established in the fortress of Kenilworth, when the pretender and his partisans landed at Fouldrey, at the southern extremity of Furness. A few friends of Lincoln and Lovel came and joined him, but the population did not rise in their favor, and the hopes of the rebels were already growing faint, when, on the 16th of June, 1487, they encountered the vanguard of the king at Stoke; the Earl of Oxford, who commanded it, gained a brilliant victory, notwithstanding the desperate courage of the assailants. His Majesty Edward VI., or, simply, Lambert Simnel, the baker's son, was made prisoner, with his tutor, the priest Simon; but the noblemen who had embraced his cause nearly all died upon the field of battle, the Earl of Lincoln at their head. Lord Lovel alone disappeared; but this time he concealed himself so well that, two hundred years later, the skeleton of a man was discovered in a vault in his castle of Minster-Lovel, in Oxfordshire: it is supposed that the unfortunate master of the house had taken refuge therein and had there perished by some accident.

Very few executions followed the revolt and the victory, but the harvest of confiscations was abundant; the priest Simon was imprisoned, and never heard of again, "the king being fond of concealing his own dangers," says a chronicler. "Lambert Simnel was placed in the royal kitchens, ignominiously turning the spit, after having worn a crown;" he became eventually one of the king's falconers. In conclusion, Henry VII. made a pilgrimage to deposit his victorious banner upon the altar of Our Lady of Walsingham.

The king had too much sense and sagacity to refuse to understand the symptoms of discontent which had manifested themselves by this revolt; he knew that he had incensed the Yorkists by the jealous obscurity in which he kept the queen, and he resolved to grant her the honor of coronation, which had hitherto been claimed for her in vain; on the 20th of November, Elizabeth of York was solemnly crowned at Westminster, while her husband, hidden behind a carved screen, contemplated the ceremony at which he had not been willing to be present.

For more than two years past, King Henry VII. had concentrated all his efforts upon the internal pacification of his kingdom, without making himself uneasy about the troubles of the Continent; but scarcely had he gained the victory of Stoke, when he saw an embassy arrive in England from the King of France, Charles VIII. While Henry VII. had been repulsing the pretensions to the throne of an impostor supported by rebels, his old protector, the King of France, had attacked a still older friend of his, Duke Francis of Brittany, who had given shelter to the Duke of Orleans, subsequently Louis XII., accused of having conspired against his cousin. A French army had entered Brittany, summoned by a certain number of Breton noblemen dissatisfied with the influence which the Duke of Orleans had obtained over their duke, and it had gained important advantages, when the ambassadors of Charles VIII., fearing an English intervention in favor of the Duke of Brittany, came to expound to the wise Henry VII. the legitimacy of a war which they described as defensive. None made allusion to the probable annexation of the duchy of Brittany to France, either by conquest or by the marriage of the young king with the heiress of Duke Francis; Henry VII. asked no indiscreet questions, and when the Bretons, in their turn, appeared at his court, begging assistance in men and money, the King of England piously offered his mediation "in order to acquit himself before God and men of all his duties of gratitude towards the king and the duke, for whom he was even disposed to go upon a pilgrimage." The French asked for nothing more; their army pursued its victorious career, but the coming and going of English negotiators from London to Paris and from Paris to Rennes, did not satisfy the Bretons, who saw themselves closely pressed. Sir Edward Woodville, one of the queen's uncles, attempted, at his own risk, a little expedition in favor of Duke Francis; but King Henry forbade any demonstration of this kind. His envoys, who were then in Paris, had been in great danger, it was said, at the news of the succor sent to the Bretons by the English.

The cause of Brittany was popular in England, and, decided though he was not to wage war, the king took advantage of this feeling to obtain from Parliament considerable subsidies; at the same time he secretly warned the court of France that he should perhaps be compelled to send reinforcements to the Bretons. Acting upon this information, Charles VIII. pushed matters vigorously; all the Breton factions had now united against the common enemy; the forces of the duke were supported by troops sent by the King of the Romans, Maximilian, and by the Count d'Albret, as well as Sir Edward Woodville's Englishmen. Duke Francis and his allies were defeated, however, on the 20th of July, 1488, by the Sire de la Trémoille, commander of the French army, at Saint Aubin-du-Cormier; the Duke of Orleans was made a prisoner, and the English were cut to pieces. Before the public voice had been raised in England to demand vengeance, the French had taken Dinan and Saint Malo, and were even threatening the Duke of Brittany in Rennes; the unhappy prince had no other resource than to sign a treaty by which he promised to summon no assistance from abroad, and never to marry his daughters, without the consent of France. One month after having suffered this humiliation, he died broken-hearted, and the little Duchess Anne, a child twelve years of age, remained alone with her council of regency, in the presence of her enemies.

The King of France claimed the guardianship of the unfortunate princess, and her barons had not yet had time to reply to this claim, which meant the same as the surrender of the duchy, when the French army again entered Brittany and took possession of several towns. This time all Henry VII.'s prudence could not suffice to repress the indignation of his people at this unequal war; the growth of the power of France, perhaps, also interfered with his views; the King of England formed an alliance with the great sovereigns of Europe to put a stop to the conquests of Charles VIII. Maximilian, King of the Romans, who was a suitor for the hand of the little Duchess Anne, his son the Archduke Philip, the King of Spain, and the King of Portugal, pledged themselves to invade France to turn aside the sword whetted for the destruction of Brittany. Henry VII. required fresh subsidies from his Parliament to continue the war.

Well supplied with money, notwithstanding the abatement which the Commons had imposed upon his demands, and possessor of two ports upon the coast of Brittany, Henry VII. at length sent to the assistance of the duchess six thousand archers in the spring of 1489; at the same time a Spanish army was crossing the defile of Roncevaux, which allowed the English, under the orders of Lord Willoughby de Broke, to hold in check the French troops remaining in Brittany;

another English corps seconded the attempts of the King of the Romans upon the north, and distinguished itself at the capture of Saint Omer. A treaty of peace was concluded at the end of the year without much glory to either party. The rigor which the tax-gatherers of the King of England had displayed in exacting the subsidies had excited an insurrection in the northern counties, and notwithstanding the prompt repression of the disturbances, the new taxes produced only the sum of twenty-five thousand pounds sterling, instead of seventy five thousand pounds voted by Parliament. Henry VII. took advantage of this to claim from the Duchess of Brittany the reimbursement of all the expenditure which he had incurred in her behalf.

While preparations were going on for the renewal of hostilities, and the English Parliament had voted a tax of the tenth and the fifteenth penny to support the war, one of the allies of King Henry, Maximilian, negotiated secretly with the counsellors of the Duchess of Brittany, obtained the promise of her hand, and privately married her at Rennes, through his ambassador, the Prince of Orange, in the month of April, 1491; he would have acted more wisely by proceeding himself to fetch the heiress of such large dominions, sought by so many suitors. Scarcely had the Sire d'Albret, a disappointed aspirant, who had at one time attempted the abduction of the young princess, been assured of the object of the Prince of Orange's mission, when he gave warning of it to the court of France, at the same time surrendering to the French the town of Nantes. In vain did the duchess, who took the title of Queen of the Romans, ask assistance from her new husband; he was occupied with a revolt of his Flemish subjects; Brittany again found itself alone, confronting the whole strength of France.

But the views of the French court towards Brittany had

changed. Charles VIII. was now of age; he had shaken off the yoke of his sister, Madame de Beaujeu; he had delivered from his captivity his cousin the Duke of Orleans, and he secretly laid claim to the hand of the Duchess Anne. Betrothed in infancy to the Princess Elizabeth of York, now Queen of England; afterwards designed by his father, King Louis XI., to become the husband of Margaret of Austria, — "Margot, the gentle damsel," daughter of Margaret of Burgundy, — he had seen his little affianced bride, who was now eleven years of age, brought up at his court, and he still publicly announced his intention of wedding her as soon as she should be of age to be married. He carried on negotiations, however, with the ladies and lords who surrounded Anne of Brittany, and when he thought himself assured of a sufficient party among them, he frankly declared his purpose, in spite of the engagements which united him to the Princess Margaret, as well as the more sacred bonds which bound the Duchess Anne to Maximilian, King of the Romans, the father of his own affianced bride. All these obstacles did not arrest the King of France, and his victorious arms were a powerful argument in his favor. Maximilian sent no assistance to his wife; the French were threatening to besiege Rennes. The question lay, with Anne, between captivity and marriage. She concluded a treaty with Charles VIII., declared void the union which she had contracted with the King of the Romans, and definitively assured Brittany to the crown of France, by wedding, on the 6th of December, 1491, King Charles, in the castle of Langeais, in Touraine. The long struggles of England and France upon Breton territory were forever ended.

The anger was great in England; perhaps Henry VII. had really been deceived; he asserted it very loudly, declaring that Charles VIII. disturbed the Christian world, and that in future he should no longer hesitate to march to the conquest of France, his legitimate and natural inheritance; at the same time he talked loudly of the alliances which he had concluded, and he obtained fresh subsidies from Parliament, the usual result of the warlike protestations of Henry VII. The raising of troops proceeded rapidly; the names of Crécy, Agincourt, Poitiers, Verneuil, were already in all mouths; the noblemen pawned their property, reserving only their horses and swords; they thought themselves certain of acquiring fine estates in France. An army of twenty-five thousand foot-soldiers and sixteen hundred horses embarked in the month of October, 1492; it was a question of conquering the whole of France, an undertaking which could not fail to be long, and winter-quarters could be taken up at Calais. Siege was immediately laid to Boulogne, without any attempt at resistance from the French; all the plan of the campaign was understood beforehand between the two monarchs, and peace had been concluded before the commencement of the war. Eight days only had been passed before the town, and no assault had been made, when letters began to circulate in the camp destroying all hope of the co-operation of the King of Spain and the King of the Romans; Henry VII. thereupon assembled his council, and submitted for its deliberation the grave question of peace with France. All the favorites of the king had been bought over in advance with French gold; they solemnly decided for the conclusion of peace. The treaties, prepared long before, were signed at the beginning of November; by the public conditions the two kings undertook always to live in peace; friendly relations between the two countries were even to subsist for one year after the death of whichever of the sovereigns should survive the other. By the secret treaty, Charles VIII. bound himself to pay by degrees to the King of England, the sum of a hundred and forty-nine thousand pounds sterling, in discharge of all his claims upon the duchy of Brittany, and in payment of the tribute due to King Edward IV. It was thus that Henry VII. knew how to sell war to his subjects and peace to his enemies. Charles VIII. found himself at liberty to proceed in his enterprises against the kingdom of Naples, and the King of England could concentrate all his attention upon his internal affairs, which threatened to give him fresh and grave cares.

A second claimant had in fact arisen for the crown. This time it was no longer a question, as with Lambert Simnel, of a living prince, easy to be confronted with the impostor; the new rival who had been raised up against King Henry VII. was no less a personage, it was said, than the Duke of York, brother of the unlucky Edward V., who had escaped from the Tower by a miracle, had wandered about the world for seven years past, and was now determined to claim his crown. He had at first presented himself in Ireland, and had soon contrived to form a party there, notwithstanding the recent remembrance of Lambert Simnel. But the Earl of Kildare still hesitated, and the young aspirant turned his steps to France. Warlike and chivalrous as he was, Charles VIII. was not destitute of the cunning natural to the son of Louis XI. It was before the war with England, and he was well pleased to frighten Henry VII.: he welcomed the adventurer, recognized his rights, and admitted him to his court, where he was soon surrounded by a guard of English exiles. Until the treaties were signed at Etaples, Charles VIII. looked with favor upon the pretender; peace with Henry VII. being once proclaimed, the self-styled Duke of York was compelled to quit the court of France, and to take refuge with the Duchess of Burgundy, the usual resource of the enemies of Henry VII. The latter had demanded that the pretender should be delivered up to him; but Charles VIII. refused this act of treachery, unworthy of his honor. Meanwhile, Margaret, the Duchess of Burgundy, hesitated, or pretended to hesitate, to recognize her nephew. She interrogated him, and made him undergo a minute examination upon the secrets of the family. Finally, she solemnly proclaimed that he was really the Duke of York, son of her brother King Edward IV., the White Rose of England; she gave him at her court the state of a prince, furnished him with a guard, and wrote everywhere to her friends in England and on the Continent, to announce the miracle which had restored her nephew to her. The English malcontents, and they were numerous, joyfully embraced this new hope. An emissary was secretly dispatched to the court of the Duchess Margaret, to verify the claims of the prince; he came back as convinced as the duchess herself. It was really, he said, the Duke of York, the legitimate heir to the crown of England, the amiable and intelligent child whose death had been mourned. The conspiracy began to spread and to be organized.

King Henry meanwhile had not remained inactive; he also had sent secret emissaries to Ireland, who asserted that the pretended Duke of York was no other than Perkin Warbeck, the son of a merchant of Tournay, a converted Jew; that he had much frequented the society of English merchants in Flanders, then had travelled in Europe in the suite of Lady Brompton, wife of an exile. Upon the faith of these instructions Henry demanded of the Archduke Philip, son of Maximilian and Mary of Burgundy, to deliver up, or, at least, to drive from his states this audacious impostor. Philip lavished assurances of his devotion, and promised to refuse all support to the pretender; but the Duchess Margaret was sovereign in her states, and none could compel her to send Perkin Warbeck away. Henry VII. interdicted to his subjects all commerce with Flanders, and he had recourse to strategy to obtain that which diplomacy refused to him. Sir Robert Clifford, being bribed, gave up the names of the conspirators; they were all arrested. Sir Simon Montford, Sir Robert Ratcliffe, and William Daubeney were immediately executed. Among those who received their pardon "few men survived long," says the chronicler; Lord Fitzwalter, among others, having attempted to escape from his prison at Calais, was beheaded without any form of trial. One greater than he was shortly going to pay with his life for the same suspicions.

Sir William Stanley, brother of the Lord Stanley, now Earl of Derby, who had placed Henry VII. upon the throne, and who had himself saved the life of the king at Bosworth, was accused by Clifford of having been concerned in the conspiracy. The king refused at first to believe it; but when he interrogated his chamberlain, Sir William was embarrassed in his answers, and ended by confessing to a certain degree of complicity. The judges of Westminster held the crime to be sufficient: Stanley was condemned to death. All reckoned upon his pardon; the king's aversion to blood was remembered, as well as the services which the family of the guilty man had rendered him; but they forgot Sir William's large fortune; he was executed, and all his property was confiscated. Terror began to seize the conspirators; they distrusted each other. The position of Warbeck became difficult in Flanders; the merchants complained of the cessation of the English commerce. The adventurer resolved to land unexpectedly in England, hoping that an insurrection would be made in his favor. He arrived near Deal on the 3d of July, 1495, while the king had gone to pay a visit to his mother, in Lancashire. He was accompanied by about five hundred men, all English exiles and of desperate courage; but the population rose against the impostor, and not for him: the peasants of Kent fought with clubs and pitchforks. The assailants were nearly all killed or made prisoners; but a small number, with Warbeck at their head, succeeded in reaching the vessels. The captives, their hands tied together, were driven to London like a flock of sheep, and were executed in a crowd in the same manner. Henry VII. lavished praises and promises upon the brave peasants who had repulsed the enemy; he, at the same time, concluded a treaty with the Flemings, promising to restore the freedom of commerce, if Duke Philip would undertake to prevent the Duchess Margaret from receiving Warbeck and his partisans. The adventurer was therefore compelled to quit Flanders; he presented himself in Ireland, where he was coldly received. It was in Scotland that he at last sought refuge. The King of Scotland was on bad terms with Henry VII., and willingly received the pretender.

Notwithstanding the numerous treaties and the projects of alliance so many times concluded between the courts of England and Scotland, Henry VII. had always been concerned in the conspiracies against James III. The brother of the King of Scotland, Albany, was dead; but the barons had not become more submissive; the malcontents rallied around the young Duke of Rothsay, the monarch's eldest son, and this unnatural war, after alternations of success and disaster, was terminated, on the 18th of June, 1488, by a sanguinary combat at Little Canglar, a wild heath at about a league from Stirling. The king was carried off by his horse, and fell to the ground in a swoon. Some peasants lifted him up without knowing him; but amid the tumult a man approached the unfortunate prince, and leaning towards him as though to succor him, he struck him two blows with a dagger. James III. was only thirty-five years of age, and his death excited in the heart of the son, who had fought against and almost dethroned him, a remorse which ended only with his life. The example of revolt which he had set bore its fruits in other ways; he lived in the midst of conspiracies and internal struggles, finding at times in his difficulties traces of the influence of Henry VII., more often being ignorant of his complicity, but convinced, notwithstanding, that the King of England was a perfidious ally with whom it was advisable to arrive at an open rupture. Perkin Warbeck furnished him with the opportunity for it. James did not look very closely into the truth of his story; he was duped, or feigned to be so, and shortly after the arrival of his "fair cousin of York" in Scotland, amid the tournaments and rejoicings with which he welcomed him, the King of Scotland married the adventurer, Perkin Warbeck, to Lady Catherine Gordon, the charming daughter of the Earl of Huntley, and through her mother a near relative of the royal house.

So many favors caused uneasiness to the King of England, who kept spies among the great Scottish noblemen, and was thus informed exactly of the movements of Warbeck. The barons of Scotland were less favorable to him than was the king, some because they had been gained over by Henry, others because they foresaw the disasters of a war undertaken in his favor. Meanwhile, the Duchess of Burgundy had sent over men and money; the court of France, displeased at the obstacles which Henry VII. placed to the attempts of King Charles upon Italy, urged Warbeck to attempt an invasion of England. Henry offered the King of Scotland a hundred thousand gold crowns if he would deliver up the pretender to him. James IV. rejected the proposal with indignation. "I have melted up my plate for him," he said; "I will not betray him." Warbeck had recently published a document, skilfully conceived, in which he related his escape from the Tower, and his wandering life, dwelt upon the tyranny of Henry VII., upon the exactions with which he burdened his people, and summoned the English to rise and rally round him. The King of Scotland accompanied him, solely through friendship, he said, and would retire as soon as an English army should be on foot. It was with these declarations that Warbeck crossed the frontier and entered England at the commencement of the year 1497.

The northern counties did not trust to the disinterestedness of the Scotch, and nobody came to meet the pretender; all the cattle had been led away, the grain and fodder had been hidden, and when the Scottish troops began to pillage to compensate themselves for the cold reception which the population gave them, the self-styled Duke of York in vain sought to restrain them, saying that he would prefer to lose the throne than to owe it to the sufferings of the English. The soldiers were dying of hunger, and were guilty of every excess. The peasants began to arm themselves: the invading force was compelled to recross the frontiers without having fought, without having even awaited the English army, as had been promised by the clever spy of Henry VII., Ramsay, Lord Bothwell, formerly a favorite of James.

The King of England meanwhile was suffering grave consequences from the war, and from the avidity which always led him to profit by it to oppress his subjects. He had obtained of the Parliament a gift of two-tenths and two-fifteenths; but the people were determined not to pay taxes so oppressive. The insurrection commenced in Cornwall; the people demanded the head of Morton, Archbishop of Canterbury, prime minister and friend of Henry VII., accused of having advised the new taxes. Sixteen thousand rebels entered Devonshire; they were soon joined by numerous adherents, at the head of whom marched Lord Audley and other noblemen. Each county which they traversed furnished reinforcements to them; they presented a formidable aspect when they arrived, on a fine day in June, at Blackheath, near London. The king's army awaited them: the agitation was great in the city; but Lord Daubeney and the Earl of Oxford advanced against the rebels. Henry VII. had prudently remained in the rear with the reserve; he had commanded that Saturday should be awaited to give battle: it was his lucky day, he said. The 22d of June, 1499, made no exception to the rule. The insurgents fought valiantly; but they had no cavalry nor artillery, and no experienced chiefs: a great slaughter took place, and many of their number were made prisoners, among others Lord Audley, a lawyer named Flammock, and Joseph, a blacksmith, who had greatly contributed to excite the revolt by the violence of his speeches against the king and the archbishop. They all three perished, but they perished alone; the mass of peasants were soon released. The king had caused the execution of all the desperate men captured at Deal in the following of Perkin Warbeck, because neither repentance nor gratitude could be expected of them; he published an amnesty to the rebels of Cornwall, and thus re-established tranquillity in the insurrectionary provinces. Henry VII. was as wise as he was provident; he was neither vindictive nor sanguinary, and there was nothing to confiscate from the poor peasants. He had, however, flattered himself too much in reckoning upon the gratitude of the county of Cornwall. Perkin Warbeck quitted Scotland in consequence of the treaty of peace concluded between James IV. and Henry VII. through the efforts of Don Pedro Ayala, the Spanish ambassador; but the delicate cares and kindnesses of the Scottish monarch followed him up to his embarkation. The Duke and Duchess of York, as they were still called, put in, in the first instance, at Cork, in Ireland; but Warbeck in vain sought to urge the Irish to insurrection.

He then conceived the project of disembarking in Cornwall, of which he had received favorable accounts; and on the 7th of September he landed at Whitsand Bay. His forces did not amount to a hundred and fifty men; but soon the relatives and friends of the men killed at Blackheath came and joined him, and Warbeck was at the head of an army, when he appeared, on the 17th of September, before the city of Exeter, having solemnly assumed the title of King of England and France, under the name of Richard IV. The *queen* had taken refuge, for greater security, in the fortress of St. Michael. Whether prince or impostor, Warbeck had contrived to gain the heart of his wife: she was devoted to his fortunes, and awaited with anxiety the result of the campaign. Exeter was defended by the Earl of Devonshire, supported by the gentlemen and citizens. The insurgents had neither artillery nor besieging machines; they sought in vain to burst open the city gate, the cannon of the ramparts swept them down without resistance. The peasants of Devonshire were beginning to retreat in small detachments; but the men of Cornwall remained firm, and promised to die to the last man for the king whom they had chosen. An advance was made as far as Taunton. There they were obliged to confront the royal army. Warbeck reviewed his rustic troops, urging them to fight well on the morrow; but in the night he saddled his fleetest horse and fled without warning any one. When the insurgents found themselves without a chief, they did not try the fortune of arms, but placed themselves at the mercy of the king, who caused the leaders to be hanged, and sent the others away, half naked and dying of hunger. The best scouts of the army were in pursuit of Warbeck; but he had forestalled them and took refuge in the church at Beaulieu, in the heart of the New Forest, before he could be reached. The king had caused men-at-arms to be dispatched to arrest Lady Catherine Gordon, whose beauty and whose tears touched him: he confided her to the care of Queen Elizabeth, who treated her captive with much kindness.

The royal troops surrounded the church of Beaulieu; but Henry hesitated to violate the sanctuary; he sent to Warbeck skilful agents, who persuaded the adventurer to accept the pardon which they were commissioned to offer to him. The self-styled Duke of York therefore quitted his refuge, without having seen the king, who had privately contemplated him, being curious to examine the features of the audacious impostor. When Henry VII. re-entered London, Warbeck formed part of his retinue: he had not been ill-treated, but he was made to pass slowly through the principal streets of the city, in order to satisfy the curiosity of the people. He was conducted as far as the Tower, and the spectators supposed they had seen him for the last time; but after a few hours he reappeared, still accompanied by his guards, and took the road to Westminster. There he came into the court, apparently free, but closely watched. Far from being degraded into the condition of a servant, like Simnel, he was treated with consideration and a certain degree of respect. He was several times interrogated before the secret council, but his avowals remained a mystery, "so much so that men, disappointed at that which they heard, came to imagine they knew not what, and found themselves more perplexed than ever; but the king rather preferred to mystify the curious than to light the braziers."

The conduct of King Henry VII. remained an enigma to his contemporaries, and time has not unveiled the secret of it. Perkin Warbeck had lived for eight months at the court, when he contrived to escape therefrom. Being immediately pursued, he took refuge in the priory of Sheen, near Richmond. The prior obtained his pardon from the king before

CONFESSION OF PETER WARBECK.

consenting to deliver him up, but the honors which had been assigned to him were withdrawn: he was placed in the stocks before the gate of Westminster, a document in hand, compelled to read his confession to the people and to suffer their insults all day. This time the prisoner avowed his humble origin, and related his whole career, cursing the ambition which had caused his imposture. After the second reading, Warbeck was shut up in the Tower, where he became the companion of the unfortunate Earl of Warwick.

One year had elapsed since the attempt of Warbeck and his public humiliation. A third pretender, Ralph Wilford, had renewed the fraud of Simnel, and assumed the name of Warwick; he had been executed, and the Augustine monk who preached his cause had been condemned to imprisonment for life. It was in the month of July, 1499, when a rumor was spread of a plot formed by Warbeck and the real Earl of Warwick to escape together from the Tower, and foment a fresh insurrection. The charm of Warbeck's mind and manners must have been great, for he had not only seduced his companion in captivity, but he had contrived to win over all his jailers. The governor of the Tower was to be assassinated, and the freed prisoners intended to take refuge in a safe place and proclaim King Richard IV., summoning to their aid all the partisans of the Duke of Clarence, Warwick's brother. Such, at least, were the allegations in the indictment, for the execution of the plot had not even been begun when it was discovered. There was enough to account for the execution of Warbeck. He had played his part long and well; but he did not retract his confessions at the last moment, and died courageously at Tyburn, on the 23d of November, 1499. His last attempt cost the life of the luckless Earl of Warwick; he was accused before the peers, not only with having sought to escape, but with having plotted with

Warbeck to dethrone the king. The poor prince was twenty-nine years of age, but, having been a prisoner since the age of seven years, he was as ignorant of the world as a child; he confessed all the crimes of which he was accused, and having been condemned to die, he was beheaded on Tower Hill on the 23d of November. With him ended the numerous attempts against the crown of Henry VII.; all the possible heirs to the throne, real or pretended, had disappeared, and political passions began to be appeased under a government regular and firm, if it was at times greedy and despotic.

Freed from all further apprehension of civil war, and more secure in his foreign relations, Henry VII. turned his views towards the settlement of his children; he had long since resolved to marry his eldest daughter, Margaret, to the King of Scotland, in order definitively to attach that sovereign to himself. At the beginning of the year 1500, he sent to King James one of the ablest among the ecclesiastical negotiators formed in his service, Fox, Bishop of Durham; and this skilful negotiator contrived to lead the young monarch into asking for the hand of the princess. The marriage was celebrated in London, in the month of January, 1502; but Margaret, who was then twelve years of age, was not sent to Scotland until the end of 1505. During this interval, her eldest brother, Prince Arthur, heir-apparent to the throne, had married the Princess Catherine of Aragon, daughter of the able Ferdinand and the great Isabella, but had died almost immediately after his marriage, and King Henry mooted the question with Ferdinand and with the Pope, whether the princess, twenty-one years of age, and widow of the elder brother, could marry the younger brother Henry, who was but thirteen years. The dispensation arrived, and the betrothal was resolved upon, for King Ferdinand, finding that matters dragged, had desired the return not only of the princess, but of the large sums paid as her dowry. Catherine lived at the court of her father-in-law, honored and beloved by all, awaiting for five years the celebration of a marriage which was to terminate so sadly.

Amid the negotiations of alliances for his children, Henry VII. had also been occupied with his own marriage. The queen his wife had died shortly after the death of Prince Arthur, and the great solicitude of the widowed monarch was to find a spouse rich enough to sensibly increase the treasures which he took so much pleasure in hoarding. His negotiations and his hopes did not prevent him from continuing to oppress his subjects. The passion of avarice grows with age. Archbishop Morton, whom the people had so often cursed, had died in 1500, but the nation had gained nothing thereby; he had been replaced in his exactions by two "leeches, two shearers," as they were called, bolder and more rapacious than Morton, less skilful than he in proving to the good English people that all was going on in a legal manner, and that the share of the subjects in the State was limited to paying the taxes cheerfully. The two new agents, Empson and Dudley, were equally detested. Dudley was of good birth and knew how to set off the exactions in a suitable form; Empson, the son of a workman, triumphed coarsely over the unfortunate people, whom he oppressed, and ridiculed their miseries. Both were lawyers well versed in their profession; each offence, crime, or misdemeanor became in their hands a matter for a fine, and that no man might escape, they kept spies everywhere charged to warn them, and juries composed of miscreants who decided all matters at their pleasure. "They hovered thus over all England," says the chronicler, "like tame falcons for their master, and wild falcons for themselves, and they amassed great riches," while filling the royal coffers.

Notwithstanding these abuses, the national prosperity went on increasing; the revival of order had sufficed to give scope to the commerce which was to found in England the middle class. The great aristocracy, decimated and ruined by the wars of the Roses, driven from power by the skilful conduct of Henry VII., remained shut up in the castles, and the younger members of the noblest houses began to devote themselves to agriculture, sometimes even to commercial enterprises, instead of recognizing no other career than arms and the Church.

The English, however, had not yet attempted the great expeditions beyond the seas which were soon to render their navy so famous. Christopher Columbus had applied to Henry VII., in his efforts to find a sovereign who would intrust a few vessels to him and conquer the New World; but Bartholomew Columbus, brother of the great navigator, had been shipwrecked before arriving in England: when he had at length accomplished his mission to King Henry, and returned to Spain to announce to his brother that he was summoned to London, Isabella the Catholic had already granted the request of Columbus, assuring to Castile the riches of the Indies. The English, therefore, had no part in the discovery of the New World, and the rumor of the treasures which were found there must more than once have made King Henry VII. pale with jealousy.

The navigators whom he had sent had brought him back neither gold nor silver. John Cabot, or Cabotte, of Venetian origin, established at Bristol, and his three sons, Lewis, Sebastian, and Sancho, had received from King Henry VII., on the 5th of March, 1496, letters-patent, authorizing them to sail with five vessels in all seas, in order there to make discoveries and take possession of them in the name of England; the prudent monarch had reserved for himself one fifth of the profits of the enterprise. It is to the first voyage of John Cabot and his son Sebastian, in 1497, that we owe the discovery of Canada; in the same year, Vasco de Gama, doubling the Cape of Good Hope for the first time, in his voyage to India, opened to commerce a new route by which all the riches of the East were to flow into Europe. Notwithstanding all the shocks and agitations which the world was yet to suffer, the time of material force, exclusive and brutal, was beginning to pass away; peaceful intelligence and activity saw a vast field of influence and efforts opening before them.

The Parliament had become the docile instrument of the king, and unresistingly voted all that he was pleased to demand; but the subsidies granted in 1504 excited great murmuring among the people. The king had claimed the feudal gifts on occasion of the knighthood conferred upon Prince Henry, and of the marriage of the Princess Margaret. The Commons offered forty thousand pounds sterling, but the king had the moderation to accept only thirty thousand pounds. The malcontents appeared to have found a chief. Edmund de la Pole, second son of the Duke of Suffolk, and brother of the Earl of Lincoln, Simnel's protector, who had been killed at Stoke, was an embittered and turbulent man. Henry VII. had refused to grant him his paternal inheritance, alleging that he inherited from his brother and not from his father, and that Lord Lincoln, being declared a traitor, had had his property confiscated; Edmund had therefore been compelled to content himself with a shred of the estates of his family and the title of *Earl* of Suffolk. He had had the misfortune to kill a man in a quarrel; the king, still jealous of all who bore the name of Plantagenet, had taken advantage of this opportunity to accuse him of murder; Suffolk had taken refuge at the court of the Duchess of Burgundy; there he hatched plots, it was said. The king caused him to be watched, charged a treacherous emissary to insinuate himself into his confidence, and, according to the instructions received by this means, he suddenly caused to be arrested the men upon whom Suffolk relied most: his brother William de la Pole, Lord Courtenay, who had married one of the daughters of Queen Elizabeth Woodville, and Sir James Tyrrel, accused of the murder of Edward V. and the Duke of York in the Tower. A few other persons were secretly interrogated. Courtenay and De la Pole remained in prison, but Sir James Tyrrel confessed the crime formerly committed upon the young princes by order of Richard III., and he was executed, as well as certain accomplices of the Earl of Suffolk, although the conspiracy of the latter was in no respect proved. The murmurs which he had been accused of encouraging were stifled, and the king, until the end of his life, dispensed henceforth with having recourse to the Parliament; he contented himself with levying taxes under the name of "benevolences;" his coffers overflowed with gold; he passed for the richest monarch of Christendom.

A favorable event happened and secured the vengeance of the king upon the Earl of Suffolk. A storm drove upon the coasts of England the Archduke Philip the Fair and his wife Joanna, who had become Queen of Castile by the death of her mother, Isabella the Catholic. The young sovereigns were on the way from Flanders to their new dominions; their counsellors urged them to face the tempest rather than to set foot upon English soil and thus to place themselves in the hands of the skilful Henry VII. Perhaps from curiosity, perhaps from fear, the archduke insisted upon landing. The King of England appeared to have foreseen all; the illustrious travellers were immediately received with all the honors which were due to them; it was announced to them that the king was coming to meet them. Philip saw that he was caught in the trap, and being in a hurry to put an end to his compulsory visit, he hastened to anticipate Henry VII. The two monarchs met near Windsor, reciprocally lavishing the most touching marks of friendship and confidence. But the wise counsellors of the King of Castile had not been deceived. Before the Spanish sovereigns were able to resume their voyage, Philip had been obliged to consent to deliver up the Earl of Suffolk, who was living modestly in Flanders; to promise to the King of England the hand of his sister the Duchess of Savoy, who was a widow and very rich; and finally to affiance his first-born son, who afterwards became the Emperor Charles V., to the little Princess Mary of England. Philip the Fair, after having besides granted great commercial advantages to the English in the Flemish markets, was at length enabled to resume the journey to Spain. Suffolk, being enticed to England, was thrown into prison, and one of the last orders which Henry VII. signed was that for his execution.

Before the negotiations for the marriage with the Duchess of Savoy were ended, Philip the Fair had died in Spain, and King Henry cast his eyes upon his widow, whom he supposed to be richer than her sister-in-law. Unfortunately Joanna was insane, hopelessly insane with grief. The health of the King of England grew more and more impaired, and it became evident to all those who approached him that it was time for him to think of death and not of marriage.

Notwithstanding his exactions and the harshness he had so often manifested, and the perfidy of his intrigues, Henry VII. was a religious prince, solicitous about the future life and the salvation of his soul; the weakening of his powers warned him to think of his end, and he multiplied his alms. His disease increasing in 1508, he for the first time lent ear to the cries of his subjects, ruined by the exactions and malversations of Empson and Dudley. The king wished to render justice, he said, and a sincere repentance for all the crimes which he had permitted appeared to have taken possession of his soul. "Nevertheless Empson and Dudley, though they could not but hear of these scruples in the king's conscience, yet, as if the king's soul and his money were in several offices, that the one was not to intermeddle with the other, went on with as great rage as ever," says the chronicler. The king's health had momentarily improved, and his conscience had been somewhat quieted; the treasures which he himself kept under lock and key in his manor of Richmond regained all their charm in his eyes. When, in the springtime of 1509, a return of his cough brought him to the verge of the grave, he had time to make his will, recommending his successor to repair the wrong which he had done, and to restore that which he had unjustly taken: he then died at Richmond in the night of the 21st of April, 1509, at the age of fifty-two years. He had reigned twenty-three years over a kingdom distracted by internal dissensions, impoverished by wars, and a prey to the most frightful disorder: he had gradually calmed men's passions, repressed or stifled insurrections and conspiracies, favored commerce and industry; but he had oppressed his subjects to wrest from them the money of which he was greedy, he had lowered the authority of the Parliaments, he had struck severe blows at the great aristocracy, and he had, above all, shrouded his policy in so many subterfuges, and pursued his end through so many intrigues and falsehoods, that even time has not been able to bring the truth to light; the real and only excuse of King Henry VII. is that he belonged to the age of Louis XI., and that he had to deal with Ferdinand of Aragon.

CHAPEL AND MAUSOLEUM OF HENRY VII.

CHAPTER XVII.

HENRY VIII. AND WOLSEY. 1509–1529.

THE reign of King Henry VIII. is characterized by three great movements, which have all left a profound impression upon the destinies of England: — the religious reform; the establishment of the absolute power of the crown in principle and often in practice; the social and even political progress of the nation, notwithstanding great outbursts of tyranny on the part of the government and of servility on the part of the people. The history of this reign is naturally divided into two periods: — Henry VIII. under the influence of Wolsey, his favorite, and soon his prime minister; Henry VIII. alone, after the disgrace and death of Wolsey. The first of these two periods extends from 1509 to 1529, the second from 1529 to 1547.

The young king ascended the throne under happy auspices. Profoundly different from his father, whose tortuous policy and avaricious prudence had often exasperated his people, Henry VIII.'s taste for display, his lively disposition, the frankness of his manners, his skill in all bodily exercises, as well as the remarkable intelligence of which he gave promise, had raised very high the national hopes. He was not yet eighteen years of age; he was tall, robust, and handsome, and people loved to see him pass through the streets when starting for the hunt, where he would tire out several horses; his vices and even his minor faults did not yet manifest themselves. His marriage with the Princess Catherine of Aragon, which took place on the 3d of June, 1509, caused keen satisfaction; the princess was twenty-five years of age, she had been living for six years in England, the language of which she spoke well; a papal bull had dissipated all doubts as to the legitimacy of the union; on the 24th of June the king and the queen were solemnly crowned at Westminster.

The young king had gathered around him most of his father's former servants, according to the advice of his grandmother, the old Countess of Richmond, whom he often consulted; but, from the first day, inspired both by a feeling of justice and by the spirit of reaction, he repudiated Empson and Dudley, making known his intention of punishing them. His counsellors identified themselves with this policy, but they would have been personally compromised if the "leeches" of the late king had been publicly accused of having sucked the blood and substance of the subjects; all the servants of Henry VII. had more or less exactions upon their consciences, and it was resolved to accuse the two lawyers of having hatched a plot to "deprive the present king of his rights and inheritance." Improbable as was the charge, the cause was judged beforehand and for peremptory reasons; Empson and Dudley were declared guilty of treason and condemned to death. They languished one year in the Tower before the execution of their sentence; all their property had already been seized, and it was rumored among the people that the queen was interceding in their favor; numerous petitions were addressed to the king asking their death, and they were executed on Tower Hill, on the 17th of August, 1510, to the great satisfaction of the nation.

Henry VIII. was young and brilliant; he had not, like his father, learned prudence in the hard school of exile; he thirsted for military glory; he willingly, therefore, allowed

HENRY VIII.

Boston... Estes & Lauriat.

himself to be persuaded by his father-in-law, the astute Ferdinand, and by the warlike Pope, Julius II., to enter into the League which they had formed against Louis XII., formerly Duke of Orleans, now King of France, who had taken up the projects of his predecessor, Charles VIII., against Italy, adding thereto his own claims to the duchy of Milan, in the name of his grandmother, Valentine of Milan. A first herald from the King of England came to command Louis XII. to abstain from making war against the pope, "the father of all Christians;" a second herald claimed the cession of Anjou, Maine, Normandy, and Guienne, a request which was equivalent to a declaration of war. Henry VIII. convoked his Parliament, and demanded subsidies. The English had not lost their taste for invasions of France, however little glorious the last might have been: money still abounded in the coffers of the old king, notwithstanding the expenses of three years of pleasure and merrymakings. A fine army was soon on foot, and prepared to embark for Calais, when King Ferdinand suggested the idea of first attacking Guienne: he at the same time sent his fleet, which was intended to transport the English troops to the foot of the Pyrenees: his son-in-law accepted his proposal, and ten thousand men embarked under the orders of the Marquis of Dorset, accompanied by a multitude of volunteers belonging to the noblest families of England.

The mouth of the river Bidassoa had been reached, and Dorset desired to set foot in France, but he was awaiting the artillery which King Ferdinand had promised him; the latter was occupied in assembling considerable forces in Biscay, and when the English thought of marching to the siege of Bayonne, they perceived that it would be dangerous to leave behind them the little independent kingdom of Navarre. Ferdinand, supported by the two armies, commenced his negotiations. John d'Albret willingly consented to preserve neutrality; but the King of Spain demanded free passage for his troops, the custody of the more important fortresses, and as a hostage, the Prince of Viana, heir to the throne of Navarre. Upon the refusal of the poor little sovereign, the Spanish army advanced into his territory, seized upon several towns, and the Duke of Albe, who was in command, proposed to the Marquis of Dorset to effect a junction with him in order to besiege Pampeluna. The English began to open their eyes; they refused to make war elsewhere than in France, and claimed the artillery and horses promised. "When we have finished," was the answer, "you shall have all that you desire." Pampeluna was taken, and Navarre joined to Spain; but the English general renewed his demands; and an offer was made to march with him against Béarn, where John d'Albret had taken refuge, instead of attacking Bayonne or Bordeaux. This was too much; Dorset refused to advance. The King of Spain dispatched an ambassador to his son-in-law; but when the credulous monarch gave the order to follow the movements of the Spaniards, the English troops fell back, and openly announced their resolution of returning to their country. This was of little importance to the Spaniards; their object was accomplished: the presence of the English army upon the Bidassoa had prevented Louis XII. from sending assistance to the King of Navarre. Vessels were provided for the revolted English, who returned to England towards Christmas, 1512, half naked, emaciated by the poor living which King Ferdinand had allotted to them, but too numerous and too much exasperated for punishment to be inflicted upon them. This first experience, however, was not destined to suffice to open the eyes of Henry VIII. regarding the policy of his father-in-law.

The check suffered by Dorset had not discouraged the

young king, and he resolved to lead his armies himself into France. Louis XII. had been driven out of Italy; his frontiers were menaced by the Holy League; he was very anxious to raise up difficulties for the King of England within his own dominions; he addressed himself to Scotland, still the faithful ally of France. King James had causes for complaint against his brother-in-law; his best commanders, Andrew and John Barton, having suffered losses at sea, the king had given them, by way of indemnity, letters of marque, of which they made use to capture English merchant ships. Sir Edward Howard, son of Lord Surrey, fell upon them as upon pirates and defeated them: Andrew Barton received a wound of which he died. The King of Scotland claimed reparations in this respect; he also demanded the jewels bequeathed by Henry VII. to his daughter Margaret, which her brother had kept. Some attempts at negotiations on the part of Henry VIII. had little result; the young king, before setting sail for France, took the precaution of causing the fortifications of the towns on the Scottish border to be repaired, and intrusted to Lord Surrey the duty of watching King James with a strong force, while his master should proceed to the Continent to attack King Louis.

The war had already begun disastrously; Sir Edward Howard, with a large fleet, appeared in the month of March, 1513, at the entry to the road of Brest, of which he made himself master. Reckoning upon his success, he had begged the king to come himself to reap the glory of it; upon Henry's refusal, Howard attacked the squadron and the town; he was repulsed, and lost his life in an attempt at boarding, throwing into the sea his chain and golden whistle, in order that those trophies might not fall into the hands of the enemies. Another son of Lord Surrey, Lord Thomas Howard, took command of the fleet, and had just repulsed the French, when King Henry landed at Calais on the 30th of June, 1513, amid the roar of the artillery of the town, and salutes from the vessels, fit emblem of the noise and splendor so dear to the young monarch.

King Ferdinand, who had drawn his son-in-law into the league against France, had recently concluded with that country a private peace, in which the annexation of Navarre to Spain was recognized; but Henry VIII.'s self-love did not allow him to retreat; he formed an alliance with the Emperor Maximilian, who promised to join him at Calais. The red rose, the favorite emblem of King Henry VIII., was to outshine the lilies of France, and while Lord Herbert was laying siege to Thérouenne, the warlike court amused itself at Calais with endless jousts and festivals, the organization of which was often intrusted to the almoner of the king, Wolsey, who grew every day in his master's favor.

The son of a rich butcher of Ipswich, Thomas Wolsey had been brought up with care; honored when very young with all the degrees of the University of Oxford, he had been recommended to his master by Bishop Fox, the favorite diplomatist of Henry VII., and the king had several times employed him in delicate missions. Upon the death of the old monarch, Bishop Fox, who saw his favor on the decline, took care to place Wolsey near the king, and soon the chaplain distanced all his rivals in the good graces of his master. Better educated than the young king, but too shrewd to allow this to be seen, skilful in the bodily exercises and amusements of his time, Wolsey shared all the tastes and already flattered all the passions of his master, even before the period when he was destined to relieve him from the embarrassments and fatigues of government.

Whilst the dancing and feasting went on at Calais, a French

LANDING HENRY VIII. AT CALAIS.

army, commanded by the Duke of Longueville and the famous Chevalier Bayard, was advancing to the relief of Thérouenne. Henry immediately hastened thither; but the French had instructions to avoid a pitched battle, and they fell back, after having placed provisions and reinforcements in the towns, — a service which the Count of Angoulême (subsequently Francis I.) continued to render to the besieged, in spite of the badly organized and badly commanded English forces. They had been for six weeks before an insignificant little town, when the Emperor Maximilian joined his brother in arms, the great King of England, the flower of the knights of Christendom. In his satisfaction at seeing under his orders, in the capacity of a volunteer, the Emperor of the West, Henry VIII. forgot that he had transmitted to him a hundred thousand golden crowns for raising troops, and that Maximilian had brought but a small escort. The reception of the emperor was magnificent; all the great English noblemen were clad in cloth of gold and silver, which suffered from the pelting rain that greeted the interview of the two monarchs. On the same day the Scottish herald-at-arms came to the camp of King Henry VIII., to transmit to him the declaration of war of his sovereign. "The Earl of Surrey will know how to deal with your master," abruptly replied the King of England. Before the return of his messenger, King James had risked and lost his game.

The French had, meanwhile, decided to advance upon Thérouenne: the English troops crossed the river to give battle to them. The Emperor Maximilian, with the red rose of Lancaster upon his helmet, directed the operations. The struggle set in briskly, but the French cavalry, after a brilliant charge, became frightened, and took flight. They carried disorder into the battle-corps, and the panic became complete. The English pursued the fugitives to the cry of "St. George;"

the efforts of the chiefs could not rally the soldiers, and nearly all were made prisoners. "It is a battle of spurs," the captives themselves said, when the king gayly congratulated them upon the ardor which the fugitives had contrived to inspire in their horses, and that name has remained to the engagement. But King Henry delayed before Thérouenne, instead of profiting by his advantages and by the arrival in France of a Swiss army to which he had furnished money. The town capitulated at the end of August, and was razed to the ground upon the advice and for the benefit of Maximilian. Just as Henry VIII. had formerly done the work of King Ferdinand, so now he was doing that of the Emperor; instead of advancing into France, he laid siege to Tournay, a French town though in Flanders, and prejudicial to the commerce of that country. Maximilian had been shrewd enough to promise the bishopric thereof to Wolsey. Tournay was taken without any great resistance on the 22d of September; but the Swiss had concluded an advantageous treaty with the King of France, and had withdrawn to their mountains. The King of England gave a great tournament, and amused himself for several days at Tournay; then returned to England on the 22d of October, after having spent large sums of money, without glory or profit. But the star of Wolsey had risen, and Henry VIII. had had the pleasure of giving orders to the Emperor.

In the meantime, the Earl of Surrey had justified his master's confidence. King James crossed the frontier on the 22d of August with a more considerable army than was usual in Scotland. He had captured several castles when Surrey met him in the environs of Flodden, an outpost of the Cheviot Hills, an advantageous situation, protected by the course of the Till, one of the tributaries of the Tweed. The English immediately saw the strength of the position, and endeavored by insulting messages to tempt King James to advance; but the Scots took no heed, and it was found necessary to make the attack. James had neglected to defend the bridge and the ford, but he came down from the hill, and advanced towards the enemy in good order, "marching like the Germans, without speaking and without making any noise." The old chiefs of the army had not advised the battle, but James would not be guided by them. "If you are afraid of the English, you may go home," he said insolently to the old Earl of Angus. The old man burst into tears. "My age renders my body of no service, and my counsels are despised," he cried; "but I leave my two sons and the vassals of Douglas in the field; may the result be glorious, and Angus' foreboding unfounded!"

It was four o'clock on the 9th of September, 1513. The guns of the two armies began to thunder; the English artillery was heavier and better served than that of the Scots; the latter were the more eager on this account to come to a hand-to-hand struggle. The Earl of Huntley and Lord Home, who commanded the left wing, attacked the English under the orders of Sir Edmund Howard; they fought furiously, and the troops of Sir Edmund, coming in great part from Cheshire, were exasperated, it is said, at finding themselves commanded by a Howard instead of a Stanley, the hereditary chief of their county. They wavered, and the Scottish corps for a long time resisted the cavalry reserve which Lord Dacre brought up. The Borderers under Lord Home's command had dispersed to plunder, and refused to renew the attack. "We have fought the vanguard," they said, "and we have made them retreat; let all do as much as we have." King James was performing wonders in the centre; he had attacked the Earl of Surrey with the flower of his chivalry, and the two generals were about to meet amid the slaughter, when confusion set in among the Highlanders, who had fallen in a disorderly manner upon the left wing of the English. Half naked and maddened with rage, the mountaineers struck before them without listening to the voice of their chiefs, as though the whole victory depended "upon the heavy blows which they gave." Being soon repulsed in this irregular attack, they were slaughtered one after the other, and the whole effort of the combat was directed towards the centre, where King James continued to fight. In an instant he was overwhelmed; the circle contracted around him; English and Scotch appeared that day to have adopted the ferocious maxim of Sir Thomas Howard, "No quarter." The Scots thronged around their sovereign, defending him with desperate valor; he fell, however, almost at the feet of Surrey; but the struggle continued around his body, which was buried under a heap of dead who had fallen in his defence. When night at length arrested the slaughter, Surrey was not yet well assured of victory; on the morrow he was compelled to engage in several little skirmishes with detached corps; but the bulk of the Scots withdrew during the night towards the frontier, and the English did not attempt to pursue them. The battle of Flodden had struck a fatal blow to Scotland; her nobility was decimated, many families had lost all their sons; but on the other hand, the struggle had exhausted their adversaries, and Surrey intrenched himself in Berwick, and disbanded, shortly afterwards, the greater part of his army. He had sent to Queen Catherine the corpse of King James, found upon the field of battle; she herself wrote to King Henry VIII. to announce the victory. "My Henry," she said, "that which God does is well done. Your Grace can see that I can keep my promises, for I send you for your banner a king's coat. I could have wished to send you the king himself, but the heart of our English people would not permit it." Upon his return, the king rewarded Surrey for his services by restoring to him the title of Duke of Norfolk, lost by his father, who had fallen on the field of Bosworth. Queen Margaret of Scotland had written to her brother, imploring him to be mindful of the ties of blood, and to spare her fatherless boy; she was appointed regent, and peace was concluded. The Council of the King of England had for a long time been aware that it was difficult entirely to subdue the Scots, and that war with that country, as poor as it was resolute, was rarely profitable, even when victorious.

Louis XII. had succeeded, by negotiations, in breaking up the league formed against him. The court of Rome received him into favor, and Maximilian became his ally upon the promise of the hand of Renée of France, the king's second daughter (subsequently Duchess of Ferrara), for Prince Charles, son of Philip the Fair and Joan the Mad, afterwards the Emperor Charles the Fifth. The young prince had not yet attained marriageable age, but he had been betrothed from infancy to the Princess Mary of England, sister of Henry VIII. The latter soon heard of the treachery which was preparing, but at the same time, and in order to appease his displeasure, Louis XII., who had recently lost his wife, Anne of Brittany, formerly widow of Charles VIII., proposed himself to marry the Princess Mary. She was sixteen years of age, and was passionately in love with Sir Charles Brandon, one of the handsomest and most gallant noblemen at the English court, who was equally devoted to her. King Louis had formerly been an accomplished chevalier; but he was fifty-three years of age, and was afflicted with the gout. When the marriage was celebrated, in spite of the sentiments of the princess, he attended in his litter the tournament at which Charles Brandon, now become Duke of Suffolk, distinguished himself by the most brilliant valor. The nuptial ceremony had taken place on the 2d of September, 1513; the king was delighted with his young wife, who reproached him with having sent back to England all her ladies and her English household. The Duke of Suffolk had also returned to London; when, on the 1st of January, 1514, Louis XII. died in Paris, exhausted by the fatigue of his long wars and the anxieties which his affairs had caused him; exhausted, also, it was said, by the efforts which he had recently made to appear at the rejoicings, in order to please his young bride. His subjects mourned him; they had given him the noble surname of the "Father of his people," a fact due above all to the wise administration of Cardinal d'Amboise. Two months after his death, his widow secretly married the Duke of Suffolk, who had come on behalf of the king her brother, at the head of the embassy which was to bring her back to England. Marriages of this kind had been frequent formerly, but the royal dignity became every year more haughty, and none was more infatuated therewith than Henry VIII.; he was very angry with his sister, and would not see her on her return. Soon, however, the supplications of Mary and the good offices of Wolsey brought about interviews. Suffolk had formerly been a favorite of the king, who was at last persuaded to forgive him. The duke and duchess reappeared at the court; Mary was more beautiful than ever, for she was now happy.

All the authority as well as all the influence in the kingdom now belonged to Cardinal Wolsey; from a plain almoner of the king he had become, in a few years, Dean of York, then Bishop of Lincoln, at length Archbishop of York; in the year 1515 he was made Chancellor of England, cardinal, and legate of the Pope. All business passed through his hands; all favors depended upon him. An able and assiduous courtier, he contrived to flatter the tastes as well as the passions of his master; he amused him with endless pleasures; he flattered his self-love; he found money to suffice for his expenses; and the king, in return, allowed him to govern the kingdom. At home, the direction which Wolsey had given to affairs was not without advantages; he strengthened the royal power upon the ruins of the aristocracy, encouraged commerce, secured the safety of the highways, and caused justice to be administered. Abroad, his personal avidity and the ambition which impelled him towards the throne of St. Peter, imprinted upon his policy a perfidious and venal character which impelled his country to fatal courses. During more than ten years the history of Wolsey was the history of England; his good and bad qualities equally influenced the entire nation, of whose destinies he was the real arbiter, since the absolute monarch who then governed the country saw only through the eyes and heard only through the ears of his minister.

In ascending the throne of France, Francis I. had hastened to confirm the alliance with England which Louis XII. had concluded by his marriage; he needed to be sure of peace in that quarter, that he might carry out his designs upon Italy, — a fatal undertaking, which seemed to afflict with madness the French monarchs one after the other, and to lead them to their ruin. Francis I. had covered himself with glory at the battle of Marignan, on the 14th of September, 1515; and Ludovic Sforza had been compelled to give up to him the duchy of Milan. Jealousy of so much success began to seize upon King Henry; he complained of the perfidy of the French, who had secretly sent to Scotland the Duke of Albany, the son of him whom King James III. had formerly banished. The French party had immediately proposed to intrust to him the regency, to the exclusion of the regent, Margaret, who had exasperated her people by marrying, less than nine months after the death of her husband, the young Earl of Angus, bold and handsome, but as ambitious as he was rash and unskilful. Albany had been born in France; he had been brought up there; his regency was necessarily unfavorable to English interests. These reasons, coupled with the counsels of Wolsey, who wished to please the court of Rome, from which he had recently received the cardinal's hat, decided Henry to conclude a fresh alliance with Maximilian, in order to drive Francis I. from Italy. An insane ambition contributed to urge the King of England into this path. The emperor, feigning to be weary of the supreme power, spoke of ceding the imperial purple to the prince who should show himself deserving of it. The vanity of Henry VIII. was aroused; he dispatched two ambassadors to Germany to see how matters stood; but his negotiators were too intelligent and honest to leave him long in error. "The imperial crown is not at the disposal of the emperor," wrote Dr. Tunstall, "but certainly of the electoral princes, and the first condition is that the person elected should be a native of Germany, or at least a subject of the empire, which your Grace is not, because never, since the origin of the Christian faith, have the kings of England been subjects; thus, I fear lest the said offer, being so specious at the first hearing, was only made to get thereby some money of your Grace."

Henry VIII. was convinced, and, according to his custom, he was driven to the opposite side by the reaction from his first feelings. Not being able to obtain the empire of Maximilian, he renounced his alliance. Francis I. had succeeded in gaining over Wolsey by rich presents; he recrossed the

Alps, intrusting to the Constable de Bourbon the government of the duchy of Milan. A treaty of alliance offensive and defensive, between France and England, was concluded on the 4th of October, 1518, promising to the little dauphin the hand of the Princess Mary, the daughter of Henry VIII., then eighteen months old. Francis I. was to buy back Tournay for the sum of six hundred thousand crowns. Wolsey had not forgotten himself in determining these conditions: he had stipulated for a pension of twelve thousand livres, to indemnify him for the loss of his bishopric. "The king intends shortly to confer some further gratification upon your Grace," wrote one of the English negotiators to the all-powerful cardinal. "I was asked what would please you most; I said that I knew nothing of that matter, but that some handsome plate or rich jewels appeared to me to be the most suitable."

King Henry's jealousy towards Francis I. appeared to have given place to a violent admiration; he proposed a personal interview, between Calais and Boulogne, to take place in the month of July, 1519. All preliminaries of etiquette had been already settled. Henry and Wolsey were busying themselves in inventing splendors of costumes and entertainments to dazzle the court of France, when in the month of January, 1519, the Emperor Maximilian died suddenly, and the great affair of the succession to the empire absorbed all minds.

For a moment Henry VIII. himself entered the lists, but without much hope or perseverance; the two rivals for the empire were still — as they had been all their lifetime — the King of France, Francis I., and the Archduke Charles, grandson of Maximilian by his son Philip the Fair. Born at Ghent, descending from the House of Austria, hereditary sovereign of the Low Countries, Charles had all the natural claims to the suffrages of the electors which were wanting in his competitor. His military renown was already brilliant, and lavish as King Francis might be of the splendid presents for which the German princes were eager, the master of the Low Countries, Spain, the kingdom of Naples, and the West Indies, was the richer of the two. In this game, as in all others, Francis I. was to be beaten by Charles V. The King of England had at first hesitated between the two competitors, but he had decided in favor of the Archduke, when the latter was definitively elected on the 28th of June. The King of France bore his check with the proud gayety natural to his race and his country. "In ambition as in love there should be no rancor," he said to the Spanish ambassador; but the expenses had been immense, and the defeat was serious. The two countries were to pay dearly for the rivalry which was thus established between their sovereigns.

Henry VIII. hastened to congratulate the new emperor by the pen of Wolsey, while the cardinal took care to explain the conduct of his master at the court of France. It was important to him, for the moment, to maintain good relations with Francis I. as well as with Charles V. The King of France claimed the performance of Henry VIII.'s promise; and the latter was too well pleased to display his magnificence to decline a proposal which had, moreover, come from him in the first place. The interview was fixed for the summer of 1520, and the ambassadors of the emperor in vain made their efforts to destroy the project.

The court of England was already at Canterbury, where the king was completing his splendid preparations, when he suddenly learned that the emperor had arrived in the Channel, and desired to pay him a visit. Wolsey was less surprised than his master; he had secretly entered into negotiations with Charles, who had promised his "very good friend the cardinal," a pension of seven thousand ducats secured by two Spanish bishoprics. Wolsey was sent by the king to meet the illustrious visitor, who, simply attired in black and scantily attended, landed amid the magnificent preparations for the Field of the Cloth of Gold. The Emperor stopped at Dover, where the King of England came shortly to meet him with great demonstrations of friendship and gratitude. They chatted together until a late hour of the night, and repaired on the morrow in state to Canterbury, the king leaving the right-hand side to the Emperor throughout, and the Earl of Derby carrying before him the sword of justice. The cardinal, with all the clergy, came forward to meet the two sovereigns, who prostrated themselves together before the shrine of St. Thomas, which King Henry VIII. was shortly to profane and despoil of all its treasures. The Emperor then presented his respects to his aunt, Queen Catherine, and appeared struck with admiration for the beauty of the Duchess of Suffolk, that Princess Mary to whom he had been betrothed in his childhood, and who had subsequently been rejected for reasons of state. The time for regrets had gone by, and the Emperor Charles V. had not come to England to occupy himself with the beauty of a woman. He securely attached Wolsey to his interest by promising him his important support in the latter's great design — the election to the pontifical throne. Presents were not forgotten, and when Charles set sail again after a short visit, he had counteracted the disastrous effects which the interview of the two sovereigns of France and England might have had upon his policy. No one was more fully aware than Charles V. of the value of splendor and magnificence, under certain circumstances; but no one knew better how to dispense with these aids in order to go directly and simply to his end, relying upon his personal influence to preserve and maintain the imperial dignity.

On the 4th of June, 1520, King Henry VIII., the queen, the cardinal, and all the court, embarked for France; the spot fixed upon for the interview was situated between Guines and Ardres; it was there that was to be established the "Field of the Cloth of Gold," which has remained famous in the history of extravagant splendor. Wolsey had been intrusted by France as well as England with the superintendence of all the festivities; but in vain did Francis I. select the cardinal for his master of ceremonies: Charles V. had promised to make him Pope.

A palace built of timber and magnificently decorated by Flemish workmen awaited the King of England; a fountain throwing forth streams of white and red wine played constantly at the front, with this invitation to all passers-by, "Make good cheer all who please." Everywhere stood gigantic figures representing savages armed with bows and arrows, and exhibiting the device which Henry had chosen to recall the advances of the Emperor and Francis I.: "*Cui adhæreo præstat*" (He whom I support prevails). Precious tapestries, magnificent hangings, gold and silver plate, ornamented the interior of this temporary palace, more substantial than the gorgeous pavilion erected by Francis I. The cloth of gold which formed the roof of this pavilion, the blue velvet, studded with stars, of the walls, its silken cords mixed with Cyprian gold, were unable to resist the gusts of wind which soon arose and beat down into the mud all these splendors; the King of France was compelled to take refuge in an old castle very near the town of Ardres. The two sovereigns had scarcely been installed in their residences, when Cardinal Wolsey, accompanied by a magnificent retinue, paid a visit to the King of France, while a deputation of French noblemen performed the same ceremony towards Henry VIII. The visit of Wolsey was, however, not a mere court formality; the marriage treaty was confirmed between him and Francis I., the King of France agreeing, in the event of the projected union being accomplished, to pay a pension of a hundred thousand crowns to Henry and his successors, so eager was he to secure the neutrality of England in the war which he foresaw. The arbitration of the affairs of Scotland was consigned to the cardinal himself, in conjunction with Louise of Savoy, the mother of Francis I. Henry had wished to have the Scots delivered up to him without reserve, but the chivalrous spirit of the King of France did not permit him to abandon, even on paper, the faithful allies who had paid so cruelly for the useful diversion made in the north of England, at the time Louis XII. had been simultaneously attacked by the English and the Swiss.

King Henry had held aloof as long as it had been a question of business; when the rejoicings and ceremonies began, he filled the scene almost alone. The two kings met and embraced on horseback, according to the ceremony decided upon in order to avoid delicate questions of etiquette; the most affectionate protestations were exchanged. The noblemen of the two courts met amicably, and when the jousts commenced, all around the lists the emblems of France and England were conjoined. For six days the combatants fought with lances, for two with swords, for two in the mellay at the barriers. Henry VIII. and Francis I. fought side by side, like two brothers in arms, facing all comers. The two kings finally essayed wrestling-matches, much in vogue in England; but King Henry, more trained, was less nimble than his adversary; he was overthrown; he demanded his revenge, but the assistants interposed; there had been combats enough. Banquets, balls, masquerades, and theatrical representations now claimed their turn.

All these diversions in common did not suffice to obliterate the old distrust born of long wars and political rivalries. King Francis resolved one morning to break the ice; he repaired alone to the quarters of the English before King Henry had risen, and touching him gayly upon the shoulder, "You are my prisoner, brother!" he said. Henry VIII. sprang from his couch, touched by this proof of confidence, and Francis, pursuing the jest, acted as his valet, assisted him to perform his toilet, and ended by exchanging presents with him. On leaving the camp, the King of France met one of his friends, the Sire de Fleuranges. "I am glad to see you again in safety, sire," said the latter; "but let me tell you, my master, that you have acted foolishly; evil be to those who advised you." "Nobody advised anything," said the king, laughing; "all came from my own head, and could come from nowhere else." Henry VIII. returned the visit familiarly on the morrow. But the moment for separation arrived; the affairs of the two kingdoms claimed the two sovereigns, and the festivities were beginning to exhaust their purses. It took years for the estates of many a nobleman to recover from the loans contracted to make a good appearance at the Field of the Cloth of Gold; it was said that most of the French were carrying all their property upon their backs.

The Emperor Charles V. had forbidden his subjects to respond to the invitation addressed to all the knights in Christendom, and it was at Gravelines that King Henry VIII. paid him a visit. The Emperor accompanied the king back as far as Calais; but the French ambassadors were unable to learn anything of the result of their conference. Before separating, Charles promised to accept his dear uncle of England as arbitrator in all the differences which might arise between the King of France and himself, — a promise easy to keep for one who held arms in his hand and could take care to submit to arbitration only questions of little importance. The king returned to London, "in good health, but with a light purse," say the chroniclers.

There had not been wanting among the citizens, and even among the great noblemen who had not accompanied King Henry to the Field of the Cloth of Gold, censures upon the insane expenditure of the court; but none had spoken more loudly than the Duke of Buckingham, and he had gone beyond the bounds of prudence. The blood of the Plantagenets flowed in his veins; he was a descendant of a daughter of the Duke of Gloucester, son of Edward III.; he was rich, magnificent, bold, intelligent. So many advantages of character and position rendered him dangerous; Wolsey profited by the first opportunity to ruin him. It was related that an astrological monk, consulted by the duke, had affirmed that his son, young Stafford, "would go far and high;" in other terms, it was concluded therefrom that the young man would succeed to the throne of Henry VIII. A similar apprehension had cost the Earl of Suffolk his head. Wolsey, many times offended by the haughtiness of the duke, caused him to be summoned to court shortly after the king returned from France. The duke set out without any mistrust; but scarcely had he arrived in London when he found himself watched and followed with more persistency than respect. He was proceeding down the Thames in his boat, when he was arrested and conducted to the Tower, to the astonishment and indignation of the people. He was accused of having urged the monk to disloyal predictions, of having plotted with the servants of the king, uttering threats against his Majesty and the cardinal. The duke maintained that not one single *fact* could be brought forward against him, but he was condemned beforehand, and the Duke of Norfolk, who presided over the tribunal, burst into tears while pronouncing the sentence which he had had the cowardice to sign. Buckingham replied with proud firmness, protesting to the end his innocence, and refusing to ask pardon of the king. The people wept at the sight of his execution, on the 17th of June, 1521; executions had not yet been sufficiently frequent under the new reign to harden and debase men's hearts.

The blood of Buckingham still reeked upon his scaffold, when Henry VIII. undertook to add to his glory as monarch and knight a splendor of a fresh kind. We have seen how the Reformation had been born in England under the inspiration of Wickliffe, or rather, how it had then, for the first time, assumed a name and proclaimed doctrines. Since that time it had never ceased to grow and develop, slowly, silently, notwithstanding the martyrdom of some persons, nearly all obscure, who perished at the stake from year to year, keeping alive the smouldering fire. But within the last four years everything had changed; Luther had applied the axe to the tree in Germany, and the renown of his work had penetrated throughout all England. Meanwhile external signs were not yet alarming for the Church of Rome, and less still for its doctrines; dissatisfaction existed mainly against the monks, then very numerous in England, whose irregularities had several times attracted the attention of the popes. Henry VIII. resolved to defend the Catholic faith against the attacks of Luther. On the 15th of May, Wolsey had given to the bishops orders to burn, in all the parishes of England, the dangerous books, and to cause to be affixed to the doors of all the churches a list of the heresies of Luther, in order to teach the people to beware of them. On the 20th of May, King Henry had written to Louis of Bavaria, asking him to burn Luther with all his books, "for the accomplishment," he said, "of which good work, sacred and acceptable to God, we offer sincerely and with all our hearts, our royal favor, our aid and assistance, and even, if necessary, our blood." But Luther had already appeared before the Diet of Worms, where, boldly maintaining his ground, he had wrested from the Emperor, who was an adept in such matters, the exclamation, "Upon my soul, the monk speaks well and with marvellous courage." The monk was in safety at the Wartburg, hidden for a while from the fury of his enemies. King Henry had no other resource against him than "the pen of a ready writer." He applied himself to the task, and published in the summer of 1521, a *Defence of the Seven Sacraments against Martin Luther*, of which a copy, magnificently written and bound, was, through the care of Wolsey, presented to Pope Leo X. in full consistory, in the month of October, by the English ambassador at Rome. After reading it, the Holy Father bestowed upon the royal author the name of *Defender of the Faith*, a glorious addition to his other titles, and one of which he was eventually to make a strange use. Luther replied to Henry VIII., refusing to believe that the treatise was the work of his pen, and then proceeding to criticise it with great severity. When afterwards Luther desired to alter his judgment and effect a reconciliation with the monarch, who, in his fashion, was placing himself at the head of the religious movement in his dominions, Henry had not forgiven the Reformer for refusing him the title of author, nor was he any more favorably disposed towards his German antagonist for attributing to him finally the composition of a work of which the latter had spoken so badly. The king published everywhere in his kingdom Luther's two letters, with a reply, and a warning to the "pious author," which testified to the small liking which he had always experienced for "this insane monk."

While Henry VIII. was examining the works of the Fathers of the Church, or causing them to be examined, and was writing a treatise on theology, the war had recommenced between France and Spain. Francis I. had invaded Navarre, but had been repulsed; his attempts upon the Low Countries had not been fortunate, and Pope Leo X. had recently formed a fresh alliance with the Emperor. In his embarrassments, Francis I. invoked the good offices of the King of England, who promised his arbitration and thereupon dispatched Wolsey to come to an understanding with the Emperor upon the dismemberment of the French monarchy. The cardinal, whom his master had intrusted with full powers, landed at Calais on the 30th of June, with a magnificent retinue, and held several conferences with the emissaries of the two sovereigns; but the first act of the comedy was not long, and Wolsey shortly repaired to Bruges, "in order," he said, "to incline the Emperor towards peaceful measures." The negotiator was accompanied by so many noblemen, his servants were so brilliantly attired and ornamented with so many jewels, that King Christian of Denmark, who was then at Bruges, was filled with amazement, especially when he saw the cardinal served by men of the highest rank, on their knees, a ceremony as yet unknown in Germany. The daily expenses of Wolsey were enormous, but he still hoped that Pope Leo X. (his junior by several years) would be carried off by some accident; it was necessary, therefore, at any price to secure the support of the Emperor. The whole secret of the English policy at this period lay there.

On the 19th of August, Wolsey wrote from Bruges to his master. The Emperor urged Henry VIII. to declare war against France; but the cardinal had said that it was necessary to await the visit of Charles to England. "He swears in the presence of Our Lady," added Wolsey, "that he holds himself bound to you forever above all other princes;" in faith of which the Emperor promised to marry the little

CARDINAL WOLSEY SERVED BY THE NOBLES ON THEIR KNEES.

Princess Mary, who had been solemnly betrothed to the dauphin four years before. The preliminaries being agreed upon, Wolsey returned to Calais, where the French ambassadors contrived to preserve their gravity and to restrain their indignation while the cardinal formally resumed the negotiations for peace. When Francis I. had rejected an unacceptable project, Wolsey, deploring his obstinacy, impartially declared, in his quality of arbitrator, that the King of France had been the aggressor, and that the King of England was bound to lend his concurrence to his ally, the Emperor Charles. A treaty was therefore signed at Calais, between the Pope, the Emperor, and King Henry VIII., according to which, "in order to check the guilty ambition of France, and to hasten the moment for a general crusade against the Turks," all the contracting parties were to fall at once upon King Francis I. from different sides.

Hostilities had not been relaxed during the negotiations, and the King of France continued to meet with disasters in the field; he had lost nearly all his conquests in Italy, when Pope Leo X., just as he was rejoicing at the capture of Parma and Piacenza, the siege of which he had urged with vigor, died almost instantly on the 1st of December, at the age of forty-six years, not without suspicion of poisoning — thus justifying the hopes which the cardinal had founded upon the accidents to which Italian princes were then particularly subject. It was a great blow to the league, but none was more interested than Wolsey, who, being informed of the event with prodigious rapidity, immediately took steps to remind the Emperor of his engagements, at the same time dispatching to Rome his secretary, Pace, to advance his interests with the sacred college, which was at that time very considerable, in consequence of the numerous appointments which had been made by Leo X.

For twenty-three days thirty-nine cardinals were shut up in conclave for the election of the new Pope, without being able to agree. Cardinal Julius de' Medici, who had distinguished himself in the recent war, had one-third of the suffrages; but he could not contrive to overstep this number; some hesitated to give to the deceased Pope a successor from his family; the cardinals of the French party and some Imperialists dreaded Cardinal Julius. Nobody spoke of Wolsey. At length one day the Medici party, seeing that they could not bring in their candidate, whose army moreover was awaiting him with impatience, themselves proposed, suddenly, Adrian, Cardinal of Tortosa, a Flemish prelate, who had formerly been the Emperor's tutor, and who was employed by him in his affairs in Spain. No one expected his election; gradually several cardinals gave their votes in his favor; Cardinal Cajetan made a great speech to celebrate the virtues and merits of the new candidate, who was unknown to most of his compeers. While Cajetan was speaking, the disposition of the conclave changed suddenly; when the votes were counted, Adrian found himself elected, by the direct and sudden inspiration of the Holy Ghost, it was affirmed. Upon his arrival in Rome, the new Pope received the compliments of Cardinal Wolsey through the medium of his secretary, Pace; the ambition of the English minister had been disappointed; but Pope Adrian VI. was old and broken in health: Wolsey waited.

Francis I. had made several attempts to regain the affection of the King of England; but as they remained unsuccessful, he suspended the payment of the pension which he had allowed to Henry VIII., placed an embargo on the English vessels in his ports, and seized the goods of the merchants. King Henry's anger had not been appeased after the most violent reprisals against the French people who were in his dominions, when the Emperor landed at Dover. The moment was propitious for the designs of Charles; Henry VIII. promised him an army of forty thousand men, and agreed to invade the north of France. Charles V. had undertaken to indemnify the King of England for the loss of the French pension, but he began by borrowing a large sum of money, notwithstanding the financial embarrassments of the English monarch. Every day, in fact, added to the latter's distress in the matter of money, for every day brought fresh festivities and prodigalities. The Emperor proceeded from one scene of display to another during his sojourn in England. When at last he set sail, Wolsey knew not where to turn to procure the necessary funds for the equipment of the army.

King Henry VIII. had imitated the example of his father's last years: he did not give himself the trouble to convoke Parliament. A loan of twenty thousand pounds sterling was forcibly exacted from the merchants of London, and scarcely had they paid it when the principal among them were summoned before the cardinal. He announced to them that they had been chosen by the king to make throughout the kingdom an inquiry concerning the property of all, upon which property his Majesty intended to raise a tenth for the defence of the kingdom. The aldermen resisted, affirming that money was as scarce everywhere else as it was in the coffers of the king; Wolsey replied that the clergy had undertaken to give up a quarter of their wealth; finally a compromise was arrived at, and the royal treasury was once more enriched with the substance of the people. But the popularity of Wolsey gave way beneath this ever-increasing oppression, and the results of the war were not of a nature to afford consolation to the unhappy persons ruined by the preparations for the struggle. The Earl of Surrey, after bringing back the Emperor to Spain, had pillaged on his return the coast of Brittany.

He then placed himself at the head of the army, which numbered fifteen thousand men only, of whom three thousand were volunteers, and one thousand German mercenaries. The season was late; the English traversed Artois, and followed the banks of the Somme, ravaging the country, burning down villages, but avoiding the castles and fortified towns. The French army had instructions not to deliver a pitched battle, but cruelly harassed the English. The rain assisting, grave distempers broke out among the troops of Surrey. In the middle of October, the English, abandoned by their foreign auxiliaries, were compelled to retreat to Béthune without having accomplished anything; the money collected with so much difficulty had been expended; the exchequer was again empty.

The King of France once more sought to obtain support in the neighborhood of his enemies; he endeavored to stir Ireland to revolt, and had addressed himself with this object to the Earl of Desmond, who claimed a certain independence, promising him troops and money if he would act in enrolling his fellow-countrymen for him. Desmond had applied himself to his task, but neither French money nor soldiers had been forthcoming, and the earl stood alone exposed to the vengeance of the English government. Affairs were not much better directed in Scotland. The regent Albany, still in contention with Queen Margaret, had obtained from his Parliament authority to repair to France to seek assistance; returning with a small body of troops, he found everything in confusion, and Margaret caused the regency of her second husband, the Earl of Angus, to be proclaimed. Having shortly afterwards quarrelled with him, she demanded a divorce, which King Henry VIII., who had not himself yet had occasion to resort to that expedient, rigorously opposed. Disorder went on increasing in Scotland; the most violent accusations were interchanged between the two parties. Albany had been recalled to power; Henry VIII. insisted that he should be dismissed as the friend of France, and upon the refusal of the Scottish Parliament, he declared war. Lord Shrewsbury made a first attempt at an invasion, which was repulsed, and the regent entered England with a considerable army. Lord Dacre, who was in command on the frontier, had scarcely any troops, but he talked so loudly of the forces that were approaching, of the anger of King Henry VIII., of the dangers which were about to fall upon Scotland, that Albany took alarm, and obtained the promise of an armistice of one month, in order that a peace might be negotiated. The skilful guardian of the frontiers allowed the retreat of the army against which he would not have been able to contend, and the Duke of Albany set sail for France.

It became necessary at length to convoke a Parliament in England; loans, taxes, benevolences were exhausted. Notwithstanding Henry VIII.'s relish for absolute power, he had a sense of necessity and knew how to submit to it. Sir Thomas More was chosen as speaker of the House of Commons; he had been drawn into the service of the court several years before; the king delighted in his brilliant and varied conversation, and gave every mark of recognition to his learning and ability. Under his direction, the Commons proved however more recalcitrant than had been anticipated; they claimed the right to inquire into affairs, and the nation supported them from without by the interest which it took in all that was said in the House. "Why do they concern themselves so much with my affairs?" the king exclaimed angrily. Wolsey hoped to intimidate the Commons by presenting himself before them in person, accompanied by a numerous retinue which filled the House; the cardinal-chancellor set forth in a pompous speech that the war promised to restore to England all that she had formerly possessed in France, and that the Commons assuredly would not hesitate to vote a tax of twenty per cent. upon property. Sir Thomas More had agreed with his colleagues that there should be no discussion in the presence of the cardinal, and this exorbitant demand was listened to in silence, with downcast eyes; no reply was made. Wolsey called upon several members one after the other; all rose at his haughty voice, then sat down again without saying anything. The minister flew into a passion. More then bent one knee, and alleged as the excuse of the Commons that they were agitated by the presence of so great a personage, and that, besides, they wished to discuss among themselves the demand which had been made to them. Wolsey was compelled to retire, and the Commons sent a deputation to the king, asking for a reduction of the tax. Wolsey returned, more and more exasperated, endeavoring to draw the members of the House into discussion by interrogating them upon their objection. The Commons remained firm, and granted only a tax of a tenth — half of what the cardinal had demanded. He was unsuccessful also before the convocation of the clergy, and, notwithstanding his power as legate, he found himself compelled to accept, instead of the fifty per cent. which he had boldly demanded at first, a gift of a tenth for five years. Reduced as were the subsidies, they still exceeded all that had ever been hitherto granted to the sovereigns of England. "I pray to the Lord Almighty," wrote at this period Mr. Ellis, a member of the House of Commons, "that the subsidy may be paid to his Grace, without reserve, and without his losing the hearts and the good will of his subjects, — treasures which I hold more precious to a king than silver and gold; the gentlemen entrusted to collect the money will not, I think, have a small task." Already during the session of the Parliament, the members had been insulted in the street by the inhabitants of London, who pulled them by the sleeve, crying, "You are going to give four shillings in the pound? Our curses go with you even to your dwellings!" Insurrections took place in several counties; but the king threw the whole obloquy of the measure upon the cardinal, and washed his hands of it, pocketing meanwhile what remained of the money after the plunderings of the tax-collectors, great and small.

A fresh expedition was in preparation against France. The Duke of Suffolk had placed himself at the head of the troops in the month of August, 1523. A powerful auxiliary was counted upon at the very court of Francis I.; the Constable Bourbon, offended by his master, pursued by the jealous hatred of Louise of Savoy, who had hoped to become his wife, had succumbed to his desire for vengeance; he had betrayed his country and undertaken to serve her enemies. As soon as the King of France should have crossed the Alps, in his expedition to Italy, the Constable, with seven thousand men, was to co-operate in the attacks of the English and Imperialists. The plot was suspected; King Francis delayed his departure, and the Constable, who had feigned illness, was compelled to fly into Italy. The allies entered upon the campaign alone and too late; they were, moreover, disconcerted in their operations by the absence of the Constable's troops. Francis I. everywhere offered resistance to the enemy in France, while his faithful servant, Admiral Bonnivet, commanded the army of Italy.

The Duke of Suffolk was not destined for more glory than the Earl of Surrey; he delayed before St. Omer, instead of effecting a junction with the Germans who had invaded Burgundy. At length, when he desired to pass, it was too late; the French army cut off his communications; he was without provisions, his troops were suffering from grave distempers.

It was necessary to fall back upon Calais. This unfortunate campaign almost cost the Duke of Suffolk his head, so great was King Henry's anger.

Pope Adrian VI. had died (4th of September, 1523) after a pontificate of twenty months, during which his austere conscience had so exasperated the Italians, that the physician who attended him in his illness was styled the "Saviour of the country." The hopes of Wolsey blossomed again; he hastened to write to King Henry to assure him of the repugnance which he should experience at leaving his good master and burdening himself with so heavy a duty as the government of Christendom. Henry understood, and caused the Emperor to be reminded of all his promises, at the same time directing the English ambassador at Rome to spare no pains to insure the election of the minister. This time Wolsey was among the number of the candidates; he had even secured sufficient votes; but the Italians, the people of Rome, came almost beneath the windows of the conclave, crying out that there had been too many *barbarians* in St. Peter's chair, and that they would have no more. This opposition, supported by the efforts of the French cardinals, secured the tiara to Cardinal Julius de' Medici. He had had the intention of retaining his name, but he was reminded that no Pope who had done so had reigned two years, and he assumed the title of Clement VII.

Wolsey was too sagacious not to conceal his disappointment; the instructions of Henry VIII. were, moreover, to assist Cardinal de' Medici if the election of the chancellor of England was impossible. The new Pope immediately confirmed Wolsey in his office of legate, authorizing him even to suppress in England the religious houses which he should find to be corrupt. The cardinal made use of this authority with moderation, employing the property of the closed monasteries in endowing the colleges and universities, in order, he said, to instruct learned doctors "capable of refuting the ever-growing and wide-spread heresies of the monster, Martin Luther."

The French army, under the orders of Admiral Bonnivet, had obtained some success in Italy, but when that commander had to deal with the Constable Bourbon, placed by the Emperor at the head of his troops, he suffered one defeat after another; the loss of nearly all the towns was crowned by the death of the brave Bayard, the flower of European chivalry. The invasion of France was resolved upon, and Charles V. besought Henry VIII. to make an attack in the north; but England was weary of making war without glory, and the king, who had, while advancing in years, conceived as little liking as he had little aptitude for the command of his armies, refused his co-operation, promising money, however, which he did not pay. Bourbon and the Marquis of Peschiera entered France; but contrary to the advice of the Constable, who wished to march upon Lyons, they delayed at the fruitless siege of Marseilles, and the generals, urged by the proximity of the army which Francis I. had gathered together at Avignon, re-entered Italy. To his misfortune, the King of France had followed them there: the struggle began before Pavia, which the French were besieging; all the forces of the empire were united there, and on the 24th of February, 1525, when the combat ceased, the French army was decimated and the king a prisoner. "All is lost, save honor!" wrote the captured monarch, who had valiantly defended himself, to his mother. He was immediately conducted to the fortress of Pizzighitone, and people rejoiced greatly in England at the victory of the Emperor, as though King Henry VIII. had not been upon the point, a few months before, of separating himself from the league, and becoming reconciled with the King of France.

The victory caused the scale to incline to the side of Charles V., and Henry hastened to dispatch ambassadors to him, promising to invade France in conjunction with the Emperor, that they might divide that kingdom amicably. As preliminaries of the treaty, the King of England proposed to ascend the throne of France, which belonged to him by right of inheritance, while Charles should content himself with the provinces formerly dependent upon the House of Burgundy. In order to accomplish this dazzling project, fresh taxes were demanded without vote of Parliament, recent experience of the temper of that body not having been favorable; but this was too much. Insurrections broke out on all sides; placards insulting to the king and the cardinal were affixed by night upon the walls; the people took up arms against the commissioners. Wolsey perceived that it was necessary to yield, and the king, more bold in words than in deeds, speedily announced that he revoked and annulled his demands; it was also repeated very loudly that the cardinal had always been opposed to this fresh *benevolence*, that it was at his entreaty that the king had abandoned it; but the people said, "God bless the king; as to the cardinal, we know him but too well."

The rejoicing had been neither general nor spontaneous in England at the time of the battle of Pavia and the captivity of Francis I. "I have heard it related," Warham, Archbishop of Canterbury, formerly a minister of Henry VII. and chancellor of his son before the cardinal, wrote to Wolsey, "that the people said in several places that it would be a subject rather for weeping than for rejoicing that the King of France was a prisoner; if he could recover his liberty and there should be a good peace, the king would no longer dream of retaking France, the conquest of which would be more burdensome to England than profitable, and the maintenance more burdensome than the conquest."

Charles V. deemed himself henceforth master of the situation, and the style of his letters changed in tone after the battle of Pavia. He was weary of the oscillations and perfidies of the English policy; he no longer wrote to his *good uncle* with his own hand, and his letters were signed *Charles*, without any reminder of the ties of kindred. He rejected the idea of invading France. "The game was in the toils," it was said; "of what use was it to chase it any longer?" Francis I. had been transferred to the Alcazar of Madrid, at his request, and was anxious to negotiate personally with the Emperor, but no interview was granted to him. The negotiators demanded of the captive king the renunciation of all his claims upon Italy, the rehabilitation of the Constable Bourbon in his rank and property, and the cession of Burgundy. Francis I. resisted upon this last point; he struggled for a long while, and even abdicated in favor of the dauphin. At one moment he threatened to starve himself to death, and the Emperor saw himself upon the point of losing all the fruits of his victory. At length, on the 14th of January, 1526, after eleven months' captivity, the King of France signed the treaty of Madrid, taking care, however, to protest before a priest, a notary, and some friends, against the constraint placed upon him; then springing upon an Arab horse, brought for him to the frontier, he galloped back to his territory, crying, "Now I am again a king!" All the conditions of the treaty were already trodden under foot.

The first notification that Henry VIII. caused to be made to Francis I. when he learned the news of the latter's liberation, was to the effect that he had concluded during the captivity of that monarch a close and advantageous alliance with Louise of Savoy, regent of the kingdom, and that a sum of two millions of crowns had been promised to him, as well as a pension of a hundred thousand crowns. The cardinal received thirty thousand crowns for the cession of the bishopric of Tournay, and a hundred thousand crowns as a reward for his services to France. The Dowager Queen of France, Mary, Duchess of Suffolk, was to have her dowry liquidated. It was moreover forbidden to the Duke of Albany to re-enter Scotland during the minority of James V. As soon as he arrived in Paris, Francis I. ratified the engagements made by his mother, assuring the emissaries of Henry VIII. that he cared for nothing when once he was in good and faithful friendship with his Grace the King of England. The league formerly concluded against the King of France was re-formed against the Emperor; the Pope absolved Francis I. from his oaths and allied himself with the kings of France and England, with the republics of Florence and Venice, and with the Duke of Milan, with a view to recommence hostilities.

Some coldness had arisen since the preceding year (1525) between King Henry and his all-powerful minister; the king had found, it was said, that the cardinal abused the authority which had been confided to him by the Pope, and that he had driven too many monks from their monasteries. The rumor of this disagreement reached Germany, and it was upon this point that Luther wrote to Henry VIII., attributing to Wolsey all the evil which had been wrought in England, and congratulating the king on his having rejected "this monster and abomination to God and man, the ruin of the kingdom and the blight of all England." The compliments of Luther were premature; the king and the cardinal had become reconciled, and Henry answered the reformer with emphatic encomiums upon Wolsey, and bitter reproaches directed against Luther for his marriage with Catherine Bora.

The two sovereigns of France and England did not keep their promises to the Pope better than those made to the

Meeting of Henry VIII and Anne Boleyn.

Emperor. All the weight of the war fell upon Clement VII., who was soon compelled to throw himself upon the mercy of Charles V. A treaty was signed between them, but less than a month afterwards the Spaniards entered Rome by surprise, and the Pope was compelled to take refuge in the castle of San Angelo. Passing from convention to convention, from perfidy to perfidy, with alternations of successes and reverses, Clement VII. found himself at length, in the month of May, 1527, besieged in Rome by the Constable Bourbon, who was killed in the assault of May 5th, at the moment when his ferocious soldiers were taking possession of the city, which they gave up to fire and sword. Not even from the Gauls and the Goths had the Eternal City suffered so much. Notwithstanding the corruption of the Romish Church and the secret indignation which was felt against her, a cry of horror was raised from one end to the other of Christendom. Wolsey wrote to Henry VIII. to remind him of his title of *Defender of the Faith*, and to ask him to act in favor of the papal authority; but the king was absorbed in matters which were destined to undermine all his old devotion to Rome. He followed the example of King Francis I., and both monarchs abandoned to his unhappy fate the ally whom they had involved in an unequal struggle.

The King of England had recently, in fact, entered upon a course which was in the end to lead him further, and to change his policy more than he had foreseen. An inconsistent and faithless husband, he had caused his wife, Queen Catherine of Aragon, many sorrows, which she had borne with grave dignity and a somewhat rigid meekness. He had, nevertheless, retained a certain respect for her; the queen was generally beloved and esteemed; but Henry VIII. had made the acquaintance of a young maid of honor of her court — beautiful, intellectual, graceful, — brought up in France, whither, when yet quite a child, she had accompanied the Princess Mary, when the latter became the wife of Louis XII., —and Anne Boleyn had awakened a violent passion in the king's heart. Did she from the first aspire to the position of her royal mistress? Did she resist the king's love through virtue or through ambition? None can say. She was of good birth; her father, Sir Thomas Boleyn, had been several times employed in diplomatic missions by the king and the cardinal; her mother was the daughter of the Duke of Norfolk. She lived constantly at the court, and the queen could not have been ignorant of an intrigue which, since 1527, had formed a subject of conversation among all the courtiers.

In order to marry Anne Boleyn, it was necessary to annul the marriage with Catherine of Aragon. King Henry VIII., after seventeen years of union, found himself smitten with scruples as to the legitimacy of his marriage with his brother's widow; he found proof of the wrath of God in the numerous bereavements which he had undergone. The queen had given him six children, but had lost all save her eldest daughter, the Princess Mary. He very ostentatiously displayed his affection for Catherine, but the delicacy of his conscience did not permit him to live in peace with her. He felt the need of obtaining learned opinions in respect to the laws divine and human which he might have involuntarily violated. Various secret motives favored the passion of the king. Notwithstanding the declarations of Henry VIII. with regard to the impossibility of the Lutheran heresies taking root in the soil of England, the doctrines of the Reformation had silently made great progress; the partisans of the new faith were aware that Queen Catherine was ardently and sincerely a Catholic; no support could be expected from her. On the other hand, Wolsey, the faithful servant of the Church of

Rome, was exasperated against the Emperor, Catherine's nephew, who had failed him in the pontifical elections, and he wished to strengthen the alliance which united his master to France, by inducing him to marry Renée, the second daughter of Louis XII. The cardinal did not foresee any serious obstacles to his project from the affair of Anne Boleyn, but the divorce served his policy. Negotiations were then in progress for the marriage of the Princess Mary with the Duke of Orleans, son of the King of France, and the ambassadors of Francis I. were enabled to assure themselves personally of the truth of the rumors which attributed to the king an insane love for Anne Boleyn. He danced with her all night at the masquerade given to the envoys. Wolsey soon afterwards proceeded to France in his turn, magnificently escorted, as was Becket in former times. When he came back, the alliance between the two crowns was closer than ever, and he had himself assured Louise of Savoy that she would soon see a princess of her blood seated upon the throne of England; but the king had spent his time during the cardinal's absence in seeking in Leviticus and in St. Thomas Aquinas arguments against his marriage with Catherine; and the first news which saluted Wolsey upon his return was the announcement made by the king of his fixed determination to make Anne Boleyn Queen of England. Wolsey fell upon his knees; his policy and his principles, such as they were, revolted equally at this marriage. In earlier times the kings of England had frequently married their female subjects; but that period was gone by, and the regal dignity was too exalted to be brought so low. At the first remonstrance, the minister perceived that discussion was useless; he bowed his head, and resolved to serve his master according to his will and pleasure; he did not, however, infuse any ardor into the business: Anne Boleyn soon perceived this, and conceived thenceforth an enmity towards the cardinal which was destined to bring about his ruin.

The task of examining the treatise upon the divorce was assigned to Sir Thomas More, but the learned jurist felt the danger of such a trust, and consulted several bishops; the greater number hesitated; all referred to the Pope the decision of so great an affair. A scruple analogous to that which had so suddenly arisen in the king's mind had preoccupied many people at the time of the marriage. The Pope's bull had satisfied all, and it was thought hard to see the question brought up again after so many years of married life. It was absolutely necessary to take the matter before Clement VII.

The Emperor had foreseen the blow, and had parried it in advance. Considering the projected divorce as an insult to his family, he had been careful, before negotiating with the Pope, besieged by the Imperialists in the castle of San Angelo, to forewarn him against the intentions of the King of England, and to make mention of them in conversation. Clement VII., meanwhile, had escaped, and from his refuge at Orvieto he awaited the approach of the French army under the orders of Lautrec. Instead of the soldiers whom he was expecting, he found himself attacked by the agents of King Henry, who demanded authorization for the cardinal legate in England to decide the question of the divorce, with the assistance of a second legate, sent from Rome. The Pope was greatly embarrassed; the army upon which he counted was partly maintained by English gold. He signed the authorization, thus letting the weight of the decision fall back upon Wolsey. The matter of the bull of Pope Julius II. was referred to a commission which was competent to revoke it if the dispensation had been obtained by means of false representations. Out of consideration for the Princess Mary, she was to be legitimated in case of the divorce of her mother. Such was the result of the negotiations which were prolonged, with various alternations, from the end of the year 1527 to the beginning of the year 1528.

This decision, which fully satisfied Henry VIII., greatly troubled the cardinal; he requested that Cardinal Campeggio should be sent to him from Rome to share the fearful responsibility which had been imposed upon him; he gently suggested to the king the doubts and difficulties which several bishops had expressed to him. The king flew into a passion, forgetting in his fury the long services of his minister. Wolsey tremblingly yielded, and caused the Pope to be implored to sign the decretal bull, which was to confirm in advance his decisions. The Pope signed, but charged Cardinal Campeggio to keep the bull secret, and to produce it only in case of absolute necessity.

An epidemic, known as the sweating sickness, which caused the death of many persons, and even placed Anne Boleyn in danger, arrested for a moment the progress of affairs: terrified by this visitation, the king became reconciled with Queen Catherine, zealously resumed all the practices of religion, and appeared to forget Anne Boleyn, who was in the country, suffering from illness. But with the danger the good resolutions of Henry disappeared, and the great noblemen of the court received an order to present themselves at the levee of the favorite as at that of the queen. Cardinal Campeggio had just arrived in England, and it was expected that the legates would at once convoke the commission. But, meantime, the aspect of affairs in Italy changed: the Emperor again assumed the ascendant in that country, and the Italian legate was too crafty to set the Pope at variance with a conqueror who might perhaps shortly be imposing laws. Lautrec, who for a while had appeared victorious, was besieged by the

Imperialists within his camp near Naples, where he died on the 15th of August from grief as much as from sickness. The miserable remnant of his army was forced to capitulate, and the Pope set on foot secret negotiations with the Emperor. Campeggio continued to procrastinate; it was necessary to gain time at any price. For a moment the Pope had been thought to be dying, and Wolsey had appeared to be very near the height of his ambition; but Clement recovered his health, and the King of France himself was negotiating with the Emperor. Henry VIII. dispatched, under the great seal, the formal order to the two legates to assemble their commission, and to proceed to the inquiry into the divorce. The court met in the great hall of the Blackfriars, on the 13th of May, 1529.

The king and queen were summoned; when his name was called, Henry replied without hesitating, "Present." Catherine, accompanied by the four bishops engaged to plead her cause, did not respond to the summons, but arose, and crossing the hall, threw herself at the feet of the king, imploring him in most touching terms, with affecting dignity and sweetness, to have pity upon her, to remember the duties which she had discharged towards him, and not to inflict upon her an undeserved disgrace. She rose amid the involuntary emotion of all present, and left the hall, whilst the king was protesting his attachment to her, and attributing all his proceedings to the scruples of his conscience. "It was not," he said, "my lord cardinal who had suggested the idea of the divorce, as the queen asserted; but the Bishop of Lincoln, his confessor, and several other prelates had enjoined him to address himself to the Pope."

Catherine had refused to be present henceforth at the sittings; the inquiry therefore proceeded without her. The advocates of the king, who alone spoke, proved, or pretended to prove, all the facts which they had advanced, and asserted the invalidity of the marriage. The king urged Wolsey, and Wolsey urged Campeggio, to pronounce judgment; but the affairs of the Pope had been arranged; he had concluded, on the 29th of June, an advantageous treaty with the Emperor, and no longer feared the anger of the king. Therefore, on the 23d of July, when the king's advocate demanded a definitive reply, "I have not come here," said Campeggio, "to satisfy a man from fear or from hope of a reward, be he king or potentate. I am old, sick, and infirm, and every day I expect death. Of what avail would it be, therefore, to me to place my soul in danger of perdition for the favor of a prince? In the doubt and difficulties which shroud this affair, wherein the defendant will not plead her cause, I defer the decision until we shall have had the advice of the Pope and other experienced persons of his council. I adjourn the tribunal until the month of October."

As he finished speaking, the Duke of Suffolk, brother-in-law of King Henry, struck his fist upon the table, exclaiming, "Never has a cardinal done any good for England." Wolsey took this reproach upon himself, and, turning towards Suffolk, he reminded him angrily of the services he had rendered him. "Without me," he said, "cardinal as I am, you would not at this hour possess a head upon your shoulders or a tongue to insult us with. We are here only as deputies charged to examine an important matter, and we cannot proceed without the decision of our supreme chief. Be calm, my lord; remember what you owe me, and what I thought never to reveal to living man for your dishonor and my glory."

The court assembled no more; but it was soon known that, a fortnight previously, the Pope had revoked the mission of the legates, and that he had received Queen Catherine's appeal. Campeggio was preparing to quit England,

and Henry VIII. was able to control his resentment so far as to take leave of him with courtesy, even offering him presents; but at Dover, at the moment when the aged legate was about to embark, a troop of men-at-arms penetrated into his apartment and searched all his coffers, pretending to seek a treasure belonging to Wolsey, but, doubtless, in quest of the decretal bull signed by the Pope, of which the cardinal was known to be the bearer. Nothing, however, was found, and Campeggio set sail, leaving his compeer of the sacred college to bear alone the whole weight of his master's anger.

As long as Anne Boleyn had not been sure of the favor of the king, she had sought the good graces of Wolsey; but now for a long time she had sworn to destroy him. All the great noblemen, weary of the yoke which weighed upon them, and ashamed of having been so long governed by a butcher's son, united themselves to her who was about to become their queen, in order to precipitate the ruin of the minister. The king lent ear to all the statements against Wolsey; he was above all seduced by the hope of confiscation: for the fortune of Wolsey was enormous. The court made a short journey, and the cardinal was not invited to take part in it. However, when he contrived to meet the king at Grafton, in Northamptonshire, Henry received him so affectionately that the conspirators were greatly discouraged. But the influence of the beautiful Mistress Anne Boleyn restored the position of affairs. On the morrow Wolsey received orders to return to London; he was never again to see his master's face.

When the Michaelmas term commenced, Wolsey took his seat in the court of chancery, but none of the servants of the king now hastened to do him honor; the hour of disgrace had come; and on the same day, Hales, the attorney-general, accused him of having illegally exercised in England the office of papal legate. No man knew better than Wolsey what was the worth of laws in the eyes of his master; they had together made and violated many; but Wolsey also knew that his ruin had been decided upon, and all his courage disappeared under this certainty. He confessed all: the crimes that he had as well as those which he had not committed; he acknowledged all the counts of the indictment, and placed himself solely at the mercy of the king. On condition of retaining his rank and ecclesiastical property, he voluntarily relinquished all that he possessed to his royal master, saying that he held all through his favor. But even this could not disarm his enemies; the Dukes of Suffolk and Norfolk brought him orders to retire to his mansion at Esher, as the king proposed to take possession of his palace of York Place (since known as Whitehall). The cardinal made no resistance; but when the emissaries demanded the great seal, Wolsey drew himself up. "The great seal of England was consigned to me by my sovereign," he said; "I hold it for life in virtue of his letters-patent, and I cannot deliver it up upon a simple word from your mouth." He remained firm, notwithstanding their insults, and only resigned the great seal on the morrow, upon an order signed by the king. "I am grieved to think that your Grace is about to be taken to the Tower," said his treasurer, Sir William Gascoyne, whom he directed to remit to the king an inventory of his wealth. "It is a cowardly falsehood!" cried Wolsey angrily; "I have done nothing to deserve to be arrested; it simply pleases the king's grace to take possession at once of this residence;" and he embarked for Esher. The people gathered in crowds on both banks of the Thames, expecting to see the fallen minister take that "traitors' highway," which was rarely traversed a second time; their expectations were disappointed; the boat glided along softly as far as Putney. As the cardinal was mounting his mule to proceed to Esher, one of the king's chamberlains, Sir John Norris, presented himself before him and gave him a ring which the king had sent to him, with some words of consolation. "Take courage," added Sir John, "and we shall see you higher than ever." Wolsey dismounted, knelt in the dust at the side of the road, and returned thanks to God for the return of favor which the king manifested towards him; then rising, "I have no longer anything to give," he said, "and your news would deserve half a kingdom." He offered, however, to Sir John Norris a small golden chain accompanied by a crucifix. "Yet," he added, "if I could send to my sovereign at least a token of my gratitude—" and as he was seeking about him his looks fell upon his jester. "Take him," he said; "for the amusement of a noble master he is well worth a thousand pounds."

The gleam of royal favor was but transitory. The king felt difficulty in separating himself completely from a friend of twenty years' standing, who had flattered, amused, served, and governed him for so long a time; but the cabal was more powerful than past services, and Wolsey, lonely and cast down, soon fell ill. "Nothing that he told me excited so much compassion in me as his appearance," wrote the French ambassador, who had been to see him; "his countenance has fallen away by one half. He is ready to give everything, even to the gown which he wears, provided the king's displeasure be withdrawn from him." The fallen minister in vain besieged the monarch with the most humble epistles. No token of royal favor came back to lighten his darkness until the moment when his life was actually in danger. Henry VIII. then relented; he sent his physician to the sick prelate, saying that he would not lose him for twenty thousand pounds; and this mark of remembrance did more than all the remedies for the cure of the cardinal. He had been condemned in the Court of King's Bench, and an indictment had been presented to the Parliament which Henry VIII. had recently convoked; but the indictment was rejected, and the king extended his protection to his old servant. At the same time he took possession of all his ecclesiastical benefices, so that Wolsey found himself deprived of everything, and in want of the necessaries of life. Henry VIII. granted his pardon, and sent to him some articles of furniture and a little money; but orders were given him to reside henceforth in his diocese. Slowly and regretfully, Wolsey set out for York, forsaking that court where he had passed his life, and where his heart still lingered. Having arrived at the seat of the duties which still remained to him, he embraced them with unexpected ardor. The fallen minister appeared to comprehend the importance of his episcopal office, and to seek from God the consolations which men refused him. His clergy, delighted, became more and more attached to him, and wished formally to celebrate his installation. Wolsey consented, on condition that no great display should be made; but on the day fixed for the ceremony, as the cardinal was at table, it was announced that the Earl of Northumberland was coming. Wolsey rose to receive him; the earl had been brought up in his house, and, doubtless, brought him good tidings from the king. Northumberland appeared agitated; he hesitated; at length, placing his hand upon the old man's shoulder, "My lord cardinal," he said, "I arrest you on a charge of high-treason." Wolsey remained dumb and motionless; when he recovered his speech, it was to burst into sobs and lamentations. His enemies had discovered a correspondence which he still carried on with the Pope and the King of France; they had persuaded Henry that it tended to prevent his marriage with Anne Boleyn.

The prelate was doomed this time to be lodged in the Tower.

He was not destined, however, to travel so far. The fatal blow had been struck. The population of his diocese was attached to him, and would have willingly attempted his rescue; but the cardinal made no resistance; he followed Northumberland like a condemned man going to his execution. On the way he was attacked by a violent indisposition, and was compelled to stay a fortnight at the residence of the Earl of Shrewsbury. When he resumed his journey, he was so weak that it was found necessary to support him upon his mule. He arrived in the evening at Leicester Abbey; entering, he said to the abbot, "My father, I have come to lay my bones among you." The monks carried him to his bed; he was never to rise from it again. Swoon followed upon swoon; his servants, who were passionately devoted to him, saw that he was dying; they summoned Kingston, the lieutenant of the Tower, who was intrusted with his keeping, and whom Wolsey had asked for. "Remember me humbly to his Majesty," said the cardinal, in a feeble voice; "beg him, in my name, to retrace in his recollection what has passed between him and me from the beginning, particularly with regard to Queen Catherine, and let him say himself whether I have offended him or not. He is a prince of royal heart and marvellous courage, for rather than renounce the smallest part of his will, he would risk the half of his kingdom. I have often begged him upon my knees, for three hours, to forego his resolution; but I have not been able to succeed therein. And I will tell you, Master Kingston, if I had served God as diligently as I have served my king, He would not have abandoned me in my old age; it is my just reward; I have not considered my duties towards God, but only my duty towards my prince."

HENRY VIII. STARTING FOR THE HUNT.

THE MONKS CARRIED HIM TO HIS BED.

Shortly after these words, which were to be repeated a hundred and fifty years later by Colbert, dying in the service of Louis XIV., Cardinal Wolsey expired, on the 29th of November, 1529, in his sixtieth year, and was buried without pomp, at midnight, in the Chapel of Our Lady, in the same monastery.

Cavendish, the cardinal's chamberlain, who had been present during his last moments, himself came to announce to the king the death of his master. Henry was at Hampton Court, a magnificent palace built by Wolsey, who had offered it to the king. He was shooting with a bow when the messenger presented himself before him; at the news he manifested a momentary emotion, then exclaimed quickly, "I know that the cardinal kept hidden in a certain place the sum of fifteen hundred pounds; do you know it?" The sum had been consigned to a priest, whom Cavendish indicated. The king caused the assertion to be repeated. "Hold your tongue about that," he said; "it is a matter between you and me; three keep a secret easily when two are cut off; if my cap knew what I think, I would cast it into the fire. If I hear a word of this spoken, I shall know who has revealed it." The king sent the chamberlain away with some praises for his fidelity towards his late master. The conscience of the sovereign acquitted him, no doubt, of all excess of kindness towards his old servant.

CHAPTER XVIII.

THE ROYAL REFORM.

PERSONAL GOVERNMENT OF HENRY VIII. 1529–1547.

WOLSEY had succumbed beneath a court intrigue, but above all, beneath the ascendency of Anne Boleyn; many other ruined fortunes were to mark the guilty passion of Henry VIII. New ministers surrounded him: the great noblemen who had overthrown the cardinal — the Dukes of Norfolk and Suffolk, and Sir Thomas Boleyn, who had become Viscount Rochford, and afterwards Earl of Wiltshire. Sir Thomas More had with regret accepted the heavy duties of chancellor, perhaps in the hope of serving the public welfare, perhaps through a weakness which was to cost him dear. All questions at that time resolved themselves into that of the divorce of Catherine of Aragon; all politics turned upon this pivot. The king had consulted all the universities of Europe, the theologians and lawyers; Oxford and Cambridge were divided thereupon, and there was much sharp discussion between the parties; but the king had gained ground among the prelates: his agents were skilful and numerous. Cranmer, formerly a tutor in a wealthy family, now a chaplain to Henry VIII., had recently published a learned treatise in favor of the divorce, insisting that the word of God alone should decide the question without any appeal to the Pope, and maintaining that the Bible, interpreted by the Fathers of the Church, interdicted marriage with a brother's widow. The opinion of the two English universities in favor of the

HENRY VIII.

divorce was obtained. The Italian universities, Bologna, Padua, Ferrara, declared themselves for King Henry: it was a question of money. The Germans had still more fear of the Emperor than taste for English gold; they were all opposed to the divorce — the Protestant theologians were as outspoken as the Catholics. "It were better that the King of England should have two wives than be divorced from Catherine to marry another," said Luther. The Pope published, in the month of March, 1530, a brief, which formally forbade the King of England to conclude a second marriage, under pain of excommunication. A few days later the Earl of Wiltshire presented himself at Bologna, where the Pope and the Emperor were at that time; the people were shocked to see the father of Anne Boleyn employed in this mission. "Let your colleagues speak, my lord," said Charles V. to him, "for you are a party to this matter." The assurance of the earl and his offers of money completed the Emperor's exasperation. "I will not sell the honor of my good aunt Catherine!" he exclaimed angrily. The embassy retired without having obtained anything, and the Earl of Wiltshire was compelled to confine his intrigues to the French universities, amid which he contrived to secure several favorable opinions. But of what use were all the decisions of the faculties when the Pope refused his assent?

This assent was of supreme importance, for the time had come when the bonds which held the crown of England to Rome were about to be broken abruptly for bad and shameful reasons, but not without a certain assent from the mass of the people. None among the prelates who surrounded the king would have dared to advise him to defy the Pope's will. Cranmer himself, who had just married secretly the daughter of a German pastor, was too timid to break a lance in the face of the court of Rome; it was a servant of

Wolsey, who had become a servant of the king, Thomas Cromwell, the son of a blacksmith at Putney, a man as bold as he was corrupt and skilful, who struck the great blow and opened up to Henry VIII. the path in which he was henceforth to walk. The king was troubled by the persevering resistance of the Pope; he had expected to obtain the divorce without great difficulty; he hesitated, and a rumor of the disgrace of Anne Boleyn was already circulated among the courtiers when Cromwell approached his royal master. "The embarrassments of your Grace arise from the timidity of your ministers," he said; and he explained that, with the favorable opinions of all the universities and the assent of the English Parliament, which it was not difficult to procure, it was easy to proceed without paying regard to the Pope. "The king could even," he added, "follow the example of the German princes, who had shaken off the yoke of the court of Rome, and declare himself purely and simply the head of the Church of England. The clergy thus depending solely upon the king, he would become the absolute master of his kingdom, instead of being only half king."

This bold conception was well suited to please King Henry VIII.; his vanity, his taste for power, and his avidity alike found satisfaction in it. Neither his conscience (such as it was), nor his convictions, ever belonged to the new faith. Internally and by doctrine he remained a Catholic, but his policy and his interest, like his passion, impelled him in another direction; he accomplished in his country a religious reform — governmental as well as liberal, aristocratic as well as popular — the effects of which were immense, and profoundly advantageous to England; but he accomplished it without religious faith, and without general principles, for the sake of his personal desires and with selfish aim. It is to God, through the hands of Henry VIII., that England owes this great step in her history; she has no obligation to be grateful for it to the despotic and corrupt monarch who severed his connection with Rome in order to repudiate his wife and to dispose at his pleasure of the ecclesiastical benefices.

The door, however, had been opened, and Parliament, being at once convoked, received a communication detailing all the proceedings of the king for the purpose of surrounding himself with learned authorities upon the question of the legitimacy of his marriage. At the same time the clergy were assembled. Very uneasy at a royal act which involved them all in a common disgrace as guilty of having seconded and supported Cardinal Wolsey, by admitting his authority as legate, — an authority which had been confirmed by Henry himself, — the prelates, accustomed to the demands of the king, immediately offered him a hundred thousand pounds sterling in order to appease his anger. Henry VIII. accepted the offering, but announced that he would grant the pardon only on condition of a vote of the ecclesiastical convention which should recognize him as "the protector and supreme head of the church and the clergy of England." Three days were occupied in discussion; the opposition was powerful and numerous, but timidity gained the ascendant; there was a disposition to admit the supremacy of the king, with this reservation: *Quantum per legem Christi liceat* (as much as it is permitted by the law of Christ).

"I will have neither tantum nor quantum," replied the king, when Cromwell came to tell him how matters stood; "return to them, and let the vote be given without quantums or tantums." The reservation was, however, maintained, and the king consoled himself with his hundred thousand pounds sterling, augmented by a small gift from the clergy of the north.

After the prorogation of the Parliament Henry VIII. endeavored to intimidate Catherine, and to compel her to accept the decision of four prelates and four lay peers. She steadily refused; being transferred from Greenwich to Windsor, and from Windsor to Hertfordshire, she was at length sent to Ampthill, where she fixed her residence. "To whatever place I may be made to go, I remain the legitimate wife of the king," she said. In the main the nation was of her opinion, and no one was more convinced of it than the chancellor, Sir Thomas More; weary of serving as an instrument of a policy of which he disapproved, but which he could not modify, he asked permission to retire, and on the 16th of May, 1532, he returned peaceably to his mansion at Chelsea, relieved from a burden which had weighed him down, and free to devote himself to the learned studies which constituted the charm of his life.

The Pope had made some overtures of reconciliation; but as the first condition was the dismissal of Lady Anne and the recall of Queen Catherine, they necessarily remained without result. The brief which excommunicated at the same time the king and Anne Boleyn was signed on the 15th of November, but without being immediately promulgated. Henry VIII. had drawn closer his alliance with Francis I. during an interview which they had at Calais, and the King of France had undertaken to intercede with the Pope for his ally; but Anne Boleyn had not waited so long to seal her victory. On the 25th of January, 1533, one of the chaplains of the king, Dr. Lee, was summoned to celebrate mass in a small chamber in Whitehall Palace; there he found the king, Anne Boleyn, two noblemen, and a lady. Henry commanded the astonished prelate to celebrate his marriage. It

PERSECUTION OF THE REFORMERS.

HENRY COMMANDED THE ASTONISHED PRELATE TO CELEBRATE HIS MARRIAGE.

is related that the chaplain hesitated; but the king asserted that he had in his closet the authorization of the Pope. The ceremony being completed, the party dispersed in silence; the court of France alone was informed of the marriage, which Henry promised to keep secret until the month of May, in order to give time to Francis I. to use his influence with the Pope.

Meanwhile the Parliament, under the influence of Cromwell, had suppressed the "annates" or first-fruits, a considerable portion of the revenues paid to the Pope in Catholic countries; the authority of the clergy in convocation had been abolished and conferred upon the crown; Cranmer, with strange inconsistency, had recently accepted the archiepiscopal see of Canterbury, not only from the king, but from the Pope, who had signed on the 22d of February, 1533, the bull which confirmed his election, and had sent him the pallium. The prelate had therefore taken an oath of obedience to the pontiff which he expected to violate, since he had been raised to his dignity with another object. The question of the divorce immediately took a new turn; the Parliament being assembled voted the "Statute of Appeals," forbidding all recourse and appeal to Rome. At the same time, and by another act, the title of Queen of England was withdrawn from Catherine, who henceforth was to be called the Dowager Princess of Wales, in the character of widow of Prince Arthur. A court of the bishops was constituted on the 8th of May at Dunstable, near to Ampthill, where Catherine resided; she was called upon to appear there; but it was carefully concealed from her that the judgment was to be definitive. The queen did not appear, and was declared contumacious; during a fortnight the summons was repeated, then, on the 23d of May, Cranmer solemnly declared the nullity of the marriage. On the 28th of May he proclaimed the union already contracted between King Henry VIII. and the Lady Anne Boleyn, who was crowned at Westminster with great pomp on the 1st of June. The task was accomplished, and the king had secured his wishes: he had worked unceasingly for this object during six years past.

The consequences were not long in manifesting themselves; on the 11th of June the Pope annulled the sentence of Cranmer, and published the excommunication of Henry and Anne, not without contriving still one chance more for reconciliation: the decree was only to be definitive in the month of September; in the interval an interview was to take place between Clement VII. and Francis I. at Marseilles. But the conduct of Henry VIII. was hesitating and inconsistent; the English ambassadors admitted to the conference at Marseilles had no power to negotiate. Francis I. demanded that the question of the divorce should be again laid before a consistory from which the Imperialist cardinals should be excluded; but an emissary of the King of England, Bonner, who arrived on the day upon which the term fixed by Clement expired, solemnly appealed from the Pope to a general council. The negotiations were interrupted, and the interview had no other result than the fatal treaty of marriage between the Duke of Orleans, the son of the King of France, and Catherine de' Medici, the niece of the Pope. Being renewed for a moment at the instance of Francis I., and by a new fluctuation in the wishes of King Henry, the relations were definitively broken off on the 23d of May, 1534, by the solemn declaration of the Sacred College assembled in consistory, clearly affirming the validity of the marriage of Henry VIII. with Catherine of Aragon. The king was requested to recall to his court his legitimate wife. The daughter of Anne Boleyn, the future Queen Elizabeth, was already six months old; she had been born on the 7th of September, to the great disappointment of her father, who, upon the predictions of all the astrologers, was expecting a son.

Whilst the Pope was hurling from the Vatican his spiritual thunders, and before the news could have arrived in London, the English Parliament had completed the severing of the bonds which for so long a time had connected England with the court of Rome. All payments as well as all appeals to the Pope were interdicted; the king was recognized as the Supreme Head of the Church, he alone being entitled to bestow bishoprics or to decide ecclesiastical questions. The royal assent was given on the 30th of March to these acts, as well as to that which excluded from the succession to the throne, the Princess Mary, the daughter of Catherine of Aragon, as illegitimate, in favor of the children of Queen Anne. All the subjects of the crown of the age of discretion, were to take the oath in favor of the new order of things; every word, deed, or pamphlet against the second marriage was placed among acts of high treason.

All these precautions and prohibitions did not prevent public opinion from being favorable to the repudiated wife. Two monks of the order of the Observants even dared to reprimand the king publicly; the popular movement encouraged the revelations of a young prophetess, Elizabeth Barton, who was called "the holy maid of Kent," and who had hitherto predicted future events without danger to her person or her friends. She had numerous partisans, dupes or intriguers, and her rhapsodies soon bore upon state matters. She had been much opposed to the divorce, declaring that if the king should repudiate Catherine, he would die within seven months a shameful death, and would be replaced upon the throne by the Princess Mary. The prophecies were printed and published; Elizabeth Barton and a certain number of her partisans were arrested and compelled to confess their imposture, on a Sunday in November, 1533, at St. Paul's Cross. Since then they had remained in prison; but on the 25th of April, 1534, by order of the Parliament, the holy maid of Kent, her confessor, and five other persons compromised in her cause, were executed and quartered at Tyburn. "I was but a poor woman without knowledge," said Elizabeth Barton while proceeding to execution; "but people persuaded me that I spoke through the Holy Ghost, which drew me into vanity and confusion of mind, for my ruin and that of the persons who are going to suffer with me."

These obscure victims were not enough to satisfy the absolute power and despotic tyranny of Henry VIII. Everything had bent before his will, and the isolated opposition which he encountered in two illustrious persons astonished as much as it exasperated him. Sir Thomas More, formerly chancellor of England, and Fisher, Bishop of Rochester, were called upon to take the oath of allegiance to the children born and to be born of Queen Anne. Neither had any objection to the political part of the oath; they willingly recognized the Princess Elizabeth as heiress to the throne, to the exclusion of Mary; but neither one nor the other could consent to declare unlawful the marriage of Catherine of Aragon, nor to legitimatize that of Anne Boleyn. Both refused the oath, explaining their reasons with more or less tact and humility, and both were sent to the Tower. Fisher was seventy-five years of age; he was ill; he was denied medical assistance and clothing. Sir Thomas More was not alone in the world like the old prelate: his daughter, Mistress Margaret Roper, ministered to his wants, while all classes of society, rich and poor, humble and great, frightened at the fate which awaited the two prisoners, unhesitatingly made the required oath, as modified by the king, and rendered more than ever adverse to the previous instructions of the clergy. At the same time, and as though for compensation, Henry VIII. caused the trial of "those people who are vulgarly called heretics," sending to the stake with indifference the Lollards, Lutherans, and Anabaptists, — melancholy witnesses to the royal orthodoxy. Some monks who had refused to take the oath of supremacy were executed and quartered at Tyburn. Acts of Parliament succeeded each other, tending to make the king a kind of lay pope, whose office it was to define and prosecute heresies, and assigning to the crown all the revenues formerly collected by the court of Rome, while intrusting to the royal wisdom the care of founding and supporting the ecclesiastical government which should seem suitable to him. Amid the general adulation, Sir Thomas More and Bishop Fisher were shortly to suffer for their courageous resistance.

The old prelate was accused of having "maliciously and treasonably affirmed that in spiritual matters the king could not be the Head of the Church." The new Pope, Paul III., had recently sent him a cardinal's hat. "Ah!" cried Henry, angrily, "I will take care that he shall not have a head to wear it;" and the bishop, being condemned as a traitor, was beheaded on the 22d of June, 1535. His head was placed upon London Bridge, turned in the direction of the diocese where he left so many to regret his loss, and his body, being first exposed to the sight of the people, was thrown without a coffin into an obscure grave. The trial of Sir Thomas More, more prolonged, ended in the same result. Often timid, sometimes inconsistent in his conduct, More had arrived at a point at which a man of honor and a Christian no longer listens to aught but to the voice of his conscience. The long months of his captivity had ruined his health, whitened his hair, and bent his form; but his soul remained firm, and his eloquence before the servile tribunal appointed to try him still caused the docile instruments of the king to shudder.

More had been deprived of all his books; the means of writing had been taken from him: his farewell to his daughter was traced with a piece of charcoal upon a paper which he had secretly procured; but before losing his pen, he had written this touching proof of gentle firmness: "I am the faithful subject of the king, and every day his interceder. I pray for his Majesty, for his, and for all the kingdom. I do no wrong, I say no wrong, I think no wrong; if that is not sufficient to preserve the life of a man, I have no wish to live. I have been dying since I came to this place; I have several times been at the point of death; and thanks be to our Lord, I did not regret it, but rather I grieved to see my sufferings abate. Thus my poor body is at the mercy of the king. Might it please God that my death should do him some good!" Before the council, More replied to offers of pardon by the assurance that he had done nothing against the marriage with Anne Boleyn. Although he disapproved of the step, he had never spoken of it but to the king himself: he had even contented himself with preserving silence upon the new title of the king as Supreme Head of the Church; now, silence did not constitute treason. His accusers desired to produce witnesses to the contrary, but they failed in their undertaking, and the judges were compelled to declare silence to be treason. More was condemned. He no longer preserved silence, and loudly declared that the new oath of supremacy was unlawful. He was led from the hall with the edge of the axe turned towards him; his son threw himself in his path to ask for his blessing. At the Tower stairs he perceived his well-beloved daughter, Margaret Roper; she made her way between the guards, and fell upon his neck, weeping. Twice she returned, unable to part from that idolized father, whose head she afterwards carried away from London Bridge, where it had been exposed. The bitterness of

LAST MEETING OF SIR THOMAS MORE AND HIS DAUGHTER.

death had passed for Sir Thomas More after this separation; upon the scaffold he appeared to have regained something of that caustic gayety which had formerly placed him in favor with the king. When he learned that Henry VIII. had commuted the horrible sentence of traitors into the penalty of decapitation, he smiled faintly. "May God preserve all my friends from royal favors," he exclaimed. He tottered upon the steps of the scaffold. "Assist me to ascend, Master Lieutenant," he said, "I shall easily descend without aid." He was not permitted to speak to those present. "I die a faithful subject and a true Catholic," he said simply; then gently putting aside his beard, he was heard to murmur, as if speaking to himself, "Pity that should be cut! That has not committed treason." His head fell on the 6th of July, 1535, to the indignation of all Europe. "We learn that your master has put to death his faithful servant, his good and wise councillor, Sir Thomas More," said the Emperor to Sir Thomas Elliot, the English ambassador. "I have not heard it, sire," replied Elliot. "It is true, nevertheless," replied Charles V.; "and let me tell you that if we had been master of such a servant, of whose merit we have had experience for so many years past, we would rather have lost our best city than so worthy a councillor." The King of France was both grieved and shocked. The pens of the greatest writers of the times celebrated the virtues of More; Erasmus, with whom he had been connected, has related the life and death of his friend; but no one has more eloquently celebrated the virtues of the former chancellor of England, no one has better exposed to public contempt the cruelty of his persecutor, than a relative of Henry VIII. himself, Reginald Pole, grandson of the Duke of Clarence, educated partly at the expense of the crown, so much had the king been charmed by the intelligence and talents of his cousin. But Pole had a conscience as intractable as that of Sir Thomas More; he refused to support the cause of the divorce, and thus voluntarily renounced the ecclesiastical dignities which the king intended for him. He had retired into the north of Italy, and it was from there that he made all Europe familiar with the infamy of the murder of Sir Thomas More, while at the same time he published his great work upon *The Union of the Church*, in which he freely unveiled the base conduct and ignoble motives of Henry VIII. No attack more profoundly exasperated the tyrant, henceforth carried away by the dangerous intoxication of absolute power.

Indignation was nowhere more violent than at Rome, and the councillors of the Pope prevailed upon him to sign a bull summoning Henry VIII. to appear at Rome within ninety days, in person or by deputies. If he should fail to respond to this appeal, he was declared to have forfeited his crown; his children by Anne Boleyn and the children of his children were incapable of succeeding; his subjects were relieved of their oaths of allegiance, and were to take arms against him; all priests were to quit his dominions; treaties of alliance with foreign princes were dissolved, and all monarchs called upon to fight against him, until he should have submitted to the Church. The bull being drawn up, the Pope did not consider the time opportune for sending it forth, and the thunderbolt still slept in the arsenal of the Vatican; but its terms were known in England, which increased the exasperation of the king. Henry VIII. opened negotiations with the Protestant princes of Germany, endeavoring to draw the King of France and the young King of Scotland into the same alliances. The functions of Supreme Head of the Church involved Henry VIII. in so much business, that he created a commission specially intrusted to provide for it; at the head of this new council he placed the secretary of state,

Cromwell, to the secret indignation of the clergy, who were little accustomed to see themselves governed by a layman; but the *Vicar-General*, as he called himself, taking, in this capacity, precedence of all the great noblemen of the kingdom, including the Archbishop of Canterbury, did not falter in the accomplishment of his duties, for the day had come for executing his promises and for filling the coffers of the king. No one knew better than Cromwell the needs of the royal treasury, for he was chancellor of the exchequer as well as vicar-general of the Church. A great number of monks had refused the oath of supremacy: the opportunity was taken to determine upon the reform of all the monasteries. Complaints were made of the morals of the monks, of their avidity; Cromwell organized a series of domiciliary visits, intended, it was said, to discover all abuses: servants, neighbors, and enemies of the religious houses were interrogated; an absolute renunciation of the authority of the Pope was demanded of the monks; finally, an inventory of the riches of each house was made, and the commissaries retired, carrying on their tablets the condemnation of the monastery. Many abbots and priors, in alarm, offered considerable sums in the hope of purchasing exemption from ruin; the money was taken, but the names were not effaced from the fatal list. The vicar-general had expected to see many monks anxious to re-enter the world, but seven small monasteries alone voluntarily opened their gates. The report prepared by the Parliament especially condemned the houses of little importance, and those of which the abbots did not take rank among the peers of the kingdom; it was there, it was said, that the disorder was intolerable. The twenty-seven abbots of the great religious houses did not defend their brothers who were threatened. All seemed smitten with stupor; some superiors prudently resigned before the crash; the royal commissioners continued their work, and when the Parliament voted the bill proposed by Cromwell, three hundred and eighty religious houses found themselves included in the act which gave to the king and his descendants all the monasteries of which the net revenue did not exceed two hundred pounds sterling, to dispose of them according to his good pleasure, upon the one condition that those whom he should endow with them should maintain an honest residence there, and cultivate every year the extent of land tilled by the monks. A revenue of thirty-two thousand pounds sterling was thus assigned to the crown; the money and plate of the suppressed monasteries were valued at more than a hundred thousand pounds sterling. After this last proof of submission, the Parliament which had modified the succession to the throne, voted the separation of England from the Holy See, and doubled the royal prerogatives, found itself dissolved at the end of six years of servile existence, without having even secured the good graces of the king, for the House of Commons had hesitated for some time to pronounce the suppression of the monasteries. It is related that the king sent for the principal leaders, warning them that he would have either the law or their heads; and the bill was passed. Commissioners were intrusted to proceed to the suppression of the monasteries; a hundred obtained compromises, and, crippled and impoverished, were founded afresh by letters-patent of Henry VIII.; the rest were invaded by the royal commissioners; monks under twenty-four years of age were sent into the world to earn their livelihood; the others were divided into two classes: those who elected for a monastic existence were dispersed in the great monasteries; it was promised that occupation should be found for the others. The nuns were abandoned to their own resources; the royal charity allowed only a secular gown when they were driven from their retreats and cast into a world of which they were ignorant. The first act of the drama had been played: the turn of the great houses was yet to come.

While this violent and arbitrary work was being accomplished under a specious veil of reform, Queen Catherine was dying in her retirement. She had obstinately refused to leave England, notwithstanding the entreaties of the Emperor: she would do nothing which might be prejudicial to the interests of her daughter, whose rehabilitation she still hoped for. She had also refused, for the same reason, to accept the title of Princess of Wales, which degraded her as a woman. She lived a sad and lonely life, separated from her daughter, who might, it was said, become imbued with her principles. Even the approach of death could not obtain for her the favor of seeing her again. The last words of the unhappy queen were, however, words of forgiveness to that cruel husband who had afflicted her with so many evils. "I forgive you everything," she said, "and I ask God to do likewise; I recommend our daughter Mary to you, begging you to be a good father to her as I have always desired. I vow to you that my eyes long for you beyond all things." It is said that the king shed a tear upon this touching message, and that he intrusted the Spanish ambassador to assure the dying queen of his affection; but Catherine had already breathed her last sigh. She died on the 8th of January, 1536, and was interred with honor at Peterborough. Her husband went into mourning, but Anne Boleyn appeared before the court in a yellow silk gown. "Now I am queen," she said, on learning the death of her whom she had outraged and overcome.

The day of retribution, however, was approaching; the same passions which had raised her to the throne in defiance of all laws, human and divine, were about to hurl her from it.

Henry had already cast his eyes upon Jane Seymour, a maid of honor of Anne Boleyn, as Anne had formerly been the maid of honor of Catherine. She was the daughter of a Wiltshire gentleman; she was beautiful, amiable, and of great gentleness of character. It is related that the queen perceived the great familiarity which already existed between Henry VIII. and Jane Seymour. The grief which she experienced therefrom was so violent that she brought into the world, prematurely, a still-born child; it was a son, and the vexation of the king was no less violent than his disappointment. Anne already felt that she was ruined: the king had left her suddenly amid a grand *fête* which she gave in Greenwich Park, and had returned to London. On the morrow, the 2d of May, she was arrested at Greenwich, as she was taking her pleasure on the river; she was accused of adultery, and immediately taken to the Tower. At the first word of accusation against her, Anne fell upon her knees, exclaiming aloud, "Lord, my God, help me, as I am innocent of this crime!" Her brother, Lord Rochford, three noblemen of the king's household, and a musician, were imprisoned at the same time.

Grief and anxiety appeared to have impaired the reason of the unhappy Anne; at times she would appeal for Divine mercy, at others, amid outbursts of laughter, mingled with tears, she would exclaim, "Why am I here? My mother will die of grief; I shall perish without obtaining justice." The lieutenant of the Tower assured her that justice was administered to the poorest of the subjects of the king; Anne laughed bitterly: she knew better than anybody what the royal justice was worth.

She had been conducted to the same apartment in which she had formerly slept on the eve of her coronation, when the king and his courtiers were equally eager to do honor to her; women had been placed around her, charged to listen to all her words; being excited by the misfortune which had befallen her, Anne talked much; all that she said was reported to the king, and contributed to her ruin. She was accused of the most degrading corruption of morals and conduct; in vain did she defend herself: the lightness of her manners, the familiar tone which she had learned, it was said, at the court of France, testified against her more than all the depositions and interrogatories of the trial. She wrote, on the 6th of May, a touching letter to the king, the authenticity of which has been contested, perhaps without reason, reminding him of the affection which he had manifested towards her, protesting her innocence, and demanding a legal trial.

". . . But if you have already determined of me, and that not only my death but an infamous slander must bring you the joying of your desired happiness, then I desire of God that He will pardon your great sin herein, and likewise my enemies the instruments thereof; and that He will not call you to a straight account for your unprincely and cruel usage of me at His general judgment-seat, where both you and myself must shortly appear, and in whose judgment, I doubt not (whatsoever the world may think of me), mine innocency shall be openly known and sufficiently cleared. My last and only request shall be that myself may only bear the burden of your Grace's displeasure, and that it may not touch the innocent souls of those poor gentlemen who, as I understand, are likewise in straight imprisonment for my sake. If ever I have found favor in your sight — if ever the name of Anne Bullen have been pleasing in your ears — then let me obtain this request; and so I will leave to trouble your Grace any further, with mine earnest prayer to the Trinity to have your Grace in His good keeping, and to direct you in all your actions. From my doleful prison in the Tower, your loyal and faithful wife,

"ANN BULEN."

In vain did Anne demand justice for herself and mercy for her companions in misfortune; she had been condemned beforehand, and her dishonor was the price of her condemnation. Within four months Henry had received the forgiveness of his two wives: one the irreproachable victim of his guilty passions; the other, who had been his accomplice, and who was suffering for her crime the most terrible reverses. The documents of the proceedings are no longer in existence, and it is now impossible to determine the question of the guilt of the unhappy Anne; she was condemned and died because the king her husband desired to marry Jane Seymour; that is what appears clearly from the facts transmitted to us by history. On the 15th of May, the sentence upon the queen was pronounced; her brother, Lord Rochford, and the four other accused persons, had been condemned since the 13th of May. A crowning affliction awaited Anne Boleyn before her supreme agony; Cranmer was compelled to declare the nullity of the marriage which he himself had formerly supported, and the Princess Elizabeth was stigmatized with illegitimacy like her sister Mary. The day on which the archbishop in agony of soul thus yielded tremblingly to the royal will, the accomplices or companions of the unhappy queen suffered their punishment on Tower Hill. The musician Smeaton was hanged; Lord Rochford and the three noblemen were beheaded; all had constantly protested their innocence, with the exception of the musician, who failed however to purchase his life by his confessions or falsehoods.

On the 19th of May, in the morning, less than three weeks after the day on which she had reigned triumphant over the

ANNE BOLEYN

festivities at Greenwich, Anne Boleyn was led out upon Tower Green. The spectators were crowded together in the narrow space. Anne had, on the previous evening, intrusted one of the women among her attendants to go on her behalf and kneel before the Princess Mary, to beg her forgiveness. She walked courageously to her death. "I have a little neck," she said to the lieutenant of the Tower; "and I heard say that the executioner was very good; he will not have much trouble." She said a few words to those who came to see her die, without bitterness towards her judges, and full of affection and respect for the king who sent her to the scaffold. "Christ have mercy on my soul! Jesus receive my soul!" she repeated on placing her beautiful head upon the block. Three years had elapsed since Henry had married Anne Boleyn, moving heaven and earth to place her upon the throne, when a blow from the axe of the executioner ended her life on Tower Green. The king waited impatiently for the signal which was to announce to him the execution of the sentence. "It is done," he exclaimed, on hearing the cannon; "that is an end of the matter. Unleash the dogs, and let us follow the stag!" He returned gayly in the evening from Epping Forest, and on the morrow morning married Jane Seymour. He had not rendered to the unhappy Anne the honor which his conscience had compelled him to pay to the virtuous Catherine; no mourning garments saddened the court of the new queen. Henry VIII. was clad in white on the day of his marriage, and on the 29th of May Jane appeared at the court decked with the royal ornaments, but she did not obtain the favor of solemnly receiving the crown; after Anne Boleyn, none of the wives of King Henry was deemed worthy of that ceremony. The Princess Mary had been received into favor by her father, not without having reluctantly signed a humiliating letter; she obtained a suitable establishment, and even appears to have been intrusted with the care of her sister, the little Princess Elizabeth. Not content with assuring the succession to the children of Jane Seymour, the king caused an act to be passed by the Parliament, which authorized him to dispose of his crown according to his own good will and pleasure. This exorbitant measure was destined to favor the Duke of Richmond, an illegitimate son of the king, eighteen years of age, whom he passionately loved. The young duke died before the act had received the royal sanction, and the king, to his great grief, found himself destitute of male children, and with two daughters whom he had himself branded with the stigma of illegitimacy.

Meanwhile the dissolution of the monasteries had inundated the country with the poor people whom they had formerly relieved; the disaffection was very great, especially in the northern counties, which were particularly attached to the old faith, from which the king was separating himself more and more. The irritation, however, was not exclusively concentrated in the lower classes; the great noblemen and gentlemen, former patrons of the monasteries, considered that the property of which they had been deprived should be returned to the families which had formerly bestowed it upon them, rather than to the royal treasury; but it was the people of Lincolnshire who first set the example of insurrection. The king sent some forces against the insurgents, under the orders of the Duke of Suffolk. The latter found the insurrection so serious, that he determined to try negotiations. The "Men of Lincoln" presented six requests, complaining particularly of the sudden destruction of the monasteries, so prejudicial, they said, to the poor of the entire country; of the excessive taxes, of the vesting of the annates and tithes in the crown, and of the agitation which certain bishops, designated by their names, had brought about in the Church of Christ by altering the faith. Upon which they prayed the king to dismiss the treacherous counsellors, who thought of nothing but enriching themselves at the expense of the poor people.

Time had been gained by asking to know the grievances of the insurgents; discord began to penetrate into their ranks; the king was enabled, without danger, to reply to them with the haughtiness which was natural to him when his supreme will was opposed. He rejected all the requests of the insurgents, demanding that a hundred of the more important among them should be delivered to him, in order that he might make an example of them. No fighting had taken place; a considerable number of the insurgents still remained united; a second letter from the king commanded them to lay down their arms in the market-place at Lincoln, if they did not wish to bring down a terrible vengeance upon their wives and children. Before the rebels of Lincolnshire had returned home, about the 30th of October, a violent insurrection had broken out on the other side of the Trent, and this movement was spreading over the whole of Yorkshire, as well as in Durham, Northumberland, Westmoreland, and Lancashire. While the fifteen hostages of the insurgents of Lincolnshire were being executed, as well as some inhabitants of the environs of London, accused of having countenanced them, the rebels of the north wanted but a chief in order to stir up a veritable civil war. They marched in the name of God, they said, for the love of Jesus Christ, of the faith and the Holy Church, to the destruction of the heretics; they assumed the name of "Pilgrims of Grace," and carried a crucifix upon their standard; nearly all obeyed the orders of a gentleman of Yorkshire, Robert Aske, who was wanting neither in ability nor character. The Duke of Norfolk was ordered to march against them; the Duke of Suffolk and the Earl of Shrewsbury watched over other positions; the towns of Hull, York, and Pontefract had opened their gates to the Pilgrims of Grace before the arrival of the royal troops, and a certain number of gentlemen had joined them when the Duke of Norfolk checked their progress before Doncaster. Negotiations were entered into at the outset as in Lincolnshire; the demands of the insurgents were almost the same, though more precise and detailed. They demanded the destruction of the heresies of Wickliffe, Huss, Luther, and Melancthon, the restitution of the Pope to the religious supremacy, the rehabilitation of the Princess Mary, and the re-establishment of the Parliament in all its ancient privileges. The king treated with contempt such of these requests as he deigned to answer. "You are very bold," he said, "to think that after having reigned so long I do not know better than you what laws are agreeable to the commoners. The affairs of the Church do not concern you, and it is strange that you should prefer to see some few villains fatten in the monasteries rather than allow your prince to have them, in discharge of all the expenses which he has undertaken in order to defend you." Henry promised no other concession but the pardon of the rebels, with the exception of the ten leaders, who were to be delivered up to him immediately. The insurgents rejected without hesitation the offers of the royal clemency, and the Duke of Norfolk, who was not sufficiently powerful to fight, found himself compelled to retreat to the southern bank of the Trent, fortifying and defending all the passes in his rear. Time was being lost; the winter was approaching; the temperature and the suspension of agricultural labor were counted upon for dispersing the insurgents.

At length the king authorized the Duke of Norfolk to make overtures to the two principal chiefs of the rebels, Lord Darcy and Robert Aske: he even expressed a desire to see them. They did not respond to this gracious invitation, but the idea of betraying their partisans began to enter into their minds. The soldiers perceived this; everywhere this proclamation was seen affixed: "Commons, be of good cheer and remain faithful to your cause; the gentlemen betray you, but you will not want leaders if there is need of them." In the month of February the numbers assembled were still very great, but the royal army had received reinforcements; the insurgent forces collapsed before the castles and towns which they were besieging; discouragement began to creep into their ranks. Lord Darcy, Robert Aske, and the greater number of the leaders were captured and sent to London, where they were executed, notwithstanding the good disposition which they had manifested. The rebels now formed only scattered bodies, and martial law was proclaimed in the northern counties. Upon the express order of the king, a great number of the inhabitants of each town, borough, and village who had taken part in the revolt were hanged and quartered in the public squares, and their bodies affixed to trees, in order to terrify the remainder of the population. The monks, who had ardently embraced the cause of the insurrection, were treated with especial rigor; the insurgent counties were everywhere strewn with bloody heads and disfigured corpses. When the amnesty was at length proclaimed and peace re-established, visitations of the religious houses still continued; nearly all the monasteries of the north were destined to be closed and to have their property confiscated, before the royal vengeance and avidity could be satisfied. The anger of Henry had increased when he had learned that Reginald Pole, installed a short time since in Rome upon the urgent solicitations of Pope Paul III., and against the advice of his relatives in England, had been nominated cardinal and legate beyond the Alps. The aim of the Pope was, no doubt, to take advantage of the insurrection of the Catholic counties in order to influence the king and bring him back into the bosom of the Church; but Francis I. and Charles V. deemed the moment ill-chosen: the cardinal was unable to see the King of France while crossing his kingdom, and the Emperor did not even allow him to enter his dominions. Pole learned at the same time that a price had been placed upon his head by Henry. Cromwell asserted that the cardinal would be brought thereby to break his heart with grief. Pending this happy result, for the bringing about of which the master and the minister were not to spare their efforts, the legate was compelled to return to Rome without having been able to accomplish his mission of sending money and encouragement to the rebels of England; the insurrection had been stifled before Pole had set foot in Flanders.

Jane Seymour had, on the 12th of October, 1537, given birth to a son, and had died shortly afterwards, thus escaping the sad fate of the wives of Henry VIII. Grief for his loss had scarcely weighed in the scale against satisfaction at the birth of a male heir to the throne; the little Edward immediately received the title of Prince of Wales, Duke of Cornwall, and Earl of Chester; the national rejoicing was mingled with the lamentations of the monks on all sides, driven from their refuge under the pretext of complicity in the recent insurrection. When nothing remained but the great abbeys, the king caused their destruction to be voted by the Parliament, notwithstanding some feeble efforts of the abbots who sat in the House of Lords. A few only escaped the wreck, at the entreaty of the population, or were consigned to the descendants of their founders. The work of spoliation was accomplished: the rich chapels, the Gothic monuments, the learned libraries, the delicate sculptures, everything was delivered up to the destructive hands of the royal agents; none dared to intervene, and treasures of science, marvels of art, were forever lost to posterity. The lands were divided among the courtiers; the valuables were nearly all reserved for the king, who contrived to remain poor notwithstanding so great an accession of riches. He was not content with plundering the living, he even went so far as to plunder the dead. From a singular animosity against the memory of Thomas Becket — of that inflexible man who would have resisted him to the death, as he had resisted Henry II. — Henry VIII. had conceived a violent dislike to his shrine at Canterbury; but he did not rest here. Becket was summoned to appear at Westminster to answer for his rebellions, and the tomb of the martyr was broken for this purpose, as though to open the prison which confined him. In presence of the silent sepulchre, the king carried on his ghastly comedy; the attorney-general spoke against the dead saint, to whom an advocate had been granted. Becket, being judged by default, was deprived of his riches and honors; two large coffers, filled with jewels deposited upon his altar, were sent to London; festivals and pilgrimages celebrated in his honor were solemnly forbidden, the portraits of the saint were destroyed, and a royal proclamation commanded the people to believe henceforth that Thomas Becket had been killed in a quarrel caused by his own obstinacy, that he had been canonized by the Bishop of Rome as the champion of a usurped authority, but that he was but a rebel and a traitor to his king, and that the faithful servants of his Majesty were to guard themselves against honoring him as a saint. Thomas Becket thus twice had the notable honor of bringing down upon himself all the royal fury; even in his tomb he was proclaimed defender of the liberties of that Church for whose sake he had yielded up his life.

So vast an amount of wealth diverted from the pious objects

to which it had been originally consecrated, troubled the conscience of Cranmer, feeble and vacillating in his conduct, but honest and sincere, notwithstanding his numerous back-slidings. He endeavored to found in his diocese some pious establishments to replace those which had been so abruptly destroyed; but the diocese was poor; he had not profited by the spoils of St. Thomas Becket, and the hospitals, the asylums for the poor and travellers, the schools for children which were formerly afforded by the convents, left a void from which the unfortunate suffered painfully. The public cry reached the king. The treasures of the monasteries had melted in his prodigal hands; he addressed himself to the Parliament, boldly demanding subsidies to indemnify him for the expenses which he had incurred for the Reformation. The two tenths and the two fifteenths which were granted to him did not suffice for his requirements, still less for those of the new bishoprics, deaneries, and colleges which the Parliament had decreed. The establishments should have been endowed with the ecclesiastical property, but there was no longer any property. Six bishoprics were founded, so poorly provided for that the prelates scarcely had sufficient to live upon. A certain number of abbeys became cathedral churches; but the king was careful before appointing the dean and chapter to confiscate a portion of the lands, so that the new dignitaries of the Church ran no risk of allowing themselves to be drawn into effeminacy by the temptations of opulence. The plain parish priests, deprived of their livings, led such a miserable existence that none would any longer enter the Church. "We have ten thousand students less in the universities than there were formerly," wrote Latimer, when asking assistance for the university of Cambridge; and it was found necessary to seek for a priest to preach from St. Paul's Cross, an honor formerly sought after by the highest dignitaries.

While the entire kingdom thus remained silent and suffering, Henry VIII. occupied his leisure in personally interrogating and judging a poor schoolmaster, named John Lambert, who had adopted the views of the German Reformers upon the doctrine of the real presence. All the arguments of the royal theologian, reinforced by those of the bishops whom he had called to his aid, could not shake the conviction of Lambert. "Resign thy soul to God," said Henry angrily. "I resign my soul to God," said the accused man, "and my body to the mercy of your Grace." "Thou shalt die then," exclaimed the king, "for I am not the patron of heretics;" and Lambert was burned alive on the 20th of November, 1538. Henry VIII. alone had found a means of combining the twofold persecution of the Roman Catholics and the Reformers; he plundered and closed the convents while he burned the heretics. Cranmer shared in the main the opinions of the unhappy Lambert, but he dared not protest, and contented himself with favoring the translation of the Bible into English, a task which had just been accomplished by Miles Coverdale; the price of the book was unhappily very high, and the circulation consequently somewhat limited.

Henry meanwhile was uneasy. The Emperor and King Francis I. had recently concluded at Nice, under the auspices of the Pope, a truce for ten years; hence the alliance of England lost the value which had often attracted the advances of the two great rivals. Paul III. again threatened to promulgate the bull so long prepared, and he sought to unite against King Henry the forces of the empire and of France. Cardinal Pole had been employed in this negotiation; it remained without result, but the distrust and jealousy of the despot had been aroused, and the fate which the family of the cardinal had so long dreaded at length overtook them. In the month of December, 1538, Lord Montacute and Sir Geoffrey Pole, brother of the cardinal, as well as the Marquis of Exeter, grandson of King Edward IV. through his daughter Catherine, were arrested and conducted to the Tower. Some months later the Countess of Salisbury, mother of the cardinal, the Marchioness of Exeter, and the son of Lord Montacute were impeached in their turn. All were condemned and all perished, with the exception of Sir Geoffrey Pole, who betrayed his kinsmen. The old countess remained for a long time in prison, as though to experience all the horrors of her situation. When she was finally led to the scaffold, at the age of seventy-two years, she refused to place her head upon the block. "No," she said; "my head has committed no treason; if you want it, come and take it." It was found necessary to seize her by force, and she resisted until the last moment.

While bathing his hands in blood, King Henry was much occupied in instructing his people in sound doctrine; he had entered seriously upon his duties as Supreme Head of the Church, and was carefully preparing the articles of faith which were to form the basis of the popular belief; woe to him who should not adhere to the six articles which the king sent to the convocation of the clergy. In the main, the doctrines expounded by the king were those of the Roman Catholic Church, with the exception of the supremacy of the Pope. The efforts which Cranmer made to bring about, by discussion with the German theologians, some modifications in the ideas of Henry, remained without result. The emissaries of the Reformed churches in vain maintained the doctrine of communion of the two kinds, the marriage of priests, and other important points in doctrine and in practice; the king thanked them for the trouble which they had taken in coming to his kingdom; he assured them of the esteem in which he held their erudition and virtues, but he sent to the Parliament of

1539 an act recapitulating the obligatory articles of faith, entirely in conformity with the teaching of the Roman Catholic Church, and threatening the most severe penalties against whosoever should reject these doctrines, or should fail to conform his life thereto. The influence of Cranmer was once more defeated, and that of Bishop Gardiner, who had constantly remained faithful to the old Church, was again triumphant. The star of Cromwell was on the wane; the first instigator of the religious rivalry of Henry VIII. with the Pope was about in his turn to succumb beneath the jealous despotism which he had contributed to raise.

The two great parties which had been formed in the Church of England after the Reformation continued to share power under the king. The bishops favorable to Protestantism had for a time prevailed, when Henry, alarmed by the alliance of the Catholic powers, sent a mission to Germany to the Protestant princes, and authorized the journey of the German theologians to England. The prelates attached to the Catholic Church triumphed when Gardiner was recalled from his retirement, and the king accepted his revision of the religious edict submitted to the Parliament. Several of the reforming bishops had already resigned, or had been deprived of their dignities, when Cromwell, still favorable to the new party, desired to furnish it with an important support by uniting the king with a Protestant queen. For several months past Henry had in vain looked for a consort among the European princesses; the Dowager Duchess of Milan replied that if she had two heads she might have thought of that alliance, but that, having but one, she declined the honor which his Majesty wished to do her. He solicited the hand of Mary of Guise, Duchess of Longueville, but she was betrothed to his nephew, James V., King of Scotland, who had lost his first wife, Madeleine of France, a few months after their marriage. King

Francis I. had refused to send to Calais the two sisters of Mary of Guise, whom Henry wished to see. Cromwell proposed the Princess Anne of Cleves, sister of the reigning duke, whose beauty, gentleness, and virtue were much extolled. Henry VIII. dispatched to Germany his favorite painter, Holbein, to bring him back a portrait of the princess; it was contained in a rose of ivory admirably carved; the casket and the contents pleased the king; he asked for the hand of Anne of Cleves, to the great joy of Cromwell. The unfortunate man had never seen the princess.

She arrived in England on the 31st of December, 1539; notwithstanding his gout and his inconvenient stoutness, the king repaired to Rochester, in order to see secretly the princess who came courageously to share with him his fatal throne. He started back in dread and anger. Anne was tall and muscular, as he had been informed, and as he wished; her features were regular but coarse; her complexion, which was fresh, bore traces of small-pox; her figure was massive, her walk awkward, and, above all, the worthy German lady was clad in the fashion of her country, without elegance or grace. The voluptuous and debilitated monarch experienced an indignation that did not permit him to show himself at first. When at length he consented to see the princess, he said but a few words to her: Anne of Cleves spoke German; the king did not know that language. He sent her a present of some furs, and returned to London to convoke his council. On perceiving Cromwell he reproached him, in violent terms, for having married him to a great Flemish nag, uncouth and awkward, ill-fitted to inspire love; he then commanded him to find some pretext for breaking off this odious union. Cromwell was politic; he trembled for his favor and, perhaps, his life; he was compelled to remind the king that, in the situation of his affairs in Germany, it would be dangerous to displease

ANNE OF CLEVES.

the German princes. "There is no remedy then! I must place my head in the halter!" exclaimed Henry piteously. He yielded, and the marriage was celebrated at Greenwich on the 5th of January. But the burden of this union became every day more insupportable to the king; he was not accustomed to find himself thwarted; the objections of Cromwell to the divorce rankled in his breast. A theological quarrel of a dependant of the minister with Bishop Gardiner completed the exasperation of the king against his vicar-general; the heterodoxy of Barnes threw doubt upon the orthodoxy of Cromwell, who had employed him in the fatal negotiation for the marriage of Anne of Cleves. The king still concealed his resentment. Cromwell opened the Parliament as usual, intrusted with the royal message, which related solely to the religious questions yet in litigation; he obtained from the Houses enormous subsidies, dispensed court favors, threatened with the royal displeasure the chiefs of the Catholic party, the Duke of Norfolk, and the Bishops of Durham, Winchester, and Bath; then, on the 10th of June, 1540, he was arrested in the very council-chamber, for high-treason. Four days afterwards he was condemned by a bill of attainder, a process which he had himself contributed to establish, and on the 28th of June he suffered his sentence as a traitor to the Head of the Church and a pestilent heretic. The king was compelled, in order to replace Cromwell, whose activity had been indefatigable, to summon to his side two secretaries of state, of whom one, Wriothesley, afterwards became his chancellor.

The ill-starred marriage with Anne of Cleves and the theological errors of Barnes were not the sole causes of the ruin of Cromwell; the beautiful face of Lady Catherine Howard, niece of the Duke of Norfolk, had played a part in the overthrow of the condemned minister. Before Cromwell perished upon the scaffold, Henry VIII. married Catherine Howard.

Anne of Cleves at first swooned on learning the intentions of the king towards her, but recovering her senses, she doubtless returned thanks to God for having preserved her from the melancholy fate of the wives of Henry VIII., and accepted without a murmur the title of "adopted sister" of the king, which was bestowed upon her by that gracious sovereign. A suitable establishment was granted to her in England; and the Duke of Suffolk, intrusted with the letters of the princess for her brother, started for Cleves, in order to explain to the duke the scruples concerning a former contract of the princess with the Duke of Lorraine, which had led the king to break off the marriage, while assuring him of the happy condition and full consent of the dethroned queen. By way of celebrating his fifth nuptials, Henry sent to the stake Dr. Barnes, the maladroit dependant of Cromwell, in company with two or three other heretics, while certain Catholics were quartered for having refused to take the oath of supremacy. The punishment alone was different: Catholics and Protestants were dragged to Smithfield upon the same hurdle, bound together, to the common indignation of both parties. "How do folks manage to live here?" exclaimed a Frenchman; "the Papists are hanged and the anti-Papists are burned." In the following month the Prior of Doncaster and six of his monks were hanged for having defended monastic institutions; all crimes became equally grave in the eyes of the despot, from the moment they thwarted his supreme will.

The triumph of Catherine Howard was destined to be of short duration and to cost her dearly. The king was much attached to her, and had taken her with him on a royal tour of inspection, during the summer of 1541, but when he returned to London in the month of August, Cranmer revealed to him a grievous discovery, made in his absence by his servants, with regard to the conduct of the queen before her

ANGER OF HENRY VIII. ON HIS FIRST VIEW OF ANNE OF CLEVES.

marriage, during her sojourn with her great-aunt, the Dowager Duchess of Norfolk. Jealous and suspicious, Henry VIII. did not demand proofs before losing all confidence in the virtue of his wife; but he wished nevertheless to have the witnesses examined, and they were all arrested and put to the torture. The queen herself, it is said, confessed her transgressions, as did the man accused of complicity with her — her cousin, Francis Dereham. The guilt of Lady Catherine Howard did not suffice, however, to ruin the queen; she positively affirmed her conjugal fidelity, and the king, whose whole love appeared to have been changed to aversion, set every means at work in order to assure himself of her alleged offence towards him. The old Duchess of Norfolk, her daughter, Lady Bridgewater, and her son, Lord William Howard, were placed in the Tower charged with having favored the bad conduct of the queen; every species of ill-treatment, every ruse, every falsehood was employed in order to extract the truth, or at least to obtain avowals capable of ruining Catherine Howard. All was in vain; "the mother and the daughter are equally stubborn," say the records of the council, and both rejected with indignation the idea of any complicity in the crimes of which the queen was accused. The two gentlemen accused, Dereham and Culpepper, were tried and condemned, and were executed at Tyburn on the 10th of December, while the Duke of Cleves was hastening to send an ambassador to King Henry, in order to induce him to take again the Princess Anne, his sister, as his wife. The proposal was rejected by Cranmer, the emissary not even being admitted into the presence of the king. Anne of Cleves remained the *good sister* of his Majesty, and the trial of Catherine Howard continued, without any one protesting in favor of the unhappy woman, deprived of all means of defence, and delivered over, bound hand and foot, to her accusers. Her uncle, the Duke of Norfolk, had abandoned her, as he had formerly done in the case of his other niece, Anne Boleyn, protesting to his Majesty "the grief occasioned to him by the abominable actions of two kinswomen towards his Grace, who might in consequence hold even himself in abhorrence." Search was being made meanwhile in the coffers and hiding-places of all the accused persons, and his Majesty had already collected in this manner large sums, when the council condemned them all to imprisonment for life with the confiscation of all their property, simply recommending that some consolations should be accorded to them in their captivity, and that certain of their friends should be admitted to them in the Tower. The king took care to cut short this indulgence, and on the same evening he caused a council to be assembled to forbid any modification in the treatment inflicted upon the prisoners, "for great and important reasons," added the conscientious monarch. The trial had established nothing except that the old Duchess of Norfolk and her children had been informed of the reciprocal love of Francis Dereham and Catherine before the marriage of the latter.

The severity which was employed towards her relatives should have enlightened the unhappy queen if she had been able for one moment to believe the promise of her life which the king had transmitted to her through Cranmer. The Parliament on the 16th of January addressed an humble petition to the sovereign, asking permission of him to proceed against Lady Catherine Howard by a bill of attainder, in order to spare his Majesty the grief of hearing the crimes of his wife recapitulated. Henry graciously consented to this delicate request, and on the 11th of February the queen was condemned by the Parliament at the same time as Lady Rochford, sister-in-law of Anne Boleyn, who had formerly given evidence against her husband and her sister. She was accused of having been an accomplice in the crimes of Catherine since her marriage. The queen and Lady Rochford were executed on the 13th of February, within the precincts of the Tower; Catherine protested even on the scaffold that she had always been faithful to her spouse, "whatever might have been the faults of her past life." The bill of attainder against Catherine Howard made it incumbent on any woman whom the king might admit to the honor of a union with his sacred person, to make a full confession before marriage. "The king had better marry a widow," it was said among the people. Henry appeared for the moment disgusted with marriage; he was absorbed in theology, that second passion of his life, which he treated almost as despotically as his spouses.

The death of Catherine Howard had not, as might have been expected, thrown the king back upon the party of the Reformation: in the month of April, 1542, he retracted the encouragements which he had given to the reading of the Holy Scriptures; he prohibited the use of the old version of Tyndal as heretical, while ordering that the new and authorized translation, without notes or commentary, should be used exclusively; above all, he forbade the reading of the Bible in public even by the orthodox, only permitting the use of the Holy Scriptures in families of the nobility and gentry. People of the inferior class were to be liable to a month's imprisonment if they dared to open the sacred volume. At the same time the revision of the *Institution of a Christian Man*, formerly published by the bishops by order of the king, was completed. The new work, which appeared in 1543, differed essentially upon several points from the first one; it was entitled *The necessary Doctrine and Erudition for any Christian Man;* the people named it the *King's Book*, and the king imposed it, in fact, as a model of faith upon his subjects, without troubling himself about the changes which his own mind had undergone since he had caused the *Bishops' Book* to be drawn up. The *King's Book* inclined more and more towards the doctrine of the Roman Catholic Church. Like the first catechism, it insisted upon transubstantiation, oral confession, and the celibacy of the clergy; it also maintained the uselessness of communion in both kinds for the faithful, and recommended masses for the dead. The new formulary was adopted by the two convocations of the clergy; all the books which were not in conformity with it were forbidden, and the primate, Cranmer, who saw the condemnation of his most cherished convictions, and the affirmation of the dogmas which he rejected, was charged with the duty of watching over the execution of the royal orders. Henry VIII. was accustomed to be obeyed; Cranmer had sent his wife and children away to Germany, since the celibacy of the priests had become legally obligatory.

The servile obedience which the king exacted from his subjects in England was not everywhere exacted with the same rigor. Henry VIII. had furnished proof of skill and foresight by his government of the almost independent principalities ranged under his sceptre. In 1536 he had definitively annexed Wales to England, subjecting the whole territory to the English laws, which hitherto had only been enforced in a portion of that country. The Welsh counties had been admitted to the privilege of sending members to Parliament, as well as the palatinate of Chester, hitherto administered according to local customs. But the most important reform which King Henry VIII. effected in this respect was the elevation of Ireland from the rank of a seigniory to that of a kingdom. From generation to generation the hereditary struggle of the Butlers, under their chiefs the Earls of Ormond and Ossory, with the Fitzgeralds, at the head of whom was the Earl of Kildare, had kept the country in a continual state of agitation;

by dint of political reverses, treasons, acts of perfidy, executions, and murders, the great Irish Houses had wearied and destroyed each other, and the government had never failed to interpose to further the work. In 1541 the king, wishing to secure the attachment of the more powerful of the Irish chiefs, elevated a certain number of them to the honors of the peerage. The eagerness of the chiefs was extreme: the great noblemen swore fidelity to the king, undertook military service, and accepted houses at Dublin, whither they were to repair to sit as members of the Parliament of Ireland. The king had granted letters-patent to them for their property, which removed their former fears of seeing the English sovereigns one day confiscate all their estates. The appropriation of the ecclesiastical property to the crown was accomplished with prudence. "Do not press them too vigorously," said the instructions of Henry VIII.; "but persuade them discreetly that the Church lands are my legitimate inheritance." The Catholic fervor of the Irish had some difficulty in accepting this mode of succession, but the work proceeded, though slowly, and did not prevent the progress of English authority in Ireland from being real and important under the reign of Henry VIII.

Scotland still remained in a body attached to the old faith. King James distrusted the treacherous manœuvres of his uncle; he had sought the hereditary alliances of his House, and his marriage with Mary of Guise, and the influence which Cardinal David Beaton exercised over him, had drawn closer the bonds which united him to France as well as to the Church of Rome. All the attempts of the King of England to bring his nephew over to his opinions, and to induce him to follow the English example by the destruction of the monasteries, had completely failed. Cardinal Beaton set out for Rome with secret instructions, a fact which troubled Henry. Hostilities broke out in the month of August, 1542. An English army crossed the frontier: they were vigorously repulsed; but the Duke of Norfolk was advancing with considerable forces; he received the reinforcements of the Earl of Angus, the father-in-law of the young king, who had come with all the members of his family, and who marched, like himself, under the English banners. The duke had scarcely advanced a few steps into Scotland when the king reassembled his forces in order to meet him. But the great noblemen were nearly all disaffected; some were secretly in favor of the Reformation: they wished to enrich themselves at the expense of the monasteries; others were bound by old friendship to the Douglases, and would not fight against them; nearly all regretted the war with England, and wished to remain upon the defensive. Norfolk having been compelled to beat a retreat, in consequence of the bad weather and the want of provisions, the king was anxious to pursue him beyond the frontiers; but his troops refused to follow him to a second battle of Flodden; one after another the barons withdrew with their vassals; the king had now no more than ten thousand men, whom he placed under the orders of Lord Maxwell. This faithful little army suddenly entered England. As they were crossing the frontier, the favorite of the king, Oliver Sinclair, produced a warrant which placed him at the head of the troops. All the noblemen refused to obey his command; disorder set in among the soldiers; the English fell upon the Scottish army, made a great slaughter, captured many prisoners of high rank, and put all the rest to flight. The troops, vanquished without a struggle, rejoined the king at Carlaverock Castle, where he awaited the result of the expedition. The blow struck home: the monarch returned in sadness of heart to Edinburgh, and took refuge in his castle of Falkland, where he spent long hours, with his head in his hands, plunged in his melancholy thoughts, without uttering a word. He was thirty-one years of age, his constitution had always been vigorous, but he was dying of a broken heart. His wife, Mary of Guise, had borne him two sons, who had both died in infancy; the birth of a daughter, the celebrated and unfortunate Mary Stuart, was announced to James V.; the sadness of the king only became greater. "It came with a lass," he is said to have murmured, remembering the daughter of Bruce, who had brought the throne to his family, "and it will go with a lass." A week afterwards, on the 14th of December, 1542, James V. expired, leaving his kingdom rent asunder by political factions and religious dissensions, a prey to all the evils of a long minority and the prospect of the reign of a woman. If he had been able to foresee the future, the last moments of the unhappy king would have been still more gloomy.

Scarcely had King Henry learned the death of his nephew, when he conceived the project of uniting the little queen, who had just opened her eyes to the light, with his son Edward, who was not yet six years of age. The alliance might have been serviceable to the two countries, but Henry claimed to take immediate possession of Scotland in the name of the future spouses, and his greedy selfishness caused all his designs to miscarry. He had enrolled in his cause not only all the Douglases, but the Scottish noblemen made prisoners at the rout of Solway Moss; they returned to their country determined to betray its most cherished interests. Cardinal Beaton had claimed the regency, according to a presumed will of the king; but the Earl of Arran, the heir presumptive to the throne and chief of the Protestant party, had been powerful enough to dispossess the cardinal; he held him imprisoned in Blackness Castle. The influence of the Catholic clergy over the common people and a certain portion of the nobility was considerable; the churches were closed, worship suspended, and the clergy worked ardently against the regent, who leaned for support upon the Douglases and their friends, who had come back into favor with him. The public voice accused the noblemen of treason and perfidy; the King of England urged them to perform their engagements. He claimed the right to hold in his hands Cardinal Beaton, and demanded the surrender of the fortresses. The truce was only to last until the month of June, and the English troops were already assembling in the northern counties; but public opinion in Scotland was aroused, and Sir George Douglas, the most active of the conspirators in the interest of England, assured King Henry that it would be impossible to lay claim on his behalf to the government of Scotland. "There is not a boy so little," he said, "but he will hurl stones against it, and the wives will handle their distaffs, and the commons universally will die in it, and many noblemen and all the clergy be fully against it." The Catholic party, uniting the cause of religious liberty with that of the state, opposed both the reading of the New Testament by the common people and the alliance with England. The restoration to liberty of the cardinal was also claimed. All the noblemen repaired to the Parliament, and the question of the marriage was there proposed without any opposition; but none dared to speak of the conditions attached by the King of England to this union so much desired by all; and the Parliament, while approving of the project of marriage, strongly objected to the plan of sending the little queen to England, at the same time taking the most jealous precautions for the maintenance of the national independence.

The anger of King Henry equalled his aspirations; he heaped the most violent reproaches upon his Scottish allies, at the same time endeavoring to attach them once more to his service by new promises. They protested their good will, but pleaded their powerlessness. Cardinal Beaton had regained his liberty, and opposed to the Earl of Arran the Earl of Lennox, an ally of the royal family, who had served with Francis I. in the wars in Italy. The treaties were renewed: the hand of the little queen was promised to Prince Edward; she was to be left in Scotland until the age of ten years; an English nobleman and his family were to form part of her household. But besides these open and reasonable conditions there was "a secret understanding": all the conspirators engaged in the service of Henry promised in case of need to take up arms in his interest and to fight for him until he should have obtained "the things agreed upon," or, at least, dominion over this side of the Firth, that is to say, over all the southern portion of Scotland.

The treaty was scarcely concluded when Cardinal Beaton raised an army in the north, and employed it at once to carry off the queen and her mother, in order to place them in safety in Stirling Castle. Arran had retained the regency, but after having signed the conditions with England, he suddenly changed his party, became reconciled with Beaton, abjured his errors, and returned to the bosom of the Catholic Church. France had sent reinforcements, and notwithstanding the assistance of Lenox, who had abandoned the patriots, the conspirators found themselves once more baffled in their attempts by the national movement brought about by Beaton.

The assistance rendered to the Scots by the King of France, excited the anger of Henry VIII.; he nourished an old grievance against that prince, for whom he had no liking, notwithstanding their frequent alliances, and he resolved to throw himself once more into the arms of the Emperor. Without effacing the stain of illegitimacy which he himself had imprinted upon his daughter Mary, he caused her to be reinstated in her civil rights by an act of Parliament, at the same time with her sister, the Princess Elizabeth, restoring to them also their title to the throne. Charles V. contented himself with this concession, and concluded an alliance with England. Emissaries were sent to the King of France, intrusted with a mass of claims, to which Francis I. would not even listen, and great preparations were begun for the invasion of French territory. Henry had recently married for the sixth time: he had espoused Lady Catherine Parr, the widow of Lord Latimer. She was beautiful, intelligent, and ardently devoted to the Protestant party; the latter fact, however, did not prevent the execution, a fortnight after the royal marriage, of three *sacramentarians*, burned alive at Smithfield.

The first detachment sent to France, under the command of Sir John Wallop, in 1540, had completely failed in their attempt, when the king went in person at the head of an army of thirty thousand men to lay siege to Boulogne. The two allied monarchs had agreed to march directly upon Paris, but sieges had an irresistible attraction for Henry VIII., and he had not yet made his entry into the town which delayed him for two months, when the Emperor entered into negotiations with Francis I., at Crespy-en-Valois. Thus they left the King of England, who had scornfully rejected the proposals of peace, free to return into his dominions after his conquest of Boulogne, exhausted by the efforts which he had had to make to raise an army and to maintain at the same time the forces which were carrying on the war in Scotland.

Intrigue upon intrigue, treachery upon treachery, succeeded each other among the Scottish factions; sometimes the Catholics and Protestants became reconciled through their hatred of England; at others some deed of violence estranged them again. Beaton, more bold and skilful than his rivals, nearly always preserved his ascendancy, but his cruel persecution of the Reformers incensed a considerable part of the nation. The English had made several irruptions into Scotland, under the orders of Lord Hertford and his lieutenants; they committed great cruelties, and finally found themselves shamefully repulsed in the environs of Ancrum. The secret manœuvres of Henry VIII., the relations which he still maintained with the nobility, and the perfidy of a certain number of great barons, prevented the Scots, however, from profiting by their advantages and by the reinforcements sent by Francis I.; the southern counties of Scotland were again ravaged by the Earl of Hertford; a fatal manifestation of the fanaticism of Cardinal Beaton occurred to add strength to the English arms and intrigues. A reformed preacher, George Wishart, celebrated among his party and passionately loved by the people, was pursued, seized, and burned alive at St. Andrew's, amid the public indignation. For a long time past the assassination of Cardinal Beaton, whom Henry VIII. regarded as the principal obstacle to his projects upon Scotland, was meditated; the moment appeared favorable, and on the 28th of May, 1546, two gentlemen of the name of Lesley, with whom the cardinal had had great personal quarrels, accompanied by some friends, took Beaton by surprise in the castle of St. Andrew's, and stabbed him in his bed. Norman Lesley hung the corpse on the wall, as the inhabitants of the town were advancing to the help of the legate. "There is your God," he said; "now you should be content; return to your homes." All the assassins received pensions from abroad, and hastened to claim the reward of their crimes. King Henry had been mistaken in his hopes; the Church of Rome in Scotland had received a fatal blow, but the national independence remained erect. The embarrassments of the finances were increasing in England; Boulogne was closely pressed by the French. Henry VIII. was now suffering from ill-health; he concluded a treaty at Campes with King Francis I., and the Scots were included therein, to the great vexation of their implacable foe. Francis I. promised money; the sum once paid, England was to surrender Boulogne, which town had been fortified at great expense since its capture. It was the end of the campaigns of King Henry VIII., which had almost uniformly proved disastrous and without any durable results, especially when the monarch had placed himself personally at the head of his troops. Hostile armies did not allow themselves to be conquered as easily as England allowed itself to be oppressed.

So many checks abroad, together with the constant pecuniary embarrassments entailed by his prodigalities at home, completed the imbitterment of the terrible character of the despot, who was now slowly dying in his palace at Whitehall. Addicted from the earliest time to the pleasures of the table, he had acquired an enormous corpulence, which rendered the least movements difficult to him. He had a difficulty in signing his name, and could not take a step without the assistance of his attendants. He suffered from an ulcer in the leg, and his morose disposition had completely metamorphosed his court, formerly so brilliant. None dared to raise his voice in favor of the most innocent victims. A lady who had access to the court, Anne Askew, young, beautiful, and learned, passionately attached to the doctrines of the Reformation, had left her husband and children to come to London to preach the Gospel; she was arrested and conducted before Bishop Bonner, who caused her to sign a confession of faith in conformity with the doctrines of the Catholic Church. But the zeal of Anne did not abate; she continued to preach: being again arrested, she was tried and condemned as a heretic. Her prosecutors were anxious to make her avow the means which she had made use of in order to spread the forbidden books among the ladies of the queen, and they put her to the torture to compel her to denounce her friends. "I have no friends at court," she repeated; "I have never been supported by any member of the council." The courage of Anne Askew remained firm at the stake as under the torture of the "wooden horse;" she died praising God, in company with a gentleman of the king's household, named Lascelles, who would not accept the doctrine of transubstantiation, and two other equally dangerous heretics. While he was ordering these executions, King Henry VIII. was delivering his last discourse to the Parliament, grieving at the lack of brotherly love among his subjects. "Charity was never so faint among you, and virtuous and godly living was never less used, nor God Himself among Christians was never less reverenced, honored, or served. Therefore be in charity one with another, like brother and brother; love, dread, and serve God; to the which, as your supreme Head and Sovereign Lord, I exhort and require you."

Perhaps Queen Catherine Parr suspected that the king needed upon his own account those religious exhortations which he had always so liberally bestowed upon his people, for she attempted, it is said, to discuss with him certain points in theology which she had studied in the heretical books, probably those very publications which Anne Askew had caused to be introduced into the royal household — a dangerous experiment which she had occasion to repent. The king flew into a violent passion. "A good hearing this," he exclaimed, "when women become such clerks; and a thing much to my comfort, to come in my old age to be taught by my wife!" The sword which had threatened Catherine so long was on the point of falling. Gardiner and Wriothesley, the new chancellor, ardent Roman Catholics, received the order to prepare the impeachment of the queen. She was warned in time; she was intelligent and skilful. When in the eventide the conversation turned again upon religious questions, the king appeared to urge her to speak; she began to laugh. "I am not so foolish as not to know what I can understand," she said, "when I possess the favor of having for a master and spouse a prince so learned in holy matters." "By St. Mary!" exclaimed the king, "it is not so, Kate; thou hast become a doctor." The queen continued to laugh. "I thought I noticed," she said, "that that conversation diverted your Grace's attention from your sufferings, and I ventured to discuss with you in the hope of making you forget your present infirmity." "Is it so, sweetheart?" replied the king; "then we are friends again, and it doth me more good than if I had received a hundred thousand pounds." The orders given to the chancellor had not been revoked; he arrived on the morrow with forty men of his guard to arrest Catherine, but the king sent him away angrily. Catherine Parr henceforth left theology in peace.

A few more executions were wanting to light up the dismal valley of death into which the king felt himself descending; the jealousies of the political chiefs of the great factions which divided the country were about to furnish matter for the last deeds of violence of the dying monarch. The ancient and illustrious house of the Howards and its chief, the Duke of Norfolk, had observed with vexation the growing power and influence of the Earl of Hertford and of the family of the Seymours. The wealth, as well as the past renown of the Howards, had nothing to fear from the new rival who had sprung up beside them; but Lord Hertford was uncle to the heir to the throne, which gave him much power in the future; he wished to secure himself against any fatal mishap by striking his enemies beforehand. The distrust and jealousy of King Henry VIII. were easily excited; the old Duke of

CATHERINE DISCUSSING THEOLOGY WITH THE KING.

Norfolk and his son, the Earl of Surrey, were arrested on the 12th of December, 1546, and taken to the Tower. At the same time, in the presence of several witnesses, the king erased their names from the list of his testamentary executors. Everything had been done to make out a strong case. Advantage had been taken of an old feud between the Duke of Norfolk and his wife, and between the Earl of Surrey and his sister, the Duchess of Richmond, to search the papers and coffers of the family, in order to discover some tokens of treason. The ladies had even been arrested, and had been severely interrogated; but all that could be alleged in the impeachment was that Lord Surrey had quartered with his own arms the royal arms of Edward the Confessor. The old Duke of Norfolk had, it was said, been guilty of seditious utterances regarding the death of the king, while manifesting his dissatisfaction at the reforms of the Church. His trial had not commenced when Lord Surrey was brought to Guildhall to reply to his accusers. He was young, handsome, valiant; he was learned and cultivated; his poems are still famous. He defended himself with as much intelligence as courage, proving that he was authorized by the decisions of the heralds-at-arms to bear the arms of Edward the Confessor, which he had constantly displayed in the presence of the king without his Majesty having discovered anything to find fault with. The court declared, however, that this simple matter of the royal arms betrayed pretensions to the throne; Surrey was condemned, and on the 19th of January the flower of English chivalry perished upon the scaffold, while King Henry VIII. was already at the point of death.

Norfolk had in vain demanded to be confronted with his accusers; he had written to the king, and his letters had remained without a reply. Henry VIII., when dying, had not forgotten the convenient arm which he had wielded so long;

the old duke, alarmed and wearied, had even gone so far as to make a gift of all his property to the sovereign, begging him to settle it upon Prince Edward. The experienced statesman knew that it would be easier for his posterity some day to recover the riches concentrated in the sovereign's own hands, than to snatch them from the hands of the greedy courtiers, who were already, in expectation, sharing them among themselves; but this manœuvre was not successful in saving him; the confession which preceded his donation served as a basis for the bill of attainder, which was voted by the House of Commons on the 20th of January, 1547. The king was no longer able to sign. On the 27th the Chancellor Wriothesley informed the two Houses that his Majesty had chosen delegates to ratify the condemnation, and an order was dispatched to the Lieutenant of the Tower to execute the Duke of Norfolk on the 28th, early in the morning. On the same night Henry VIII. expired, after a reign of thirty-seven years. Not until the last day of his life had the boldest of his courtiers dared to suggest to him the possibility of his approaching end, and proposed to bring a priest to him. "No other than Archbishop Cranmer," he said; "but not yet: when I shall have rested." When the archbishop was at length asked for, the king could no longer speak; Cranmer reminded him of the mercy of God through Jesus Christ, and Henry grasped the hand of the prelate with his remaining strength; a moment afterwards he was no more.

For some years past, endeavors have been made to place the memory of King Henry VIII. in a more favorable light. No one has labored in this direction with more zeal and ability than Mr. Froude; but no party passions can annihilate the facts of history; the personal character of the king must still be regarded as corrupt and cruel: relations with him were fatal to all who approached him, wives and ministers. A monarch despotic and arbitrary, violent and unjust, he was at the same time a capricious and perfidious ally, a vain and harsh pedant. The reform which he undertook in England was the work of his private interest and his tyrannical pride, not of a settled and sincere conviction. In his heart he still remained a Catholic, and only wished to rid himself of the supremacy of the Pope, who thwarted him, and of the monasteries, the spoliation of which enriched him. Illegalities and abuses of all kinds were increasing with the servility of Parliament, with the long duration of the reign, and the development of the vices of the king. At the time of his death the subjugation of England had become complete.

Notwithstanding so many crimes, oppressions, and errors, England gained much in the reign of Henry VIII.; the king had overwhelmed his people with taxes, but he had maintained public order, and favored the development of commerce; he had persecuted both Catholics and Protestants, but by separating violently from the court of Rome he had implanted in the English soil the germ of that religious liberty which was destined never to perish; he had labored to construct a peculiar edifice, filled with strange contradictions, and he had called it the Church of England in order to place himself at its head as the supreme chief; but he had imprinted upon the English reform its peculiar character, at once governmental and liberal, aristocratic and popular. He infamously plundered the monasteries, but he thereby involved in the party of reform the great noblemen enriched by the spoils: he shed upon the scaffold the noblest blood of England, but he followed the policy of his father in raising to power obscure men drawn from that growing middle class which was one day to constitute the greatness and strength of his country. Without brilliant military genius, without great political talents, he had contrived to maintain himself abroad as an arbiter respected by the greatest sovereigns of Europe, causing the scale to incline to the side to which his capricious vanity impelled him. The royal coffers were full at the death of Henry VII.: they were empty at the time of his son's death, notwithstanding the enormous exactions which had filled them so many times; but sixty years of comparative peace had enriched the nation, so long crushed under the weight of civil and foreign wars; it had regained its breath. In vain had Henry VIII. oppressed it; in vain had he reduced the Parliament to servile dependence; the new spirit inspired by the Reformation had done its work; in spite of the stake, religious sects were already multiplying: the day of the Puritans was about to dawn; the obstinate resistance of weakness under a powerful oppression was already preparing. Protestant England had sprung into existence.

CHAPTER XIX.

THE REFORMATION.—EDWARD VI. 1547–1553.

THE oppressive tyranny of Henry VIII. had ceased, and the child who succeeded him was destined to reign without attaining manhood. The ambitions and animosities of the great, the sincere passions and the intrigues of theologians, were about to occupy the scene, to divide and agitate all minds; but the work which was to make England Protestant and free had begun, and was continuing silently, and in obscurity. Henry VIII. had thought to regulate the religious movement in England as he had shaken off the supremacy of the Pope, but all his despotism could not arrest the effects of the new convictions, powerful especially among the lower clergy and the inhabitants of the towns. It was there that the Reformation numbered every day more numerous and more zealous adherents; it was there that the changes soon brought about by Cranmer in the organization of the Church met with the most ardent sympathy; and it was there that the persecution set on foot by the fanatic zeal of Queen Mary was to find the firmest resistance and the most heroic martyrs. Henry VIII. had accomplished the royal reform in order to satisfy his passions and his personal animosities; the English people, under the reign of his son, accomplished noiselessly and without proclamation a reform in a far different way, solid and deep. The country districts were still Catholic and long remained so; a portion of the bishops and the high clergy refused to admit the new doctrines; but the religious reform progressed none the less; it was no longer in the power of man to arrest the work begun in the hearts and consciences of a mass of people as obscure as they were sincere. The young king, moreover, never had the desire to do so. During the short reign of Edward VI., through the weaknesses and vacillations natural to childhood, the prince was seen to pass from one to the other of the great noblemen who were contending together for power; never did he change in opinion or in religious tendency, and his influence always weighed on the side of the Reformation. Edward VI. was destined for a long while yet to remain the most Protestant of English sovereigns.

Henry VIII. had scarcely been dead four days, his obsequies had not yet taken place, and already all that he had wished and ordained for the government of England during the minority of his son was destroyed. Formerly the House of Lords possessed the privilege of designating the regent and the members of the council of regency; Parliament had granted this power to the king by the Act which had allowed him to dispose at his pleasure of the succession to the throne. Henry had accordingly made use of his right in designating in his will sixteen persons destined to constitute the privy council, and to be intrusted with the executive power. A second commission of twelve members was to be consulted in grave cases; the two bodies united composed the council of regency. Among the more important members of the privy council were to be read the names of Cranmer, Chancellor Wriothesley, Lord Hertford, Lord Lisle; but the Earl of Hertford did not limit his ambition to a seat in the council. He had taken his steps and had secured partisans among the testamentary executors of the king; at the first meeting he contrived to accomplish his project. It was proposed to select a president. Wriothesley violently opposed this, saying that the will placed all the councillors in the same rank: he counted, no doubt, upon taking possession of the principal part of the power: he found himself alone upon his side, and finally gave way. When the Lords reassembled on the 1st of February around the young king, had heard the list of the members of the two councils read, Wriothesley added that the executors had resolved to place at their head the Earl of Hertford as Protector of the Kingdom and governor of the royal person; on condition, however, that he would take no steps in any matter without the assent of the majority of the members of the council. All the peers spiritual and temporal applauded this selection, and the last wishes of Henry VIII. were thus unceremoniously violated.

Some intentions were attributed to the late king, however, which met with more respect: a clause of the will commanded the executors to accomplish all the promises which he might have made; it was even asserted that he had repeated this injunction to those who surrounded his deathbed. The royal promises might be of great extent and entail grave consequences; inquiries were promptly resorted to; according to the statement of Sir William Paget, secretary of state, Sir Anthony Denny and Sir Fulke Herbert, gentlemen of the bedchamber, to whom the king had spoken on the subject, it was a question of a promotion to the peerage and a distribution of legacies in money among the testamentary executors. Lord Hertford was to be made Duke of Somerset; the Earl of Essex to become Marquis of Northampton; Lord Lisle, Earl of Warwick; Wriothesley, Earl of Southampton; Sir Thomas Seymour, brother of Lord Hertford, Baron Seymour and Lord High Admiral; all were to receive from the ecclesiastical property still at the disposition of the crown, revenues proportioned to their new dignities. The servants of the new king rewarded themselves in advance, and with their own hands, for the services which they were to render to him. Public opinion was shocked at this: people went so far as to call in question the alleged intentions of the late king as they had been reported by Sir John Paget. The elevation of Somerset was received with great joy among the Protestants, to whom he was favorable; the Catholics counted upon Wriothesley, who had become Lord Southampton, but he committed the imprudence of commissioning four delegates, under the great seal, to attend in his absence to the affairs of the chancellorship, without having previously consulted his colleagues; this act was declared illegal, and the fault being grave enough to deprive the chancellor of his office and his seat in the privy council, he gave in his resignation, and was kept a prisoner in his house, until the council had decided the amount of the fine which he was to pay. Henceforth Somerset found himself without a rival; none protested when he caused all the executive powers to be conferred upon himself, abolishing the two councils, and confounding all the testamentary executors under the common title of councillors of the king. Matters were arranged; an amnesty had been proclaimed for all state offenders, with the exception of the Duke of Norfolk and Cardinal Pole, and the Protector was preparing to sign the treaty of alliance between France and England, renewed in London on the occasion of the accession of Edward VI., when he learnt the news of the death of Francis I. This monarch had been painfully affected by the decease of the King of England; he was convinced, it was said, that he should only survive him a short time. And such indeed was the fact; the French king died at Rambouillet, on the 31st of March. By his death Protestant interests received a fatal blow in

Germany and in Scotland: in Germany, because the Emperor Charles V., set free from his rival, was becoming master of the country; in Scotland, because the Guises, the brothers of the dowager queen, were all-powerful with the new king of France, and because the latter immediately concluded a close alliance with the Earl of Arran, now placed at the head of the Catholic party. At the same time Henry II. refused to sign the treaty of London, and sent ships to Scotland to assist the regent in the siege of the Castle of St. Andrew, which the assassins of Cardinal Beaton had been able to retain. The latter sought help in England, promising to support the marriage of the little Queen Mary with the young King of England; but before the Protector had had time to assemble his forces, the castle was captured, razed to the ground, and all its defenders conveyed to France. Five weeks elapsed before the English troops were able to cross the frontier. It was on the 10th of September that the two armies met, not far from Musselburgh. Arran was there encamped behind the river Esk, with considerable forces; nearly all the great Scottish noblemen had joined him, notwithstanding party rivalries. The first challenge which the English received was that of Lord Huntley, who proposed to the Protector to fight him man to man, or with the assistance of ten knights on each side, after the fashion of the Horatii and Curiatii. Somerset smiled. "Tell your master," he replied to the herald, "that it is a want of judgment on his part to make such a proposal to me, who, by the grace of God, am intrusted with so precious a jewel as the person of a king and the protection of his kingdom." Warwick wished to accept the challenge of Huntley, but the duke did not permit it. "Let them come to us upon the field of battle," he said, "and they shall have blows enough."

The Scots, eager to come to close quarters, committed the imprudence of quitting the advantageous position which they occupied, to advance and meet the enemy. The combat began by a charge of Scottish cavalry, taken in flank, as they were crossing the bridge of the Esk, by a broadside from the English vessels drawn up along the coast. The English had found time to take possession of the hill upon which was situated St. Michael's church; the fray soon became general. The English wavered at first before the long lances of the Scots; but the ardor of the latter led them so far forward in the pursuit that, in re-forming, they found themselves involved in the hostile ranks; the arrows of the English archers, who were drawn up on an eminence, thinned the ranks of the Scottish men-at-arms; the firing from the vessels was incessant; the knights at length gave way and took to flight. The pursuit was vigorous, and the massacre horrible; quarter was given only to the great noblemen capable of paying a heavy ransom; eight thousand Scots, it is said, lay dead upon the battlefield of Pinkie, so called from the name of a neighboring mansion belonging to the Douglases. The Earl of Huntley, Lord Yester, Lord Wemyss, and several other persons of distinction, were made prisoners.

For four days the victors continued their work of pillage at Leith and in the environs. People expected to see them march upon Edinburgh, but Somerset suddenly ordered a retreat, no man in Scotland being able to explain this unexpected deliverance. It is probable that matters of importance recalled him to the court of the young king.

Lord Seymour, brother of the Protector, and Lord High Admiral of England, was as ambitious as Somerset, and more courageous and enterprising; he had been deeply offended by the unequal partition of the power, and during the absence of the Protector had labored to establish his influence with

DEATH OF ANNE ASKEW.

BATTLE OF PINKIE.

the little king. He married, in the month of June, 1547, Catherine Parr, the late king's widow, who had always loved him, it was said, notwithstanding the two other unions which she had contracted, and finding himself thus brought nearer to the person of the king, who often saw his step-mother, and being enriched by the fortune which Catherine had amassed as Queen of England, he took care to win the good graces of Edward VI., by supplying him with the funds which he wanted for his pocket-money and charities, liberalities which the Protector did not encourage. Seymour had also gained the favor of the king's household by distributing many gifts among them. In the month of November, 1547, the admiral persuaded the young king to address a letter to the Parliament, requesting that the office of guardian of the royal person should be conferred upon his uncle, Lord Seymour. The project became known and steps were taken; the admiral was threatened with the Tower, and a reconciliation was effected between the two brothers; Seymour shortly afterwards received a fresh dotation.

The ambition of the admiral could not be satisfied with money. Catherine Parr had recently died in childbed, and a rumor was in circulation that she had been poisoned. Her husband had already turned his views higher; he was paying his addresses to the Princess Elizabeth, whose governess he had completely gained over; he did not aspire to a secret marriage, which, according to the will of Henry VIII., would have impaired the right of succession, but he gave aid to all the members of the council, endeavoring to arouse among them sufficient disaffection to secure the approval of his union with the princess. The Protector resolved to rid himself of so dangerous a rival. The opportunity was propitious: Sharrington, the director of the mint at Bristol, was accused of having enriched himself by means of numerous malversations. The admiral defended him vigorously; but

Sharrington, to save his life, suddenly betrayed his advocate; he stated that he had promised to coin money for Lord Seymour, and that the latter could count upon an army of ten thousand men, with whom he hoped to change the aspect of the state. Less than this was needed to send the Lord High Admiral to the Tower. His courage was not cast down, and he demanded to be confronted with his accusers. Somerset had been brought up in the school of Henry VIII.: he knew how to use bills of attainder. The little king, terrified, had abandoned his uncle Seymour. When the House of Commons made some opposition, asking that the accused should be heard, a royal message silenced the objectors, and the bill was voted without further difficulty. Lord Seymour was executed on the 20th of March, 1549, protesting his innocence to the last. Two letters were seized, it was said, written from the Tower to the Princesses Mary and Elizabeth, to incite them to jealousy towards their brother. The Protector gave the young king a terrible example of cold barbarity, by being the first to sign the death-warrant of *his* brother.

The war continued in Scotland, with alternations of successes and reverses; but its principal aim, the marriage of King Edward VI. with the little queen, had been thwarted by Henry II., King of France, who destined her for the Dauphin. The Parliament even consented to send the child to France, there to receive her education in safety. Mary of Guise remained in Scotland, but the little queen, Mary Stuart, crossed over to Brest in a French vessel, and she was conducted to St. Germain-en-Laye, to be solemnly betrothed to the Dauphin. Warfare continued upon the frontiers, but the thoughts of the government were elsewhere; a great popular insurrection, which had taken its rise in the south, had gained the eastern counties, and a portion of England was in commotion.

Various causes had contributed towards the insurrection: the alteration of the currency under the reign of Henry VIII. had brought about an excessive rise in the nominal price of commodities, but labor was not remunerated in proportion; workmen were, on the contrary, less employed and less paid than in the past. A great quantity of arable land had been transformed into pasture-ground, in consequence of a considerable increase in the price of wools. The monasteries no longer gathered in intelligent peasants to make monks of them; monastic charities no longer relieved the misery of the poor; the vast spaces belonging to the parishes, where the villagers were wont to let their cattle graze, had been, by degrees, swallowed up by the neighboring proprietors, who had inclosed all the waste lands, thus depriving the poor, at a time of great distress, of a resource to which they were accustomed. Vagrancy had increased in such a manner, that in the first year of the reign of Edward VI. a barbarous law had been voted by Parliament, delivering up to any man, in the capacity of a slave, any individual sojourning for three days in any place without a fixed residence. Being declared a vagabond, he was to be branded upon the chest with a red-hot iron; his master had the right to compel him to work by every possible punishment; he could chain him up, let him out to hire, or sell him: a veritable slave-market being thus suddenly instituted for a few years in that free England which, three centuries later, was to be the first to put its hand to the work of destroying slavery throughout the whole world. These rigors had not sufficed; the vagabonds were not the only unhappy or exasperated persons; the religious feelings of the Catholic inhabitants were galled by the rapid progress of the Reformation. The insurrection was so grave that the Protector, always greedy of popularity, vainly endeavored to appease it by a hurried measure, forbidding the inclosure of all waste lands accessible to the peasants, and ordering that they should everywhere be restored to their former uses. This concession only served to put arms in the hands of the peasantry, some of whom broke down the fences, while others defended them: the government was everywhere obliged to send troops. But for the auxiliary corps raised in Italy, Spain, and Germany for the war with Scotland, the Protector would have found himself much embarrassed.

The demands of the insurgents and the aims of the insurrection differed greatly in different parts of the country. The south almost everywhere claimed the re-establishment of the old religion; the men of Devonshire, at the head of whom marched Humphrey Arundel, were secretly urged by the priests; they had laid siege to Exeter, and Lord Russell, badly provided with men and supplies, could not effectually succor the town. The proclamations of the young king in vain succeeded each other in answer to the requisitions of the insurgents. Exeter was closely pressed for five weeks, and famine was already in the city, when Lord Russell, having received troops and money, at length defeated the rebels and caused the siege to be raised; the insurrection was drowned in blood, and the soldiers ravaged the country. Arundel and some of the chiefs were taken to London, where they were executed.

The insurrection in Norfolk had a more political character; it had begun in like manner by the question of the inclosures. A tanner of Norwich, named Ket, had placed himself at the head of the insurgents, and established his camp upon a little elevation called Mousehold-heath, at the gates of Norwich. There, surrounded by malcontents from the environs, to the number of twenty thousand it is said, he declaimed against the oppression of the commoners by the nobles, and against the new religious service, asserting that he had only taken arms with the object of placing around the king honest councillors, favorable to the wishes of the people. A first attack upon the rebels, directed by the Marquis of Northampton, completely failed; they had been allowed time to assemble; they pillaged at their ease in the environs, then gathered again under the *Reformation Tree*, as they called an oak in the centre of their camp, bringing with them the noblemen whom they had made prisoners. It was not until the 25th of August, when the disorder had already lasted for nearly two months, that the Earl of Warwick, detained several days in Norwich for want of men and supplies, was able, on the arrival of some reinforcements, to attack the camp of Ket. The rebels were completely defeated, and the massacre was terrible. Ket and his brother, being sent to London to be tried, were hanged, one from the belfry of Wymondham, the other in the citadel of Norwich, and nine of the principal leaders were suspended from the nine branches of the *Reformation Tree*. The revolt in Norfolk was at an end, and the insurrection which manifested itself shortly afterwards in Yorkshire having been stifled, tranquillity was restored in the country; it was not so at the court.

The checks which the policy as well as the arms of England had suffered in Scotland, the encroachments of King Henry II. in the territory surrounding Calais and Boulogne, the proposals of Somerset to the Emperor to deliver the latter town to him, had slowly undermined the influence of the Protector, he still remained popular among the lower classes, who called him the *good Duke;* but the nobility were discontented, incensed at the arrogant tone of the "Duke of Somerset by the grace of God," as he styled himself. Indignation was aroused at the palace which he had raised in the Strand, at the cost of a church and three episcopal dwellings, and public opinion began to assign him a rival in the person of a man long since destined by the animosity of the former chancellor, Wriothesley, to accomplish the ruin of his enemy. Lord Warwick, equally ambitious, equally vain, but more bold and enterprising than Somerset, had already acquired a great military reputation, which was increased by his recent services in Norfolk. The two rivals nearly came to blows in the month of October, 1549. Twenty members of the council joined Warwick in London, and the Protector, who remained at Hampton Court with the young king, began to assemble forces. Edward VI. has related in his journal the negotiations between the Protector and the malcontents, the alternations of resolution and weakness of Somerset, the decision of the noblemen congregated around Warwick. The overtures of the Protector, though more and more moderate, were all rejected; the trouble of answering him was no longer taken, when at length he convoked the council at Windsor. All the nobility repaired thither, and decreed without hesitation the arrest of Somerset; on the 14th of October he was conducted to the Tower, accused of high treason, and the young king was brought back to Hampton Court. Warwick was henceforth master. Southampton in vain hoped to share the power with him; he was not even re-established in the office of chancellor, and the earl who had hitherto appeared to be in favor of the Roman Catholic party, abandoned it completely and turned towards the Reformers. The wind blew from this quarter, and the principles of Warwick had never impeded in anything the pursuit of his interests.

The Duke of Somerset was, at first, treated gently; he shrank from no humiliation in order to secure the mercy of the king, and confessed all that was desired, upon his knees, before the council. Deprived of all his offices, and smitten with a heavy fine, he appeared to accept his downfall meekly,

EDWARD VI. WRITING HIS JOURNAL.

remaining at court and behaving so modestly that he was again admitted into the privy council. The eldest son of Warwick, Lord Lisle, even married, on the 3d of June, 1550, Lady Anne Seymour, the daughter of the Duke of Somerset. But secret intrigues increased every day; notwithstanding solemn reconciliations the hostility of the two rivals remained unaltered. Warwick had taken the precaution of causing himself to be appointed warden of the Scottish frontiers, in order to cut off on the north the Duke of Somerset's retreat if the latter should attempt to excite civil war; he was at the same time ambitious of equalling him in rank, and caused himself to receive the title of Duke of Northumberland; his friend, the Marquis of Dorset, became Duke of Suffolk, and a few days after this promotion it suddenly became known that the Duke of Somerset had been arrested and conducted to the Tower, charged with conspiracy and high treason. The duchess was also arrested, as well as a certain number of the duke's friends.

The charges against Somerset were grave and numerous; he had plotted, it was said, the assassination of the principal noblemen of the council — Northumberland, Northampton, Pembroke, and others; a revolt was at the same time to be fomented in London, and the duke was to take possession of the king's person. This time the prisoner was publicly conducted to Westminster Hall, to be tried by his peers, that is to say, by the councillors of the king, whom he was accused of having intended to assassinate; but he was not confronted with the witnesses against him, the prosecutors contenting themselves with reading to him their depositions. He confessed to murderous designs against his powerful enemies, but these he had abandoned, he said, and he absolutely denied any intention of rebellion or insurrection. He was accordingly acquitted upon the count of treason, but the count of felony was proved, and this sufficed to ruin him. The people, who thronged in the Hall and the streets, did not understand the sentence; the axe, which had been borne before him so long as he was accused of high treason, had disappeared from the procession; they cried out that the *good duke* had been acquitted, and the favor of the population of London did not incline Northumberland to show mercy. On the 22d of January, 1552, six weeks after his condemnation, less than five years after the day on which he had made himself master of the supreme power, the former Protector of England was conducted to that scaffold so often bathed in the most illustrious blood. He died with more resolution than he had shown during his life, his young nephew, convinced, it is said, of his crime, having made no effort to show mercy to him. Somerset no doubt called to mind on Tower Hill the brother whom he had formerly sent to the same fate. Four of his friends only were executed in like manner, protesting their innocence. "Every time the Duke of Northumberland places his head upon his pillow, he will find it wet with our blood," exclaimed Sir Ralph Vane, addressing the people. They listened silently, without much emotion; the nation was growing accustomed to see its great noblemen fall beneath the executioner's axe instead of perishing bravely, as in other days, sword in hand, upon the field of battle.

Boulogne had been definitively restored to France by a treaty of peace in which Scotland was included; the seal of the new alliance was to be the marriage of Edward VI.; but the health of the young monarch had been declining for some months past, and the ambitious Northumberland had already entered upon the scheme which was destined to bring about his ruin. He had married his fourth son, Lord Guildford Dudley, to Lady Jane Grey, the eldest daughter of the Duke of Suffolk, and granddaughter, by her mother's side,

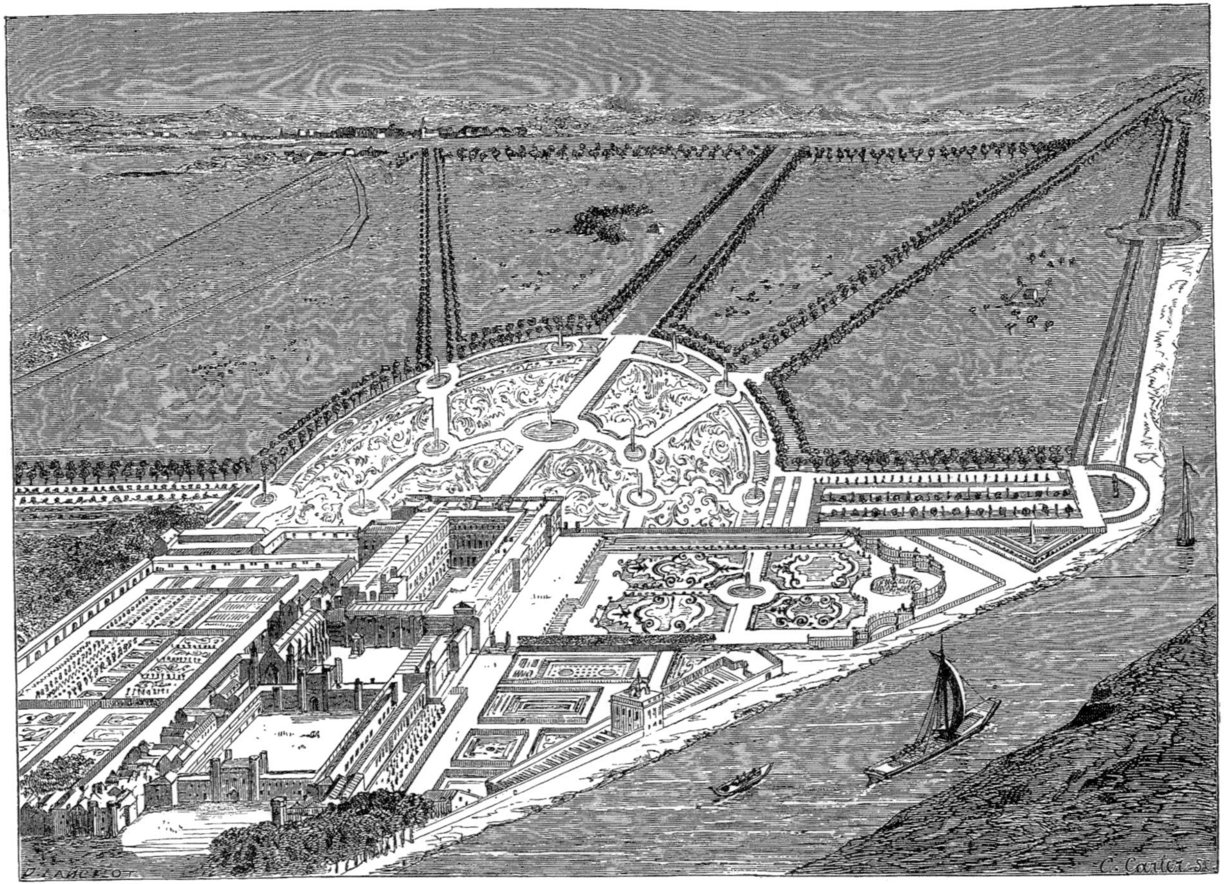

BIRD'S-EYE VIEW OF HAMPTON COURT.

of Mary, queen-dowager of France, and sister of Henry VIII. He thus united his family to the royal blood, while he caused his other children to contract powerful alliances. His aim was no other than to exclude from the succession to the throne the princesses Mary and Elizabeth, who had never been rehabilitated in respect to their legitimacy, in the interest of the Duchess of Suffolk, the mother of Lady Jane Grey, who was disposed to renounce her rights in favor of her eldest daughter. The duke counted upon obtaining support in his undertaking from the Protestant party, who were uneasy, and with good reason, at the prospect of the Princess Mary's accession to the throne. He urged the same argument upon the young King Edward: it was, in truth, the only one which could operate upon him. The dying youth had, naturally, never played the part of a statesman: he appears even not to have taken much interest in public life, but he was sincerely pious and attached to the Protestant faith. The progress of the Reformation had been the great desire of this mind of precocious gravity, and he had it at heart to protect the new religion after his death; he knew himself to be in most precarious health, and consented willingly to the proposals which Northumberland made to him upon this subject. Perhaps he thought, moreover, that he had the right to exercise the same privilege that his father had claimed, of designating a successor to the throne. The poor lad did not perceive into what new troubles and dangers he was about to plunge his kingdom by exposing it once more to the disasters of a contested succession and the rivalries of the great lords.

Three social forces, meanwhile, had made immense progress in England — regard for public order, the idea of the royal legitimacy, and the spirit of the Reformation. This last power which Northumberland thought to enroll in his service, had taught men to govern themselves, to decide freely and rationally in respect to their own affairs, and not even the dread of an ardently Roman Catholic reign was able to turn them aside from the path of justice. These three motives united frustrated the ambitious designs and plots of the great nobles. Subsequently, in the reign of Elizabeth, the same influences were destined to establish Protestantism forever in England. The reformed faith had made rapid strides since the death of Henry VIII. The silent struggle between the progressive and the retrogressive parties had continued; Cranmer and Gardiner still confronted each other, but Cranmer now had the upper hand. Gardiner had at first been placed by Henry VIII. on the list of the privy council, then his name had been erased from it through motives of prudence; the Archbishop of Canterbury had all the members of the council at his disposal, with the exception of the Chancellor Wriothesley, and Tunstall, Bishop of Durham. It has been seen how Wriothesley was driven from power; Tunstall was relegated to his diocese. Cranmer, therefore, found the coast clear, but he was determined to proceed with more moderation, for fear of arousing a fresh *pilgrimage of grace;* he did not completely succeed in averting the grave displeasure which his innovations caused among the populations remaining Catholic.

The first care of the archbishop was to establish in each diocese *royal visitors*, half lay, half ecclesiastical. Wherever they presented themselves, their authority was supreme; they established in all churches the use of a collection of homilies intended to be read every week, and composed, in great part, by Cranmer; none could preach without the authorization of the Protector or the Metropolitan. This prudent prohibition, intended to favor the extension of the new doctrines, did not escape attention; Gardiner immediately protested against the homilies and against the paraphrase of the New Testament by Erasmus, introduced into the church service in each parish. The reactionary bishop demanded that neither the doctrine nor the practice established by the late king should be interfered with until the majority of the young Edward VI. The intervention of Gardiner was not successful; he was arrested and held in prison during the continuance of the Parliamentary session.

The property which the religious communities, churches, and colleges yet possessed, had been placed by Parliament at the disposal of the king, as a trust-fund for the endowment of schools and livings. Cranmer opposed without success this fresh spoliation, foreseeing that it would turn to the profit of the courtiers: but the measures voted by the two Houses were of a consoling nature: the law against the Lollards, the prohibition against reading the Scriptures, and the statutes of the six articles of faith, were revoked; marriage was allowed to the clergy; communion of the two kinds was granted to the laity, and soon the order was given for celebrating the service in the English language, without any modification being yet made in the text itself of the Mass. Such were the changes already accomplished a year after the death of Henry VIII. The royal power had at the same time extended itself and gathered strength; the election of the bishops had been withdrawn from the deans and chapters, and made to depend solely upon the king, and it was by a simple royal decree that the bishops were invited to suppress in their dioceses certain Catholic observances by taking care to destroy all images that might still remain. In the month of January, 1549, appeared the great work which the Archbishop of Canterbury had been preparing for some time, the Catechism and the Prayer-Book of the Church of England. This latter production, skilfully composed by a commission of bishops and theologians, had for a basis the missals and breviaries of the Catholic church, deprived of all that might clash with the Protestant faith, yet carefully adapted to the convictions and sentiments of the Catholics. It was a work of conciliation effected with skill and with the most praiseworthy intentions; but the archbishop did not deceive himself regarding the repugnance which it encountered among the population, and he took care to surround it with an efficacious protection; from Whitsuntide, the use of any other book for Divine service was prohibited under severe penalties. The insurrections which shortly afterwards arose proved that Cranmer had not been mistaken; the new service was especially an object of complaint to the rebels of Devonshire. Cranmer soon perceived that it was necessary to begin an attack upon those prelates who were hostile to the innovations; they were numerous, but the majority were timid and contented themselves with proceeding slowly to make the reforms ordained by the government; some few were bolder; it was towards these that the efforts of Cranmer were directed.

For two years Gardiner had been confined in the Tower, in consequence of a sermon declared to be seditious, and he had not been brought to trial. The Bishop of London, Bonner, reprimanded for his want of zeal, was commissioned by the council to preach at St. Paul's Cross; his text had been chosen and all the divisions of his discourse settled beforehand, when he appeared before the crowd; he was to overwhelm with ecclesiastical thunders the rebels of Devonshire and Norfolk, to refer to the king and his religious authority, and to point out that, the rights and power of the sovereign not depending upon his age, King Edward VI. was as competent to decide questions of faith as he could be in later years. Bonner completely omitted this last point of the sermon, and was immediately summoned before the council. He excused himself upon the ground of the weakness of his memory, affirmed that he had lost his notes, declaring at the same time that he was prosecuted not for a trifling act of forgetfulness, but because he had firmly maintained the Roman Catholic doctrine of the real presence. He was condemned, deprived of his see and sent to prison. Ridley, Bishop of Rochester, was summoned to London in his place; but the bishopric was despoiled of a portion of its possessions, as well as of those which became vacant by successive deprivations. The court profited by the conscientious obstinacy of the bishops.

Gardiner was more skilful than Bonner, and quite as resolute; he embarrassed his enemies by his self-possession and his intellectual resources, and he refused to sign the formula of submission which was presented to him, so long as he should continue to be unjustly detained. He accumulated so much evidence, and called so many witnesses to prove the plot long since formed against him, that Cranmer cut short the proceedings. Gardiner was deprived of his bishopric, and, like Bonner, he was detained in prison, as well as two other prelates, Heath and Day, Bishops of Worcester and Chichester. It was at this period that the great Scottish reformer, John Knox, being in London, preached before the king with so much talent and vigor that the primate was instrumental in offering to him the bishopric of Rochester, which had become vacant by the translation of Poynet to Winchester, where he replaced Gardiner. Knox declined, but the proposal shows upon what path the Church of England, formerly so violent against the friends and partisans of Knox, had entered. Ridley, Latimer, Hooper, all prelates ardently attached to the Reformed faith, replaced the deposed bishops; Hooper was so profoundly imbued with Calvinistic principles, that much difficulty was experienced in inducing him to accept the consecration of the primate, and allow himself to be invested with the sacerdotal ornaments.

Effectually to introduce the new religion it was not enough to secure convinced and faithful ministers; it was necessary also firmly to establish its doctrines. Towards the end of the year 1551, the prelates finished drawing up the articles of the national faith in forty-two propositions, containing the same principles as the thirty-nine articles subsequently voted under Queen Elizabeth, which still remain the rule of faith of the Church of England. In the main, and under different forms, they come very near the doctrines of the Reformation on the Continent, inclining, sometimes towards Calvinism, sometimes towards Lutheranism, but always resting firmly upon the Bible.

The resource of removing the bishops had always been open to the government when it had been found impossible to triumph over their resistance; but it was more difficult to compel the Princess Mary to practise the new forms of worship. She had been warned, by an order of the council, at the time of the institution of the prayer-book, that the celebration of mass would no longer be permitted even in her private chapel; and for two years the intercession of the Emperor in her favor remained ineffectual; the chaplains of the princess were arrested, she was finally called before the council, and the young king himself vainly endeavored to convince her. The Emperor went so far as to declare that he would wage war with England rather than suffer his relative to be constrained in her conscience. Cranmer counselled the young king to temporize; but Edward VI. wept, lamented the obstinacy of his sister and the obligation which he was under of allowing mass to exist in any place in his kingdom. The attempts were renewed with Mary several times; she remained inflexible in her resolution. "If the chaplains cannot say mass, I shall not hear it," she said; "but the new service shall not be established in my house; if it is introduced there by force, I shall leave the place." "Mat-

"THE NEW SERVICE SHALL NOT BE ESTABLISHED IN MY HOUSE."

THE CORPSE PASSED UNDER HER WINDOWS.

ters remained thus," says Burnet, "and I think that Lady Mary continued to have her priests and to have mass said, so secretly that it could not be complained of."

In truth, and notwithstanding the removal of the bishops and some deplorable executions of poor heretics who attacked the very foundations of Christianity, persecution was at a stand-still under the reign of Edward VI. In this new stage of the Reformation, no Catholic suffered seriously for his attachment to his faith.

The obstinacy of the Princess Mary had left a profound impression upon the mind of the young king, and contributed, no doubt, to the effect of Northumberland's insinuations in favor of a Protestant succession. Edward was unwilling, however, to compromise any of his councillors, and he drew up with his own hand the project for a law which was to regulate the succession to the throne; he then caused the judges to be summoned, with the attorney and solicitor-general, to commission them to prepare the act. They hesitated; the king peremptorily commanded them to obey, and only reluctantly granted them time to examine the precedents, before fulfilling the wishes of his Majesty.

When the lawyers returned they were still undecided, or rather they had convinced themselves that the law required of them by the sovereign would involve an act of treason both on the part of the framers of the act and on that of the council. The king insisted; the Duke of Northumberland, who was present, flew into a passion; the lords of the council, before whom the judges explained their scruples, had been won over by the intrigues of the duke. Cranmer, who had at first been opposed to this step, yielded to the solicitations of the young monarch; the measure was resolved upon, and the act, prepared by the lawyers, received the great seal as well as the signatures of all the members of the council.

Northumberland had made an attempt to take possession of the person of Mary; but she had been warned in time, and instead of obeying the summons which was made to her in the name of the king her brother, she retired precipitately to her manor of Kenninghall, in Norfolk. Here she soon received the news of the death of Edward VI., who expired at Greenwich on the 6th of July, 1553, at the age of fifteen years and a half. The time had come to make a trial of the new basis upon which Cranmer had sought to found the religion of the kingdom. The question whether England was to be Catholic or Protestant was about to be decided.

CHAPTER XX.

PERSECUTION. — BLOODY MARY. 1553–1558.

THE Duke of Northumberland was more ambitious than able, and more bold than skilful. In seeking to disturb the natural order of succession he had undertaken a task above his strength; nor had he appreciated the relative power of the two religions now existing side by side: he had thought the Catholics more weakened than they were, and the Protestants more disposed to sacrifice all for the accession of a Protestant sovereign than they showed themselves to be; the hope which he had conceived of taking possession of the two princesses, Mary and Elizabeth, was thwarted from the first. The death of the young king was kept secret, and an express dispatched to his sisters to bring them to him. It was the second time that Mary had been summoned, and notwithstanding her repugnance, she had set out, when a note from the Earl of Arundel warned her of the state of affairs; she immediately retraced her steps, and shut herself up in Framlingham Castle. Elizabeth had also been warned in time. Northumberland henceforth had to struggle against a rival at liberty, and aware of his sinister designs.

Edward VI. had been dead three days, and precautions had been taken in London, when Lady Jane Grey, who had retired to Chelsea during the last weeks of the king's life, was recalled to Sion House, the palace of her family. She was there alone on the 10th of July, 1553, occupied, it is said, in reading Plato in Greek, — for Lady Jane was as learned as she was gentle and modest, — when the arrival of the Duke of Northumberland, her father-in-law, accompanied by several lords of the council, was announced. Indifferent subjects were talked about; but the young woman was troubled by the watchful looks and respectful tone of her visitors, when her mother-in-law entered with the Duchess of Suffolk. "The king, your cousin and our sovereign lord, has surrendered his soul to God," said Northumberland; "but before his death, and in order to preserve the kingdom from the infection of Popery, he resolved to set aside his sisters, Mary and Elizabeth, declared illegitimate by an act of Parliament, and he has commanded us to proclaim your Grace as queen and sovereign to succeed him." At the same moment the lords of the council knelt before Lady Jane, vowing fidelity to her; she started back, uttered a cry, and fell to the floor. She was young, timid, in delicate health, fond of retirement, and addicted to serious studies; she protested, asserting that she did not feel herself capable of governing. "But if the right is mine," she said at length, raising her head with modest confidence, "I hope that God will give me strength to bear the sceptre for his glory and the happiness of the people of England." She was immediately conducted to the Tower, the usual residence of sovereigns before their coronation; at the same time, the death of King Edward VI. and the accession of Lady Jane Grey were proclaimed in the streets and market-places, while the reason of the exclusion of the princesses was explained. The crowd listened in silence, without any tokens of satisfaction, and the name of Mary was whispered among them. The violation of the ordinary rules of succession was evidently viewed with no favor by the people of London.

In the country the movement was more vigorous. Mary had written to the council, haughtily claiming her rights in

LADY JANE GREY

a tone befitting the sovereign power, and the lords had not yet replied to this appeal, when a certain number of noblemen and gentlemen hastened to join their legitimate queen. The Catholics were not alone, for Mary promised to change nothing in the laws and the religion established by King Edward. She had a small army under her orders, when the Duke of Northumberland, who had hesitated to leave London, and the conspirators whom he held in some degree captive, decided at length to march against Mary, leaving the Duke of Suffolk with his daughter to govern in her name. He had scarcely left the capital, when the members of the council crept out of the Tower under different pretexts, and met at Castle Baynard, the residence of the Earl of Pembroke. The Earl of Arundel was the first to announce his resolution of passing over to Queen Mary. "If reasons do not suffice," exclaimed Lord Pembroke, "this sword shall make Mary queen, or I will die in her cause!" All the nobles responded with acclamation, and the Duke of Suffolk, who had rejoined his colleagues, united his voice to theirs, basely abandoning his daughter. Mary was proclaimed in the streets of London, in the places where a week before the name of Lady Jane had resounded, and at St. Paul's Cross, where Bishop Ridley had preached on the preceding Sunday in favor of the Protestant succession. This time people applauded, and the Catholics triumphed; the Protestants had not learned to connect religious principles with political freedom, or did not foresee the evils which they were about to suffer. On leaving London with his troops, Northumberland himself had augured ill from the coldness of the population. "They come to see us pass," he said, "but no man cries 'God bless you!'" He was at Cambridge when he learned at the same time the proclamation of Mary in London, the defection of the members of the council, and that of the forces which he had raised in the north, who had now rallied round Mary. Tears flowed down his cheeks when he repaired to the public square of the city, and, throwing his cap in the air, was the first to proclaim Queen Mary. On the morrow he was arrested and taken to the Tower, which Lady Jane had quitted to return to Sion House as soon as Mary had been recognized by the council. But the young queen of ten days had been arrested, as well as her husband; the gloomy fortress began to be peopled by all the actors in the drama of which this poor girl was to be the victim. Mary advanced by short stages to London, where she entered on the 3d of August amid the joyful acclamations of the populace: her sister, Elizabeth, came to meet her with a thousand noblemen and gentlemen. The conduct of Elizabeth had been as skilful as it was prudent, and worthy of the wise policy which she was to practise upon the throne, and she was already indebted for this to the counsels of the Secretary of State, Cecil. When Northumberland had caused the accession of Lady Jane to be announced to her, proposing land and riches to her in exchange for her rights to the throne, Elizabeth replied that she had no rights to renounce, since her elder sister, the Princess Mary, was alive. Then, giving out that she was ill, she had awaited the event, timing her movements so as to arrive first in London, muster her friends, and salute the new sovereign upon her entry into the capital. During the five years of her sister's reign all the prudence of Cecil was destined to be required for the service of the mistress whom he had chosen.

The first care of the queen was to repair to the Tower; the prisoners were expecting her, not those whom she had just sent thither, but the old Duke of Norfolk, a captive for so many years, the Duchess of Somerset, and Bishop Gardiner, who delivered in the name of all a brief speech of welcome to the sovereign whose accession restored them to liberty. Mary was moved to tears. "You are *my* prisoners," she said, embracing them. The bishops Bonner and Tunstall were also delivered from their long captivity; the latter was admitted into the council as well as Gardiner, who soon became chancellor and prime minister. The corpse of King Edward had scarcely been interred, his obsequies being performed according to the English rites, before the sermons at St. Paul's cross had changed their character. Bourn, canon of St. Paul's, soon afterwards Bishop of Bath and Wells, rose against the innovations introduced into the church under King Edward, declaiming against those who had kept Bonner, the legitimate bishop of the diocese, for four years in prison. The people were not accustomed to such tirades; the canon was in danger of his life; two reformed preachers, who were shortly to seal their testimony by death, Bradford and Rogers, had great difficulty in conducting him back to his residence in safety.

Queen Mary had been a fortnight in London, and six weeks only had elapsed since the death of Edward VI., when the Duke of Northumberland, his eldest son, the Earl of Warwick, and the Marquis of Northampton, were brought before the council as prisoners charged with high-treason. The crime was manifest, but the judges assembled to condemn the guilty men were also implicated in it themselves. Northumberland endeavored to take shelter behind the members of the council, who had all signed the edict emanating from the personal will of the deceased king; the councillors maintained that they had obeyed, under the penalty of their lives. The Duke of Norfolk, who had but just escaped from the Tower, presided over the court; Cranmer and the Duke of Suffolk signed the sentence. All the base acts of Northumberland could not save him; in vain did he ask to confer with the doctors sent by the queen in order to enlighten his conscience;

the only favor granted to him was that of being simply beheaded. The Earl of Warwick behaved with more self-respect. Four secondary accomplices were condemned with the three great noblemen; but Northumberland, Sir John Gates, and Sir Thomas Palmer alone suffered their sentence. They died on Tower Hill on the 22d of August; the duke was interred in the chapel of the Tower, beside the Duke of Somerset, formerly his victim; on the right and left lay the remains of Anne Boleyn and Catherine Howard. The queen had been urged to rid herself also of Lady Jane Grey and her husband; but Mary called to mind the youth of the poor little usurper, saying that she had been but a tool in the hands of her father-in-law, and contented herself with detaining them in the Tower.

The Catholic party was triumphant. The Emperor Charles V. had recommended prudence, advising that only some few dangerous enemies should be struck down, but that the new religion should not be touched, trusting to time the work of modifying errors, and taking care not to plunge the people into despair by too much severity. This wise policy agreed neither with Mary's fervent convictions nor with the firmness of her character, imbittered by long misfortunes, by reiterated acts of injustice, and by shattered health. "God has protected me in all my misfortunes," she said, "it is in Him that I confide. I will not testify my gratitude slowly and in secret, but at once and openly." The public declaration promised to molest none of her subjects for religion: but Mass had already been re-established in the principal churches in London, Cranmer and Latimer were sent to the Tower, and the Princess Elizabeth, prudently bowing her head before the storm, had renounced the practice of the Protestant worship to return to the Catholic faith, of which she always preserved some remains at the bottom of her heart; she accompanied her sister to Mass, had a chapel established in her residence, and devoted a portion of her time to embroidering church ornaments. Mary was crowned on the 1st of October at Westminster, by the hands of Gardiner. Five days afterwards the Parliament assembled; a month had scarcely elapsed before the edifice raised with so much care by Cranmer and the English Protestants had fallen to pieces; matters had returned to the point at which Henry VIII. had left them: the prayer-book was set aside, the service in the vernacular tongue abolished, the marriage of priests and communion of the two kinds prohibited; the married bishops and those in favor of the reformed doctrines were deprived of their sees, while the marriage of Henry VIII. and Catherine was declared alone valid. The queen did not, however, renounce the title of Head of the Church; it was thought best not to alarm the Protestants by placing them at the outset under the yoke of Rome, and above all to avoid touching upon the question of the restitution of clerical property, which would have raised all the House of Lords against the new régime. The queen contented herself by setting the example of making restoration to the Church of all the estates annexed to the crown. Being reassured by this indulgence, Parliament voted all that was desired, and destroyed all that it had formerly established. The convocation of the clergy returned in a body to the old practices; those priests who had sincerely embraced the Protestant faith, and who refused to repeat Mass, were replaced without difficulty by the monks who were everywhere issuing forth from their hiding-places. The prisons were soon filled by the refractory; those who were not prisoners might go about begging on the high-roads with their wives and children; a certain number fled abroad. Violent persecution had not yet commenced; Cranmer was acquitted upon the count of treason, but he was sent back to the Tower as a heretic. The sentence of death pronounced against Lady Jane Grey and her husband had not been executed; the captives even enjoyed a kind of liberty in their prison. Queen Mary was occupied in a more important matter; although now thirty-seven years of age, moved by the solicitations of her councillors, she was thinking of marriage.

Many illustrious alliances for the Princess Mary had been successively contracted and broken off. While she was yet in her cradle, the Emperor, the King of France, the Dauphin, had each in turn aspired to her hand; but it was whispered at court that the queen had some partiality for Lord Edward Courtenay, son of the Marquis of Exeter executed in 1538. Scarcely had she released this handsome young man from the Tower, when she conferred on him the title of Earl of Devonshire, with all the confiscated estates of his father, and it was asserted that her favors did not stop there. Edward Courtenay did not know how to take advantage of fortune; he was thoughtless and dissipated; his convictions did not incline to the side of Roman Catholicism, and he preferred, it was said, the society of the Princess Elizabeth to that of her royal sister. The queen manifested much coldness towards the princess, who retired to her residence at Ashridge in Buckinghamshire, closely watched by two agents of the court. A union with Cardinal Pole, a cousin of the queen, and who was not then in orders, was also spoken of; but he was fifty-three years of age, he was living in retirement by the Lake of Garda; and, although there was a project at that time at Rome for sending him as legate to England, the Emperor increased the obstacles to his departure, in order to have time to accomplish an undertaking which he had greatly at heart, and which the presence of Pole might have hindered.

Queen Mary had learned during her misfortunes to depend upon Charles V., who had never failed her: since she had been upon the throne she had taken his advice in all her affairs; the Emperor took advantage of this circumstance to ask her hand for his son, the Archduke Philip, soon afterwards Philip II., who had recently lost his wife, Isabella of Portugal. The foreign powers, and especially France, seconded by the ambassadors of Venice, dreaded this union, which was calculated to cause the balance in Europe to incline against them; their opposition was favored by a powerful party in the very bosom of the council; Gardiner was at its head. He vigorously represented to the queen the aversion which the English had always experienced towards foreign sovereigns, the discontent which the haughtiness of Philip had aroused among his own subjects, the continual hostilities with France which must result from this marriage, the anger and uneasiness of the Reformed party. The Commons even presented an address praying the queen to choose her husband from among the distinguished men of her kingdom. Courtenay was the soul of all the intrigues, encouraged and nourished by the French ambassador, M. de Noailles. But opposition only aroused the obstinacy of Mary; she was a worthy daughter of Henry VIII., and on the very day when the Houses had manifested to her their aversion to a foreign prince, she caused the Spanish ambassador to come into her private chapel, and there, throwing herself upon her knees before the altar, she took God to witness that she plighted her troth to Philip, Prince of Spain, to belong to him and no other as long as she should live. The marriage treaty was communicated to Parliament on the 14th of January, 1554: the Emperor had been very accommodating in the conditions, counting, no doubt, upon the influence which Philip would acquire over his wife. The queen was to remain sole mistress of the government in England, without any foreigner being allowed to participate in the offices or dignities; Burgundy and the Low Countries were secured to her children, and in the event of Don Carlos, Philip's son by the first marriage, happening to die, all the possessions of the crown of Spain were to devolve upon the posterity of Mary. Gardiner himself unfolded before the two Houses and the burgesses of the City all the advantages of this alliance which he had so ardently opposed.

The arguments of the chancellor did not convince the country. Conspirators were encouraged by the promises of France; projects were various: some wished to place Elizabeth upon the throne, giving her Courtenay for a husband; others counted upon releasing Lady Jane Grey and proclaiming her again. They appeared to have determined on this project, when, on the 20th of January, the queen learned that Sir Peter Carew had taken arms in Devonshire, resolving to oppose the disembarkation of Philip, and had already taken possession of the city and the citadel of Exeter. Almost at the same time it was discovered that Sir Thomas Wyat was inciting the population of Kent to rebellion. He was a Catholic, and had distinguished himself at the siege of Boulogne, but he had conceived the most violent horror of Spain, and he appears to have been disposed to support the claims of the Princess Elizabeth, for he had refused, from the first, to enter into the plot in favor of Lady Jane Grey. The alarm was great in London: the guards at the gates were doubled; the Duke of Suffolk, whom Mary had pardoned, took refuge in Warwickshire, and loudly protesting against the marriage of the queen, he called the population to arms without much effort. The boldest as well as the most popular of the conspirators was Wyat, who held the city of Rochester, against which place the old Duke of Norfolk was advancing with Lord Arundel. As the duke was ordering the assault, five hundred men of the London train-bands, whom he had brought with him, suddenly stopped at the entrance of the bridge, and the

QUEEN MARY CALLS GOD TO WITNESS THAT SHE PLIGHTS HER TROTH TO PHILIP.

captain addressing them said, "My masters, we are going to fight against our fellow-citizens and friends in an unjust quarrel; they have assembled here to resist the evils which would fall upon us if we were subject to the proud Spaniard, and I know not who is the Englishman who could say nay to them." The train-bands immediately began to cry, "A Wyat! A Wyat!" at the same time turning their field-pieces against the royal troops. The Duke of Norfolk was compelled to retire in haste, and his return spread terror in London. The queen alone remained firm, repairing with her ladies to the City, protesting to the Lord Mayor, the aldermen, and burgesses, that she only wished to be married for the honor and advantage of her kingdom; that nothing compelled her to marry since she had delayed so long, and that she counted upon her good subjects to help her to subjugate the rebels. On the same day she learned that the Duke of Suffolk and Sir Peter Carew had been defeated in the inland shires and in the west. A full amnesty was promised to all the insurgents of Kent, the noblemen excepted; a price was set upon the head of Sir Thomas Wyat. He had delayed in his march, but on the 3d of February he entered the suburb of Southwark with a considerable force, without doing any damage except to the residence of Bishop Gardiner, which was pillaged. Wyat had counted upon the goodwill of the inhabitants of London, but the gates of the city remained closed, and the population of Southwark, who had received him well, soon begged him to retire, when the cannon of the Tower began to roar, and the cannon-balls to rain upon the bridge and the two churches fortified by Wyat. Thereupon the insurgents directed their efforts to another point, and succeeded in crossing the river at Kingston; but Lord Pembroke awaited them at the head of the royal troops, and when Wyat, with a handful of brave men, had opened up a passage for himself, the ranks closed behind him; he found himself caught in the streets. The citizens did not rise in his favor, as he had hoped. He made a brave defence, but, overwhelmed by numbers, was captured and sent to the Tower; a great many of his followers were taken and hanged. The insurrection had miscarried.

The courage of Queen Mary had not for a moment failed her; while her terrified courtiers were hastening to bring the grievous news to her, she shamed them for their terror, asserting that she would herself enter into a campaign to support the justice of her cause, and die with those who served her rather than yield an inch to a traitor like Wyat; but she had already caused her anger to be felt by those whom she suspected of having taken part in the plot. Three of her councillors had by her orders arrived at Ashridge, where they found Elizabeth in bed. It was late, and the emissaries had insisted upon entering the residence of the princess. "Is the haste such that it might not have pleased you to come to-morrow in the morning?" asked Elizabeth haughtily. "We are right sorry to see your Grace in such a case," said the councillors. "And I," replied Elizabeth, "am not glad to see you here at this time of night." It was necessary, however, to obey and to get into the litter which the queen had sent; Mary wished to see her sister, "dead or alive," she said. The house was surrounded by soldiers; they set out; the journey was slow: Elizabeth dreaded the arrival in London; some few noblemen who came to meet her reassured her. She learned, however, that Courtenay had been sent to the Tower. She had not yet seen the queen when she was informed of the sad fate of Lady Jane Grey.

The insurrection had scarcely been stamped out and Wyat made a prisoner, when Mary signed the order to execute Lady Jane and her husband, both of whom had been condemned to death several months before. The royal clemency had allowed a last interview between husband and wife, but Lady Jane refused this favor. "I shall see him again shortly," she said. She saw him, indeed, before the eternal reunion, but dead and mutilated; the corpse passed under her windows on the return from Tower Hill. A few hours later, on the 12th of February, 1554, Jane in her turn mounted the scaffold, within the precincts of the Tower, after having firmly repelled the Dean of St. Paul's, who pursued her with his arguments in favor of the Roman Catholic religion. She died in the faith which she had believed from childhood, serene and grave, without a complaint or a tear, simply avowing to the few spectators of her execution that she deserved death for having consented, although with regret, to serve as an instrument to the ambition of others. She implored the mercy of God and delivered herself up into the hands of the executioner, moving all hearts by her constancy and meekness. Her father was beheaded several days after her, on Tower Hill, without arousing the compassion of any one. Passing from one treacherous act to another, he had at length found himself on the scaffold.

Executions succeeded each other without intermission. To the last moment Sir Thomas Wyat maintained that the Princess Elizabeth had been ignorant of all his projects. The jury had the courage to acquit Sir Nicholas Throgmorton, a devoted friend of the princess, compromised in the conspiracy; the verdict saved his life, but this unusual independence was to be dearly paid for by the jurymen; they were all sent to prison, and only regained their liberty after a long captivity, and upon payment of a fine. Meanwhile, appearances were unfavorable to Elizabeth; she had in vain solicited an audience of her sister, and finally wrote to her, absolutely disclaiming all complicity in the insurrection, and denying the correspondence which she was accused of having carried on with the King of France. The order was nevertheless given to conduct her to the Tower, and on Palm Sunday, while the population of London thronged the churches, the princess, conducted by Lord Sidney, was brought by the Thames to the Traitors' Gate. She refused at first to land; then, as one of the guards offered her his hand, she repelled him abruptly, and placing her foot upon the gloomy stairs, she exclaimed, "Here landeth as true a subject, being a prisoner, as ever landed at these stairs; and before Thee, O God, I speak it, having none other friend but Thee above." She sat down for a moment upon the stone; the lieutenant of the Tower begged her to take shelter from the cold and rain. "Better sitting here than in a worse place," she said; "for God knoweth whither you bring me." She entered, however, and found herself within the walls of a prison, fearing in the recesses of her soul the fate of her mother: and soon afterwards she was still more terrified when a new governor, Sir Henry Beddingfield, was appointed to the Tower. He had the reputation of being harsh and cruel, and several times Elizabeth asked the guards whether the scaffold of Lady Jane had been removed, expecting to ascend it in her turn. On the 19th of May, however, Elizabeth was taken to Richmond, and thence to Woodstock, where she remained, closely watched by Sir Henry Beddingfield, while Courtenay was removed to Fotheringay. The arrival of Prince Philip was now expected, and the preparation for the marriage occupied all minds, whether gratified or discontented. The population of London daily manifested its aversion to the Spanish alliance and its attachment to the doctrines of the Reformation; the queen's preachers began to look upon the pulpit erected at St. Paul's Cross as a dangerous spot. One of them, Doctor Pendleton, received a shot there, from which he narrowly escaped death, and the use of fire-arms was prohibited.

The manœuvres of the Emperor had succeeded; his confidential ambassador, Renard, had prevailed over the intrigues of Noailles. Philip arrived in England with the title of King of Naples, Charles V. being unwilling, he said, that so great a queen should unite herself to a simple prince: the marriage was celebrated with great pomp, on the 25th of July, 1554: but the royal bridegroom had taken care to surround himself with troops at the moment of his landing, one of his emissaries, Count Egmont, having been assailed shortly before by the people, who mistook him for his master. The first care of the Houses of Parliament, when they assembled on the 1st of November, was to increase the precautions against the Spanish influence in the councils of the queen; all Philip's liberality, and all the money he had brought from Spain, could not lull the distrust, which on the other hand was nourished by the haughtiness of his manners and the rigid etiquette with which he surrounded himself.

The first Parliament convoked by Mary had voted the re-establishment of the Roman Catholic worship; the second had adopted the treaty of marriage; the third was summoned to declare the reunion with Rome; but the interests of the House of Lords were opposed to this measure. Before repealing the act of supremacy, the Lords, enriched by the spoliation of the monasteries, required guaranties from the court of Rome; the Pope gave them through the mouth of Cardinal Pole, who had arrived in England as legate: the Parliament then became submissive, and presented a petition to the king, queen, and cardinal, begging them to intercede with the Holy Father to obtain pardon for the English people and their reconciliation with the Holy See. Pole was furnished with the necessary powers, and he pronounced the absolution. The work of Henry VIII. as well as that of Edward VI. was destroyed, and the conscience of Queen Mary could now rest in peace. The Parliament thought it had done enough; but Mary desired to feel her way towards securing the royal crown to her husband. She encountered so much opposition that she was obliged to renounce her project; the Commons also refused the subsidies which she had caused the Emperor and his son to expect, as an assistance in prosecuting the war with France. Philip in vain endeavored to win a little popularity by interceding with the queen in favor of the prisoners of state detained at the Tower. Several were restored to liberty; Courtenay received authority to travel upon the Continent, and the Princess Elizabeth reappeared at court. She did not long remain there; her position was difficult; she was constantly watched by jealous eyes; when she returned, however, to her residence at Ampthill, the queen began to look upon her sister with less uneasiness, for she was herself now expecting an heir to the throne.

The year 1555 opened under sinister auspices for the Reformed Church; the laws against heretics had been put in force again, and on the first day in January the Bishop of London, Bonner, followed by a great procession, repaired to St. Paul's, to return thanks to God for the light with which He had once more illumined the sovereign and the nation. A court commissioned to try heretics was soon formed. The prisons were filled with the accused; the first who was summoned belonged to the clergy of St. Paul's; Gardiner presided over the tribunal. "Did you not pray for twenty years against the Pope?" cried the prisoner, driven to extremities by the questions of his judge. "I was cruelly forced to it," replied the bishop. "Why, then, do you wish to make use of the same cruelty towards us?" asked Rogers. But this simple notion of liberty of conscience had not yet penetrated into the most enlightened minds, Catholic or Protestant; each party in turn had recourse to force to bring about the triumph of what it regarded as the truth, and William of Orange, for loudly proclaiming toleration towards the Catholics in a country which he was snatching from the horrors of the Inquisition, drew down upon himself the censure of his Protestant friends. Rogers was condemned to be burned; he was refused the consolation of saying farewell to his wife. She was at the foot of the stake with her nine children, the youngest at her breast, and she encouraged her husband until the last moment. He died worthy of her, augmenting by his firmness that long series of martyrs of the Reformed faith with whom the fanaticism of Mary was about to enrich the Church. Executions succeeded each other. Hooper, the dispossessed Bishop of Gloucester, an eloquent and austere divine, and Robert Ferrar, Bishop of St. David's, were burned in their former dioceses. Condemnations and executions increased every day. Gardiner, weary of so many horrors, had ceased to preside over the court commissioned to try heretics, and the zeal of Bonner himself did not suffice to satisfy Philip and Mary. Cardinal Pole had in vain endeavored to moderate the persecuting ardor of the queen; the gentleness of his character and the experience which he had acquired in Germany, equally rendered him averse to executions as a means of conversion; but the conscience of Mary was pledged to her enterprise; she desired to make England Roman Catholic; and notwithstanding the terror of some, the hesitation of others, and the servility of a great number, she found her task greater and more difficult day by day: it was not the moment for relaxing her efforts.

Upon the accession of Mary, the relative strength of the two religions was about equal in the kingdom, although irregularly divided according to localities. The Protestants were numerous in nearly all the towns; the Catholics remained powerful in the north; but important influences contended against the royal authority, passionately engaged as it was in the struggle; the great noblemen were imperfectly assured of the security of their possessions, notwithstanding all the protestations and promises of the Pope. The Protestant faith had taken firm hold upon a great number of souls among the clergy and the people. The ranks of the nobility did not furnish any religious martyrs, but the uneasiness which their temporal interests caused them contributed to keep up the agitation which produced so many political victims, and the masses of the people sealed their convictions with their blood. Two bishops and a great number of priests had already perished at the stake, in company with a host of unknown and obscure martyrs. The most illustrious witnesses of persecuted Protestantism were still captives; two bishops and an archbishop, all three celebrated for their eloquence and the part which they had played in the past, — Ridley, Latimer, and Cranmer, — had been conducted to Oxford, in the month of March, 1554, there to argue in public with the Catholic doctors; all three had boldly maintained their opinions, and all three had been declared obstinate heretics. They had been awaiting their sentence for eighteen months, when, on the 12th of September, 1555, the royal commissioners arrived at Oxford. In his capacity of former Primate of England, Cranmer, a prisoner, was summoned to appear at Rome within eighty days, according to the forms of the canon law. Ridley and Latimer were condemned to die forthwith. A learned Spanish theologian was, however, dispatched to them to enlighten them upon their errors. Latimer refused to see him, Ridley combated all his arguments. Bishop Ridley was learned, eloquent, admirably versed in the Holy Scriptures, and it was he who had maintained, with the most brilliant results,

DEATH OF LATIMER AND RIDLEY.

ELIZABETH'S CORONATION PROCESSION.

the discussions with the Catholic doctors. The day for argument had gone by, that of martyrdom was arriving. On the 16th of October, 1555, the two prelates were conducted to the stake prepared for them near Baliol College, where the monument now stands which commemorates their execution. Latimer was old and feeble; he walked with difficulty. Ridley, who had preceded him, ran to meet him and embraced him. "Be of good heart, brother," he said, "for God will either assuage the fury of the flame or strengthen us to bear it." The old man smiled, suffering himself to be divested of his clothing by the guards; Ridley removed his garments himself, distributing them among the bystanders. When both were clad in their shrouds and fastened back to back at the stake, the old bishop drew himself up, as though suddenly endowed with that superhuman strength which his companion in martyrdom had promised him. "Be of good comfort, Master Ridley!" he cried, "and play the man, and we shall this day light such a candle by God's grace in England as I trust shall never be put out." The flames immediately suffocated him, but Ridley suffered longer. One of the bystanders at length had the humanity to stir up the fire, and the bag of gunpowder which had been attached to the necks of the victims having ignited, Ridley died by the explosion, while the prophetic words of old Latimer were still ringing in every ear, and in many hearts.

Gardiner died on the 12th of November, and the queen confided the seals to the Archbishop of York, Heath, a prelate more zealous than his predecessor in the persecution of heretics, but less skilful and prudent in the conduct of public affairs. Upon the assembling of Parliament, Mary touched a tender chord; she asked for authority to restore to the Holy See the first-fruits and tithes, annexed under the reign of her father to the crown. "I set more value upon the salvation of my soul," she said, "than upon the possession of ten kingdoms such as England." The Houses did not oppose the salvation of the sovereign's soul, but they trembled to see her lay hands upon *their* property, and the subsidies rendered necessary by the decrease in the royal revenues which the return of the annates to the court of Rome involved, were voted with ill-humor, and not without objections. The queen was obliged to have recourse to many vexatious methods in order to procure the money which her husband constantly demanded of her, thus increasing every day the unpopularity of the Spaniards in the kingdom. All the English detested Philip. Mary alone loved him, with the sad tenderness of an unrequited affection. The king was almost always away from his wife, and only replied to her constant letters when he demanded of her the sums which he needed to maintain the wars with France. It was in vain that English prudence stipulated that peace should be maintained between France and England. What could laws effect against the devotion of the queen to her husband?

The weakness and timidity of Cranmer, deprived of the firm example of his companions in captivity, had been counted upon with good reason. The eighty days had elapsed, and the Primate, not having appeared at Rome, was declared guilty, degraded from his holy office, and delivered up to the secular power. Then began the attempts at conversion. The prisoner was transferred to the house of the Dean of Christchurch, where indulgences were lavished upon him. It was represented to him that he was still in the prime of life, healthy and vigorous; why should he be obstinate in his errors and die like Latimer, who had only renounced a few years of a miserable existence? The unhappy archbishop suffered himself to be gained over, and signed six abjurations successively, each time adding something to his shame. At the end of these humiliations, at the moment when he believed that he had at last purchased his liberty, it was announced to him that repentance did not absolve from punishment, that his return into the bosom of the Church insured, indeed, to him eternal life, but could not save him from the stake, and that he was condemned to die on the 21st of March. In view of this perfidy, which deprived him of the reward of his recantations, Cranmer at length understood the greatness of his fault, and from the platform, where he was placed to read to the people his last confession, he boldly rejected the Papal authority and the doctrines to which he had assented a few days previously, protesting his attachment to the Reformed religion, and his resolution to die faithful to it. At the same time he humbled himself before God and men for the base fear of death which had led him to be false to the truth and his conscience. The excitement of the crowd was great; something totally different had been expected. "Play the Christian man," Lord Williams called out to him; "remember yourself; do not dissemble." "Alas! my lord," the archbishop answered, "I have been a man that all my life loved plainness, and never dissembled till now, which I am most sorry for." When he was conducted to the stake, before the flames had reached him, he thrust his right hand into the raging fire to punish it for having signed his abjuration. "This hand hath offended," he exclaimed. Motionless in the midst of the flames, he appealed neither to the mercy nor the justice of men. "Lord Jesus receive my spirit," he said, and expired. The impression produced by his execution was immense; he redeemed, by his firm courage at the stake, all the vacillations and inconsistencies of his life, and his executioners placed the seal upon his glory as the Reformer of the Church of England, by employing against him a base act of perfidy rare even in the annals of the Marian persecutions.

Those from whom abjuration had been obtained sometimes died of remorse, as happened to the diplomatist, Sir John Cheke; they were rarely dragged to the stake.

Cardinal Pole was immediately appointed Archbishop of Canterbury; but his counsels could not arrest the persecutions, stimulated by the violent zeal of Pope Paul IV., recently raised to the pontifical throne. Eighty-four persons perished that year by the flames. Nor did the living only suffer condemnation; the bones of Martin Bucer, who had died in England, whither he had been summoned by Cranmer during the reign of Edward VI., were disinterred and publicly burned. The body of the wife of Pierce, the martyr, suffered the same outrage; her grave was first desecrated, and she was afterwards buried in a dunghill. The reign of Mary lasted only five years; but in this short space of time two hundred and eighty-eight persons were legally condemned to execution on account of religion, and it would be impossible to enumerate the obscurer martyrs who died of hunger or suffering in the prisons. Most of the victims belonged to the middle class and to the people; it was here that was manifested the most faithful attachment to the doctrines of the Reformation. The great, enriched by the spoliation and governmental reform of Henry VIII., cared only to preserve their possessions. The poor defended in their way their precious faith by dying for it. Secret discontent was great even among the Roman Catholic population; the Spaniards were detested; crimes increased. Notwithstanding the stern repression which they had undergone in the time of Henry VIII., — seventy-two thousand murderers, thieves or vagabonds, had, it is said, perished upon the gallows during his long reign, — the executioners of Queen Mary had also much to do: repeatedly, men of good family, who had degraded themselves to the condition of highwaymen, were detected and seized. Certain parts of the kingdom remained in a state of dull discontent; it was amid this general uneasiness that Philip, who had become King of Spain in 1556, upon the abdication of the Emperor Charles V., at length succeeded in involving his wife and England in his quarrels with France.

The personal influence of Philip over Queen Mary was alone able to obtain this concession; the king was aware of this, and he arrived in England in the month of March, determined to recruit his armies with English forces. The whole of Mary's council, with Cardinal Pole at their head, at first opposed this measure. In vain did Philip threaten his wife that he would leave her forever; the ministers of the queen appealed to the marriage contract, affirming that England would find herself reduced to the state of a vassal if she allowed herself to be dragged at the heels of Spain into a war of no interest to herself. An enterprise attempted by an English refugee in France, Thomas Stafford, who crossed the British Channel with some few troops, and took the castle of Scarboro' by surprise, happened to second the solicitations of Philip II. Being made a prisoner, Stafford asserted that the King of France, Henry II., had encouraged him in his attempt, and the queen eagerly seized this pretext to satisfy the wishes of her husband by declaring war against France. When Philip quitted England, upon the 6th of July, 1557, never to return, he was shortly afterwards joined, before Saint-Quentin, by a thousand English knights and six thousand English foot-soldiers, commanded by the Earl of Pembroke. Queen Mary had great difficulty in raising this small corps; perhaps for the first time, war with France was not popular in England.

It was soon to become even more unpopular, notwithstanding the successes of the King of Spain in France. The capture of Saint-Quentin, and the fear of seeing the victorious army advance against Paris, recalled the Duke of Guise from Italy, where he was threatening the territories of Philip; the latter had just taken up his winter-quarters in Flanders, when the French general laid siege to Calais. The Spaniards had foreseen the danger and had proposed to strengthen the garrison, but the English council had jealously rejected this offer, and were preparing to send reinforcements. Meanwhile the French appeared before Calais on the 1st of January, 1558; on the 8th, after a skilful attack upon the ramparts, the town capitulated and the garrison issued forth with their arms and baggage, while the English troops were waiting at Dover until the state of the sea should permit them to proceed to the assistance of their fellow-countrymen. On the 20th, Guisnes succumbed in its turn, and the English lost the last foot of ground which they possessed in France. Calais had been in their hands two hundred and eleven years, and its loss was bitterly painful to the queen and the people. Parliament immediately voted subsidies to prosecute the war more vigorously. The Dauphin, subsequently Francis II., had recently married the young Queen of Scotland (April 24th, 1558), and the Scotch took up arms upon the border, thus associating themselves with the quarrel of their sovereigns by one of those aggressions towards which they were always disposed. They refused, however, formally to declare war against England, as they were urged to do by Mary of Guise, the regent of Scotland in the name of her daughter. The English fleet, under the orders of Lord Clinton, had ravaged the coast of Brittany without much result; but a small squadron of ten vessels contributed to the victory of Gravelines by ascending the Aa, as Egmont was beginning the combat, and opening fire upon the right wing of the French. The Marshal de Termes and a great number of French noblemen were made prisoners in this battle, which cost dear to France, yet brought nothing to England but a little glory in the wake of the Flemish general.

Meanwhile Mary was ill; she had seen her deceitful hopes of issue fade away, and the eyes of all turned towards the prudent Elizabeth, in retirement at her manor of Hatfield. The princess professed a scrupulous attachment to the practices of the Roman Church, following, in that matter, without difficulty the counsels of her politic adviser, Cecil. She had refused the proposals of marriage made her by several princes, among others the Duke of Savoy and Duke Eric of Sweden. Philip II. would have been glad to rid himself of his sister-in-law by causing her to marry, but Elizabeth contrived to thwart his projects without offending her sister, who as a rule adopted all the wishes of her husband. Elizabeth replied to the emissaries of the King of Sweden, who addressed themselves directly to her, that she could not think of listening to any proposal which had not been sanctioned by her Majesty. Mary was touched by this confidence, and she manifested more friendliness to the princess, who always walked with caution upon the brink of abysses into which the imprudence or the ill-timed zeal of her friends might have precipitated her. The great nobles attached to the Reformation lived, as she did, in retirement. The earls of Oxford and Westmoreland, as well as Lord Willoughby, had been reprimanded by the council, upon a question of religion. The Earl of Bedford had even suffered a short imprisonment. Sir Ralph Sadler, one of Henry VIII.'s trusted agents, and destined to be often thus employed by Elizabeth, had quitted the court, weary of the fanaticism which was displayed there. All awaited in silence the death of Mary, bowing their heads under a yoke which could not last long. The queen, always delicate, had for several months been suffering severely with slow fever. She had vainly hoped to recover her strength at Hampton Court. She was brought back to London, and expired in St. James's Palace, at the age of forty-three, on the 17th of November, 1558, without having again seen the king her husband. She sighed so bitterly at the last that the ladies asked her if she were suffering, commiserating her for the absence of King Philip. "Not that only," she said, "but when I am dead and opened you shall find Calais lying in my heart." The following morning, at nearly the same hour, Cardinal Pole died at Lambeth. The two pillars of the Catholic Church in England fell at the same time. Pole had hoped to insure the triumph of his cause by gentleness and justice; Mary had supported it by steel and fire. Both were equally sincere and conscientious. Mary was of a narrow mind; her character, naturally stern and harsh, had been imbittered by injustice and suffering; but she was upright and honest, avoiding the subterfuges and deceits which Queen Elizabeth too often practised; she was animated by a fervent faith, which she deemed it her right and duty to impose by force upon all her subjects. The sufferings of heretics excited little compassion in her breast; she was hardened against them, but in her private life, and towards her servants, she was kind and generous, capable of affection and of devotion. She blindly loved her husband, who neglected and despised her on account of her age, and the few charms which nature had bestowed upon her. Mary, however, was learned; she wrote pure Latin, she had studied Greek, and spoke French, Spanish, and Italian with ease. She was a good musician, and danced gracefully. Her household was a model of order and regularity. The queen set an example of piety and virtue. The memory of these good qualities and misfortunes pales in the presence of a supreme fault: a terrible stain remains imprinted upon the brow of the unfortunate queen by her fanaticism and her conscientious cruelty. She persecuted piously, she burnt sincerely; her acts, more than her character, merit the odious name which history has given her. On examining her life closely, one is tempted to pity Bloody Mary.

CHAPTER XXI.

POLICY AND GOVERNMENT OF QUEEN ELIZABETH, HER FOREIGN RELATIONS. 1558–1603.

ELIZABETH was at Hatfield when Mary died, a striking proof of the distrust which reigned between the two sisters, and which banished one from the deathbed of the other. The princess was devoting herself, as usual, to the serious occupations which were dear to her. Still more learned than her sister, brought up with care by the famous Roger Ascham, Elizabeth had continued the practice of reading some Greek every day; she even translated the rhetorician Isocrates. These literary recreations were interrupted by more urgent cares when the mortal illness of her sister began to bring about her the worshippers of the rising sun. Philip II. had sent to her an ambassador upon whom he depended. The Count de Feria had seen the princess before the queen's death, and the king believed her to be gained over to the great Catholic confederation, and compelled to rely upon him and to regulate her conduct according to his advice. She did not, however, consult him upon the course to be pursued when she was apprised of the death of her sister. Sir William Cecil, secretary of state under Edward VI., who, being in disgrace under Mary, had prudently submitted to the Roman Catholic requirements, had received all his orders in advance. Parliament was in session; Chancellor Heath repaired to the Houses, and there announced the accession of Queen Elizabeth, "the legitimate and rightful heir to the throne." Cries

PORTRAIT OF ELIZABETH.

were raised of "Long live Queen Elizabeth!" Couriers were dispatched by Cecil to all the sovereigns of Europe, announcing the accession; and the Lords hastened to Hatfield to present their homage to the new sovereign. They asked themselves, on arriving, what attitude she would probably assume. The Protestants, delivered from an odious yoke, rejoiced, being convinced that, under her sister's reign, the princess had concealed her real opinions. The Catholics, in some anxiety, counted upon the influence of Philip II. The first remarks of Elizabeth did not enlighten them; she was cautious and moderate, announcing no intention of abrupt changes. One indication alone, though slight in itself, soon showed from which quarter the wind blew: when the queen arrived at Highgate, the bishops came to meet her, and all kissed her hand, with the exception of Bonner, Bishop of London, the principal persecutor of the Reformers, upon whom she turned her back. Notwithstanding the solemnity of the Catholic services performed in honor of Queen Mary and the Emperor Charles V., who had died a short time before, judicious observers saw the queen inclined towards the party of the Reformation. Her ministers were more decided than herself. Cecil, Pembroke, Northampton, and Lord John Grey, her intimate councillors, were all convinced of the immense progress which Protestantism had silently made during the Marian persecutions. They perceived, moreover, that the throne of their mistress rested exclusively upon the Protestant principle. Submissive to the Pope, England must reject Elizabeth as illegitimate, since the marriage of Henry VIII. with Anne Boleyn had not been sanctioned by the Catholic Church, and the succession would lie between Lady Catherine Grey, the younger sister of the unhappy Jane, grand-daughter of Mary Tudor, and Mary Stuart, Queen of Scotland, Dauphiness of France, grand-daughter of Margaret Tudor, wife of James IV., King of Scotland. The legitimacy of Elizabeth and her right to the throne sprang naturally from the Act of Supremacy. At her coronation, on the 15th of January, all the bishops, with the exception of Doctor Oglethorpe, Bishop of Carlisle, refused to officiate, striking a fatal blow to Roman Catholic influence in the kingdom by the hostile attitude which they thus assumed from the outset, either at their own instance, or in obedience to orders emanating from Rome. Elizabeth was, however, crowned by Oglethorpe with all the ancient ceremonies, to the passionate delight of the population of London, always favorable to the Reformation; they crowded the streets through which she was to pass upon her issuing forth from the Tower, where she had been formerly detained in terror of death: flowers rained into her carriage, shouts of gladness resounded on every side. Elizabeth received them with that kindly condescension which bound the hearts of her people to her, smiling when she heard the old men in the crowd declare that she resembled King Henry. "Be ye well assured," she said to the multitude that thronged around her in front of Guildhall, "I shall stand your good queen." Amid many faults and some crimes, Elizabeth kept this promise.

The Protestants were eager to enjoy their triumph, and the more eager because they were a little anxious; the queen had preserved in her chapel a crucifix and a holy-water basin; she had forbidden controversial preaching and the sermons at St. Paul's Cross. These measures were taken in the interest of peace and concord, it was said, but they did not satisfy the ardor of the Reformers. Lord Bacon relates that the day after the coronation one of the courtiers presented to Elizabeth a petition in favor of certain prisoners, entreating, since she had in honor of her accession set free many captives, that she would please also to release the apostle Paul and the four evangelists, so long detained in prison in a foreign tongue, so that they could not converse with the common people. The queen gravely replied that it was necessary first to ascertain from them whether it would be agreeable to them to be released. She had, however, already authorized the reading of the liturgy in English; a commission of theologians had been secretly appointed to revise the Prayer-book of Edward VI., before restoring it to use. Elizabeth did not approve of all the reforms instituted by Cranmer; the crowd of English who had taken refuge abroad on account of their religion, and who had returned to England at her accession with a zeal increased by persecution, would soon have drawn the Church of England into a path which was not hers, if the secret tendencies of Elizabeth towards Romanism and her resolution to maintain the royal prerogative had not energetically resisted their influence. When Parliament met, on the 25th of January, 1559, the queen made no proclamation, leaving to Cecil and to the Keeper of the Seals, Nicholas Bacon (father of the great Chancellor Bacon), the duty of making known her wishes. She allowed the bill of supremacy and the restoration to the crown of the tithes and annates to be proposed and voted. She allowed the laws of King Edward concerning religion to be re-established, and also the Prayer-book as modified by her orders; but the law to reinstate the married clergy, who had been dispossessed under the reign of Mary, was set aside by her desire. She never could tolerate the marriage of priests. She also discountenanced the project for a code of canon law, being uneasy, no doubt, concerning the discussions which might spring from it. This twofold check dissatisfied the party ardent for the Reformation. Elizabeth subsequently asserted that the Protestants had impelled her in her course at the moment of beginning her reign. This was untrue; Parliament had not as yet asserted its rights. It was under the prolonged influence of the Reformation that it was destined to foster noble instincts of liberty, and even at times to triumph over the firm will of Elizabeth.

Everything depended upon the queen's marriage, and of this all parties were sensible. The great bulk of the nation were not so anxious about the selection of a husband as about the husband himself. They ardently desired to see the succession assured, and in the first session of Parliament in 1559, a deputation was sent to the queen at Whitehall, with the message that the Commons conjured her Grace to think of marriage, in order that her posterity might reign over the kingdom. On this occasion for the first time Elizabeth proclaimed that aversion to marriage which was definitively to triumph over so many assaults and momentary hesitations. "From my years of understanding, knowing myself a servitor of Almighty God," she said, "I chose this kind of life in which I do yet live as a life most acceptable unto Him, wherein I thought I could best serve Him, and with most quietness do my duty unto Him." Then, laying stress in a few sentences upon the difficulties which she had overcome during the reign of her sister, in remaining faithful to her resolution, she added, without promising the Commons to marry, that she would never choose any husband but one as devoted as herself to the happiness of her people. "I take your petition in good part, for it is simple, and containeth no limitation of place or person. If it had been otherwise, I must have misliked it very much, and thought it in you a very great presumption, being unfit and altogether unmeet to require them that may command. And for me, it shall be sufficient that a marble stone declare that a queen, having reigned such time, lived and died a virgin." The Commons retired without having obtained anything definite. The same demand was to be repeated many times, and to receive answers of different kinds; but until the end of her life Elizabeth took pleasure in keeping the world in suspense by her grave coquetries, expecting a marriage which she herself never seriously desired.

While the Parliament of England was imploring the queen to take a husband, the King of Spain, Philip II., solemnly determined, by a conscientious sacrifice, to do her the supreme honor of offering her his hand. Being resolved to preserve the place which he had acquired in England, and to retain that powerful kingdom in the bosom of the Catholic Church, he had written to Feria on the 10th of January, 1559, enumerating the objections which might be made to his union with his sister-in-law, and the inconveniences and sacrifices which must result to him from the step; but with a magnanimity which he himself was the first to admire, Philip had resolved to set aside all obstacles. "You will understand in this what service I render to our Lord; through me her allegiance will be regained to the Church." Philip ended by settling beforehand all the conditions to which Elizabeth must conform, all the acts of submission which she must make to the Pope and to the Church, before she could aspire to the elevation which the King of Spain destined for her. Paul IV. had been unfortunate in preparing the way for the contrition of Queen Elizabeth. Immediately upon her accession, when that event had been communicated to the Holy See, as well as to all the sovereigns of Europe, the Pope had abruptly replied that, the Princess being illegitimate, she must beware of laying hands upon the crown, and must relinquish it instantly until he should have declared concerning her rights. This claim did not incline the queen to appreciate Philip's generous sacrifice; she gently put aside the advances of the Count de Feria, asserting that the friendship of her brother of Spain was as dear to her as his love could be, and that the Pope himself could not unite her to the husband of her sister.

Feria spoke of the Queen of Scotland. Elizabeth did not suffer herself to be frightened, and without positively refusing the honor which the King of Spain did her, she said laughingly, that she was afraid he might be a bad husband, since he would come to England simply to marry her, but would not sojourn there with her. The confidential letters of Philip had transpired: Feria understood that the definitive reply would be unfavorable, but Elizabeth loaded the ambassador with attentions. A peace with France was negotiating at Cambray, and the queen, who hoped to recover Calais, wanted the support of Philip in this important business. When peace was at length signed at Cateau-Cambrésis, and the violence of the English resentment was appeased, on the 2d of April, by the promise of the surrender of Calais at the end of eight years, Philip II. transferred to another Elizabeth the honor which he had wished to do his sister-in-law, by marrying the young Elizabeth of France, daughter of Henry II. "My name brings good fortune," said the Queen of England on learning, not without vexation, the conditions of the treaty, with that singular coquetry which impelled her all her life to make use of every means to retain around her the suitors to whom she would grant nothing. The alliance between England and Spain still subsisted. "You will assure the queen that I remain her good friend," wrote Philip II. to Feria. He feared that she would turn towards the court of France, which was making her great advances. He might have reassured himself. France was then represented, in the eyes of Elizabeth, by Mary Stuart, and that princess had recently committed an offence forever inexcusable in the eyes of Elizabeth, by quartering upon her escutcheon the arms of England with those of Scotland and France. The Dauphin, in confirming the treaty, had also taken the title of King of England, Scotland, and Ireland: a fatal pretension, and one which was destined to engender many crimes.

The Parliament was dissolved when Elizabeth called upon the bishops to conform themselves to the laws which had recently been re-established. All refused to do so with the exception of Kitchen, Bishop of Llandaff, formerly a Benedictine, whose habit it was to adopt at all times his sovereign's religious belief. A certain number of dignitaries of the Church followed the example of the bishops, who found among the lower orders of the clergy very few adherents. Several bishoprics chanced to be vacant at the accession of Elizabeth. She gave pensions to a few of the clergy who retired on account of their religion, and filled all the livings by placing in them the greater number of the exiles driven forth by the fanaticism of Mary. The Church of England was forever lost to the Holy See, whatever hopes in the future the Catholic party might conceive. The two statutes generally known under the names of the "Act of Supremacy," and the "Act of Uniformity," debarred from public offices all conscientious Catholics who refused to recognize the religious authority of the queen, and forbade them at the same time the practice of their form of worship. Then began for the Catholics a quiet, scrutinizing, continuous persecution, penetrating into families, maintained by espionage, always vexatious, sometimes bloody, mingling with politics and drawing therefrom the pretext for tyranny. This oppression did not break out at first; it was in 1561 only that Sir Edward Waldegrave and his wife were sent to the Tower for having entertained in their house a Catholic priest. The bishops themselves were at first simply deposed; but their injudicious zeal having led some of them, towards the end of 1559, to present a petition imploring the queen to follow the example of her sister, of blessed memory, Elizabeth, greatly incensed, sent the petitioners to prison. Bonner was detained there until his death; the other prelates were at length released and even installed, sometimes with the Protestant bishops who had succeeded them, at other times with the rich clergy, to the great displeasure of both. The monasteries recently restored by Mary were once more closed, and the crown again took possession of the property of the Church, of which restitution had been made under the last reign. In the main, and notwithstanding a few modifications, the work of Cranmer and of Edward VI. was restored. The opinion of the majority of the nation and prudent policy had overcome, in Elizabeth's mind, her personal tastes and tendencies.

Political motives were about to unite her more and more with the Protestant party in Europe. When she learned the impertinent pretension of the Dauphin to the title of King of England, she exclaimed, "I will take a husband who shall cause the head of the King of France to ache; he does not know what a rebuff I intend to give him." Upon this, public rumor immediately attributed to the queen the intention of uniting herself in marriage to the Earl of Arran, son of the former regent of Scotland, now known under the French title of Duke of Châtelherault, heir-presumptive to the throne of Scotland, after the Stuarts. The Earl of Arran had ardently embraced the Protestant faith, and was in London in 1559, at the moment when Mary Stuart mortally offended "her good sister of England." He had a secret interview with the queen at Hampton Court, and immediately set out, under a fictitious name, for Scotland, accompanied by Randolph, Elizabeth's confidential emissary. The state of Scotland had become both complicated and aggravated by the death of the King of France, Henry II. Francis II., the husband of Mary Stuart, had determined, it was said, to expend all the property of France, if it were necessary, to put an end to the insurrection. It was to the support of the insurgents that the Protestant policy, then represented by Cecil, wished to pledge Queen Elizabeth, in order to bring about her marriage with the Earl of Arran, after he

G. Staal del. Ferd. Delannoy sc.

MARIE STUART

Estes and Lauriat, Boston

should have become King of Scotland, and thus to achieve that union of the two crowns which Henry VIII. had contemplated in his plan for the marriage of Edward VI. with Mary Stuart.

Nowhere had the Catholic Church offered so many vulnerable points to the Reformers as in Scotland, for nowhere were the clergy so corrupt. The Protestant doctrines, in their most austere and aggressive form, had made such great progress there, that Knox may be regarded as the real chief of that insurrection which everywhere held the regent, Mary of Guise, in check. The violence of religious passions had already occasioned the destruction of a great number of churches and monasteries; already had the greater part of the nobility abandoned the regent, and formed themselves into a "Congregation of the Lord," under the direction of Lord James Stuart, illegitimate son of James V., and brother of Mary Stuart. The troops coming from France were the sole support of the regent against the insurgents; but these reinforcements were numerous and efficient. A French garrison had taken possession of Leith and threatened Edinburgh, when the agents of Queen Elizabeth set themselves to work: Randolph in Scotland; Sir Ralph Sadler at Berwick, whither he had been officially sent to negotiate with the emissaries of the regent concerning the question of outrages upon the borders. The negotiations with the Lords of the Congregation were taking their course, still profoundly secret. Elizabeth was naturally parsimonious, and she had found the finances of England in great disorder; however, at Cecil's instigation she sent to Sadler considerable sums for the support of the malcontents. No blows had been struck since the last agreement between the regent and the great noblemen, and it was not until the month of October, 1559, that the insurgents laid siege to Leith. Hitherto Elizabeth had haughtily denied all relations with the Lords of the

Congregation; but one of her agents had been arrested, having in his possession a sum of two thousand pounds sterling. The hesitations and doubts of the queen often impeded the action of Cecil. She had no liking for the ardent Presbyterians. Knox, in particular, was odious to her; she had never forgiven him for a pamphlet upon female government, entitled, *The First Blast of the Trumpet against the monstrous Regiment of Women.* "I like not the audacity of Knox, whom you have well brought down in your answer," wrote Cecil to Sadler; "it does us no good here, and I suppress it as much as I can; however, fail not to send me what he writes." The subsidies did not suffice to maintain courage and discipline in the Scottish army. Being repulsed before Leith, the Lords of the Congregation evacuated Edinburgh, and fell back during the night to Stirling. Elizabeth resolved to adopt more efficacious measures. On the 27th of February, 1560, through the agency of Maitland of Lethington, formerly secretary of the queen regent, but now among the insurgents, she concluded a treaty of alliance with the great Scottish noblemen, for the whole duration of the marriage of the Queen of Scotland with the King of France, undertaking not to lay down arms so long as the French should remain in Scotland. An English army crossed the frontier, under the orders of Lord Grey of Wilton; an English fleet, commanded by Winter, entered the Frith of Forth; and the Lords of the Congregation, having assembled all their forces, on the 6th of April laid siege to Leith. The siege was still in progress on the 10th of June, when the queen regent, Mary of Guise, expired in Edinburgh Castle, where Lord Erskine had received her, as upon neutral ground. This death precipitated the conclusion of a peace desired by both parties. The French surrendered Leith and returned to their vessels, thus delivering Scotland from their presence; and a council of twelve noblemen, chosen partly by the queen, partly by the Parliament, was empowered to govern the country in the absence of the sovereign. The court of France recognized Queen Elizabeth's right to the throne, and "her good sister Mary" gave up bearing the English arms. The treaty of Edinburgh secured in Scotland the supremacy of Protestantism, which had now become the religion of the majority of the population. The vote of the Scottish Parliament, in the month of August, 1560, officially severed all bonds with the court of Rome, by adopting a confession of faith drawn up by Knox and his disciples, according to the doctrines of Calvin, and striking at the root of ecclesiastical organization, as well as at the rites and ceremonies of the Roman Catholic faith. Matters having gone thus far, Parliament deigned to think of the assent of the queen. Sir James Sandilands, formerly Prior of the Hospitallers, was dispatched to France to ask for a ratification, which was at once refused. It was said that Mary's uncles, the Duke of Guise and the Cardinal of Lorraine, were making preparations to invade Scotland, when the young King of France, Francis II., expired suddenly, on the 5th of December, 1560, after a reign of seventeen months. The power of Mary Stuart was suddenly eclipsed; the bright morning of her life was about to disappear behind a dark cloud heavy with misfortunes and with crimes.

While Mary, but lately Queen of France, was preparing to return to her cold and rugged country, Elizabeth was keeping in check the suitors who were contending for her hand. The King of Sweden, who had already been ambitious of the honor of becoming her husband when he was but heir-apparent, and she scarcely better than a prisoner at Hatfield, dispatched his brother, the Duke of Finland, to renew his proposals. The ambassador was courteously received and treated with distinction by the queen; but no sooner had he been installed by order of Elizabeth in the bishop's palace at Southwark, than the King of Denmark sent his nephew, the Duke of Holstein, as an aspirant to the same honor. "It is said that the Archduke of Austria is on the way here," wrote Cecil, "without pomp, and, so to say, in secret. The King of Spain is earnest for him. I would, in God's name, that her Majesty might accept one, and that the rest should be honorably sent back." The Archduke Charles, son of the Emperor Ferdinand, did not come; like Elizabeth herself, he hesitated. The King of Sweden was not easily put off with refusals, but his ambassador was obliged to depart without having obtained anything. The Duke of Holstein carried away at least, for his uncle, the Order of the Garter, and received a pension for himself. The queen trifled with all these suitors, taking pleasure in keeping them upon the alert by her coquetry, but was more tenderly interested in a young nobleman of her court than in all the princes who were seeking her alliance. For several months past the attention of the courtiers had been excited by the signal favor which she had manifested towards Lord Robert Dudley, son of the Duke of Northumberland and brother of Lord Guildford Dudley, the husband of Lady Jane Grey. The passing fancy which Elizabeth had displayed for Sir William Pickering and for Lord Arundel had given place to a more durable attachment. Lord Robert, subsequently known in history under the title of the Earl of Leicester, had taken possession of the queen's heart. He nourished the hope of marrying her, but he had a wife whom he kept in a secluded spot in the country. One day this lady fell down a staircase and broke her neck, without any one being a witness of the accident. Court rumors were unfavorable to Lord Robert; he was loudly accused of having caused the death of his wife, and the queen felt how strongly public opinion in England was opposed to her desire to marry the man whom she loved.

Mary Stuart had returned to Scotland. Elizabeth, always uneasy in respect to her rival's claims to the English crown, had tartly refused an authorization to pass through her dominions, which Mary had asked, and the bitter feeling always existing between the two princesses had only increased. The Lords of the Congregation had begged for the Queen of England's support, when Mary Stuart refused to ratify the separation which they had decreed between Scotland and Rome. Scarcely had the young widow, leaving with regret that France in which she had been brought up, set foot within her own kingdom, before she encountered the violent opposition of her subjects to the worship which she had sincerely at heart. Her Roman Catholic friends, among others the Bishop of Ross, had urged her to land in the Highlands, and surround herself with the forces of the Earl of Huntley, a fervent Catholic, before making her entrance into Edinburgh. She rejected this clumsy proposal, which placed her at the outset in strife with the majority of the nation, and the plaudits of the people greeted her at Leith, on the 19th of August; but, on the first Sunday after her arrival, when the fierce Protestants saw the altar prepared in Holyrood Chapel, an outcry was raised against the Mass, and Lord James Stuart was obliged to remain before the door, with his sword drawn during the whole time of the service, in order to prevent an outbreak. He did not succeed in preventing a visit from Knox. That ardent and indomitable preacher repaired to the residence of the queen, now urging her with pious solicitations, now loading her with reproaches. Mary wept; but she refused to listen any longer to Knox, and the Reformer from this time forward made it a practice to refer to her from the pulpit under the name of Jezebel. The abyss was already beginning to open between Mary Stuart and her people; the crimes of both were soon to render the evil irreparable.

Queen Elizabeth had opened negotiations for persuading her "good sister of Scotland" publicly to renounce all claim to the English crown, but Mary demanded to be recognized as the second person of the kingdom, heiress to the throne in case of Elizabeth's death without issue. This claim the queen would not admit; she experienced an inexpressible reluctance to settling the succession to the crown. Mary Stuart was not destined to be the only sufferer from this mean jealousy. Elizabeth was at times more than a man, as her minister, Robert Cecil, son of the great Burleigh, said subsequently, but she also became sometimes less than a woman. She had conceived suspicions concerning Lady Catherine Grey, sister of Lady Jane, and heiress to the latter's rights, such as they were. It was discovered that Lady Catherine had secretly married Lord Hertford, son of the Duke of Somerset, formerly Protector. She was imprisoned in the Tower, as though she had conspired against the life and power of the queen. Her husband, who was travelling in France, was peremptorily recalled and thrown into prison in his turn. The marriage was declared null, and the child that had recently been born to this pair was pronounced illegitimate. Without any other pretext but state reasons the husband and wife were detained in the Tower, where Lady Catherine Grey died in 1569. The same cause had already cost the lives of two daughters of the Duchess of Suffolk; the third was shortly afterwards to pay, like them, for the royal blood which ran in her veins.

Arthur and Anthony Pole, nephews of the Cardinal, had made a vain attempt in favor of Queen Mary, who would marry, it was said, one of the two brothers, when they should have placed her upon the throne of England; but the queen had felt no uneasiness from this source, and she pardoned all the accused persons. She could not, however, conceal from herself that the Catholic princes in general looked upon her with distrust, and would willingly seek a pretext in the illegitimacy of her birth to conspire against her in favor of the Queen of Scots. This secret motive, far more than her religious convictions, led Elizabeth to maintain abroad the cause of the oppressed Protestants, who turned their eyes towards her for help. In France, the Reformers, under the orders of the Prince of Condé and Admiral Coligny, had risen at the beginning of 1562, upon the violation by the Duke of Guise of the recent treaties and his massacre of the Protestants at Vassy. They immediately besought the assistance of Queen Elizabeth. Philip II., who had recently sent six thousand men to support the Duke of Guise, advised him to keep out of the quarrel and to remain neutral; but Elizabeth had adopted the theory that she was seconding the wishes of the King of France by fighting against the Guises, who endeavored to tyrannize over him. Under this pretext she sent three thousand men to France, with instructions to take possession of Havre, as a pledge for the good intentions of the Huguenots towards her. At the same time she furnished money to the Prince of Condé. An English detachment, sent to the assistance of the besieged city of Rouen, was cut to pieces upon the occasion of the capture of the town. But the garrison of Havre had been reinforced; the Earl of Warwick, brother of Lord Robert Dudley, was in command of the town; he remained firm for nine months both against treachery and the armies of the French. He only yielded to the plague, and after infection had thinned his forces. Wounded and ill himself, he was concerned only for the fate of the soldiers whom he brought back when he returned to England in the month of July, 1563, bringing with him the pestilence which had triumphed over all his efforts. Thousands of victims succumbed to the plague which ravaged London during the months of September and October. Elizabeth was negotiating with Queen

Catherine de' Medici. The Protestants had been vanquished, but the Duke of Guise was dead, assassinated by Poltrot. Peace was signed on the 11th of April, 1564, at Troyes, and the last hope of regaining Calais vanished with the departure of the hostages whom France had given shortly before; Elizabeth received in exchange the sum of a hundred and twenty thousand crowns, a sum very useful to her treasury, which was then empty.

The Parliament of England had, nevertheless, voted considerable subsidies in the preceding year, not without repeating its constant request in relation to the queen's marriage. The Commons had added on this occasion another petition, which sounded ill in the royal ears. In the event of her Grace having decided forever against marriage, she was implored to permit Parliament to designate and recognize her legitimate successor. Once more Elizabeth led her people to hope that she was thinking of marriage. She was at this time engaged in the Scottish intrigues respecting the marriage of Mary Stuart, more probable, although as much debated as her own. Religious and political parties continued to rend Scotland asunder. The Catholics, under the orders of the Earl of Huntley, had been defeated at Corrichie by the Earl of Murray, formerly Lord James Stuart, at the head of the Protestants. It was constantly repeated that such or such a one of the great opposing noblemen aspired to Queen Mary's hand, and they were not the only aspirants. Her beauty, her charms, and the prospect of the crown of England added to the Scottish crown, drew upon her the eyes and the ambitious hopes of a crowd of princes. The King of Spain proposed his eldest son, Don Carlos, and the negotiation had been considerably advanced by the care of the skilful ambassador of Philip in London, the Bishop of Quadra, when that prelate died, and the matter was given up. The Guises spoke of the Duke of Anjou, who subsequently became Henry III., of the Duke of Ferrara, and of several others; but all these suitors were Catholics, the Scottish nation was hostile to them, and Queen Elizabeth did not conceal the fact that any union with a foreign prince, opening up to her enemies the road to her dominions, would bring about war. A personal interview had been projected between the two queens. Mary was, it was said, desirous of consulting "her good sister," and of proceeding according to her advice, but Elizabeth, vain as she was and willing to let her beauty be extolled by her courtiers at the expense of her rival's charms, had no wish to risk the comparison; the two princesses never saw each other. The Queen of England, meanwhile, proposed for Mary Stuart's husband the man whom she herself loved, Lord Robert Dudley, whom also she soon raised to the rank of Earl of Leicester. Did she act sincerely? Did she honestly wish to make the fortune of Leicester at Mary's hands, when state policy and her personal scruples did not allow her to raise him to her own level? These questions can never be answered; but the negotiations were renewed several times, Elizabeth continuing to insist upon marrying the Queen of Scotland to a great English nobleman, and refusing to hear of any but Leicester. People spoke of Lord Darnley, the eldest son of the Earl of Lennox, and grandson, by his mother Lady Margaret Douglas, of the Earl of Angus and of Margaret Tudor, Queen of Scotland, and aunt of Elizabeth. He was, therefore, cousin to Mary Stuart, and his father, who had long been exiled from Scotland, but had now recently returned thither, had immediately undertaken to bring about his marriage with the queen. Darnley's birthplace was in England, and he was an English subject, but Elizabeth was not in favor of his pretensions. Resting her hand upon Leicester's shoulder, she said to Melville, the skilful and faithful emissary of Mary Stuart, "What do you think of this man? Is he not a good servant? Yet, ye like better of yon long lad," referring to Darnley, who bore the sword of justice before her. Notwithstanding these objections, Darnley arrived in Scotland at the beginning of the year 1565, and was well received by Queen Mary. He was handsome and of good figure; his mother was skilful and intriguing. The confidants of Mary were all gained over; the queen was not opposed to this union. Lord Murray, who counted upon retaining power, counselled the marriage, and Parliament did likewise. Queen Elizabeth was informed of what was going on; her anger was violent. Cecil still hoped that Mary Stuart would marry Leicester and would ward off from the head of his mistress the danger of a union which constantly occupied his thoughts. The grave objections of "her good sister" were made known to the Queen of Scotland. Elizabeth went further: the property which the Lennoxes possessed in England was confiscated, and the Countess of Lennox and her second son were sent to the Tower. Sir Nicholas Throgmorton, in whom Elizabeth had confidence, was dispatched to Scotland, to intrigue with the Lords of the Congregation; by slow degrees they separated themselves from Mary, and Murray was the first to blame what he had himself advised a short time before. The preachers thundered against the possibility of a union with a Roman Catholic king, and Mary was solemnly invited by the assembly of the Church to conform herself to the Protestant faith, and abolish everywhere in her dominions the Catholic worship. Plots succeeded plots, but Mary was, she said, too much involved to draw back, and, on the 12th of July, Darnley, whom the queen had recently raised to the rank of Earl of Ross and Duke of Rothsay, married Mary Stuart in Holyrood Chapel, and was proclaimed king at the Cross in the market-place of Edinburgh. The Earl of Murray and most of the Lords of the Congregation immediately rose in insurrection; but before they could gather their forces, the queen marched upon them at the head of the royal army, with pistols at her saddle-bow. The lords turned their horses' heads and retired without fighting. The Earl of Murray and the Duke of Châtelherault only stopped in their flight when they had crossed the frontier. They were ill received by Elizabeth, though she had encouraged them in their revolt, for she liked neither insurgents nor men who had been vanquished, and she did not intercede in their favor with Mary when the latter had obtained from her Parliament a bill of attainder against the chiefs of the insurrection. At this time Mary committed the error to which she had for a long time been solicited by her uncles of Guise: she united herself to the great Catholic alliance formed many years before between France and Spain, and renewed, it was said, at Bayonne in 1564. The continual difficulties caused by the rebellions of the great nobles and by the intrigues of England naturally tended to throw Mary into the arms of the Catholic sovereigns; it was a fatal mistake on the part of the Queen of Scotland, but her guilt lay in another direction.

Darnley was both incompetent and unmannerly, violent and weak. The affection which he had inspired in Mary Stuart soon disappeared and gave place to contempt. Nor, according to public rumor, was this all: the niece of the Guises, brought up by Catherine de' Medici amid all the dissoluteness of the French court, had a bad reputation among the austere Presbyterians, and her inclination to surround herself with young men, foreigners, and artists, was attributed to the most disgraceful motives rather than to the elegant tastes and the love for frivolous pastimes which were probably its real cause. No one was more disliked among Mary's favorites than an Italian, David Rizzio, who had won her favor by his musical talents, and to whom she had gradually confided important trusts. Rizzio had especially aroused the jealousy of Darnley; the Italian had, it was said, taken the liberty of reproaching the young king with his behavior towards Mary; he also encouraged the queen in her refusal to confer upon Darnley the crown matrimonial instead of the vain title which he bore. A plot was formed against the life of Rizzio. At the head of the conspirators was Lord Ruthven, who had been a short time before in a dying condition, and who arose from his sick-bed to take part in a deed of blood with Lord Morton, chancellor of the kingdom. Their aim was to recall the Earl of Murray and the exiled lords, by revoking the acts passed against them by Parliament.

On the 9th of March, 1566, Mary was at supper in her apartment with her ladies, and Rizzio was in the room, when the young king came in, followed almost immediately by Ruthven. The queen rose in much alarm when the other conspirators also entered. Ruthven ordered Rizzio to leave the apartment, but Mary placed herself before her favorite, who clung to her dress. Darnley seized the hands of his wife; the table was overthrown; the unhappy Italian cried, "Mercy! justice! justice!" George Douglas seized Darnley's dagger and struck Rizzio. Andrew Ker, one of the conspirators, drew his pistol upon the queen, who was begging them to spare her favorite. He was dragged out, and was pierced by numerous dagger-thrusts in the antechamber, while Morton, outside, guarded the doors of the palace with a troop of armed men. When Mary learned that Rizzio was dead, she is said to have exclaimed, "I will then dry my tears and think of revenge." Darnley endeavored to console the queen; she suffered him to believe that she accepted his excuses, and when her brother, Lord Murray, presented himself on the morrow at Holyrood with the banished noblemen, she received him without anger, and succeeded in detaching him from those who had exerted

"GEORGE DOUGLASS SEIZED DARNLEY'S DAGGER AND STRUCK RIZZIO."

themselves in his behalf, perhaps without his knowledge. Morton and Ruthven, abandoned by Darnley and Murray, immediately took flight, while the Earl of Bothwell and Lord Huntley brought to the queen an army of eighteen thousand men, levied upon the spur of the moment. Mary was once more mistress of the situation. Two obscure accomplices in Rizzio's murder alone bore the penalty of the crime, and on the 9th of June, 1566, the queen gave birth to a son, who was to become James VI. of Scotland and James I. of England. Elizabeth had promised to act as godmother to the child of the Queen of Scotland. As soon as the prince was born, Melville departed in all haste to bear the news to London. Cecil was the first informed; he repaired to Greenwich; the queen was dancing after supper. "But," wrote Melville, "so soon as the secretary, Cecil, whispered in her ear the news of the prince's birth, all her mirth was laid aside for that night. All present marvelled whence proceeded such a change, for the queen did sit down, putting her hand under her cheek, bursting out to some of her ladies that the Queen of Scots was mother of a fair son, while she was but a barren stock." On the morrow Elizabeth had regained her composure, and she graciously congratulated the ambassador, dispatching the Earl of Bedford to Scotland with her gifts, to be present at the baptism of the little prince. Darnley refused to take part in the ceremony; he knew that the Queen of England had forbidden her emissaries to render to him royal honors.

He had, besides, other causes for dissatisfaction. A growing coldness existed between his wife and himself. The apparent reconciliation which had followed Rizzio's murder had not lasted, and Darnley was intending to leave Scotland and travel on the Continent. Queen Mary had addressed a letter to the privy council of Elizabeth, claiming the recognition of her hereditary rights, a matter which had recently been mooted in the English Parliament, to the great exasperation of her Majesty. The Commons had been more urgent than usual, notwithstanding the ordinary promise of the queen to think of marriage. Elizabeth had recently been ill, and the terrors of a contested succession had drawn forth the members from their ordinary state of submission. When Mary's request arrived, the Queen of England abruptly imposed silence upon the Commons. "Under the pretexts of marriage and succession, many among you conceal hostile intentions," she said; "but I have learned to distinguish my friends from my enemies; and take care, whoever be the sovereign who holds the reins of government, not to wear out his patience as you have done mine." She instructed the Earl of Bedford to induce Mary to ratify the treaty of Edinburgh, which yet remained pending, and which contained verbally the renunciation of the rights which Mary claimed, promising to regulate the question of the succession by a fresh treaty. Mary refused, but, not to irritate her powerful rival, she consented at Bedford's request to pardon Morton, Ruthven, and Lindsay, who had taken refuge in England after the murder of Rizzio. Darnley no doubt experienced fears at the news of Morton's return, for he immediately left the court and sought retirement at the residence of the Earl of Lennox near Glasgow.

Scarcely had the young king arrived at his father's house when he caught the small-pox. He was in great danger, and the queen sent her physician to him, without going to see him herself, so long as he was seriously ill. She remembered, no doubt, that, being apparently in a dying condition in the preceding summer, at Jedburgh, her husband had not troubled himself to go and see her. When Darnley was convalescent, Mary consented to a fresh reconciliation. She repaired to Glasgow and brought the king back with her to Edinburgh.

She took up her residence as usual at Holyrood, but the fear of contagion caused Darnley to be installed in an isolated house, where the queen visited him. Rumors of conspiracy were already afloat; the insolent Darnley had few friends and many enemies. He was, however, warned by the Earl of Orkney that if he did not promptly quit this place, he would lose his life there; but the king had been smitten again with a capricious passion for his wife. He judged by appearances only, and a word from Mary's mouth was enough to quiet his suspicions. On the 9th of February, 1567, the queen took supper with him, then left him at eleven o'clock for a ball which she was giving at Holyrood, in honor of the marriage of one of her household. Three hours after her departure, at two o'clock in the morning, the house in which Darnley had remained alone with five servants was blown up, and the body of the unhappy king was found in the garden, near that of a page, without trace of fire or of any violence, while the other victims remained buried beneath the rubbish. No one had escaped. The blow had been struck by a sure hand, and Mary was again a widow.

Public rumor immediately accused the Earl of Bothwell. His violent passion for the queen was known; it was even whispered that the affection was mutual, notwithstanding the signs of grief shown by Mary, who remained shut up in an apartment hung with black. The details of the crime indicated long premeditation and skilful accomplices. Nearly all the ministers of the queen, Maitland especially, were implicated in the suspicions of the public. No one laid hands upon the principal person accused, even when the Earl of Lennox demanded his arrest. He was allowed to take possession of Edinburgh Castle before a warrant of arrest was made out against him. He appeared at the bar of the court of justice, but rather in triumph than as an accused person. The Earl of Lennox, alarmed at the attitude of the assassins of his son, had fled, taking refuge in England. Bothwell was acquitted, and bore the sceptre before the queen at the opening of Parliament. Darnley had been sleeping but a month in his bloody tomb, and already the rumor was afloat that the queen was about to marry the Earl of Bothwell, whom current opinion regarded as her husband's murderer. Bothwell, moreover, had been married six months before to the sister of the Earl of Huntley.

The faithful friends of the queen — and she had yet a few, in this court agitated by such violent passions and pierced by such dark deeds of treachery — warned her of the sinister rumors which circulated concerning her. Her honest envoy, Melville, relates how he took her a letter coming from England upon this subject; the queen showed it to the secretary, Maitland. "Bothwell will kill you," said the statesman; "retire before he comes within this place." And as Melville persisted, the queen sharply replied that matters had not yet come to that, without being willing to enter into more details.

Bothwell had in the meantime taken his precautions and secured powerful partisans. He brought together at a banquet all the principal members of the Parliament, and there, protesting his innocence of the murder of Darnley, he announced his intention of marrying the queen. Whether from fear or from interested motives, the guests signed a paper which Bothwell had prepared, recommending the earl for the husband of Mary, and they undertook to favor the marriage by every means. Four days later Bothwell had gathered a thousand horse, and posting himself in the way of the queen, who was returning from Stirling, between Linlithgow and Edinburgh, whither she had been to see the little prince, he attacked the royal escort, and, himself laying hands upon the bridle of Mary's horse, he carried her off, with her principal councillors, to Dunbar Castle, exclaiming at the moment of the capture, that he would marry the queen, "who would or who would not; yea, whether she would herself or not." He detained her for five days in his fortress, without her subjects making the slightest effort for her rescue. On the 29th of April, when she was restored to liberty, the queen appeared in the session court, and there declared before the chancellor that notwithstanding the outrages which the Earl of Bothwell had made her suffer, she was disposed to pardon him and to raise him to still greater honors. On the 15th of May the marriage was celebrated at Holyrood, publicly according to the Protestant rites, and in private according to those of the Catholic Church. Bothwell had legally separated himself from his wife; the murderer had obtained the object of his crime.

Hitherto silence had been preserved as to Bothwell's guilt, but the public conscience was shocked by this marriage. All at once the plots burst forth which had long been in preparation to hurl Mary from the throne. Scarcely had she, whether willingly or under compulsion, concluded this odious union, when revolt suddenly threw off the mask. The great nobles had signed an engagement with Bothwell; now they loudly accused him of the murder of Darnley, made public their fears for the life of the little prince, and announced their intention of delivering the queen from her husband's yoke. An attempt to take possession of Bothwell's person having failed, the confederates marched upon Edinburgh, where they seized the government. But Mary rarely shrank from violence; she was resolute and quick. On the 15th of June, a month after her marriage, she was at Carbery Hill at the head of the troops that she had raised, in the face of the insurgents' army. No engagement took place. The ambassador of France, the aged Le Croc, endeavored to negotiate between the two parties. The forces of the confederates increased every moment; the soldiers of the queen appeared valiant. Bothwell proposed single combat to the hostile chiefs. Several accepted, but without result. It was at length agreed to let Bothwell go unimpeded, provided the queen would consent to return to her capital, where her faithful subjects would receive her with honor and respect. Two hours later Bothwell departed at a gallop, a free man; but Mary was a prisoner, and she was conducted to the house of the Provost of Edinburgh, where she remained shut up for twenty-four hours without being approached by any one. On the morrow, after nightfall, a numerous guard took the captive to Lochleven Castle, under the custody of William Douglas and his mother, who was also the mother of Murray, Mary's illegitimate brother. Bothwell soon left the kingdom.

The anger of Elizabeth, at the news of Mary's arrest, was violent and unfeigned. Not that she took much interest in the rival whose authority she had incessantly endeavored to undermine, through fear of the enterprises which the latter might attempt against England, but the outrage suffered by the Queen of Scotland was an insult to all sovereigns. It was a blow to the regal dignity, a fruit of the pernicious principles propagated by Knox and his adherents. Sir Nicholas Throgmorton was sent to the confederate noblemen to command them to set at liberty their queen; but Cecil was not in such a hurry as was his mistress to see Mary out of prison. His private instructions in some slight degree abated the negotiator's ardor. The lords of the council meanwhile lost no time. Lord Lindsay appeared at Lochleven, the bearer of an act of abdication in favor of the little prince. The queen was desired to sign it; she refused. Lindsay grasped her arm with his iron gauntlet. "Sign," he said, "if you do not wish to die as your husband's murderess." The queen signed without looking at the paper, then raised her sleeve to show to those present the marks of the violence which she had just suffered. The uncouth warrior was himself ashamed. "I did not know that a woman's flesh was like new-fallen snow," he muttered; but he carried away the document. King James VI. was proclaimed and crowned on the 20th of June, and on the 22d of August the Earl of Murray, who had returned to Scotland after a prudent absence, was declared regent of the kingdom. He paid a visit to his sister at Lochleven, and afterwards asserted that he had only accepted the office out of consideration for the prayers and tears of Mary. In the month of December, an act of the council declared the queen an accomplice in the murder of her husband and the abduction of her person by Bothwell. The deed was proved, it was said, by a correspondence between Mary and Bothwell recently discovered by the Earl of Morton. The responsibility for the queen's deposal fell entirely upon her own head, and was but the just punishment of her crimes.

The violence or the justice of men could take everything from Mary Stuart except the power of her charms. Even at Lochleven she was able to make partisans and to find friends. On the 2d of May, 1568, the lords of the council suddenly learned that the queen had escaped from Lochleven through the skill of a young man who had contrived to steal the keys. She arrived by night at Hamilton Castle, and had already revoked her abdication. Before the end of the week she had gathered an army around her.

The situation was critical, but the regent and his friends knew how to meet the emergency. As Mary advanced towards Dunbarton Castle, she encountered a body of troops, small in number, but disciplined and well armed; her partisans sprang to the combat with more zeal than strategy, and they were soon defeated and put to flight. The deserted queen at first escaped the pursuit of her enemies, but she felt that she was closely pressed. The thought of the horrors of a prison chilled her with fear; she had expected death before when she was in the hands of her revolted subjects; and she now resolved to place herself under the protection of "her good sister," Queen Elizabeth, and to escape into England. The friends who yet surrounded her were opposed to this project. The Archbishop of St. Andrew's implored her upon his knees to abandon it; but Mary would listen to nothing; crossing the Solway in a little fishing-boat, she landed at Workington on the 16th of May, a fortnight after her escape from Lochleven, and thence directed her course at once towards Carlisle. Arrived there she dispatched a messenger to solicit an interview with Elizabeth. The fugitive queen was already lodged in the fortress, rather as a prisoner than as a sovereign, when she received Elizabeth's reply to her request. The Queen of England could not see her, it was said, until she should have cleared herself of all suspicion with regard to the death of her husband.

Elizabeth had refused to grant the title of Regent to Murray, and she had appeared to espouse Mary's cause; but the policy of Cecil received too opportune an assistance from the imprudent confidence of the Queen of Scotland, to allow the opportunity to pass without profiting by it. The captive committed the mistake of asking, that, if the queen could not protect her, she would at least allow her to traverse her kingdom, to go and beg the support of foreign princes, "the King of France and the King of Spain being bound to come to her assistance on this occasion." The Catholic confederation in Scotland, at the threshold of England, was too real a danger to escape Elizabeth's sagacity. She consented to Cecil's proposal, and made an offer to serve as arbitrator between the Queen of Scotland and her subjects, by means of an English commission. Mary indignantly refused. She could not and would not degrade the crown of Scotland to the condition of vassalage: she was a queen and independent. The arbitrators proposed to her had at all times fomented the disaffections in her kingdom, and had supported her enemies. She asked no other favor than liberty to return to Scotland, or to repair to France. She had come into England upon the faith of the assurances of friendship which Queen Elizabeth had transmitted to her while she was at Lochleven. "Being innocent, as, thank God, I know I am, do you not," she asked, "do me a wrong by keeping me here?"

In reply to this appeal, which in common justice it was difficult to reject, Mary was transferred from Carlisle to Bolton Castle. The agents of Elizabeth, in all the European courts, appeared to have agreed to alarm their mistress concerning the consequences of the liberation of the Queen of Scotland. "Her Grace now holds the wolf that would devour her," wrote, from Paris, Sir Henry Norris; "it is said that there is a conspiracy between the King of France, the King of Spain, and the Pope, to ruin her Majesty, and to put the Queen of Scotland in her place."

Elizabeth sent a messenger to Scotland, to summon the regent and the confederate lords to cease hostilities; but her representations had little effect, while the arguments of the Scottish insurgents produced a powerful impression upon her. She began to believe in the crime of which Mary so vigorously protested her innocence, and she insisted that the Queen of Scotland should exculpate herself fully in her eyes, promising to place Mary again upon the throne if her innocence should be proved; for, at the bottom of her heart, and in her royal sympathy for sovereigns, she had been and remained shocked at the audacity of the Scots, who had dared to dethrone their queen, whatever might have been her faults. The regent had replied to the reproaches and threats of the Queen of England, that "if Elizabeth wished to wage war against them, they would not sacrifice their lives, and would not risk their possessions, by passing as rebels in the world, when they had in their hands the means of justifying themselves, whatever regret that might occasion them."

The die was cast; the accusers of Queen Mary, her brother, Lord Murray, and her constant enemy, Lord Morton, were to come from Scotland, to be confronted with her before the commission of English judges. All parties were equally uncertain respecting the result of the conference, for all distrusted Queen Elizabeth, who had lavished upon both sides the most contradictory promises. Mary counted upon her to replace her again upon her throne. "I have abandoned dispatching my letters to the courts of France and Spain, relying upon the promises of your Grace, and wishing, if I am to be restored to the throne, that it may be solely by the means of the court of England." However, Cecil had assured Murray "that it was not intended to re-establish the Queen of Scots if her crime is proved, whatever her friends may say."

The conferences opened at York, upon the 4th of October. There were repeated all the arguments, there were enumerated all the facts which have since been well known in history. Mary threw the guilt of the crime not only upon Bothwell, but upon his accomplices, causing it to be clearly understood that her accusers had good reasons for making the whole weight of it fall upon her. She resolutely denied the genuineness of the letters found in her casket, of which copies only had been produced at first, and she demanded to be admitted to the queen, to defend herself in her presence. The conferences were transferred from York to Westminster. The Queen of England and her ministers felt the necessity for following more closely the dark intrigues which intersected each other in all directions around the captive queen. The secretary, Maitland, had opened a negotiation for the marriage of the Queen of Scotland with the Duke of Norfolk, affirming that the Protestantism of the great English nobleman would reassure the reforming party in Scotland, and would definitively re-establish the throne of the queen. It is probable that the designs of the skilful intriguer went further. He was aware of the secret discontent of the English Catholics, of the powerful friends whom Norfolk could rally around him, and he hoped no doubt to raise a revolt in England. The wisdom of Cecil saw through the manœuvre. Mary's liberty was forever lost, even could her innocence have been proved, which it assuredly was not. Mary in Scotland constantly threatened the throne of Elizabeth. The servants of the Queen of England went so far even as to fear for her life. Mary in prison was dangerous, no doubt, but the peril was less, and the question of the justice of the detention of a sovereign who had voluntarily come to place herself under her relative's protection, did not at all enter into the matter. On the 11th of January, 1569, after three months of conferences and of intrigues, Elizabeth publicly declared to the regent, Murray, that nothing had been proved against his honor or that of his partisans, but that the crimes imputed to Queen Mary had not been demonstrated with sufficient clearness to inspire her with a bad opinion of "her good sister." Nevertheless, Murray returned a free man to Scotland, supplied with the money which was necessary to him for the support of his government, and Mary remained in prison, in spite of her protestations and her anger. Elizabeth had several times caused her to be advised to relinquish the crown and to lead a peaceful life in England, but Mary had firmly replied that she was resolved to die rather than to do such a thing; that justice required that she should be re-established upon her throne, after which "she would show as much clemency to the authors of her troubles as should appear to her compatible with her honor and the good of her kingdom." The captive had also protested that she would not consent to proceed further away from the frontier; but, on the 26th of January, in cold and gloomy weather, the beautiful queen was compelled to mount a wretched horse, and accompanied by some ladies and a small number of servants, to proceed as far as Tutbury Castle, in Staffordshire, a fortress belonging to the Earl of Shrewsbury. This nobleman was henceforth intrusted with her custody, a constant anxiety to the sovereign who under the influence of female jealousy had belied the nobler side of her character, and who could now find no place strong enough, no jailer vigilant enough to keep the prisoner whom she was unjustly detaining.

The affairs of Queen Elizabeth were as complicated abroad as at home, and her foreign policy was not more honorable or more sincere. The oppression of the United Provinces by the King of Spain had aroused a general discontent which brought about insurrections in the towns, and the beginning of that indomitable rebellion which was to end in the dismemberment of the Low Countries. The Prince of Orange had placed himself at the head of the oppressed people, protecting the religious and political liberties of his country, and his great struggle with the terrible Duke of Alba had begun. Everywhere the Protestants felt themselves threatened, and conspiracies recommenced in France. The Prince of Orange and the Prince of Condé both applied to Queen Elizabeth to obtain assistance and money. The queen secretly supported them in a niggardly and unwilling fashion, though urged by Cecil, whose policy was more firm, whose intelligence was more clear-sighted, and whose views were broader than those of his mistress; but she took care loudly to protest her friendship for the King of Spain and Charles IX., while encouraging the enemies, declared or secret, who strove against their power. Upon every stage and in every country of Europe the policy of the sixteenth century constantly presents that character of duplicity and falsehood which necessarily results from the absence of publicity and control, but which renders history difficult to understand and more difficult to relate.

In presence of the embarrassments which the claimants of the succession to the English crown caused her, Elizabeth had resumed — if indeed she had ever abandoned — her matrimonial negotiations. The Archduke Charles was yet unmarried, and in 1567 the queen solemnly sent the Earl of Sussex as ambassador to Vienna, to deal with the great question of religion. The archduke had never come to England, although he had often been invited so to do, and the queen declared that she would never marry a man without having seen him. Sussex lavished upon her descriptions of the archduke's person and of his estates, also insisting much upon the high position which he occupied at the court of the Emperor. He assured the prince that this time the queen was quite in earnest in the matter, that she was free to marry whomsoever she pleased, and that she had never inclined towards any other union. The archduke professed himself much honored, but when the question of religion came up, he frankly declared that his religion was that which his ancestors had always professed, that he recognized no other, and would never change it. Elizabeth then urged the Protestant feeling of her subjects, without, however, breaking off the negotiations, which only ended on the day when the archduke married the daughter of the Duke of Bavaria.

The embarrassments of Elizabeth in England were complicated through the progress of the intrigue having for its object the marriage of Mary with the Duke of Norfolk. Elizabeth had openly spoken of it to the duke, who had excused himself, affirming that he could never think of uniting himself to a princess who had raised claims to the throne of England, nor to a woman whose husband could not sleep peacefully upon his pillow. This allusion to the fate of Darnley had for a moment lulled the queen's distrust, but Cecil was keenly alive to all the dangers which threatened his mistress. He had a short time before discovered the marriage of Lady Mary Grey, sister of Lady Jane and Lady Catherine. "Here is an unhappy chance and monstrous!" he wrote. "The serjeant-porter, being the biggest gentleman in this court, hath married secretly the Lady Mary Grey, the least of all the court. They are committed to several prisons; the offence is very great." And the jealousy of Elizabeth towards any who had claims, nearer or more remote, upon the throne was so excessive, that the unhappy Mary remained in prison until her death, without ever seeing her husband again. Deplorable end of a family doomed to the most tragic reverses!

Cecil had personal reasons for watching the intrigue for Mary's marriage with the Duke of Norfolk. The Earl of Leicester, always jealous of the influence of the great minister with his mistress, endeavored secretly to undermine a power which he dared not openly attack, and now exerted himself to make a friend of the powerful Norfolk by urging him in his perilous undertaking. The duke hesitated, but the Earl of Arundel and the Earl of Pembroke, uniting themselves with Leicester, dispatched to Queen Mary articles of marriage, intended to insure the security of Elizabeth by the total renunciation by Mary of her pretensions to the crown of England, and by an alliance, offensive and defensive, with the English queen. Mary Stuart was to allow the reformed religion to be established in Scotland, and to give her hand to the Duke of Norfolk.

In order to escape from prison people are willing to accept harsh conditions, especially when they are not firmly resolved to observe them. Mary promised all that was desired, merely stipulating that the consent of Elizabeth should be obtained to the marriage. "All my misfortunes," she said, "have arisen from the anger of my sister, when I married Darnley." Leicester was counted upon to obtain this favor, and the duke wrote the most impassioned letters to Mary, through the agency of the Bishop of Ross, who was still faithful to his mistress. The consent of the kings of Spain and France had been asked for, and Murray was to propose to the Scottish Parliament the liberation of the queen.

This he did, though probably without any great sincerity. Mary had brought many misfortunes and few benefits to Scotland, and her brother had not that attachment for her which causes all other considerations to be forgotten. The articles coming from England were rejected; the question of the divorce which Bothwell had caused to be declared in Denmark was not even examined, and Queen Elizabeth was warned of what was preparing in the dark. She was at Farnham; the rumor of the marriage circulated at the court. Leicester had as yet said nothing to his mistress. Norfolk was there, not daring to go away; he dined at the table of the queen, who one day said to him with a significant air, which recalled to him his own words: "Good evening, my lord duke; be careful upon what pillow you rest your head." Norfolk took alarm. A few days afterwards the court was at Titchfield. Leicester fell ill; the queen hastened to his bedside, and there, impelled by remorse and keeping up the farce of passion, Leicester avowed to her with tears that he had acted disloyally towards her, by endeavoring, unknown to her, to marry her rival to the Duke of Norfolk. Leicester obtained his pardon, but the royal displeasure rested upon the Duke of Norfolk. The disfavor of Elizabeth was dangerous; the duke retired to Kenninghall, whence he was soon recalled. A French servant of Mary Stuart, arrested in Scotland, had, it is said, made fresh revelations upon the complicity of his mistress in the murder of Darnley: the servant was executed, but the imprisoned queen remained exposed to the anger and indignation of Elizabeth. An insurrection in the north was feared, for the earls of Arundel and Pembroke had both quitted the court. Norfolk was conducted to the Tower; the Bishop of Ross was arrested, although he pleaded the privilege of an ambassador, and all the noblemen compromised in the intrigue received an order to retire to their homes. The anxieties of Elizabeth, real or feigned, were not without some foundation. The Catholics of her kingdom, groaning under a secret but cruel oppression, naturally looked towards the Queen of Scotland, in their eyes the legitimate heiress to the throne, sanctified by her misfortunes, surrounded by the double fascination of her charms and of that faith towards which she had always manifested the most sincere attachment. The Huguenots had recently suffered great disasters at the battle of Jarnac, where the Prince of Condé had been killed, and also at the battle of Moncontour. The English gentlemen whom the queen had gradually allowed to pass into the service of the French Protestants were compelled to return to England, whither they brought back gloomy tales of the cruelty of the victorious Catholics, and their resolve to cause Catholicism to triumph everywhere, no matter by what means. To complete the hostility of the Continent, Queen Elizabeth, always greedy for money, had seized in time of peace upon a fleet of Spanish galleons, bearing to the Duke of Alba the sums sent to him by the King of Spain, which fleet had taken refuge near the English coast in order to escape some Huguenot vessels. It was asserted at the court of England that the money did not belong to Philip II., but to some Genoese and Lombard bankers, who could not object to lending it to Queen Elizabeth. The vessels of the English merchant navy had all become pirates, stopping and pillaging the Spanish and French ships, seconding the attempts and projects of the Huguenots upon all coasts, and bringing arms and supplies to them. Convoys setting out for La Rochelle were even accompanied by royal vessels, and the queen secretly authorized a great number of noblemen to take service in the army of the Huguenots, or in that of the Prince of Orange, while she replied to the complaints of the Spanish and French ambassadors by the assurance of her friendship for their sovereigns and of her wish to preserve the peace. Treachery was met by treachery. A conspiracy, half Spanish, half French, was preparing upon the Continent to encourage the insurrection of the Catholics. Ridolfi, an agent sent from Italy, had communication with the Duke of Alba on passing through the Low Countries. Designs were secretly entertained against the life of Elizabeth, and the representations of the governor-general, who did not believe in the possibility of success, having had no effect upon his master, the intrigue went on in the north of England, Elizabeth's tyranny having itself paved the way.

Captive princes always find means of communicating with their partisans, however close may be their prison, and however strict the supervision may appear. Mary Stuart had entered into relations with all the great Catholic noblemen of Yorkshire, Durham, and Northumberland. An attempt at escape had even been organized, which was to place her at the head of her little army, but the project failed, and, on the 16th of November, 1569, the earls of Northumberland and Westmoreland, with a great number of noblemen and retainers, raised the standard of revolt, with the intention of marching upon Tutbury, to deliver and proclaim the captive queen. Upon the way the insurgents burned in the churches the prayer-books, announcing everywhere that the Catholic religion was re-established, and summoning all good Catholics to join them. But Mary had already been transferred from Tutbury to Coventry. The people did not respond to the appeal of the rebels; the southern counties took up arms against them. A goodly number of Catholics united with the royal army assembled at York. Uneasy and irresolute, the two earls fell back upon Raby Castle. They besieged Sir George Bowes, in Barnard Castle, compelled him to capitulate, and planted themselves in the little port of Hartlepool, hoping to receive Spanish assistance through the Low Countries.

Meanwhile the Earl of Sussex, who had delayed so long at York that suspicions had been aroused as to his loyalty, at length advanced against the rebels with the reinforcements which the Earl of Warwick had brought to him. The insurgents fell back slowly towards the frontier of Scotland, and soon took refuge, without fighting, in that kingdom, the support of which they had hoped for. Elizabeth at once demanded the surrender of all the chiefs. Murray could not or would not satisfy this requirement. The Earl of Northumberland alone was in his hands. The Earl of Westmoreland, Egremont, Ratcliff, and the other great noblemen, were in safety at the residences of their Scottish friends, who furnished them with means for proceeding to the Spanish Low Countries. The regent sent his prisoner to Lochleven, saying that he would exchange him for Queen Mary; but before the negotiation had begun, even before Lord Leonard Dacre, the last of the insurgents who still held out in England, had been in his turn obliged to take refuge in Scotland, Murray was assassinated on the 22d of January, 1570, in the streets of Linlithgow, and Queen Elizabeth wreaked her vengeance upon the counties which had taken part in the insurrection. "There are so many guilty persons to condemn," wrote the Bishop of Durham to Cecil, "that difficulty is experienced in finding enough men innocent of all rebellion to make juries of them." A royal declaration was read in all the churches, in the peaceful districts as well as in the regions bristling with gibbets, which reminded the people of the tranquil years that England had enjoyed under the reign of Elizabeth, and affirmed that she claimed, as chief of the Church, no other authority than that which her predecessors had exerted, her noble father, King Henry VIII., and her dear brother King Edward VI. She did not intend to put a constraint upon the conscience of her subjects, provided the Christian religion, as it was established in the Acts of Faith, was in no wise molested, and that people conformed themselves to the laws of the kingdom for the practice of public worship. Liberty, as understood by Queen Elizabeth, consisted in doing exactly as she commanded.

The death of Murray, the only man sufficiently skilful and influential to maintain a little order in unhappy Scotland, had again delivered up that kingdom to the dissensions of parties. The Duke of Châtelherault and the Earl of Argyle immediately took possession of the government in the name of Queen Mary; but Morton, at the head of the *king's men*, as the partisans of James VI. were called, had taken up arms, summoning England to his aid. Elizabeth sent him an army and a regent. She had taken back into favor the Earl of Lennox, father of Darnley and grandfather of the little king, and dispatched him to Scotland, to govern in the name of his grandson, while the English troops several times entered

Scotland, devastating all the southern counties, burning the towns and villages, and supporting the efforts of the new regent, who was implacable in ravaging the domains of the Duke of Châtelherault and of all the family of the Hamiltons. When Sir William Drury returned to Berwick, on the 3d of June, after the recent campaign, the ravages had been so great that the authority of Lennox appeared to be established upon the ruin of all his adversaries.

Catholic arms as well as Catholic conspiracies had failed. Pope Pius V. proposed to try the spiritual thunders of the Vatican. A bull declaring the excommunication of Elizabeth, depriving her of her pretended rights to the crown of England, and absolving her subjects from their allegiance, had been for some time prepared; it was signed after the insurrection had failed, and several copies of it were sent to the Duke of Alba, but Philip II. prohibited the publication of them in the Low Countries. On the 13th of May, 1570, however, the bull was posted upon the door of the palace of the Bishop of London. During the investigations which were immediately made in courts of law, of evil notoriety both in political and religious affairs, it was ascertained from a student under torture, that he had received a copy of the bull from a rich Catholic gentleman named Felton. The latter was arrested, and he avowed without hesitation that he had posted up the bull, but no punishment could make him reveal the names of his accomplices. Being condemned to a traitor's death, he walked to the place of execution as to a martyrdom, designating the queen by the name of "Pretender," and remaining firm in his enthusiasm until the last moment. While upon the scaffold, however, he asked that the pardon of Elizabeth might be solicited for aught in which he had offended her, and sent to her, in remembrance of him, a magnificent ring of great value, which he took from his finger. Even in the case of those who contended against her with the greatest tenacity, Elizabeth had been able to win from her people so sincere and loyal an affection, that condemned persons sent presents to her, and criminals whom she had caused to have a hand cut off for having written against her, seized their hats with their left hands and waved them above their heads, exclaiming, "God bless Queen Elizabeth!"

The faithful attachment of the English nation to its sovereign did not, however, prevent the progress of a new principle of liberty which grew with the firm and independent opinions of a portion of the Protestant population. Elizabeth had preserved at the bottom of her heart much liking for Catholic doctrines, and still more for the Catholic forms of worship. She loved sacerdotal vestments and pompous ceremonies. She retained candles and a crucifix in her chapel, and she had a horror of married priests. All the weight of her authority did not prevent the most fervent Protestants of her kingdom from being convinced, especially among the middle classes, that the Reformation had been too quickly checked in England, and had not been sufficiently thorough. They thus inclined more and more towards the religious practices and doctrines of the Continent in their austere simplicity. The "Puritans," as they were already called, were in bad odor with Elizabeth, and she often persecuted them, with all the more severity because she attributed to them, and not without reason, the republican and democratic tendencies spread abroad in Scotland by Knox, the effect of which had appeared in the revolts against Mary Stuart. A certain number of bishops and many great noblemen secretly inclined towards the Puritan ideas. Even Cecil was not hostile to them, although he had the royal favor more at heart than all sects and doctrines of whatever kind. In the Parliament of 1571 the Puritans for the first time asserted themselves. Thomas

Cartwright, a distinguished professor, who occupied, at Cambridge, the Margaret Professorship of Theology, maintained that the Episcopal system was opposed to the Holy Scriptures. He was suspended, not without commotion among the public. The laws proposed in Parliament were hostile to the Catholics; they prohibited, under the penalties of treason, claiming the succession to the crown, for any person whatsoever, during the queen's lifetime; they placed an absolute veto upon all communications with the Pope and all obedience rendered to his bulls; but at the same time they required assiduity in the worship established by the State, and, four times a year, reception of the sacrament in the Anglican Church. This last article was abandoned by the queen, but the Anglican worship was as odious to the Puritans as to the Catholics. They presented in Parliament seven bills for the progress of reform and the repression of abuses. The queen, in a passion, ordered Mr. Strickland, the member who had proposed them, to abstain from appearing in the House; but the Puritans had gained more ground than the queen was aware of; they introduced a motion to summon Strickland to the bar, and to cause his exclusion to be explained to him, declaring that the House which could decide the right to the throne had the privilege of occupying itself in ecclesiastical matters. The prudence of Elizabeth prevailed over her anger. Strickland reappeared on the morrow, and took his seat amid the acclamations of his colleagues: the queen had been vanquished, and her aversion to the Puritans was thereby increased. This was the first triumph gained by the fathers of the liberties of England over the political and religious despotism which was growing up in the shadow of the Tudor throne. At the end of the session, after the Commons had been reprimanded for their indocility by Nicholas Bacon, Lord Keeper of the Seals, Parker, Archbishop of Canterbury, caused Mr. Wentworth, one of the great orators of the House of Commons, to be summoned, and demanded of him how they had dared to suppress some of the articles of faith which had been presented to their vote. "We were so occupied in other matters, that we had no time to examine them, how they agree with the Word of God," boldly replied Wentworth. "What?" said the bishop; "surely you mistake the matter; you must refer to us in this." "No," said the Puritan, "by the faith I bear to God, we will pass nothing without understanding what it relates to, for that were but to make you Pope; it will not be by our hands." However, notwithstanding the haughty resistance of the Houses, the bishops continued to insist upon the observance of the newly issued Articles of Faith, under thirty-nine heads, which had replaced the forty articles of Edward VI. A complete submission was required of the pastors, and they were deprived of their livings at the first refusal declared before the court of high commission, to which was intrusted the decision of all ecclesiastical disputes. "Matters will soon be ended with them," wrote Parker to Cecil, speaking of the nonconformist ministers, "for I know them to be cowards." The learned archbishop was never more completely mistaken. The courage of the Puritans remained firm through all persecutions. A hundred years were not destined to elapse without bringing the day of its triumph.

The friends of Queen Mary had resolved upon her marriage. The Duke of Norfolk being in the Tower, a plan was formed for marrying the Queen of Scots to her brother-in-law, the Duke of Anjou. Elizabeth was alarmed, and, to cut short this new intrigue, she made overtures on her own behalf to the court of France. Her most skilful diplomatist, Walsingham, was sent to Paris, intrusted with this negotiation, complicated by the secret support which the queen continued to give to the Huguenots. The parleyings lasted for several months, until finally the Duke of Anjou positively refused to change his religion; whereupon people turned their eyes towards the Duke of Alençon, the youngest son of Catherine de' Medici; he had scarcely reached his eighteenth year; the queen was drawing near her fortieth. The negotiations nevertheless took their course, amusing Elizabeth by outward tokens of gallantry, in which she still took delight, and, at the same time, preventing all the assistance which the court of France might have brought to the unfortunate Mary Stuart. Charles IX. had claimed for his sister-in-law permission to live in France; but, piqued at the reports of the French ambassadors in respect to the relations of the captive with the King of Spain, and by her correspondence with the Duke of Alba, he at length exclaimed, "Ah! the poor fool will never cease till she lose her head; in faith, they will put her to death. I see it is her own fault; I meant to help, but if she will not be helped, I can do no more." The prospect of the throne of England for the Duke of Alençon was too brilliant to be sacrificed to the interests of Mary; Queen Catherine negotiated an alliance, offensive and defensive, with Walsingham.

Abandoned by her relatives and her friends in France, Mary Stuart had not ceased to conspire with Spain; but her agents were so closely watched, the supervision of Cecil was so strict, that several emissaries fell, one after another, into his hands. On one occasion, the Bishop of Ross, recently restored to liberty, contrived to substitute innocent letters for the compromising papers which his messenger had brought; but enough was soon known to make it certain that Mary was urging the Spaniards to attempt an invasion of England, and that the Duke of Alba promised to make arrangements with a person designated in cipher. Suspicion immediately fell upon the Duke of Norfolk. The plague having broken out in the Tower, he had been guarded in his house in London for fifteen months. He was taken back to his prison, and his trial began. The duke at first made a bold denial; then, when he was shown the confessions wrung by fear or torture from his servants and the agents of Queen Mary, including the bishop of Ross, he admitted certain things, still maintaining that he had never conspired against the queen, that he had even engaged in the negotiation for the marriage only because he thought she was informed of it, and that in marrying Queen Mary he would do nothing prejudicial to her Majesty. He solemnly denied all accusations of correspondence abroad or with the rebels during the insurrection. No witness was confronted with him; only the depositions taken after torture were communicated to him. He was accused of having maintained relations with the Pope; Norfolk, the old pupil of Fox, the author of the Protestant martyrology, declared that he would rather be torn to pieces by wild horses than change his religion. He recalled the solicitations which the Earl of Leicester had made to him, before he had become concerned in this affair. Leicester sat at the council, listening without pity to the complaints of his confiding victim. He voted the death of the duke, who immediately turned towards his judges. "This is the judgment of a traitor, my lords," he exclaimed: "but I am a true man to God and the queen as any that liveth, and always have been so. I do not now desire to live. I will not desire any of your lordships to make petition for my life; I am at a point. And, my lords, as you have banished me from your company, I trust shortly to be in a better company. This only I beseech you, my lords, to be humble suitors to the queen's Majesty, that it will please her to be good to my poor orphan children." Even in his letters to the queen, full of repentance for having offended her, and for having acted in several matters without her knowledge, the duke never asked for mercy, and refused to make any confession which might involve other victims in the doom which awaited him. Norfolk had been condemned since the middle of January, and the queen signed his sentence on the 8th of February; but during the night she became agitated, and caused Cecil, whom she had raised to the rank of Lord Burleigh, to be summoned. She forbade him to have the sentence executed, saying that she wished to reflect further; three times the sentence was signed, and three times Elizabeth recalled it, hesitating to put to death her relative and former friend.

At length Parliament intervened. The nation was profoundly agitated by rumors of plots. The documents found upon the emissaries of Mary had circulated among the public; already they saw the Duke of Alba, the ferocious butcher of the Low Countries, invade England at the head of those Spanish soldiers whose cruel exploits had terrified Europe. On the 16th of May the Commons presented to the queen a petition, in which the Lords concurred, desiring the execution of the duke for the security of the country. This time the sentence was not withdrawn, and on the 2d of June, 1572, the Duke of Norfolk was beheaded on Tower Hill, protesting to the last his devotion to his sovereign, and his attachment to the reformed faith. He refused the handkerchief with which it was proposed to bind his eyes. "I do not fear death," he said. When his head fell, the crowd wept as they had wept twenty-five years before at the death of his father, the Earl of Surrey, beheaded on the same spot by order of King Henry VIII. Two months later, on the 22d of August, the Earl of Northumberland, captured by treachery, when he thought himself delivered at the price of an enormous ransom paid by his wife, died upon the scaffold at York. He was seized upon the vessel which was to take him to the Low Countries, and the attainder which overtook him avoided the

EDINBURGH CASTLE.

embarrassments of a trial. His father had also died upon the scaffold, upon the same day, nineteen years before.

All these trials and executions tended towards the same end. Mary Stuart was condemned before her accusation had been spoken of. Protestant opinion, Protestant fears, were violently excited against her. Burleigh and Walsingham were both convinced that the repose of England was only to be purchased at the price of her blood. Parliament, always ardent in such cases, had proposed to proceed against the prisoner by means of an attainder, but the queen opposed this. The Houses contented themselves with depriving Mary of her hereditary rights, and declaring her unfitted to succeed to the English throne. The captive queen was at this time at Sheffield, in the custody of Sir Ralph Sadler and of the Countess of Shrewsbury. None of the details of the Duke of Norfolk's death had been spared to her; and she had refused to leave her apartment during all the time of the trial. Her faithful servants were everywhere losing ground in Scotland. The Archbishop of St. Andrew's, seized by Lennox in Dunbarton Castle, had been hanged without process of law, and the murder of Lennox himself by the Hamiltons was not enough to compensate for the disasters to the Catholic cause. The new regent, the Earl of Mar, was less powerful than Morton, the queen's fiercest enemy. However, Edinburgh Castle still held out for Mary, and the Highlanders recognized no other sovereign.

A crime committed in another country, and for which she was in no wise responsible, was destined to bring the unfortunate Mary to the scaffold, however long the alternations between hope and fear might yet be. On the night of the 23d and 24th of August, 1572, St. Bartholomew's Day, the Protestants, assembled in great numbers in Paris, upon the occasion of the marriage of the King of Navarre to Marguerite of Valois, sister of King Charles IX., were suddenly massacred in their beds, in the streets, or while escaping over the housetops; and the same slaughter, spreading like a conflagration from town to town, soon extended through the whole of France. Thirty or forty thousand persons perished thus in a few days. Almost all the chiefs of the Protestants were gone. The most illustrious, Admiral Coligny, was killed in his apartment, and his body thrown out of the window. It was to free themselves from the preponderating influence which he was beginning to exert over the king that Catherine de' Medici and her son, the Duke of Anjou, formerly an aspirant to the hand of Elizabeth, and at this time king-elect of Poland, had concerted and accomplished this massacre, for which they had obtained the authorization of Charles IX. only by dint of harassments which had almost reduced the monarch to imbecility.

The public outcry was terrible in all Protestant countries; nowhere, however, greater than in England, whither refugees, fleeing for their lives, now hastened from all parts of France. The queen went into mourning, and refused for several days to receive the French ambassador, M. de la Mothe-Fénelon; but she felt no real sympathy for the French Huguenots, and the horrors which caused the blood of her subjects to boil in their veins had not interrupted the negotiations of her foreign policy. Walsingham courteously thanked the king that his house had been spared during "the riot." The excuses and explanations of Charles IX., transmitted by his ambassador, were accepted. The project of marriage with the Duke of Alençon was not abandoned: only Walsingham gave Queen Catherine to understand that it was not a favorable moment for the visit of the Duke of Alençon to England, by reason of the extreme exasperation of the population against the Catholics.

The first-fruits of this exasperation were the counsels which Queen Elizabeth received from all quarters to put an end to the life of her rival, who had been so long her prisoner. The bishops, in a body, advised her to rid herself of the Queen of Scots, "the origin and source of all the evils;" but Elizabeth as yet shrank from the state crime which has sullied her name in the eyes of posterity. She would have been glad to have the natural enemies of Mary Stuart, the subjects whom she had misgoverned and who had revolted against her, imbrue their hands in their sovereign's blood. She dispatched Killigrew, one of her most skilful agents, to negotiate for Mary Stuart's liberation, who was to be consigned to the justice of her people, in exchange for certain hostages from the great families of Scotland. It was becoming too difficult to keep the Queen of Scots, Killigrew was to say; she drew too many dangers upon the kingdom, and the queen preferred to consign her into the hands of her subjects.

This attempt failed through the loyal uprightness of the Earl of Mar, at that time engaged in the difficult task of reconciling the factions. After taking part in a banquet at the residence of Lord Morton, in the course of his patriotic negotiations, he fell ill and died, not without suspicion of foul play, and on the 24th of October, 1572, Morton, who had long been a dependant of Elizabeth, was raised under her auspices to the dignity of Regent. Killigrew assisted him in negotiating for the surrender of Edinburgh Castle, which was reduced to the last extremities by the private treaty concluded by Lord Huntley and the Hamiltons. The secretary, Maitland, shut up in the castle with the brave Kircaldy of Grange, poisoned himself a few days after the capitulation, ending by suicide a life of subtle and ingenious intrigues which were almost always doomed to failure. Kircaldy was hanged as a traitor, and Queen Mary lost her last friends in Scotland.

Charles IX. had refused to send assistance to the faithful defenders of the citadel of Edinburgh, for fear that Elizabeth might support the Protestants, who depended upon La Rochelle. Secretly, she had several times assisted them, and she encouraged the naval expedition of the Earl of Montgomery in their favor. When the unhappy Charles IX. died in 1574, haunted even to his deathbed by the remembrance of his victims, the efforts of the French Reformers were suddenly seconded by the support of the Duke of Alençon, leagued with them against his brother, Henry III., who had returned from Poland to ascend that throne of France whereon the sons of Catherine de' Medici sat successively, to the misfortune and shame of their country. When the new king had discovered the plot, the Duke of Alençon was already engaged, in concert with the young King of Navarre, in raising an army: both of the brothers asked assistance of Elizabeth, but she preferred the position of mediator, and it was through her good offices that the peace of St. Germain's was concluded in 1576, securing to the Protestants the free exercise of their religion, and to the Duke of Alençon the appanage and title of Duke of Anjou. The peace was not of long duration, and the formation of the League, the progress of the influence of the Guises in the kingdom, their authority over King Henry III. as well as over the fanatical party, soon put arms once more into the hands of the Reformers. A brilliant prospect opened at the same time in the Low Countries to the new Duke of Anjou.

The affairs of the Prince of Orange and the cause of liberty in the United Provinces had steadily been advancing since the commencement of the struggle; amid defeat, disaster, and oppression, the indomitable courage of William the Silent and his fellow-citizens had by degrees gained so much ground, that Spain was on the point of losing forever half of the

Low Countries. The Duke of Alba had been recalled after that government, whose fearful memory yet makes us shudder. His successor, the Grand Commander Requesens, died in 1576. Shortly afterwards the Prince of Orange, not knowing where to look for support in his growing embarrassments, offered the protectorate of Holland and Zealand to Queen Elizabeth, as the descendant of the former sovereigns of the country through Philippa of Hainault, wife of Edward III. The Queen of England refused, not desiring, she said, to encourage in revolt the subjects of her good brother, the King of Spain. William the Silent then offered the sovereignty to the Duke of Anjou. Don John of Austria, at that time governor of the Low Countries, longed to invade England, to deliver Queen Mary, marry her, and sit with her upon Elizabeth's throne. The project was chimerical, it was not encouraged by Philip II.; but it was a plausible pretext for Elizabeth with regard to the King of Spain. She affirmed that the offensive and defensive alliance which she had concluded with the Prince of Orange, was intended solely to defend the Low Countries against the encroachments of France, and to protect England from the invasions of Don John. Queen Elizabeth had already sent a great deal of money to the revolted provinces; she gave yet more upon the pledges which the States-general furnished her; but the Duke of Anjou took no steps, and the patriot armies were twice defeated by Alexander Farnèse, nephew of the King of Spain. The French prince excused himself for his tardiness by his fear of offending the Queen of England, with whom he had lately resumed his matrimonial negotiations. The agent whom he had sent to London, M. de Simier, a man of talents and of pleasant manners, obtained great influence over the queen, and revealed to her a circumstance of which she was ignorant, namely, the secret marriage of the Earl of Leicester with the widow of the Earl of Essex, then very recently deceased. Elizabeth flew into a passion, the man who had occupied for thirty years the first place at her court was closely confined in his mansion at Greenwich.

Simier did still more: he induced his master to attempt a romantic venture with the queen; in the middle of the summer of 1580 the Duke of Anjou appeared in England under a disguise. He was short, thin, marked with the small-pox; but his amorous ardor, his youth, his journey, pleased the queen. When the duke was about to return it seemed that, for the first time, Elizabeth really wished to contract a princely union. The council was much divided: the queen was forty-eight years of age, the prince was very young and a Catholic. The most skilful politicians could not contrive to discover the secret feelings of their sovereign; but the time of petitions for her marriage had gone by; the queen bitterly felt it. The negotiations with Simier continued with alternations of favor and discontent on the part of Elizabeth. It was at length announced that the marriage would take place in six weeks. The States-general of the Low Countries had proclaimed the Duke of Anjou, and when he entered the provinces with an army of sixteen thousand men, Elizabeth sent him a present of a hundred thousand crowns. After having achieved some successes and delivered the city of Cambray, besieged by the Spaniards, the Duke of Anjou returned to England, where he was favorably received. The queen gave her ring to him, and commanded that the contract should be prepared. In Paris and in the Low Countries there was rejoicing at the marriage. Even in England it was believed that the queen was at length about to take a husband. This was on the 22d of November, 1581. When the duke appeared before the queen on the 23d, in the morning, he found her pale and in tears; it is said that she had changed her mind during the night upon the representations of her ladies, and at the idea of the danger which threatened her if she should have children; she declared to the prince that she would never marry. The Duke of Anjou, in a passion, returned to his residence; he threw the queen's ring upon the floor, accusing the women of England of being as capricious as the waves of their seas. The change which had been wrought in Elizabeth's designs was not yet made public: the Protestant preachers continued to thunder against the Catholic marriage, and libels against the Duke of Anjou abounded, severely punished by the queen, who accompanied him as far as Canterbury, weeping bitterly at his departure. She was never to see him again; the defeats suffered by his arms in the Low Countries, his retreat into France, and his death in the month of June, 1584, caused the queen so much sorrow, that her Majesty's ambassador in Paris dared not write to his mistress the details of the duke's death, for fear of "ministering cause of grief" to her.

The affairs of Scotland caused grave anxieties to Queen Elizabeth. So long as Morton governed she was assured of the support of a mortal enemy of Queen Mary; but the great Scottish noblemen had become wearied of the iron hand of a master sullied by so many crimes; and in 1578 a convention of the nobility declared the young king, then thirteen years of age, competent to exercise his authority personally. Morton retired to Lochleven Castle, then he reappeared at the court, powerful with the young king, and abusing his power as usual; but the ground was mined beneath his feet: King James had a favorite, the first of a long list, Esmé Stuart, his cousin, son of a brother of the Earl of Lennox. The young monarch had conferred upon him the title of Duke of Lennox; he was seconded by another Stuart, James, son of Lord Ochiltree: both accused Morton of the murder of Darnley. The earl was arrested. Queen Elizabeth sent Randolph, her former agent, to Scotland, to intercede in his behalf. It was even attempted to intimidate the Scots by movements of troops; but all was useless. Elizabeth was not willing to wage war for the sake of saving Morton's life; he was condemned, and perished upon the scaffold. The young Duke of Lennox and James Stuart, who had become Earl of Arran, governed the kingdom in the name of James VI.

This revolution in Scotland, this resistance to the pressure of Elizabeth and even of the Protestant princes of the continent, revived the hopes of the Catholics. James had been brought up with great care in the Protestant religion. His tutor, George Buchanan, a learned and able man, was specially distinguished for his attainments in theology, and had inspired the young king with a taste for that science; but it was hoped that the Catholic blood of the Guises would assert itself, and that the desire of delivering his mother might inspire in the young monarch opinions favorable to the intrigues which were still forming on her behalf. The Earl of Arran, who wished to supplant Lennox in James's favor, lent himself to these manœuvres. Queen Mary offered to legalize the irregular accession of her son, and to abdicate in his favor. But at the moment when the agents of the Catholic party abroad brought to James the subsidies of the Pope and of Spain, he was lured into the residence of the Earl of Gowrie, son of the old Ruthven, and suddenly found himself a prisoner there. The power fell again entirely into the hands of the Protestant lords. Arran was cast into prison. Lennox fled to France, where he perished shortly afterwards, and Queen Mary, trembling for her only son, wrote to Elizabeth to implore her to preserve the young king's life. James had already succeeded in delivering himself from the snares of his enemies; he had promised pardon, he was free, and lived in the midst of a crowd of contradictory and confused intrigues which occasionally embarrassed even the penetration of Walsingham, who had been sent to Scotland by Queen Elizabeth. However, the presence of the son upon the throne of Scotland had awakened the hopes of the mother in her prison, as well as the ardor of her friends in England and on the Continent. A number of isolated Catholic plots, of no serious importance, were constantly renewed and were inevitably followed by torture and the gallows. The penal laws against Catholic priests were applied with an extreme rigor, often favored by public opinion, which saw in them so many conspirators. The most celebrated victim of this persecution was the Jesuit Campion, a distinguished and able man, whose execution excited a certain amount of compassion. Burleigh was compelled to exculpate himself from the charge of putting him to the torture. The wooden horse had been applied so gently, he affirmed, that the Jesuit had been able to walk at once, and to sign his confession. The prisons were filled with Catholics: those whom the persecutors dared not send to the gallows sometimes died there of grief and physical suffering. This was the case with the Earl of Arundel, son of the Duke of Norfolk, formerly in great favor with Elizabeth. Having become a Catholic and fallen into disgrace, he had been arrested when endeavoring to escape: being thrown into the Tower, he languished there for several years, and finally died without being permitted to see his wife and children again. The formidable abuses of absolute power manifested themselves all the more vigorously, because the strong intellect of Burleigh had not, any more than that of his mistress, conceived the least idea of the rights of conscience. While Elizabeth was forbidding Catholic priests to say mass until as late as 1589, she continued to expel the nonconformist ministers from their livings, and caused heretics and anabaptists to be burned. A circumstance which aggravated the situation of the Catholics was the suspicion, very often well founded, that they had a secret understanding with foreign powers, and mixed politics with their religious interests. In 1584, the ambassador of Spain, Mendoza, received his passports and quitted the kingdom, much compromised by the revelations of Francis Throgmorton, who was condemned to death for having conspired against the queen, with the object of delivering Mary Stuart. Parliament voted fresh measures against the Catholic priests; these measures were attacked by a Welsh member named Parry, and he was sent to the Tower; whereupon his confessions were so complete, he denounced so many accomplices, he revealed dangers so imminent, that he was suspected of being simply a tool of the Protestant party, employed to prove the peril which surrounded the queen. But if Parry had counted upon pardon, he was mistaken; he was executed on the 25th of February, 1585, retracting at the last moment all his revelations, and exclaiming upon the scaffold, "God grant that in taking my life Queen Elizabeth may not have killed the best keeper in her park." It was supposed that Parry was mad, but his accusations had agitated the Catholics, who protested loudly against any disloyal project, and in particular against the theory of *permissible assassination*, which Parry had attributed to their Church. The gentleman who presented this protest to the queen was cast into prison, where he died. A Protestant association was formed to protect the life of her Majesty, and to avenge her death in case of crime. The Earl of Leicester placed himself at the head of this movement, which received the sanction of Parliament. Mary Stuart looked upon this league as her death-warrant; she trembled, with good reason, in her prison, for her son made no effort in her favor; he was negotiating with the Queen of England a treaty of alliance against the Catholic powers, without the name of Mary

HOLYROOD PALACE.

NAVAL ENGAGEMENT, TIME OF ELIZABETH.

being once mentioned between them. In reply to Mary's pathetic appeals James VI. had contented himself with replying that she was Queen-Mother, and had nothing to do with the affairs of Scotland. "I love my mother, as I ought, by duty and by nature," he said to the French ambassador, "but I cannot approve of her conduct, and I know that she wishes no more good to me than to the Queen of England." The end of the long drama was approaching.

The Protestant policy had completely gained the ascendant in the councils of Elizabeth: she was still officially at peace with Spain; but for many years her great admirals, Drake, Hawkins, and Sir Walter Raleigh, furnished with letters of marque, scoured the seas, seizing all Spanish vessels which they encountered, pillaging at times Spanish towns, and constantly invading the Spanish settlements in America. For a long while, moreover, the cause of liberty in the Low Countries had been secretly protected by the money and assistance of Elizabeth, and she had just now conspicuously lent her support to it by sending an army of six thousand men, under the orders of the Earl of Leicester, to carry on the war which, a year before, on the 10th of July, 1584, had lost its illustrious chief, William the Silent, beneath the dagger of Balthazar Gérard, an assassin in the pay of Philip II. The Queen of England had again declined the Protectorate of the United Provinces; but she had accepted as a pledge of her close alliance with that rising state the surrender of the towns of Brill and Flushing. Acting independently, and without consulting the queen, Leicester even went so far as to cause himself to be appointed governor by the States-general of the Low Countries. But he had presumed too much upon his past influence over Elizabeth; she had never forgiven him for his marriage with the Countess of Essex; he had gained no success in the Low Countries; his military talents were no greater than was his political skill. The queen became so angry that it caused much uneasiness to the members of the council; great difficulty was experienced in preventing her from recalling Leicester at once, and the States-general, who believed themselves giving satisfaction to the court of England, soon perceived with grief that Elizabeth was growing cold to their cause.

A fresh effort was in preparation in Queen Mary's behalf, the last link in the long succession of plots which were to bring her to the scaffold. Anthony Babington, a young man of good family, a fervent Catholic, rich, and for a long while devoted to the unhappy captive, engaged in a project of conspiracy, supported, it was said, by the Duke of Parma, Alexander Farnèse, who was to make a descent upon England as soon as Queen Elizabeth's death should have been brought about. Babington was desirous of delivering Mary Stuart and placing her upon the throne; he paid little heed to the means proposed to him by Savage, the prime mover in the plot, and he gathered around him a few friends as bold and imprudent as himself. It appears certain that from this point Walsingham was aware of the conspiracy, but he allowed matters to proceed until Queen Mary had written twice to Babington. As soon as the captive was compromised, the accomplices were all arrested. Savage and Babington alone had desired and plotted the murder of the queen; a few of the conspirators had contemplated only the deliverance of Mary Stuart, others had limited themselves to keeping silence concerning the conspiracy. "It is my cruel destiny," exclaimed Jones before the tribunal, "that I should betray my friend whom I love as myself, or fail in my allegiance and become a false friend or a miserable traitor. My tender feeling for Thomas Salisbury has ruined me, but God knows that I meditated no treason." The less guilty among the conspirators were condemned to be hanged; the chiefs of the conspiracy suffered the horrible punishment of traitors. They were so young and of such good appearance that their punishment caused a certain degree of emotion in London. These were the last victims of the beauty and misfortunes of Mary Stuart.

The captive queen had been transferred from prison to prison, each day more closely confined, each day treated with less consideration and respect. She had at one time reproached Lord Shrewsbury for too much severity, but she felt herself protected by his honor; Lord Shrewsbury was no longer her guardian: she was intrusted to Sir Amyas Pawlet and Sir Drew Drury, fierce Protestants, almost Puritans, who felt no pity for the corrupt, murderous, and idolatrous woman whom they held in their hands. A few days before the arrest of Babington, Mary had been removed from Chartley Castle in Staffordshire; when she was taken back there, she found all her cabinets open, her papers abstracted; her two secretaries, De Naou and Curle, had been taken to London. She looked for a moment at the havoc, then turning towards Pawlet, "There are two things, sir, which you cannot take from me," she said, with dignity: "the royal blood which gives me the right to the succession, and the attachment which unites me to the faith of my ancestors." Alas! Mary would have been glad to buy back her life and liberty at the price of her ancestral faith; she had once made this offer to Elizabeth, but the approach of a death which she felt to be inevitable brought her back to the real convictions of her soul. Amid all the faults and crimes of her life she had been sincerely a Catholic; purified by long sufferings, she was to die a Catholic, leaving to a rival whose life she had imbittered the odious stain of her execution.

Parliament had passed a law, which, without naming Mary, condemned her by anticipation. Elizabeth's council urged the queen to place the captive upon trial. The repeated plots of which she had been the occasion, the inexhaustible interest which she excited in Europe, appeared to Burleigh, Walsingham, and Sadler, sufficient reasons for Mary's destruction. Elizabeth hesitated, irresolute and perplexed; she foresaw, perhaps better than her councillors, the harm which would come to her from the death of her relative, a person who had taken refuge under her protection and was defenceless in her hands. Leicester, who had recently returned to England, proposed to have recourse to poison; Walsingham openly opposed this suggestion; he was specially intrusted with the matter. Burleigh was old, and perhaps, like the queen, was reluctant to strike the final blow; but Walsingham insisted upon a trial in due form and a public condemnation. "That conduct is alone worthy of your Grace," he said. He carried with him the majority of the council, and the queen nominated a commission to try "her good sister, the Queen of Scots," according to the new law of Parliament, against "any person claiming the succession who might have encouraged or supported plots, invasions, or attempts against the safety of the kingdom and the person of the queen." It was scarcely necessary to bring together the great names which formed the commission to sign a sentence which was already written in the law itself.

Mary had quitted Chartley, and had been brought, a few days after the execution of Babington, to Fotheringay Castle, in Northamptonshire. Here the commissioners arrived on the 11th of October, 1586, the bearers of a letter from Queen Elizabeth, which informed the captive that she was compromised in the recent conspiracy, and that she was about to be tried upon that count, as well as upon several others, according to the laws of England, under the protection of which she had lived. Mary was old before her time, feeble, and overwhelmed with sorrows, but her royal pride was aroused by this arrogant claim on the part of her rival. "Whereas the queen hath written," she replied, "that I am subject to the laws of England, and to be judged by them because I have lived under the protection of them, I answer that I came into England to crave aid, and ever since have been detained in prison, and could not enjoy the protection or benefit of the laws of England; nay, I could never yet understand from any man, what manner of laws these were. But I will not derogate from the honor of my ancestors, kings of Scotland, by submitting to be tried as the subject of my sister of England, and as a criminal." The commissioners were before her when she made this protest. "We will try you then as absent and contumacious," said Burleigh. "Look to your conscience, and remember that the theatre of the whole world is much wider than the kingdom of England," replied Mary. "Show your innocency," insisted the vice-chamberlain, Hatton, "lest, by avoiding trial, you draw upon yourself suspicion, and lay upon your reputation an eternal blot and infamy." Mary at length yielded, on condition that her protest should be admitted. Protestation and resistance were alike useless.

On the 14th of October, the commissioners assembled in the great hall of Fotheringay Castle. A throne, with a canopy, occupied the place of Queen Elizabeth; lower down a chair without a canopy awaited Queen Mary. The judges were surrounded by their assistants, and furnished with tables for their documents. The accused queen had neither counsel, advocates, nor documents; but her pride, her skill, her presence of mind sufficed, for two days, to hold in check the ablest lawyers of England. It was no longer a question of defending herself against past accusations, the murder of her husband, or her complicity with Bothwell; she was accused of having participated in plots for the overthrow and death of the Queen of England, and, notwithstanding her denials, it is difficult for history to exculpate her of this crime. She had probably been implicated in conspiracies against Elizabeth even at the time when she was yet a sovereign and free. What a temptation to take part in them when she was detained a prisoner, in defiance of justice as well as of royal hospitality! The lovely eyes which had made so many victims were now dulled, the elegant figure bent; but the subtile wit, the stately grace, the infinite seductiveness, which had been the danger and the charm of Mary Stuart, existed still. She covered her face with her hands when the Earl of Arundel, still in prison in the Tower, was mentioned. "Alas!" she exclaimed, "what hath that noble House of the Howards endured for my sake!" She had asked that her two secretaries, whose depositions had been read, should be brought before her. They were in London, and she challenged the authenticity of their testimony, as well as that of a letter written, it was said, by her, to provoke an invasion of England; which letter, she declared, she believed to be the work of Walsingham, "to bring her to her death." The secretary rose, protesting that he had never acted through malice, and had done nothing which was unworthy of an honest man. He, no doubt, congratulated himself inwardly on having rejected the proposal of poison put forth by the Earl of Leicester. The weight of the accusations rested upon the recent conspiracy of Babington and upon the testimony of the two secretaries. Mary demanded to be heard by Parliament and to see the queen in person. The instructions of the commissioners were positive. Elizabeth was not willing to see the captive. When the judges quitted Fotheringay and assembled at Westminster, the witnesses were summoned before them, but the accused was not there. On the 25th of October, 1586, in the Star Chamber, the commissioners declared that Mary Stuart, daughter of James V., known under the name of Queen of Scotland, had taken part in the conspiracy of Anthony Babington and in several others, to the prejudice of and against the life of her Majesty the Queen of England, in the name and under the pretext of her pretended rights to the crown; consequent upon which, she was condemned to death, without this sentence being in any wise prejudicial to James VI., King of Scotland, who retained all his rights and privileges as though the said condemnation had not existed.

The sentence was pronounced, but Elizabeth hesitated to put it in execution, as she had hesitated to bring her royal cousin to trial. Parliament made an effort to deliver her from the odious responsibility which she dreaded, and on the 12th of November the two Houses implored the queen to provide for her own safety, by causing, as soon as possible, the deserved punishment to fall upon the criminal. Elizabeth replied to her faithful subjects, asserting the absence of any rancor in her soul: "If we were two milk-maids, with pails upon our arms, and it was merely a question which involved my own life, without endangering the religion and welfare of my people, I would willingly pardon all her offences." She prayed God to enlighten her upon the course to follow, promising to make known her resolution within a short time. In the meanwhile she caused the two Houses, through the chancellor, to be asked whether there were not some means of placing her life in safety without interfering with that of Mary. Parliament replied in the negative. But Elizabeth's hesitations were not yet at an end; a fresh speech expounded her scruples to her people. "I have," she said, "since first I came to the crown of this realm, seen many defamatory books and pamphlets against me, accusing me to be a tyrant. Well fare the writers' hearts: I believe their meaning was to tell me news. And news indeed it was to me to be branded with the note of tyranny. But what is it which they will not write now, when they shall hear that I have given consent that the executioner's hands should be imbrued in the blood of my nearest kinswoman? But so far am I from cruelty that, to save mine own life, I would not offer her violence; neither have I been so careful how to prolong mine own life as how to preserve both, which that it is now impossible, I grieve exceedingly. I am not so void of judgment as not to see mine own perils before mine eyes; nor so mad to sharpen a sword to cut mine own throat; nor so careless as not to provide for the safety of mine own life. And now for your petition. I pray you for this present to content yourselves with an answer without answer. Your judgment I condemn not; neither do I mistake your reasons, but pray you to accept my thankfulness, excuse my doubtfulness, and take in good part my answer answerless. If I should say I would not do what you request, I might perhaps say more than I think. And if I should say I would do it, I might plunge myself into peril, whom you labor to preserve." The sentence of death was, however, posted up in all parts of London, and greeted with cries of joy by the populace.

Lord Buckhurst had been chosen to announce her condemnation to Mary; it was hoped that some confession might be obtained from her, in her agitation and despair at approaching death. But whatever might have been Mary's crimes in the past, and her misdeeds towards Queen Elizabeth, her courage had not relaxed in misfortune, and it did not fail her at the supreme hour. A bishop had accompanied the fatal messenger; the queen refused to see him, asking for her chaplain. "I am a-weary of this world," she said, "and glad that my troubles are about to end." She repeated that she had never taken part in any plot against the life of Elizabeth, and her last care was to write to the Pope and to the Archbishop of Glasgow to enjoin that her reputation should be cleared of all stain, it was a task above the power of those to whom it was intrusted by this unfortunate woman, who could not appeal to her son to defend her. As a condemned criminal, the Queen of Scots was now deprived of all the honors which had hitherto been rendered to her. Her jailer, Sir Amyas Pawlet, sat down in her presence without permission.

"I am an anointed queen," said the fallen sovereign; "in spite of the Queen of England, her council, and her heretical judges, I will still die a queen." Mary's last letter to Elizabeth was truly a royal epistle, without complaints or recriminations, thanking God that He had deigned to put an end to a sorrowful pilgrimage, and asking no other favor than that of dying in the presence of her servants, to whom she begged the queen to cause to be given the small legacies indicated in her will. It was in the name of Jesus Christ, of their kinship, of the memory of Henry VII., their ancestor, and of the royal dignity which was common to them, that the captive, about to die, proudly besought these trifling favors from her triumphant rival.

The King of France, Henry III., had not absolutely abandoned his sister-in-law in her extremity; he sent to the court of England an ambassador extraordinary to plead her cause. Elizabeth delayed before giving him an audience; when she admitted him into her presence, with great ceremony, it was not without emotion that she affirmed that the Queen of Scots had three times attempted her life. All Bellièvre's arguments were useless; when he declared that his sovereign would consider as a cause of rupture the execution of a dowager queen of France, Elizabeth became angry. The envoy received his passports. The resident ambassador, M. de l'Aubespine, accused of being implicated in a fresh conspiracy against the queen's life, saw his secretary cast into prison. A third emissary was no more successful.

While he was interceding for Mary with the Queen of England, King Henry III. was endeavoring to awaken in the breast of James VI. the natural feelings of a son for his mother. What severer condemnation of the conduct of the King of Scotland can be imagined than the fact that it shocked and scandalized Henry III.! He succeeded in obtaining a preliminary mission to Elizabeth, but by a personage of so little importance, and so deep in the interests of England, that France was not satisfied with this proceeding, which had, nevertheless, aroused the anger of Queen Elizabeth. James hastened to write to her, excusing himself humbly, alleging that he in no wise imputed to her the blame of what had been done against his mother. Sir Robert Melville accompanied the second embassy. "Why does the Queen of Scots seem so dangerous to you?" asked the emissaries. "Because she is a Papist, and they say she shall succeed to my throne," said Elizabeth bluntly. "Does her Grace still live?" said Melville tremblingly. "I think so," replied the queen, "but I would not answer for it in an hour." Mary's old servant interceded passionately for her, but his colleague, Gray, assured the ministers that it was not a dangerous affair, adding coarsely, "A dead woman does not bite." Walsingham was seriously astonished that a Protestant monarch like James should not feel that his mother's existence was incompatible with the safety of the Reformed churches in England and Scotland. The king recalled his ambassadors, and contented himself with recommending his mother to the prayers of all his subjects; the greater number of the Presbyterian pastors refused obedience to his orders.

Elizabeth had repelled all foreign interventions; and still she hesitated; she was heard to mutter to herself in Latin,

Aut fer aut feri, that is, "Either bear strokes, or strike;" and, *Ne feriare, feri*, "Strike, lest thou be stricken." The warrant had been ready for six weeks, when the queen signed it, in private, on the 1st of February, consigning it to the secretary of state, Davison, "without other orders," as she subsequently asserted. She made the suggestion that Sir Amyas Pawlet might have spared her all this trouble, and she commanded that he should be written to in that strain. Pawlet refused in set terms, saying that his property and life were at her Majesty's disposal, but that God did not permit him to sacrifice his conscience, nor to leave an infamous stain upon his name. None would incur the responsibility of the crime; the queen did not even command the warrant to be sent. It went, however, without her having informed herself on the subject: a precaution which was useful to her subsequently. On the 7th of February, while the scaffold was being erected in the court-yard of Fotheringay, Elizabeth told Davison that he must write again to Sir Amyas. "It is useless, I think," began the secretary. She did not allow him time to explain himself, and turned towards one of her ladies who was entering. Davison was never to see his mistress again.

The Earl of Shrewsbury had arrived at Fotheringay. Queen Mary immediately understood what the arrival of the Earl-Marshal meant. When the sentence had been read, Mary made the sign of the cross, and said tranquilly that death was welcome, but that she had not expected, after having been detained twenty years in prison, that her sister Elizabeth would thus dispose of her. She at the same time placed her hand upon a book beside her, swearing that she had never contemplated nor sought the death of Elizabeth. "That is a Popish Bible," exclaimed the Earl of Kent brutally; "your oath is of no value." "It is a Catholic testament," said the captive, "and therefore, my lord, as I believe that to be the true version, my oath is the more to be relied on;" and she asked what would be the time of the execution. "To-morrow, at eight o'clock," said Lord Salisbury, in great agitation. "Your death will be the life of our religion," said Kent; "as, contrariwise, your life would have been its death." The queen smiled bitterly. She was left alone with her servants: she bade farewell to them, drinking to their health at her last repast, and asking pardon of them all. She passed a portion of the night in writing to her confessor, to the King of France, and to the Duke of Guise. At eight o'clock the sheriff of the county entered the oratory where she was at prayer; she rose immediately, took the crucifix from the altar, and advanced with a firm step; she was clad in the rich and sober costume of a dowager queen. At the door of the antechamber she found her faithful servant, Melville, who for three weeks had waited in vain to be permitted to see her. He threw himself upon his knees before her, weeping and sobbing. "Cease to lament, good Melville," said the queen, "for thou shalt now see a final period to Mary Stuart's troubles; the world, my servant, is all but vanity, and subject to more sorrow than an ocean of tears can wash away. But I pray thee, take this message when thou goest, that I die true to my religion, to Scotland, and to France. Commend me to my son, and tell him that I have done nothing to prejudice the kingdom of Scotland." She asked that her servants might be present at her execution. The Earl of Kent refused; she insisted with warmth. "I know my sister Elizabeth would not have denied me so small a matter," she said, "that my women might be present even for honor of womanhood." The point was conceded: two of the ladies of the queen accompanied her to the scaffold, as well as Melville and a few servants. When the sentence had been read, Mary reminded the spectators that she was

MARY STUART SWEARING SHE HAD NEVER SOUGHT THE LIFE OF ELIZABETH.

a sovereign princess, and had nothing to do with the laws of England; that she died by injustice and violence, without ever having conspired against the life of Elizabeth. The Dean of Peterborough began a discourse; the queen interrupted him several times. "I am fixed in the ancient religion," she said, "and by God's grace, I will shed my blood for it." Seeing that she could not impose silence upon him, she turned round looking away from him; but he followed her movements, and proceeded to place himself in front of her. While he prayed aloud in English, the queen repeated in Latin, with profound contrition, the Penitential Psalms. When the dean had finished, she prayed aloud in English for the Church, her son, and Queen Elizabeth. She kissed the crucifix; the Earl of Kent exclaimed, "Madam, you had better put such Popish trumpery out of your hand, and carry Christ in your heart." "I can hardly bear this emblem in my hand without at the same time bearing Him in my heart," said the queen. The executioners had laid hands upon her to undress her; as her women burst into sobs in their indignation, she placed a finger at her lips and embraced them, saying to the spectators, "I am not used to be undressed by such attendants, nor to put off my clothes before so much company." Her eyes were bound with a handkerchief embroidered with gold, and the executioners conducted her to the block. She laid her head upon it without trembling. "Into thy hands, O Lord, I commend my spirit," she said aloud. The executioner was more agitated than the victim; he was obliged to strike three times. When he raised the bleeding head, exclaiming, "God save Queen Elizabeth!" the dean and the Earl of Kent alone replied, "Thus perish all her enemies." No one said "Amen." The queen's little lapdog had hidden himself in her clothing, nor could he be separated from the body while it remained upon the scaffold.

The news of the execution had spread abroad in London, and many people were manifesting their joy thereat, before any one had dared to announce the fact to the queen. She feigned great anger, shedding tears, and asserting that she had given no order. The secretary of state, Davison, was sent to the Tower; Burleigh and the other ministers were disgraced. Walsingham had been prudent enough to absent himself; when he reappeared, his colleagues were not long in returning into favor; but a victim was necessary. Davison remained in prison during all the remainder of the reign of Elizabeth, and his whole fortune was confiscated to pay the fine which was imposed upon him.

Elizabeth's first care had been to communicate to King James the grief which she experienced at the unhappy event which had occurred without her knowledge in her kingdom. The king wept on learning the death of his mother, asserting that he would move heaven and earth in his vengeance. His anger, however, was soon appeased: the pension which he received from Elizabeth was increased; one of the obstacles which might impede his succession to the throne of England had disappeared. The royal aspirant consoled himself with this expectation. "Could an only son forget his mother?" Mary Stuart had asked on learning her condemnation. The conduct of King James proved that it was possible.

King Henry III. would have been much embarrassed to accomplish his threats and to wage war in England to avenge his unhappy sister-in-law. He was groaning under the yoke of the League and of the Guises, and no doubt easily forgave Elizabeth the blow which she had struck at the haughty House of Lorraine. L'Aubespine reproached Elizabeth for the assistance which she had so long been giving to Henry of Navarre. "I have done nothing against your sovereign," said the queen, resorting to her former argument; "I support the

MARY STUART.

King of Navarre against the Duke of Guise." L'Aubespine did not persist.

For a long time past, the expeditions of the English buccaneers in the West Indies had completed the exasperation caused to Philip II. by the assistance which Elizabeth furnished to the rebels of the Low Countries. The death of Queen Mary supplied him with a natural pretext for the explosion of this resentment. The Queen of England made some efforts to propitiate him as she had propitiated the kings of France and Scotland. In the Netherlands her arms had not been triumphant. Leicester was the weakest and the most incompetent of the generals, and during his absence in England, to assist in the condemnation of Mary Stuart, a body of his troops, commanded by malcontent officers, had restored Deventer to the King of Spain, passing over at the same time into his service. The earl's return into the Low Countries did not repair matters. The Dutch were discontented and uneasy; the queen recalled her forces, retaining merely the hostage towns, and she accepted the provisional appointment of Maurice of Nassau, son of William the Silent, as stadtholder of the United Provinces. She had even opened a secret negotiation with the Duke of Parma, who still held out in the Low Countries; but while endeavoring to preserve peace, she understood that war was becoming imminent, and the great preparations in which the King of Spain was employed were not unknown to her. As a preliminary to hostilities, Sir Francis Drake was dispatched with a fleet of thirty vessels, and with orders to destroy, even in their ports, all the Spanish vessels which he might encounter. Never was mission executed with more satisfaction and success. On the 19th of April, 1587, the bold seaman forced the entrance of the port of Cadiz, where he destroyed thirty great vessels; then, following the coast-line as far as Cape St. Vincent, he captured, burnt, and sunk a hundred other ships, and destroyed on his way four fortresses. At length he entered the Tagus, recently become tributary to Philip II., who had taken possession of Portugal to console himself for the loss of Holland, and there took possession, under the very shadow of the Spanish standard, of the St. Philip, a ship of the largest size, laden with a precious cargo. The exploits of Drake delayed by more than a year the expedition which the King of Spain contemplated, and gave time to Elizabeth to complete her preparations. "I have singed the King of Spain's beard," said the victorious admiral on returning to England. Philip's anger redoubled under these insults. The Pope, Sixtus V., supplied him with money and renewed the bull of excommunication against Elizabeth. All the vessels of the kingdoms of Naples and Sicily were confiscated for the service of the king. The republic of Venice and that of Genoa lent him their fleets. In all the ports of Spain ships were in course of construction. A fleet of flat-bottomed vessels, prepared in Flanders, were to transport to England the Duke of Parma and his thirty thousand soldiers. The humblest Spanish sailor thought himself assured of the conquest of England. Philip II. promised himself the triumph of the Catholic faith in this haunt of heretics. We may doubt whether Pope Sixtus V. was equally sure of success. *Un gran cervello di principessa*, ("She has the mind of a great princess,") he often said in speaking of Elizabeth. But Europe, Protestant or Catholic, had not yet lost the habit of trembling before the power of Spain. All eyes were fixed upon England, against which so many preparations were going forward.

England, meanwhile, did not remain idle. In the month of November, 1587, the queen convoked a council of war, to which she summoned all her distinguished soldiers and the great sailors of that time, who were destined to be the founders of the English navy. Sir Walter Raleigh took a large share in the deliberations, and vigorously maintained the opinion that it was necessary both to meet the enemies at sea, and to prepare for them on land. Elizabeth's fleet was not large. She had not made war, and the money of which she could dispose did not suffice for the appeals which she received from all the Protestant countries of Europe, oppressed and struggling for their faith. Thirty-six vessels composed the royal navy, but merchant ships abounded. The country had greatly increased in wealth under the reign of Elizabeth; the devotion of her subjects provided for everything; private individuals fitted out merchant ships for war, and offered them to the queen, while the great seamen who had acquired experience and fame as buccaneers against the Spanish in all seas, — Drake, Hawkins, Frobisher, — took command of the vessels, under the orders of the High Admiral, Lord Howard of Effingham. One hundred and ninety-one ships were at length gathered together, and the Dutch sent to the assistance of their allies sixty more, manned by the fierce Zealanders, ever eager to fight against the Spaniards. The fleet was disposed in squadrons to cover the coasts, while the land forces, under the orders of Leicester, assembled from all parts to resist invasion. All the ancient fortifications were repaired, and new works were raised as if by magic. A camp was formed at Tilbury Fort, opposite Gravesend. The queen repaired thither herself to review the troops. Her subjects had vied with each other in devotion. Catholics as well as Protestants had generously responded to her appeal. The Catholic gentlemen, when a command had been refused them, enrolled themselves as common soldiers. One hundred and thirty thousand men had been raised in the different parts of the territory. When the queen assembled her forces at Tilbury, she had around her more than sixty thousand men.

The earls of Essex and Leicester marched at the bridle of her war-horse; she carried in her hand a marshal's baton. All her courage shone in her eyes. "My loving people," she said, "we have been persuaded by some that are careful for our safety to take heed how we commit ourselves to armed multitudes, for fear of treachery, but I assure you that I do not desire to live to distrust my faithful and loving people. Let tyrants fear! I have always so behaved myself that, under God, I have placed my chiefest strength and safeguard in the loyal hearts and good will of my subjects; and therefore I am come among you at this time, not as for my recreation and sport, but being resolved in the midst and heat of the battle to live or die among you all, to lay down for my God, for my kingdom, and for my people, my honor, and my blood even, in the dust. I know that I have but the body of a weak and feeble woman; but I have the heart of a king, and of a king of England too, and think it foul scorn that Parma or Spain should dare to invade the borders of my realms. To which rather than any dishonor shall grow by me I myself will take up arms." The popular enthusiasm was great, but the general alarm equalled the enthusiasm. The terrible reputation of the Spanish troops had preceded them. The raw recruits who formed the greater portion of the land forces would have been unable to resist the veterans of the Duke of Parma; but the English navy was destined to save England.

The Invincible Armada, as the Spaniards arrogantly called it, issued forth from the Tagus on the 29th of May, 1588. It numbered about one hundred and thirty ships, of which some were of very large size. The sea appeared to fight in favor of England; on their way to Corunna, where the fleet was to receive reinforcements, in the vicinity of Cape Finisterre, a storm arose which dispersed the squadron and destroyed a number of vessels. The news of the disaster arrived in England; the people thought themselves delivered from the enemy. Elizabeth, always economical, immediately wrote to Lord Howard to lay up four of the largest vessels of the fleet, and to discharge the crews. The admiral refused to do so, saying that he would rather pay them out of his private fortune. This was a most fortunate decision, for the Armada had reformed, and on the 19th of June it was signalled in the vicinity of Plymouth. It advanced majestically in the form of a crescent, covering the sea for an extent of three leagues. An immediate landing was expected, but the orders of Philip had been to approach the coast of Flanders, there to be reinforced by the Duke of Parma, his fleet and his soldiers. Lord Howard was following the enemy, in readiness to attack any ships separated from the squadron by accidents of the sea. Thus began a series of combats, all disastrous to the Spaniards, though often impeded on the side of the English by the failure of munitions. On the 22d, 23d, 24th, 25th, and 26th of July, Howard, Drake, Hawkins, Frobisher, engaged either in concert or separately, fought almost without intermission. On the 28th, at length, "this morris-dance upon the waters," as Sir Henry Wotton called it, was approaching its end. The Duke of Medina-Sidonia, a Spanish admiral, had sent for assistance to the Duke of Parma; he was in the vicinity of Calais, but the English vessels blockaded the Strait between Nieuport and Dunkirk. The Flemings could not pass, and a great battle began. The Spaniards presented a compact mass which impeded the movements of the English vessels, smaller than theirs. During the night, fire-ships were launched against them. The Spaniards had terrible experience of this method of warfare employed by the Dutch in the Scheldt; confusion set in among the ranks of the squadron. The vessels quitted their positions and crowded all sail to escape the explosion of the fire-ships; in vain did their admiral endeavor to reassemble them; the English attacked the isolated vessels at their ease. Everywhere minor encounters were going on; almost everywhere the English were the victors. The Duke of Medina-Sidonia decided to abandon the invasion, and return to Spain by doubling Scotland. The English pursued him. "We have the Spaniards before us," wrote Drake to Walsingham, "and mind, with the grace of God, to wrestle a pull with them. God grant that we have a good eye to the Duke of Parma, for with the grace of God, if we live, I doubt it not but ere it be long so to handle the matter with the Duke of Sidonia, as he shall wish himself at St. Mary's Port among his vine-trees." The failure of ammunition put an end to the pursuit, and the Spaniards were abandoned to the mercy of the sea. A terrible storm assailed them near the Orkney Islands. A great number of vessels went aground upon the coast of Scotland, and the crews were made prisoners. Those ships which were driven to Ireland did not save a single man. The English colonists cut them to pieces to prevent them from seconding the Irish insurrection. When the Duke of Medina-Sidonia returned, in the month of September, to Santander, in the Bay of Biscay, he had but sixty vessels left, and those in bad condition, while their crews, worn out with fatigue, looked like spectres. The English had lost but one ship of importance.

For some time people feared a descent of the Duke of Parma, "who," wrote Drake, "I take to be as a bear robbed of her whelps;" but the alarm soon subsided, and the queen caused the camp at Tilbury to be broken up. The army was disbanded, and the Earl of Leicester set out for his castle at Kenilworth. He died there, on the 4th of September, shortly after his arrival. The queen, whose favorite he had been for thirty years, did not appear greatly afflicted at his loss; she caused his effects to be sold at auction to pay his debts to the public treasury. She had chosen a new favorite, as yet almost a boy, the Earl of Essex, son-in-law of Leicester. The charm of his person, his gayety, and the frankness of his manners, amused Elizabeth. She was fifty-five years of age; Essex was not twenty, when, in 1587, she made him Knight of the Garter, and captain-general of the cavalry. At the death of Leicester, he was raised to the dangerous position of favorite at the court of an imperious, exacting woman, accustomed to the most extravagant flatteries, and, moreover, still vain of her beauty and personal charms. The greatness of Essex was to cost him dearly.

A fruitless expedition to Spain, in favor of Don Antonio, who aspired to the crown of Portugal, did more honor to the bravery of the Earl of Essex than to his military talents. When he returned to England, he imprudently entered into a fierce struggle against the influence of the Cecils. Walsingham had died, in 1590, and Burleigh desired the vacant place for his son, Robert Cecil. Essex supported the cause of the unhappy Davison, unjustly disgraced for several years; the queen gave the office to Burleigh, authorizing him to employ his son as his assistant. Hence arose a constant hostility which was to end in the ruin of Essex. Elizabeth had often differed in opinion from her great minister, she had been rude to him, had ill-used him, and contradicted him, but none had ever succeeded in destroying his influence with her. Leicester had attempted it in vain. Essex strove in his turn to do it, and with as little chance of success. The queen knew to whom she owed in great measure the prosperity of her reign, and the memory of the father was destined later to increase in her eyes the services and the merits of the son.

The Earl of Essex consoled himself for his defeat at court by setting out for France at the head of the troops sent by

Elizabeth to the assistance of Henry of Navarre, now become Henry IV., King of France. Henry III. had been stabbed by Jacques Clément, on the 21st of July, 1589, and since then, his legitimate successor had been laboring to obtain his kingdom from the Leaguers, obedient to the Duke of Guise, and supported by Spain. Henry was besieging Rouen when the Earl of Essex joined him, at the head of the English reinforcements. He distinguished himself in skirmishes, in one of which his brother, Walter Devereux, was killed: but the impatient fondness of his mistress recalled him to England. Duplessis-Mornay advised Henry IV. to send Essex back to the queen, if he wished to obtain of the latter fresh aids in men and money, which were becoming every day more necessary against the Duke of Parma, who had recently entered France. The war was popular in England, and English gentlemen had always been eager to enroll themselves in the ranks of the Huguenots. The queen had been for a long while the faithful ally of Henry of Navarre. When he decided, in 1593, to secure the peace of his kingdom and the establishment of his throne by abjuring Protestantism, the indignation in England was violent. Elizabeth accused the king of treachery, but the Edict of Nantes soon satisfied the English Protestants by assuring to their brethren the free exercise of their religion, and the hostilities which continued between France and Spain served Elizabeth's policy too well for her to withdraw from her ally the efficacious support which she had always given to him. The moment would not have been propitious for abandoning him; for the Spanish armies had again penetrated France, and in the month of April, 1596, the Archduke Albert of Austria took possession of Calais, which Elizabeth claimed of Henry IV. in return for her services. Amiens, Doullens, Cambray, were captured in succession. "I have enacted the King of France long enough,"

G. Staal del.

Ferd. Delannoy sc.

HENRI IV.

Estes and Lauriat Boston.

exclaimed Henry IV., on placing himself at the head of his troops; "it is time to play the part of King of Navarre," referring to his early renown as a soldier; and he repulsed and defeated his enemies, while Queen Elizabeth, carrying war along the coast, sent the Earl of Essex to Spain with Sir Walter Raleigh. The fleet commanded by Lord Howard bombarded Cadiz. Essex stormed the town and took possession of it; he would have been glad to retain his prize, but, the council of England not approving of that measure, Cadiz was delivered up to the flames before the English weighed anchor to return to their country. A second expedition, directed against the Azores, had but little result. The influence of the Cecils with the queen was still hostile to Essex, notwithstanding an apparent reconciliation. The earl withdrew to Wanstead House, occupied by his wife, the daughter of Walsingham, and widow of the celebrated Sir Philip Sydney, the Christian hero of the chivalry of the sixteenth century, slain at thirty years of age, before Zutphen. The jealousy and the affection of the queen soon recalled Essex to court; he was appointed earl-marshal.

Notwithstanding the opposition of England, the King of France had concluded, in 1598, with Philip II., the treaty of Verdun, and Sir Robert Cecil, who had been sent to Paris, brought back the Spanish proposals for peace. Essex, who only lived for war, and who could not exert his authority at other times, vigorously opposed these overtures. The queen was not in favor of peace, but the Cecils dwelt upon the embarrassments of the situation, upon the gravity of affairs in Ireland, upon the distress of the treasury. Burleigh, drawing from his pocket a book of Psalms, showed this prophetic verse: "The bloodthirsty man shall not live out half his days." The quarrel became bitter. Essex lost his temper, and being reprimanded by the queen, turned his back upon her. Elizabeth started up and gave a box on the ear to her insolent subject. Essex had his hand upon his sword. "I would not have taken such an affront from the hands of the king, her father," he said, "and I will not accept it of a petticoat." Lord Howard grasped his arm, and the earl impetuously quitted the council, and at once proceeded to Wanstead, where he remained in retirement four months. When he reappeared at the court, still apparently powerful, Burleigh was gone: he died on the 4th of August, 1598, at the age of seventy-eight. His loss had caused the queen bitter tears. Sir Robert Cecil, able and sagacious, but less upright than his father, and less faithfully attached to the interests of the queen, could not replace with Elizabeth the sincere and steadfast union of the sovereign and the minister during forty years. The queen's great consolation at this period was the death of Philip II. The war soon languished, and peace being concluded at the end of the year 1598 between the Spaniards and the United Provinces, delivered Elizabeth from the enormous subsidies which she had for a long time furnished to her Dutch allies. The States-general acknowledged their debt towards her Majesty, and undertook to discharge it by degrees. People in England were now only occupied with the plots, real or imaginary, which were discovered every day against the queen's life, some devised, it was said, by the Catholics, who still groaned under the weight of very oppressive penal laws, others attributed to the Spanish influence. The King of Scotland was even accused of a project of assassination. He defended himself warmly against the charge. The queen wrote to him that she could not believe him guilty; but her confidence in his honor was so like a pardon for the alleged crime, that King James was not content, and demanded the trial of the accused, one Valentine Thomas. The court of England contented itself with detaining in prison the wretch who had

ELIZABETH ROSE AND GAVE A BOX ON THE EAR TO ESSEX.

dared to tarnish the name of James VI.; when the latter succeeded to the throne, he gave himself the pleasure of sending Valentine to the gallows.

The condition of Ireland had for a long while occupied the thoughts of Queen Elizabeth and her ministers. A serious insurrection at the beginning of the reign had for a moment placed Shane O'Neil at the head of all the Irish of pure race. He had been betrayed and assassinated, but his country had not been subjugated. The projects of colonization of the Earl of Essex, father of Elizabeth's favorite, and encouraged by her, had not succeeded better than the devastating campaigns of the Lords-Lieutenant, Sir Henry Sidney and Lord Fitzwilliam. The English had undertaken to civilize Ireland by destroying its inhabitants, as they had undertaken to establish Protestantism by prohibiting the Catholic worship in a country entirely devoted to that religion. Both efforts had justly failed, and the jealous rivalries of the Irish noblemen, the ever-recurring quarrels of the Butlers and the Fitzgeralds, the revolts, the submissions, the arrests, the murders of the chiefs of these two houses, the rival pretensions of the Earls of Ormond and Desmond, wearied the patience of the queen and council, exhausted the public treasury, and kept alive the hopes of the enemies of England. Two adventurers, Stuckely and Fitzmaurice, conceived the idea of taking advantage of the papal pretensions to the possession of the islands, to attempt a bold stroke upon Ireland. They had obtained a bull relieving the Irish of their allegiance to Elizabeth, besides assistance in money, a few soldiers, and some arms. Stuckely remained in Portugal, and perished at the battle of Alcazar against the Moors; but Fitzmaurice, brother of the Earl of Desmond, landed in Ireland, in 1579, in the hope of bringing about an insurrection. He was coldly received, and compelled to take refuge at the residence of his brother.

A reinforcement of pontifical soldiers, besieged in the fortress of Smerwick, were put to the sword by Sir Walter Raleigh. The Earl of Desmond, suspected of having taken part in the insurrection, was beheaded by the English troops, who seized him in a hut; Lord Grey de Wilton, who had become Lord-Lieutenant, restrained the revolt with a hand of iron, without obtaining any amelioration in the moral or material situation of the country. Sir John Perrot succeeded him in 1585; as severe as Lord Grey, but more just, he had had the misfortune to give himself up, in a fit of exasperation, to bitter words, not only against the queen, but against her "dancing chancellor," Hatton. The vengeance of the minister and the anger of the sovereign had appeared to slumber, but when Perrot, weary of asking in vain for assistance and money, had obtained his recall, he was accused of high treason, overwhelmed by the testimony of the men whose excesses he had restrained during his government, and soon condemned to death. His son had married a sister of Essex, and the influence of the earl counterbalanced that of his enemies. Grief or poison saved him from a death on the scaffold. He died on the 20th of June, 1591, at the moment when the position of the Earl of Tyrone, Hugh, son of O'Neil, Baron of Duncannon, was becoming important in Ireland. This nobleman was regarded by his fellow-citizens as the legitimate sovereign of Ulster. He claimed for his country liberty of conscience and the maintenance of the ancient local customs, — savage privileges quite incompatible with civilization. He also claimed all the estates which had formerly belonged to his ancestors. Handsome and skilful, he had been able to discipline his fierce soldiers, and he led them in battle array against the queen's troops. Sir John Norris had died of grief and anger. Sir Henry Bagnall had been defeated and killed at Blackwater, in County Tyrone, and the insurrection was spreading throughout the whole of Ireland. It was asserted that the Pope and the King of Spain had promised assistance to the rebels. In this perilous situation, the council of the queen decided that no other than the Earl of Essex should take the command of the army. For a long time he refused. The viceroys of Ireland had all suffered disgrace or death. He finally yielded to the personal entreaties of Elizabeth, and quitted London in the month of March, 1599, accompanied by the flower of the English nobility. His absence was to inflict upon him a mortal blow. The troops were dispatched slowly, ill armed, ill fed. In vain he demanded reinforcements. Sir Walter Raleigh and Sir Robert Cecil assured the queen that her general had no other desire than to prolong the war. When he entered the province of Ulster, the centre of the rebellion, he had not six thousand men with him. He concluded an armistice with the Earl of Tyrone, then, without waiting for permission, he embarked in haste for England. Immediately on his arrival in London, he repaired to the palace; the queen was at her toilet; he entered and threw himself upon his knees before her, kissing her hands. When he issued forth, he appeared radiant, congratulating himself that after having suffered stormy troubles and inward griefs while far from home, he had found peace and quietude again in his own country. On the morrow everything was changed. The earl received orders to remain a prisoner in his apartment. Sir John Harrington, who had accompanied Essex to Ireland, was summoned to appear before the queen. "She chafed much, walked to and fro, looked with discomposure in her visage," says Sir John, "and when I kneeled to her, she catched at my girdle, saying, 'By God's Son, I am no queen, that man is above me! Who gave him command to come here so soon? I did send him on other business.' She bade me go home; I did not stay to be bidden twice.

If all the Irish rebels had been at my heels I should not have made better speed." The next day Essex was summoned before the council. He replied with gravity and moderation. He was consigned into the custody of the Keeper of the Seals. All the affection of the queen for the earl appeared to have turned to anger. She forbade the friends, the physicians, and particularly the wife of the prisoner, to have any access to his person. Essex was ill and had been now detained for eight months, when in the month of May, 1600, he wrote to the queen, reminding her of her former favor, of which his enemies had been so jealous that they continued to hate him habitually, now that he was forgotten and thrown into a corner, like a dishonored corpse. On the 26th of August, liberty was restored to him, but orders were given to him not to appear at the court. Terrible is the intoxication of power and royal favor! Essex was a scholar; he had a taste for literature and the arts; he might have retired into the country, and hidden his disgrace. But he preferred to try his fortune once more. His secretary, Cuffe, an enterprising and unprincipled man, urged him to attempt by a bold stroke the ruin of his enemies. He was beloved by the population of London. An insurrection might rid him of Cecil, Raleigh, Cobham, the court party as they were called. The earl opened the doors of his house to all malcontents, and assembled together the officers who had served under him. He involved in his cause King James VI., asserting that Cecil and his friends were endeavoring to banish the Scottish king from the succession, in favor of the Infanta of Spain, Clara-Eugenia, daughter of Philip II., married to the Archduke Albert. Secret advices warned the earl that his projects were known to the council. He resolved to act. He was surrounded by his friends on Sunday, the 8th of February, 1601, preparing to march to the City, to rouse to insurrection the populace assembled at St. Paul's Cross, at the moment of the sermon, and thus make his way to the queen with the assistance of the mob. The Lord-Keeper Egerton and Sir William Knollys arrived at his house at the same moment, demanding an explanation of this noisy assemblage. "There is a plot against my life; letters have been forged in my name; men have been hired to murder me in my bed!" exclaimed Essex violently; then, as the magistrates promised justice, he conducted them into an inner room, and bolted the door upon them. Essex then hastened to the city with Lord Rutland, Lord Southampton, and a few others. The streets were deserted; there was no preaching at St. Paul's Cross. The citizens remained shut up in their houses in obedience to orders which the lord mayor and aldermen had received from the queen. Essex called every one to arms; none responded. He had great difficulty in getting back to his house, which he in vain endeavored to defend. At the sight of cannon levelled against the walls, he surrendered with his friends, and was conducted to the Tower with the Earl of Southampton. When the two noblemen appeared, on the 19th of February, before the House of Lords, Essex asserted that he had only obeyed the law of nature in defending his reputation and his life. The prosecution was supported by Francis Bacon, whose career was soon to present so strange a mixture of greatness and infamy. He owed his elevation to the friendship and the protection of the Earl of Essex. He was less violent than his colleague Coke, who accused the earl of having desired to raise an insurrection. "He would have called a Parliament, and a bloody Parliament would that have been, where my Lord of Essex that now stands all in black would have worn a bloody robe; but now in God's just judgment he of his earldom shall be Robert the Last, that of a kingdom thought to be Robert the First." All the arguments of Essex were demolished by Bacon, although Essex reminded the lawyer of the language which he had himself used regarding the party which he now supported. No witness was confronted with the accused, whose condemnation to death was unanimously pronounced by the peers.

When the usual question was put to the two earls, whether they knew any reason why they should not be condemned, Essex did not complain of the fate which awaited him. He was himself weary of life, he said, but he interceded warmly for his friend, Lord Southampton. He was urged to ask mercy of the queen. "Do not accuse me of pride," said the earl, "but I could not ask for mercy in that way, though with all humility I pray her Majesty's forgiveness. I would rather die than live in misery; I have cleared my accounts, and have forgiven all the world." A confession signed by Essex was circulated, but many people believed it to be forged. It was also asserted that he had expressly asked to be executed in secret, and the fact was formally denied by King Henry IV. "Quite the contrary," said that monarch, "he would have desired nothing so much as to die in public." The popularity of the Earl of Essex was dreaded, and the prolonged emotion which his death caused proved that this apprehension was not unfounded. He was beheaded on the 25th of February, 1691, at eight o'clock in the morning, in an outer court of the Tower. He was not thirty-three years of age. Sir Walter Raleigh witnessed the execution from a window, as well as that of several of the earl's friends. He did not know that the day would come in like manner when other eyes would in their turn come to contemplate his death. The Earl of Southampton remained in prison until the accession of King James, with whom he was soon in great favor.

If the King of Scotland had then found himself, as his mother had been, "under the protection of English law," he would have incurred serious dangers. His correspondence with Essex had compromised him so much that he felt compelled to send ambassadors to London to exculpate himself with Elizabeth. Sir Robert Cecil, faithful to the instinct of the courtier, who turns to the rising sun, was in the service of the King of Scotland. The queen was appeased, and augmented the pension of her successor. If the chroniclers do not wrong her, she had shortly before been concerned in a strange plot, in which the king had narrowly escaped perishing by the hand of the sons of the Earl of Gowrie, beheaded for rebellion in 1584. The queen and her destined successor had little liking for each other, and bitter recollections separated them. In dispatching his emissaries to London, the King of Scotland had recommended them to walk prudently between the two precipices of the queen and the people. The envoys were sufficiently skilful to secure the best of guides. It was then that Sir Robert Cecil began with King James a correspondence which would have cost him his head if his mistress had been aware of it. Less skilful, Sir Walter Raleigh and Lord Cobham did not contrive to gain in time the good graces of the future monarch, a fatal imprudence, as one of them afterwards found.

The war continued in Ireland, supported by a considerable body of Spaniards. Lord Mountjoy had shut them up in Kinsale and pressed the siege vigorously, when the Earl of Tyrone advanced at the head of six thousand Irish, to second his allies. He was repulsed after a desperate fight; the Spaniards were obliged to capitulate and to re-embark in their vessels. Mountjoy pursued Tyrone from one hiding-place to another, until he was compelled to surrender, towards the end of 1602. The expenses of the war were enormous; the queen convoked her Parliament for the last time in the month of October, 1601. She was sick and depressed; but she appeared before the Houses more magnificently attired than ever, and obtained considerable subsidies. The Commons, however, had determined to cause their favors to be paid for. They protested violently against the monopolies granted or sold by the Crown, which allowed the possessors to fix the price of articles of first necessity as suited them. The sale of wine, oil, salt, tin, steel, and coal, were each of them a monopoly. It was asked why bread was not on the list. "If no remedy is found for these," said a member, "bread will be there before the next Parliament." The discussion, formal and categorical in its nature, lasted four days. The ministers endeavored to defend the prerogative, but the Parliament held firm; the Puritan spirit had been constantly gaining ground during recent years, and the queen was compelled to yield. A promise was given to abolish the existing monopolies, and not to grant fresh ones. This engagement was not strictly kept, but the worst features of the evil had diminished. Elizabeth no longer governed as of old. The energy of her will yielded to the growing feebleness of her body. She had always been able to recognize the moment when concessions must be made; and she felt, besides, with bitter sorrow, that her popularity had decreased among the nation.

The day of complete decline was approaching. The anxieties of absolute power, remorse for past cruelties, regret for the death of the Earl of Essex, weighed upon that head bent with age and illness. Elizabeth sought no confidants; secret in her griefs as in her resolves, she bore alone the burden of her weariness; but the beginning of the year 1603 saw her strength diminishing day by day. She no longer showed herself in public, alleging the sorrow which she experienced at the recent death of the Countess of Nottingham. She no longer slept, and scarcely ate. "She remained seated upon cushions," wrote the French ambassador, at the beginning of March, "refusing to take any medicine or to lie down." Her eyes remained fixed upon the ground, and days elapsed without her saying a word. On the 21st of March her women put her to bed, and she listened attentively to the prayers of the Archbishop of Canterbury, Whitgift. On the morrow, the 22d of March, Cecil, the Lord Admiral, and the Lord Keeper of the Seals, approached the dying queen, begging her to name her successor. She trembled. "I tell you my seat has been the seat of kings; I will have no rascal to succeed me." The lords looked at each other, uncertain as to the meaning of her words. "I will that a king succeed me," she said; "and who but my nearest kinsman, the King of Scots?" "Is your Grace quite determined?" asked Cecil. She made a sign indicating Yes, asking that she should be left in peace. She had again seen the archbishop, and she was speechless when the lords of the council returned. "Will your Grace deign to make a sign to indicate if you have chosen the King of Scotland for your successor?" they asked again. She raised herself, and joined her hands above her head as though to form a crown. Then she sank back upon her pillows and died in the night of the 24th of March, 1603, without having uttered a word. She was nearly seventy, and had wielded the sceptre for forty-five years.

Throughout her reign Queen Elizabeth had willed and accomplished great things. She had governed England despotically, but was skilful, nevertheless, in observing the national tendencies and in yielding to them when resistance was becoming dangerous. Under the influence and upon the advice of her faithful minister, Lord Burleigh, she had often been the arbitrator of Europe, constantly the patron and protector of the persecuted Protestants. She tarnished the brilliancy of her reign and forever sullied her glory by feminine follies and evil passions, while obstinately refusing to accept the duties and enjoy the legitimate happiness of a woman's life. Brave, proud, far-sighted, and persevering, she displayed much intellectual ability, and certain fine moral qualities, but rarely or never the tender and modest virtues which inspire and retain private affection. And yet for many years she was able to inspire sentiments of another nature. When in the midst of her glorious career, Elizabeth one day asked a lady of the court how she preserved the affection of her husband, the lady replied, "By assuring him of mine, madam." "Thus it is," exclaimed the queen, "that I possess the love of my many husbands, the people of England, making them feel that which I bear to them." She did indeed possess the love of her people, and she made common cause with them during long years, and through great trials. When she died, the evils and dangers inherent in absolute power had done their work; the English nation were beginning to grow weary of the rule of its great queen, and to dream of political and religious liberties which had no place in the mind or in the heart of Elizabeth Tudor.

In ascending the throne, Queen Elizabeth had found England profoundly divided upon religious questions, impoverished by the excessive exactions of her father and her sister, still agitated by the bloody dissensions of the great nobles and by the insurrections among the lower classes during the reigns which had just elapsed. She governed for forty-five years, amid religious dissensions yet subsisting, although stifled under her powerful hand. She oppressed the Catholics, and their number, which at her accession perhaps equalled that of the Protestants, rapidly diminished under the measures which she applied to them. Men who can neither practise the rites of their religion, nor quit the kingdom, who cannot leave their homes without authorization, who are incessantly exposed to vexations and acts of injustice, not to mention the terrible risk of an accusation of treason, abandon their faith if they are weak, or take refuge in exile if they are energetic and zealous. Upon this destruction of the liberty of her Catholic subjects Elizabeth firmly established the Anglican Church; but the protection with which she surrounded it, while injuring the rights of the Catholics and the nonconforming Protestants, did not prevent the Catholic nucleus from subsisting in England, or the Puritan faith from developing itself. With all their exaggerations, their narrow minds, the severity of their principles, the Puritans were to become for their country the salt of the earth. They were to save it successively from despotism and from corruption, from the ruin both of liberty and of morals. Few things contributed more towards this progress of the Protestant faith in its austere simplicity, than the reading of the Bible in the English tongue. The translation of Miles Coverdale had replaced that of Wicliffe, and the venerable translator, imprisoned in his youth under Henry VIII., a bishop under Edward VI., and again persecuted under Mary, had paid dear for the privilege of placing within reach of his brethren the bread of life; but as literature and science advanced, his translation was found defective and full of errors. Parker, the first Archbishop of Canterbury under the reign of Elizabeth, caused the undertaking of a new version, which was ardently carried out by a commission of learned men. It was completed in 1572, and published under the name of Bishop Grindall's Bible, the latter having, in 1575, succeeded Parker as Primate. Grindall was in favor of the reading of the Scriptures, and was even a friend of the Puritans, who increased during his episcopate, notwithstanding the harshness of the queen towards them, and the severe measures everywhere employed to bring about uniformity of worship. Notwithstanding the fines of twenty pounds sterling per month, imposed upon those who did not attend the services of their parish church, the "Brownists," a Puritan sect of the most radical kind, originated at this period and endured without flinching a violent persecution. A great number of the Fathers of the American States had frequented the assemblages of the Brownists, before taking the course of abandoning their country to worship God in liberty. After the death of Grindall, in 1583, the Puritans found an implacable foe in the new archbishop, Whitgift. The struggle began between the Primate and the nonconformist clergy; it lasted long; but during the later years of the life of Elizabeth it became less violent. The Puritans at that time grounded upon the succession to the throne of a Presbyterian prince hopes which were to be cruelly deceived.

If Queen Elizabeth at home oppressed those of her subjects who did not purely and simply accept the religious doctrines which she offered to them, she always supported upon the Continent the political and religious efforts of the Reformers. We have seen with what prudence she acted, and how her powerful instinct of government, her taste for absolute power, and her horror of rebellion, often compelled Cecil to urge her into the way of that great policy which tended to make England the protectress and chief of Protestantism in Europe. Amid all the duplicities, timid counsels, and meannesses of Queen Elizabeth towards the French Huguenots and the Dutch Protestants, it must yet be admitted that hers was the only aid constantly at the service of the continental Reformers, and it was only through an economy hitherto unknown in the royal expenditure that she was able to meet their oft repeated demands. Her father, Henry VIII., had confiscated the property of the monasteries and that of the subjects whom he put to death, and he had overwhelmed his people with unheard-of taxes. Her brother and her sister, for different reasons, had left their finances in the saddest disorder. Under the wise direction of Cecil, and thanks to Queen Elizabeth's economy, the treasury of England was enabled to satisfy the constant calls from without and to provide for the requirements within, notwithstanding the reduction in the public burdens. The development of commerce and industry was encouraged. "The money which is in the pockets of my subjects is as useful to me as that in my treasury," said the queen, — a great economical maxim which the kings her predecessors had neither known nor practised.

Elizabeth had taken measures to second the industrial efforts of her people. In order to give an impetus to national manufactures, a sumptuary law of 1581–82 prohibited to certain persons expensive silk clothing and laces manufactured abroad; at the same time, as the exportation of wool formed the greater part of the commerce of England, the rearing of sheep was everywhere encouraged. Pasture-grounds had increased in all directions, in many parts of the country taking the place of ploughed land, and the cloth manufactories every day employed more hands. Linen cloth also began to be manufactured. The persecutions of Philip II. in the Low Countries brought to England skilled workmen, who gave fresh life to different branches of manufacture. It was at this period the happiness and honor of England to receive those who fled from the tyranny of the Spaniards, as she was subsequently to give shelter to the French Huguenots after the revocation of the Edict of Nantes.

Commerce and industry prospered under the reign of Elizabeth; but the predominant achievement of this period was the formation of the English navy, which at her accession was yet only in its infancy, but which had become queen of the seas before her death. The protectionist system, practised in all its rigor by King Henry VIII., soon gave way to the wise liberality of Cecil. An Act of the first Parliament of Elizabeth relaxed the navigation laws, authorizing trading by foreign vessels on certain conditions, and favoring the development of the great commercial companies. In 1566 the Royal Exchange of London was built under the auspices of Sir Thomas Gresham, and the relations with the Low Countries, Germany, and the kingdoms of the north suddenly took a fresh impulse, making up for the progressive decrease of the fisheries. "Fish is no longer eaten," said Cecil regretfully.

A new trade for England, the monopoly of which had hitherto been left to Spain and Portugal, was the odious slave-trade. An English sailor, John Lock, had been the first to embark in this traffic. Hawkins engaged in it with success, seizing a shipload of negroes upon the coast of Guinea, and selling them in St. Domingo; but this detestable commerce was not to attain its full development until later: it was the Spaniards and their colonies, not the unhappy blacks, whom the English sailors of the time of Elizabeth regarded as their legitimate prey.

Under the reign of Queen Elizabeth began the great voyages of discovery which gave rise to the abuses of buccaneering, at the same time that they opened a vast field to the enterprise and researches of the human mind. Martin Frobisher first entered upon this career in 1567. He desired to find a new route to India; but he stopped in the vicinity of Hudson's Bay, where he took possession of certain territories in the name of England, and discovered the strait which still bears his name. Hence was conceived the first idea of a northwest passage, subsequently sought for ardently by John Davis, who, as well as his predecessor, gave his name to a strait. Frobisher made three voyages to this region, where he thought that he had found gold, but he was finally employed in the queen's service, commanded one of the vessels which repulsed the Spanish Armada, and was killed in 1594, in attacking a fortress near Brest, which held out for the Leaguers against Henry IV.

While Frobisher was seeking the polar passage, Drake accomplished the journey round the world, an undertaking which had yet only been attempted by the Portuguese, Fernando Magellan, who has given his name to a well-known strait. His voyage had been secretly authorized by Elizabeth, in defiance of the claim of the Spaniards to the islands and seas of America, which had been, they said, solemnly conceded to them by the Pope. Drake paid no heed to their complaints, pillaging the coasts, capturing ships, and accumulating by his acts of piracy enormous wealth, of which he brought her share to the sovereign, who received him honorably upon his return, without recognizing the errand upon which he had been employed. The little vessel in which Drake made his voyage was preserved at Deptford until it fell to pieces.

The projects of Sir Walter Raleigh had not been exclusively directed, like those of Hawkins and Drake, towards those parts of the world occupied by the Spaniards. He had conceived the hope of enriching his country and himself in other ways than by buccaneering, and had attempted several successive expeditions towards the southern part of North America. He had already failed twice, and had lost his brother, Sir Humphrey Gilbert, in one of his voyages, when, in 1584, he set sail, with the authorization of the queen, to take possession, with full ownership, of the lands he might discover, upon condition of reserving a fifth part of the produce of the mines for the crown. It was in this expedition that he accidentally discovered the territory which now composes the states of Virginia and North Carolina, possessions which Queen Elizabeth deigned to distinguish by the name of Virginia. The letters-patent granted to Raleigh were confirmed by an act of Parliament, and in the following year Sir Richard Grenville, a relative of Sir Walter, sailed for the new colony with eight hundred emigrants, who established themselves in the island of Roanoke. They had nearly perished from hunger and privation, when, in the following year, Sir Francis Drake, returning from an expedition against the Spanish territories, received them on his ship. Two other attempts at colonization had the same result, and Virginia remained abandoned to the savages without having yielded any other result to England than the discovery of tobacco, which for a long time bore the name of Virginia grass.

We have seen that at the time of the attack of the Spanish Armada the royal navy was of little importance; but the number of merchant vessels was considerable. The latter had increased by a third in fifty years. Whale-fishing, which began to develop in 1575, soon employed a large number of vessels. The protracted war with Spain and Portugal having hindered the arrival of the productions of India, a company of traders was formed in the city of London to undertake voyages to the East Indies. In December, 1600, Queen Elizabeth granted a charter to them: this was the origin and the modest germ of the great East India Company. The political and religious animosity which nourished the buccaneering expeditions against Spain, and the cruel revenge which the Spaniards took upon the English sailors who fell into their hands, served to develop the taste for remote enterprises, and to form that race of bold sailors who have so powerfully contributed to the grandeur and independence of their country.

At the same time that material and social prosperity received so powerful an impulse under the reign of Elizabeth, literature burst forth into a splendor whose light has not yet in the least degree faded. The intellectual movement had preceded all the others. It began towards the close of the civil war and the desolations which it brought in its wake. Scotland had had its share in this glory as well as England, although civil war was still prevailing in that country. From 1494 to 1584 seven colleges had been founded at Oxford and eight at Cambridge; the university of Aberdeen in 1494, that of Edinburgh in 1582, two colleges of the university of St. Andrew's founded between 1512 and 1537, the university of Trinity College at Dublin in 1591, assured in Great Britain the development of learning. The suppression of the monasteries retarded this movement momentarily, but Reformers were not regardless of the danger. Cranmer in particular made serious efforts to remedy the evil. The so-called grammar-schools, then established in great numbers, spread abroad elementary education and a certain degree of intellectual culture; but the higher instruction, and, in particular, the study of the classics, had received a blow from which they were long in recovering. Great disorder reigned in the universities: morals there were lax and the studies very deficient. The revival of letters began with the study of foreign languages. We have seen that Queen Mary, like Queen Elizabeth, understood French, Italian, and Spanish, as well as Latin and Greek. From this usage, more and more diffused, sprang a strange abuse of foreign words, which introduced something like a new tongue into the English language. Under the reign of Elizabeth the lords and fine ladies at the court spoke a language designated by the word "Euphuism," composed of the harmonious syllables of all languages, which is now difficult to understand, and especially to read aloud. Traces of it are found even in the poems of Spenser.

Amid this momentary decline of learning, a natural result of violent convulsions, it is impossible not to recognize the fact that the sixteenth century furnished, in England as elsewhere, a great number of men as learned as they were distinguished by natural gifts. Without going beyond the reign of Elizabeth, we may mention Roger Ascham, her tutor, born in Yorkshire in 1515, whom the Queen retained beside her in the capacity of secretary, until his death in 1568. His most esteemed work is entitled *The Schoolmaster*. The tutor of King James VI. of Scotland has left a name even more celebrated. A historian and a poet, George Buchanan, born at Killearn, in 1506, began by being a soldier. He lived for a time in France, in Portugal, in Piedmont, leading a life crowded with adventures, and returned to Scotland in 1560. Being appointed by Queen Mary to a post of public instruction, he nevertheless continued to attack her, and to write violent pamphlets against her. The Scottish Parliament appointed him tutor to the young king, whom he instructed with considerable care. When he was accused of having made his pupil a pedant, he replied, "That is the best thing I could make of him." His *History of Scotland* possesses real interest, although it is characterized by much partiality. He died at Edinburgh in 1582.

Doctor Hooker had no disposition to take part in the great agitations of his time. He was born in 1554, and domestic dissensions, caused by the temper of his wife, led him to seek a modest and retired life. He had been Master of the Temple in London, but a preacher, who was his colleague, an ardent Puritan, made existence so hard for him that he retired to a country living, where he wrote his great work *Of the Laws of Ecclesiastical Polity*, a book full of judgment, moderation and learning, a model of the most beautiful English style. He died in 1600, being only forty-seven years of age, shortly after he had ended his book.

The courtiers did not abandon exclusively to the learned

SHAKESPEARE.

the cultivation of letters. Lord Surrey, beheaded during the last days of Henry VIII., has left some charming verses. The Lyon King-of-Arms of Scotland, Sir David Lyndsay of the Mount, was also a poet. The type of knight and gentleman, Sir Philip Sidney, nephew of the Earl of Leicester and son-in-law of Walsingham, who has left in a lifetime of thirty-two years an accomplished model and an ineffaceable remembrance to posterity, wrote in prose and in verse. His romantic allegory of *Arcadia* is the most important of his works. He had dedicated it to his sister Mary, Countess of Pembroke, a worthy friend of such a brother. It was said of her that to love her was of itself a liberal education. She died young, like himself, having published the book which her brother had left to her, and which had an immense success.

We have mentioned the learned and the lettered courtiers. We now come to the real poets. England numbers two under the reign of Elizabeth: the one charming, elegant, and prolific; the other, unique in the history of the world: Spenser and Shakespeare. Edmund Spenser was born in London in 1533. He wrote at first some poems of little importance, but he devoted several years to the composition of the *Faery Queene*, of which Sidney was the first patron, and which was completed under the auspices of Raleigh. We might have placed Spenser among the courtiers, if that had not been to do too much honor to the latter, for his patrons often employed him among them, and he ended by obtaining considerable estates in Ireland out of the confiscated estates of the Earl of Desmond. The *Faery Queene* was dedicated to Queen Elizabeth, who is constantly celebrated in the poem. She granted a pension to Spenser, and the success of the work was the greater from the fact that the court took pleasure in searching for the persons concealed beneath the allegorical names. An inexhaustible imagination, the most elevated sentiments, and the most charming descriptions, cause one to forget the peculiar taste of the time, the confusion and complication of incidents, as well as the strange form of versification. Read without pausing, the *Faery Queene* may appear tiresome, but a great number of detached portions will always remain masterpieces. Spenser died in 1598, after having been obliged to flee from Ireland, then a prey to insurrection.

William Shakespeare * was born on the 23d of April, 1564, at Stratford-upon-Avon, in the county of Warwick. Prosperity and respectability undoubtedly belonged, at this period, to his family, as his father became chief magistrate of his native town five years afterward. We may therefore suppose that Shakespeare's education, in his earlier years, was in conformity with the circumstances of his father; and when a change in his fortunes, from whatever cause it may have arisen, occasioned an interruption of his studies, he had probably acquired those first elements of a liberal education which are quite sufficient to free the mind of a superior man from the awkwardness of ignorance, and to put him in possession of those forms which he will need for the suitable expression of his thoughts. This is more than enough to explain how it was that Shakespeare was deficient in those acquirements which constitute a good education, although he possessed the elegance which is its usual accompaniment.

In the year 1576, the brilliant Leicester celebrated the visit of Queen Elizabeth to Kenilworth by festivities, whose extraordinary magnificence is attested by all the chronicles of the time. Shakespeare was then twelve years old, and Kenilworth is only a few miles from Stratford. It is difficult to doubt that the family of the young poet participated, with all the population of the surrounding country, in the pleasure and admiration excited by these pompous spectacles. What an impulse would the imagination of Shakespeare be sure to receive! Neverthe-

* M. Guizot, *Shakespeare et son temps.*

SHAKESPEARE'S TOMB.

less, the information which we possess regarding the amusements of his youth gives no hint whatever of the tastes and pleasures of a literary life.

In 1582, at the age of eighteen, he married; and two years later we know that he left his family and went up to London in search of the means of subsistence, or of some opportunity for the display of his talent. We can say very little with regard to the employment of the early part of Shakespeare's residence in London, to the circumstances which led to his connection with the stage, and to the part which consciousness of his talent may have had in forming the resolution which directed the flight of his genius. A tradition, which was preserved among the actors of the time, represents him to us as filling at first the lowest position in the theatrical hierarchy, namely, that of call-boy, whose duty it was to summon the actors when their time came to appear upon the stage. But, when turning his mind to the theatre, is it likely that Shakespeare would have stopped short at the door? At the time of his arrival in London, in the year 1584 or 1585, he had a natural protector at the Blackfriars' Theatre; for Greene, his townsman, and probably his relative, figured there as an actor of some reputation, and also as the author of several comedies. According to Aubrey, it was with a positive intention to devote himself to the stage that Shakespeare came to London; and, even if Greene's influence had not been able to secure his reception in a higher character than that of call-boy, it is easy to understand the rapid strides with which a superior man reaches the summit of any career into which he has once obtained admission. But it would be more difficult to conceive that, with Greene's example and protection, a theatrical career, or, at least, a desire to try his powers as an actor, would not have been Shakespeare's first ambition. The time had come when mental ambitions were kindling on every side; and dramatic poetry, which had long been numbered among the national pleasures, had at length acquired in England that importance which calls for the production of masterpieces.

Even before Shakespeare's advent, theatrical representations had constituted, not only the chief gratification of the multitude, but the favorite amusement of the most distinguished men. A taste so universal and so eager could not long remain satisfied with coarse and insipid productions; a pleasure which is so ardently sought after by the human mind, calls for all the efforts and all the power of human genius. This national movement now stood in need only of a man of genius, capable of receiving its impulse, and raising the public to the highest regions of art.

Years nevertheless elapsed before Shakespeare made his appearance on the stage as an author. He arrived in London in 1584, and is not known to have engaged in any employment unconnected with the theatre during his residence in the metropolis; but *Pericles*, his first work according to Dryden, though many of his other critics and admirers have rejected it as spurious, did not appear until 1590. How was it possible that, amid the novel scenes that surrounded him, his active and fertile mind, whose rapidity, according to his contemporaries, "equalled that of his pen," could have remained for six years without producing anything? A probable supposition is that the poet spent his labor, at first, upon works which were not his own, and which his genius, still in its novitiate, has been unable to rescue from oblivion.

Shakespeare's comrades doubtless soon perceived what new successes he might obtain for them by remodelling the uncouth works which composed their dramatic stock; and a few brilliant touches imparted to a ground-work which he had not painted — a few pathetic or terrible scenes intercalated in an action which he had not directed — and the art of turning to account a plan which he had not conceived, were, in all probability, his earliest labors, and his first presages of glory. In 1592, a time at which we can scarcely be certain that a single original and complete work had issued from his pen, a jealous and discontented author, whose compositions he had probably improved too greatly, speaks of him, in the fantastic style of the time, as an " upstart crow, beautified with our feathers; an absolute *Johannes Factotum,* who is, in his own conceit, the only Shakescene in the country."

It was, we are inclined to believe, while engaged in these labors, more conformable to the necessities of his position than to the freedom of his genius, that Shakespeare sought to recreate his mind by the composition of his *Venus and Adonis*, in which a metre singularly free from irregularities, a cadence full of harmony, and a versification which had never before been equalled in England, announced the "honey-tongued poet;" and the poem of *Lucrece* appeared soon afterwards to complete those epic productions which for some time sufficed to maintain his glory.

The date of these two poems is uncertain, but whatever it may be, their place among Shakespeare's works is at a period far more remote from us than any of those which filled up his dramatic career. In this career he marched forward, and drew his age after him; and his weakest essays in dramatic poetry are indicative of the prodigious power which he displayed in his last works. Shakespeare's true history belongs to the stage alone; after having seen it there, we cannot seek for it elsewhere; and Shakespeare himself no longer quitted it. His sonnets—fugitive pieces which the poetic and sprightly grace of some lines would not have rescued from oblivion but for the curiosity which attaches to the slightest traces of a celebrated man—may here and there cast a little light on the obscure or doubtful portions of his life; but, in a literary point of view, we have in future to consider him only as a dramatic poet.

We have already seen what was the first employment of his talents in this kind of composition. Great uncertainty has resulted therefrom with regard to the authenticity of some of his works. Shakespeare had a hand in a vast number of dramas; and probably, even in his own time, it would not have been always easy to assign his precise share in them all. For two centuries, criticism has been engaged in determining the boundaries of his true possessions; but facts are wanting for this investigation, and literary judgments have usually been influenced by a desire to strengthen some favorite theory on the subject. It is, therefore, almost impossible, at the present day, to pronounce with certainty upon the authenticity of Shakespeare's doubtful plays.

It is also a subject of controversy which of the works unquestionably his own appeared first in the order of time. In this unimportant discussion, one fact alone is certain, and becomes a new subject of surprise. The first dramatic work which the imagination of Shakespeare truly produced was a comedy; and this comedy will be followed by others: he has at last taken wing, but not as yet towards the realms of tragedy. How could it be that the frivolous spirit of comedy was his first guide in that poetic world from which he drew his inspiration? Why did not the emotions of tragedy first awaken the powers of so eminently tragic a poet? Was it this circumstance which led Johnson to give this singular opinion — "Shakespeare's tragedy seems to be skill; his comedy to be instinct"? Assuredly, nothing can be more whimsical than to refuse to Shakespeare the instinct of tragedy; and if Johnson had had any feeling of it himself, such an idea would never have entered his mind. The fact just stated, however, is not open to doubt; it is well deserving of explanation, and has its causes

The merry Wives of Windsor.

in the very nature of comedy, as it was understood and treated in the Elizabethan age.

At the advent of Shakespeare, the nature and destiny of man, which constitute the materials of dramatic poetry, were not divided or classified into different branches of art. When art desired to introduce them on the stage, it accepted them in their entirety, with all the mixtures and contrasts which they present to observation; nor was the public taste inclined to complain of this. The comic portion of human realities had a right to take its place wherever its presence was demanded or permitted by truth; and such was the character of civilization, that tragedy, by admitting the comic element, did not derogate from truth in the slightest degree. In such a condition of the stage and of the public mind, what could be the state of comedy, properly so called? How could it be permitted to claim to bear a particular name, and to form a distinct style? It succeeded in this attempt by boldly leaving those realities in which its natural domain was neither respected nor acknowledged; it did not limit its efforts to the delineation of settled manners or of consistent characters; it did not propose to itself to represent men and things under a ridiculous but truthful aspect; it became a fantastic and romantic work, the refuge of those amusing improbabilities which, in its idleness or folly, the imagination delights to connect together by a slight thread, in order to form from them combinations capable of affording diversion or interest, without calling for the judgment of the reason.

The great poet, whose mind and hand proceeded, it is said, with such equal rapidity that his manuscript scarcely contained a single erasure, doubtless yielded with delight to those unrestrained gambols in which he could display without labor his rich and varied faculties. He could put anything he pleased into his comedies, and he has, in fact, put everything into them, with the exception of one thing which was incompatible with such a system, namely, the *ensemble* which, making every part concur towards the same end, reveals at every step the depth of the plan and the grandeur of the work. It would be difficult to find in Shakespeare's tragedies a single conception, position, act or passion, or degree of vice or virtue, which may not also be met with in some one of his comedies; but that which in his tragedies is carefully thought out, fruitful in result, and intimately connected with the series of causes and effects, is in his comedies only just indicated, and offered to our sight for a moment to dazzle us with a passing gleam, and soon to disappear in a new combination.

In Shakespeare's comedy, the whole of human life passes before the eyes of the spectator, reduced to a sort of phantasmagoria — a brilliant and uncertain reflection of the realities portrayed in his tragedy. Do not expect to find probability, or consecutiveness, or profound study of man and society; the poet cares little for these things, and invites you to follow his example. To interest by the development of positions, to divert by variety of pictures, and to charm by the poetic richness of details — this is what he aims at; these are the pleasures which he offers. There is no interdependence, no concatenation of events and ideas; vices, virtues, inclinations, intentions, all become changed and transformed at every step. Thus negligent and truant is the flight of the poet through these capricious compositions! Thus fugitive are the light creations with which he has animated them! But, then, what gracefulness and rapidity of movement, what variety of forms and effects, what brilliancy of wit, imagination, and poetry! — all employed to make us forget the monotony of their romantic frame-work; and who but Shakespeare could have diffused such treasures over so frivolous and fantastic a style of comedy?

Five only of Shakespeare's comedies, the *Tempest*, the *Merry Wives of Windsor*, *Timon of Athens*, *Troilus and Cressida*, and the *Merchant of Venice*, have escaped, at least in part, from the influence of the romantic taste. Of these, the *Merry Wives of Windsor* may be said to be almost perfect in its composition; it presents a true picture of manners; the *dénouement* is as piquant as it is well-prepared; and it is assuredly one of the merriest works in the whole comic repertory.

According to tradition, this comedy was composed by order of Queen Elizabeth, who, having been greatly delighted with Falstaff, in the play of *Henry IV.*, desired to see him once again on the stage. Falstaff is, indeed, one of the most celebrated personages of English comedy, and perhaps no drama can present a gayer one. Born to move in good society, as we see him in *Henry IV.* he has not yet renounced all his pretensions of this kind; he has not adopted the coarseness of the positions to which he is degraded by his vices; he does not make a merit of his intemperance, nor does he base his vanity upon the exploits of a bandit. If there were anything to which he would cling, it would be to the manners and qualities of a gentleman; to this character he would pretend, if he were permitted to entertain, or able to maintain, a pretension of any kind. At least, he is determined to give himself the pleasure of affecting these qualities, even should the gratification of this pleasure gain him an affront; though he neither believes in it himself, nor hopes that others believe in it, he must at any cost rejoice his ears with panegyrics upon his bravery, and almost upon his virtues. This is one of his weaknesses, just as the taste of Canary sack is a temptation which he finds it impossible to resist; and the ingenuousness with which he yields to it, the embarrassments in which it involves him, and the sort of hypocritical impudence which assists him to get out of his dilemmas, make him an extraordinarily amusing personage.

The *Merry Wives of Windsor* presents a different action, and exhibits Falstaff in another position, and under another point of view. He is, indeed, the same man; it would be impossible to mistake him; but he has grown older, and plunged deeper into his material tastes, and is solely occupied in satisfying the wants of his gluttony. Elizabeth, it is said, had desired Shakespeare to describe Falstaff in love; but Shakespeare, who was better acquainted with the personages of his own conception, felt that this kind of ridiculousness was not suited to such a character, and that it was necessary to punish Falstaff in a more sensitive point. Even his vanity would not be sufficient for this purpose; for Falstaff could derive advantage from every disgrace in which he was involved; and he had now reached such a point as no longer even to seek to dissemble his shame. The liveliness with which he describes to Mr. Brook his sufferings in the basket of dirty linen is no longer the vivacity of Falstaff relating his exploits against the robbers of Gadshill, and afterwards so merrily getting out of the scrape when his falsehood is brought home to him. The necessity for boasting of himself is no longer one of his chief necessities; he wants money, money above all things, and he will be suitably chastised only by inconveniences as real as the advantages which he promises himself. Thus the buck-basket and the blows of Mr. Ford are perfectly adapted to the kind of pretensions which draw upon Falstaff such a correction; but although such an adventure may, without any difficulty, be adapted to the Falstaff of *Henry IV.*, it applies to him in another part of his life and character; and if it were introduced between the two parts of the action which is continued in the two parts of *Henry IV.*,

H. Hofmann del. — R. Goldberg sc.

Shylock, and Jessica. — The Merchant of Venice.

it would chill the imagination of the spectator to such a degree as entirely to destroy the effect of the second part.

It would be superfluous to seek to establish in a very accurate manner the historical order of these three dramas in which Falstaff appears; Shakespeare himself did not bestow a thought upon the matter. We may, however, believe that, from the uncertainty in which he has left the whole affair, he was at least desirous that it should not be altogether impossible to make *The Merry Wives of Windsor* the continuation of *Henry IV.* Hurried, as it would appear, by the orders of Elizabeth, he at first produced only a kind of sketch of this comedy, which was nevertheless acted for a considerable period, as we find it printed in the first editions of his works; and it was not until several years afterwards that he arranged it in the form in which we now possess it.

The story of the *Merchant of Venice* is of an entirely romantic character, and was selected by Shakespeare, like the *Winter's Tale*, *Much Ado about Nothing*, *Measure for Measure*, and other plays, merely that he might adorn it with the graceful brilliancy of his poetry. But one incident of the subject conducted Shakespeare to the confines of tragedy, and he suddenly became aware of his domain; he entered into that real world in which the comic and the tragic are commingled, and, when depicted with equal truthfulness, concur, by their combination, to increase the power of the effect produced. What can be more striking, in this style of dramatic composition, than the part assigned to Shylock? This son of a degraded race has all the vices and passions which are engendered by such a position; his origin has made him what he is, sordid and malignant, timid and pitiless; he does not think of emancipating himself from the rigors of the law, but he is delighted at being able to invoke it for once, in all its severity, in order to appease the thirst for vengeance which devours him; and when, in the judgment scene, after having made us tremble for the life of the virtuous Antonio, Shylock finds the exactitude of that law, in which he triumphed with such barbarity, turned unexpectedly against himself — when he feels himself overwhelmed at once by the danger and the ridicule of his position, two opposite feelings, mirth and emotion, arise almost simultaneously in the breast of the spectator. What a singular proof is this of the general disposition of Shakespeare's mind! He has treated the whole of the romantic part of the drama without any intermixture of comedy, or even of gayety; and we can discern true comedy only when we meet with Shylock — that is, with tragedy.

It is utterly futile to attempt to base any classification of Shakespeare's works on the distinction between the comic and tragic elements; they cannot possibly be divided into these two styles, but must be separated into the fantastic and the real, the romance and the world. The first class contains most of his comedies; the second comprehends all his tragedies — immense and living stages, upon which all things are represented, as it were, in their solid form, and in the place which they occupied in a stormy and complicated state of civilization.

In the year 1595, at latest, *Romeo and Juliet* had appeared. This work was succeeded, almost without interruption, until 1599, by *Hamlet*, *King John*, *Richard II.*, *Richard III.*, the two parts of *Henry IV.*, and *Henry V.* From 1599 to 1605, the chronological order of Shakespeare's works contains none but comedies and the play of *Henry VIII.* After 1605, tragedy regains the ascendant in *King Lear*, *Macbeth*, *Julius Cæsar*, *Antony and Cleopatra*, *Coriolanus*, and *Othello*. The first period, we perceive, belongs rather to historical plays; and the second to tragedy properly so called, the subjects of which, not being taken from the positive history of England, allowed the poet a wider field, and permitted the free manifestation of all the originality of his nature.

It cannot be doubted that, between historical dramas and tragedies, properly so called, Shakespeare's genius inclined in preference towards the latter class. The general and unvarying opinion which has placed *Romeo and Juliet*, *Hamlet*, *King Lear*, *Macbeth*, and *Othello* at the head of his works, would suffice to prove this. The power of man in conflict with the power of fate — this is the spectacle which fascinated and inspired the dramatic genius of Shakespeare. Perceiving it for the first time in the catastrophe of *Romeo and Juliet*, he feels himself suddenly terror-struck at the aspect of the vast disproportion which exists between the efforts of man and the inflexibility of destiny — between the immensity of our desires and the nullity of our means. In *Hamlet*, the second of his tragedies, he reproduces this picture with a sort of shuddering dread. A feeling of duty has prescribed to Hamlet a terrible project; he does not think that anything can permit him to evade it; and from the very outset he sacrifices everything to it — his love, his self-respect, his pleasures, and even the studies of his youth. He has now only one object in the world: to prove and punish the crime which had caused his father's death. That, in order to accomplish this design, he must break the heart of her he loves; that, during the course of the incidents which he originates in order to effect his purpose, a mistake renders him the murderer of the inoffensive Polonius; that he himself becomes an object of mirth and contempt — he cares not, does not even bestow a thought upon it: these are the natural results of his determination, and in this determination his whole existence is concentrated. But he is desirous to accomplish his plan with certainty; he wishes to feel assured that the blow will be legitimate, and that it will not fail to strike home. Henceforward accumulate in his path those doubts, difficulties, and obstacles which the course of things invariably sets in opposition to the man who aims at subjecting it to his will. By bestowing a less philosophical observation upon these impediments, Hamlet would surmount them more easily; but the hesitation and dread which they inspire form part of their power, and Hamlet must undergo its entire influence. Nothing, however, can shake his resolution, nothing divert him from his purpose: he advances, slowly it is true, with his eyes constantly fixed upon his object; whether he originates an opportunity, or merely appropriates one already existing, every step is a progress, until he seems to border on the final term of his design. But time has had its career; Providence is at its limit; the events which Hamlet has prepared hasten onward without his co-operation; they are consummated by him, and to his own destruction; and he falls a victim to those decrees whose accomplishment he has insured, destined to show how little man can avail to effect, even in that which he most ardently desires.

The *Othello* is derived from an Italian story by Giraldi Cinthio, which Shakespeare changed by slightly varying the *dénouement.* In other respects, he has retained and reproduced every incident; and not only has he omitted nothing, but he has added nothing. He seems to have attached almost no importance to the facts themselves; he took them as he found them, without giving himself the trouble to invent the slightest addition, or to alter the slightest incident. He has, however, created the whole; for, into the facts which he has thus exactly borrowed from another, he has infused a vitality which they did not inherently possess. The narrative of Giraldi Cinthio is complete; it is deficient in nothing that seems essential to the interest of a recital; situations, incidents, progressive development of the principal

Hamlet. — Hamlet.

BOSTON. ESTES & LAURIAT.

event, external and material construction, so to speak, of a pathetic and singular adventure — all these things are contained in it, ready for use; and some of the conversations even are not wanting in a natural and touching simplicity. But the genius which supplies the actors to such a scene, which creates individuals, imparts to each his peculiar figure and character, and enables us to witness their actions, to hear their words, to anticipate their thoughts, and to enter into their feelings; that vivifying power which commands facts to rise, to go onward, to display themselves and to effect their accomplishment; that creative breath, which, diffusing itself over the past, resuscitates it, and fills it in some sort with a present and imperishable vitality; — this is what Shakespeare alone possessed; and by means of this, from a forgotten novel, he made *Othello.*

So far as we are able, at the present day, to form any idea of Shakespeare's character, from the scattered and uncertain details which have reached us regarding his life and person, we have every reason to believe that he never bestowed much care either on his labors or on his glory. More disposed to enjoy his own powers than to turn them to their best account — docile to the inspiration, rather than guided by the consciousness of his genius — vexed but little by a craving after success, and more inclined to doubt its value than attentive to the means of obtaining it — the poet advanced without measuring his progress, discovering his own ability at every step, and perhaps retaining, even at the end of his career, some remains of ingenuous ignorance of the marvellous riches which he scattered so lavishly in every direction. His sonnets alone, of all his works, contain allusion to his personal feelings, and to the condition of his soul and life; but we rarely meet in them with the idea, so natural to a poet, of the immortality which his works are destined to achieve.

He could not have been a man who reckoned much upon posterity, or who cared at all about it, who displayed so little anxiety to throw light upon the only monuments of his private existence which have been left to posterity for a possession.

Externally, meanwhile, his life seems to have pursued a tranquil course. All the documents which we possess exhibit Shakespeare to us placed at last in the position which he was rightfully entitled to occupy, and valued as much for the charm of his character as for the brilliancy of his talents, and the admiration due to his genius. A glance, too, at the affairs of the poet will prove that he was beginning to introduce into the details of his existence that order and regularity which are essential to respectability. We find him successively purchasing, in his native town, a house and various portions of land, which soon formed a sufficient estate to insure him a competent income. The profits which he derived from the theatre, in his double capacity of author and actor, have been estimated at two hundred pounds a year, a very considerable sum at that time; and if the liberalities of Lord Southampton were added to the economy of the poet, we may conclude that, at least, they were not unwisely employed.

Who would not suppose that a life which had become so honorable and pleasant would long have retained Shakespeare in the midst of society conformable to the necessities of his mind, and upon the theatre of his glory? Nevertheless, in 1613, or 1614 at the latest, three or four years after having obtained from James I. the direction of the Blackfriars Theatre, without having apparently incurred the displeasure of the king to whom he was indebted for this new mark of favor, or of the public for whom he had just produced *Othello* and *The Tempest*, Shakespeare left London and the stage to take up his residence at Stratford, in his house at New Place, in the midst of his fields. It certainly is not easy to discern the causes which led to his departure from London; although perhaps the arrival of infirmities may have warned him of the necessity of repose; perhaps, also, the very natural desire of showing himself in his native place, under circumstances so different from those in which he had left it, made him hasten the moment of renouncing labors which no longer had the pleasures of youth for their compensation.

New pleasures could not fail to spring up for Shakespeare in his retirement. A natural disposition to enjoy everything heartily rendered him equally adapted to delight in the calm happiness of a tranquil life, and to find enjoyment in the vicissitudes of an agitated existence. The first mulberry-tree introduced into the neighborhood of Stratford was planted by Shakespeare's hands, in a corner of his garden at New Place, and attested for more than a century the gentle simplicity of the occupations in which his days were spent. A competent fortune seemed to unite with the esteem and friendship of his neighbors to promise him that best crown of a brilliant life, a tranquil and honored old age, when, on the 23d of April, 1616, the very day on which he attained his fifty-second year, death carried him off from that calm and pleasant position, the happy leisure of which he would doubtless not have consecrated to repose alone.

We have no information regarding the nature of the disease to which he fell a victim. His will is dated on the 25th of March, 1616; but the date of February, effaced to make way for that of March, gives us reason to believe that he had commenced it a month previously. He declares that he had written it in perfect health; but the precaution taken thus opportunely, at an age still so distant from senility, leads to the presumption that some unpleasant symptom had awakened within him the idea of danger. There is no evidence either to confirm or to set aside this supposition; and Shakespeare's last days are surrounded by an obscurity even deeper, if possible, than that which enshrouds his life.

K. Hofmann del. Tob. Bauer sc.

Othello and Desdemona.

CHAPTER XXII.

JAMES I. 1603–1625.

SCARCELY had Queen Elizabeth's soul quitted her body, when a distant cousin of the great sovereign, Sir Robert Carey, set off for Scotland, being advised of her death by his sister, Lady Scrope, who formed part of the royal household. Cecil and the members of the council, distanced by the zeal of the courtier, had at least the advantage, in dispatching their messengers to Edinburgh, of being able to announce to the king that he had been solemnly proclaimed in London a few hours after Elizabeth's death. The wise promptitude of Cecil forestalled any other pretension. The only person who might have urged a claim to the throne, Lady Arabella Stuart, cousin, on her father's side, to the King of Scotland, and a descendant, like himself, of Henry VII., was in safe-keeping. None thought of stipulating for a few guaranties in favor of the liberties of the country or for the reform of the abuses grown old with the royal power. The lords of the council were expecting the reward of their intrigues in behalf of the new king, and the public mind saw with satisfaction the prospect of a union with Scotland, which promised to put an end to the continual wars between the two kingdoms. The Scots were hoping to enrich themselves in England.

No one was more in need of such an opportunity than the king. His Majesty, James VI. of Scotland, now also James I. of England, was so poor that he could not set out for his new kingdom until Cecil had sent him money. He had, besides, no desire to see, even after her death, the sovereign whom he had so much dreaded during her lifetime, and the journey, begun on the 6th of April, proceeded so slowly that Elizabeth had for three weeks been sleeping in her tomb when her successor at length arrived, on the 3d of May, at Theobalds, in Hertfordshire, the country house of Sir Robert Cecil, where all the members of the council awaited him. He had lavished on his way the honor of knighthood upon all who asked for it: since his departure from Scotland he had made a hundred and forty-eight knights. Cecil took advantage of the sojourn which the king made at Theobalds to gain his favor completely. Alone, among the colleagues of whom he was jealous, the Earl of Northumberland contrived to preserve his honors. Lord Cobham, Lord Grey, and especially Sir Walter Raleigh, were disgraced. The first concession granted to the wishes of the nation was the suspension of all the monopolies. This favor was proclaimed, on the 7th of May, upon the entrance of the king into the city of London. Severe measures with regard to the chase immediately followed the arrival of the monarch, who was passionately fond of that amusement.

The plague had lately broken out in London, and it delayed the coronation, but it did not hinder conspiracies. The powerful hand of Elizabeth had been able to keep down, but not to prevent them. Her successor might disparage the wisdom and the political sagacity of the great queen who had raised him to his throne; but he was destined to see his authority often threatened and despised. He had begun by making a dangerous enemy in depriving Raleigh not only of his place in the council, but of the honors and monopolies which constituted his fortune. The favor which the king manifested naturally enough to his Scottish friends had made other malcontents. The Catholics, at first allured by the promises of James, had seen him go over to the side of the

PORTRAIT OF JAMES I.

Anglican Church. "I make the judges," he said sportively, during his journey from Scotland to England; "I make the bishops. By God's wounds, I do as I please, then, with the law and the Gospel." He naturally inclined to the side of power. Raleigh, Cobham, Grey, encouraged for some time by the Earl of Northumberland, always an enemy of Cecil, found support among the priests and lesser Catholic gentlemen, to whom the Puritans allied themselves. The conspirators proposed to seize upon the person of the king, in order to induce him, they said, to change his ministers. Before the day appointed all the conspirators were arrested. Sir Walter Raleigh and Lord Cobham were conducted to the Tower. The plague delayed the judgment as it had delayed the coronation. The trial of Raleigh was, besides, difficult to conduct. Cecil took all the care therein that the matter deserved. Lord Cobham, in cowardly alarm, betrayed his accomplice. Both were accused of having sought to assassinate James in order to raise to the throne Lady Arabella Stuart. Raleigh defended himself in person with all the intelligence, all the animation, all the indomitable courage of which he had so many times given proof during his adventurous life. He was nevertheless condemned as well as Lord Cobham and Lord Grey. All three were pardoned when Cobham and Grey were already upon the scaffold. The tragic adventures of Sir Walter Raleigh were not yet at an end.

The king had hunted in peace since the conspirators, who so greatly alarmed him, had been in the Tower. He also amused himself with theological polemics. While king of Scotland he had been obliged to accept the yoke of the Puritans. Happy to escape from them, he pursued them in his new kingdom with bitter rancor. Suddenly converted to Episcopacy, he discussed in person with the doctors favorable to Presbyterian principles. "No bishops, no king," cried

James, and left his adversaries no opportunity to reply to him. Then, making use of the prerogative which he so resolutely claimed, he gave orders to all his subjects to conform themselves to the ordinances, doctrines, and ceremonies of the Church of England, authorizing the bishops to dismiss from their livings all clergymen who should refuse to obey. More than three hundred pastors were thus deprived suddenly of their occupation as well as of their means of subsistence. A great number left the country; others remained at home, and the spies, formerly exclusively commissioned to ferret out the Catholics who dared to hear mass, added to this duty that of discovering the secret meetings which the dismissed pastors often held even in their former parishes. King James was preparing by religious persecution that great Puritan party which was to contribute so powerfully to the overthrow of his son.

The Parliament had assembled on the 19th of March, 1604, and the leaven of opposition which had already appeared under Elizabeth, had not been wanting in the first relations of the new sovereign with the representatives of his people. The contested election of Mr. Goodwin marked the commencement of the struggle; the Commons had the audacity to complain of some abuses, and they did not prove themselves generous in the voting of supplies. King James was profoundly imbued with the doctrine which he had set forth in a pamphlet entitled *The True Law of Free Monarchies*, namely, that the king has the right of commanding, and the subject the duty of obeying. He dissolved Parliament as quickly as possible; but the Commons had, nevertheless, time to call the royal attention to the Papists, recommending them to all the rigor of the laws. The bishops and the Puritans were agreed upon this point. The enormous fines regularly imposed upon Catholics for their absence from the established worship, were exacted with a severity that filled the coffers of the king while ruining numerous families. James required payment of all arrears for the past year. The wealthy Papists were threatened with judicial prosecutions. They knew the sentence beforehand. Many ransomed their lives by the payment of large sums. The king had begun to hunt again, forbidding anybody to speak to him of business on the days which he devoted to that pastime. The counties which he honored with his presence groaned under the burden. One of the hounds of his Majesty appeared one morning bearing upon his neck a petition addressed to him in these terms: "Good Medor, we beg you to speak to his Majesty, who hears you every day and does not listen to us, that he may kindly return to London to his business, for our provisions are exhausted, and we have nothing left to give him to eat." The king laughed and remained where he was; but matters were preparing in London to recall him.

Among the Catholics ruined by the successive exactions which they had suffered was Robert Catesby, a renegade in his youth, who had, however, returned with zeal to the faith of his fathers, and had been since then engaged in all the Catholic intrigues. Weary of persecution, and seeing no hope of relief either in the earlier promises of the king, or in the influence of Spain which had been counted upon to some extent, he conceived the atrocious idea of destroying all the persecutors at a blow — King, Lords, and Commons — upon the opening of the Parliament convoked for the 7th of February, 1605. Prudent and circumspect, he sought accomplices. Thomas Winter, a gentleman and a Catholic like himself, formerly employed by Spain in the Low Countries, only consented to enter into the plot after having asked the Spaniards if they had no longer any hope. Upon his return from Ostend, with a reply in the negative, he brought back a former comrade, Guy Fawkes, a soldier of fortune, resolute and fanatical like the two other conspirators. Seven persons in all were bound by the most solemn oath, when the plotters set at work in a house which they had hired adjacent to Whitehall, under the name of Percy, one of the conspirators, an officer of the royal household. Their plan was to dig a mine extending under the Houses of Parliament. "No one set to work to dig or to transport the powder who was not a gentleman," said Fawkes in his examination. "While the others worked I acted as sentinel, and the work was stopped if any passer-by appeared." The stores were deposited at Lambeth, on the other side of the river. They were brought in small quantities as the subterranean passage progressed.

Twice the work was suspended: the prorogation of the Parliament was delayed; at first until the month of October, then until November. The conspirators, who were no longer pressed for time, separated in order not to arouse suspicion. At the end of May the work was completed. They had been able to hire a cellar which extended beneath the floor of the House of Lords, and thirty-six barrels of powder were deposited therein. But to these minds, agitated by dark designs and burdened with a weighty secret, idleness was fatal. They were, besides, nearly all without resources, and the successive delays brought about in their enterprise had reduced them to great difficulties. The want of money induced Catesby, still the prime mover in the plot, to admit among the conspirators two rich men upon whom he thought he could rely. One, Sir Everard Digby, promised to invite to a great hunting expedition all the Catholic gentlemen, members of Parliament, whose lives it was desired to save. The other, Tresham, a relative of Catesby, and already compromised with him in certain intrigues, undertook to provide the necessary funds; but scarcely had he taken the oath

GUNPOWDER-PLOT OF GUY FAWKES.

when the confidence with which Catesby had hitherto been animated suddenly failed him. He became dispirited: day and night he felt himself haunted by the most sinister forebodings.

All was ready. Prince Charles, the second son of King James, was to be proclaimed by Catesby at Charing Cross at the moment of the destruction of Whitehall. Tresham was to depart in a vessel chartered for that purpose, and repair to Flanders to invoke the assistance of the Catholic powers. Guy Fawkes was designated to set fire to the mine. The rendezvous was at Dunchurch. The uneasiness of the greater number of the accomplices was concerning their friends, who they were afraid might be the victims of their scheme. Catesby had, it was said, taken steps for keeping a great number of Catholics away from Whitehall. "But were they as dear to me as my own son, they should be blown up with the rest rather than cause the affair to fail," he added. Meanwhile, on the 26th of October, ten days before the opening of Parliament, Lord Monteagle, father-in-law of Tresham, received a letter in a disguised hand, enjoining him not to repair to Whitehall on the 5th of November. "The Parliament will receive a terrible blow," said the anonymous writer, "and yet they shall not see who hurts them."

Lord Monteagle immediately carried the warning to Cecil. On the morrow the conspirators learned that they were betrayed. Nothing happened, however, to show that the mine had been discovered. Guy Fawkes recognized all his secret marks again, and, notwithstanding the growing uneasiness engendered by the information received, he continued to mount guard in the cellar. The other conspirators waited the event with a courage bordering on insanity. On the 4th, in the daytime, Fawkes was at his post when the Earl of Suffolk, High Chamberlain, intrusted with the preparations for the opening of Parliament, appeared at the door of the cellar. He cast a careless look around him. The barrels of powder were hidden beneath a heap of wood and fagots. "Your master has made great provision of fuel," he said to Fawkes, who had represented himself as the servant of Percy, and he quitted the dangerous cellar. Fawkes hastily gave intimation to Percy, who had remained in London, then he returned to his mine. At two o'clock in the morning he was arrested.

All the conspirators had fled. Catesby still hoped to rouse the Catholics to insurrection, but none responded to the appeal. On the 7th of November they were assembled in a house at Holbeach, upon the borders of Staffordshire, being resolved to perish to the last man in defending themselves. Sir Robert Walsh, sheriff of Worcester, caused the residence to be surrounded by his troops. There was no means of escaping, the house had already been fired. "Stay, fool!" cried Catesby to Winter, "we will die together." Both grasped their swords and sprang upon the assailants. They were immediately killed. Several others perished likewise. Sir Everard Digby was arrested, as well as other less distinguished conspirators. Tresham had remained quietly in London, counting upon his treachery to save him. He was arrested and taken to the Tower with his accomplices.

Guy Fawkes, meanwhile, questioned by the king himself, remained indomitable even in the ruin of his hopes and the mortal peril in which he was situated. "How could you bear the thought of destroying my children and so many other innocent persons?" said King James. "For desperate ills there must be desperate remedies," replied the bold conspirator. "Why did you collect so much powder?" asked a Scottish courtier. "I had purposed to cause all the Scots to be blown as far as Scotland," Fawkes said gravely. He was several times put to the torture, always refusing to tell the names of his accomplices. He was assured they had fled and were arrested. "It is useless, then, to name them," maintained Fawkes, "they have named themselves." It was through Bates, a servant of Catesby, that the complicity of the Jesuits Greenway and Garnet was discovered. Tresham had also given evidence against them, but being attacked in his prison with a serious illness he retracted his accusations, and died on the 23d of December, not without some suspicion of poison.

Greenway had succeeded in escaping; but Garnet, a provincial of the order of Jesuits, was arrested with Oldcorne, one of his brethren. Both were submitted to the torture; both finally confessed their knowledge of the plot, which, they said, they had always opposed, the order of Pope Paul V. being to suffer all and to win by patience the crown of life. In spite of the skill and eloquence of Garnet the two Jesuits suffered death, but Garnet himself was not executed till the 3d of May. All the conspirators who had fallen into the hands of justice had expiated their crime on the 30th of January. Oldcorne died at the end of February.

The terror which the plot had occasioned, the horror excited in all classes of society, of which we still find traces in the custom of burning in the streets, upon the 5th of November, an effigy bearing the name of Guy Fawkes, fell back upon the Catholics, who were persecuted in a mass with fresh rigor, even though they were strangers to the conspiracy. Parliament urged the king forward in this fatal path. The ministers were obliged to moderate the ardor of the members who had been threatened with being blown into the air with his Majesty.

Royal visits amused James, and relieved him for a while from the anxieties which his people occasioned him. The King of Denmark, brother-in-law of the King of England, who had married Anne of Denmark, and the Prince of Vaudemont, of the House of Guise, spent a few weeks in England, setting to the courtiers an example of debauchery which did not, however, prevent James from continuing to discuss all the theological questions of the time, in writing or by word of mouth, with Catholics as well as with Puritans. He had always the resource of throwing his adversaries into prison when their arguments became too powerful, especially when it happened, as in 1607, that an insurrection broke out during the discussions. A question had arisen, as in the days of Edward VI., of the right of enclosure. The people of Northamptonshire, Warwickshire, and Leicestershire, claimed, with arms in their hands, the pasturage of waste lands. When the king was assured that it was not a plot of his theological antagonists, the insurrection was soon repressed, but not without revealing the extreme weakness of the government and the indolence of the king as well as of his ministers.

The Parliament meantime rejected the favorite project of James, who desired to unite not only the two crowns, but the two nations of England and Scotland by common laws and a common religion. The plan was good and useful, but premature. Scotland rejected it angrily, fearing to be subjected to England. The latter rejected it with scorn, asserting that the beggars of Scotland were coming over into England in sufficiently numerous bands, without its being necessary to make Englishmen of them. The subsidies were not voted. The king, dissatisfied, abandoned his proposals; but for two years he did not convoke Parliament. It was necessity alone which compelled him, in 1610, to claim the co-operation of his people in filling the treasury. Cecil, who had become successively Lord Cranborne and Earl of Salisbury, now sat at the Treasury and proposed enormous subsidies to the Commons; but Parliament presented a petition of grievances, and refused to vote anything without being assured of the redress of their wrongs. Negotiations were carried on for several months. Parliament at length granted a greatly reduced subsidy, without having obtained all that they demanded in return. A weak, indolent monarch, often indifferent concerning the most important affairs, James was as obstinate when it was a question of his prerogative as he was in matters of theology. Cecil died, it is said, of the anxieties and vexations which Parliament had compelled him to endure in the two sessions of 1610 and 1611. He expired on the 24th of May, 1612. As crafty and as avaricious as his father, he had not always exhibited that breadth of view and firmness of resolve which had made Burleigh the worthy minister of Queen Elizabeth.

While the king was maintaining an argument with the Dutchman Conrad Vorstein, upon the nature and attributes of the Divinity, and demanding of the States of Holland the banishment of his adversary, — Lady Arabella Stuart, whose name had so often served as a watchword for conspiracies, without her ever having been implicated in them herself, for the first time in her life had become a plotter. Her object, however, was simply to marry William Seymour, grandson of the Earl of Hereford, to whom she had been attached from infancy. When the secret was discovered, the princess was imprisoned at Lambeth, and her husband thrown into the Tower. She saw him, however, sometimes, and was forcibly removed to Durham. She contrived to escape. Seymour also fled from his prison. Both desired only to live together abroad; but the husband alone reached a free country. The unfortunate Lady Arabella was arrested on board the vessel which was taking her across the Channel, and consigned to the Tower for the remainder of her life. She lost her reason, and died in 1615, after having been long forgotten even by those who had dreaded her name.

The favorites of James I. succeeded each other in the royal household without intermission, often arousing the jealousy of the queen. These favorites were loaded with riches and honors while they were all-powerful, abandoned and forgotten when they were replaced by another, unless they possessed some dangerous secret. Robert Carr, or Ker, of an old border family, had recently taken possession of this envied position, when Cecil died, in 1612. Still young, but having already become Viscount Rochester, a member of the Privy Council, and Knight of the Garter, he was created Lord Chamberlain, and fulfilled the functions of Secretary of State, thanks to the assistance of one of his friends, Sir Thomas Overbury, who was destined to pay dearly for the honor. Sinister rumors soon began to circulate concerning Rochester himself.

Prince Henry, the eldest son of James, was the idol of the people. Handsome in face and figure, brave and strong, skilful in all bodily exercises, he had, it was said, chosen the Black Prince for his model, and was studying the science of war with more pleasure than letters and theology. His father's pedantry was odious to him, and he did not scruple to blame his actions. A great admirer of Sir Walter Raleigh, who was still imprisoned in the Tower, he often said that no other king than his father would keep such a bird in a cage. "He has become a man too soon to live long," it was said among the people. Yet the greatest hopes were founded upon him. His life was regular, and his opinions appeared to incline to the side of the Puritans, the real party of the people, who looked upon him as the liberator promised by the Scriptures. King James was afraid of his son. "Will he bury me alive?" he said, when he heard of the multitude which surrounded the young prince. He was endeavoring, meanwhile, to marry his son, now to the Infanta of Spain, now to the Princess Christine of France; but the negotiations proceeded slowly, and the English people flattered themselves with hopes of a Protestant alliance, like that which had recently been concluded for the young Princess Elizabeth, betrothed to the Count Palatine Frederick V. This prince had just arrived in England, on the 16th of October, 1612, for the celebration of the marriage, when Prince Henry, who had been ill for some time, suffered a sudden relapse. He was weak, and appeared to be in a state of stupor. An energetic will still triumphed, however, over the disease; he rallied several times, appeared in public and dined with the king. But the young man's strength was declining rapidly, and his physicians were not agreed as to the nature of the illness. On the 5th of November the king was informed of the desperate condition of his son. The prince was in London; but the king dreading the affliction which awaited him, immediately set out for Theobalds, of which Cecil had given up the ownership to him, and awaited the event from afar. The prince died on the 6th of November, 1612, amid general grief, mingled with indignation; Rochester was everywhere accused of having poisoned him, although the accusation seems to have been without just grounds. Henry had grown too rapidly, and had not had strength to bear the attacks of a putrid fever. The king did not manifest for his son the same regret as his people. He immediately resumed for Prince Charles the negotiations of marriage begun for Prince Henry, and also celebrated on the 13th of February the nuptials of his daughter with a pomp and splendor which were to be the only satisfaction of the young princess, who was destined to suffer to the last degree from the difficulties and trials of the regal state.

The king was more than ever embarrassed for money. He had endeavored to contract loans; he had re-established and increased all the monopolies; he had sold to all comers the honors of knighthood, a new order intermediate between the nobility and the common people, which was soon after to take the title of "baronetage;" but the avidity of the courtiers, the prodigality of the king, in ministering both to his own pleasures and to those of his favorites, as well as old debts which oppressed him, exhausted all resources. It was necessary to have recourse to Parliament. Sir Francis Bacon, formerly a dependant of the Earl of Essex, afterwards his accuser, one of the greatest minds and the most despicable characters in a period accustomed to such contrasts, promised James to undertake the task of making the Parliament obey. Rochester, who had become Earl of Somerset, joined him. They were called with regard to this the *undertakers*. The Commons assembled in ill humor. They had got intelligence of the audacious project formed to constrain them. They consulted the Lords upon the right of the king to establish various taxes. The Upper House refused the conference, but the subsidies were not voted. The king caused Parliament to be warned that he would dissolve it if it did not fulfil its task, the only one for which it was convoked. Parliament replied that it would not vote as long as the grievances were not redressed. It was dissolved not to be recalled for six whole years. This Parliament did not pass a single act, but it powerfully contributed to establish that independence of the House which was soon to strike a deathblow to absolute power in England.

Already in the horizon was dawning the star of a new favorite, who was destined to have a hand in shaking the foundations of the throne. George Villiers, known in history under the name of Buckingham, was beginning to replace the Earl of Somerset in the king's affections. The latter had recently married the Countess of Essex, who had been separated by divorce from her husband, the son of the unfortunate favorite of Queen Elizabeth. Somerset and his wife were accused by the public voice of having imprisoned, then poisoned a former friend of theirs, Sir Thomas Overbury. The growing favor of Villiers gave to the enemies of the declining favorite courage to denounce him to the king. The great judge Coke, rival of Bacon, adopted the vulgar calumny circulated against Somerset, and accused him of having poisoned Prince Henry. Several accomplices were arrested and the assassination of Overbury was proved; but the connivance of Somerset remained doubtful. The prosecution went on slowly and as though regretfully; the tone of the earl was often haughty; the king intervened in his favor: the favorite was in possession of many important secrets. Bacon conducted the affair with consummate prudence and ability. The countess was separately condemned to death. Somerset being declared guilty in his turn, was pardoned, as was his countess; and the earl received royal gifts even after retirement to his country-seat, which was soon afterwards granted to him as a prison. Either through fear or from a lingering affection, James I. did not abandon his former favorite, notwithstanding his growing passion for a new face. George Villiers was henceforth to reign undividedly over the father as well as the son. Prince Charles had assumed the title of Prince of Wales; his friendship for Villiers equalled that of the king.

Fourteen years had passed since James had quitted Scotland, and he had never visited his hereditary kingdom; he had had no money for that purpose; but the States of Holland, free from the war with Spain since the recognition of their independence in 1609, had recently paid their debts to England, and the journey to Scotland was resolved upon. The king, besides, had a great task to achieve there; he was laboring to establish religious uniformity among his subjects. Twelve years previously he had undertaken to introduce

Episcopacy in Scotland. Persecution, imprisonment, exile, had by degrees disposed of the chiefs of the opposition. Welch and Decry, condemned to death, then to banishment, had left the country. Old Andrew Melvil, called to London for a conference, and forcibly detained as his nephew had already been, had left the latter in his prison in Scotland, where he had died, and was himself living at Sedan, ever indomitable in his aversion to Episcopacy and in his support of the rights of a free-born Scot. James had in Scotland an agent as able as he was unscrupulous. Sir George Hume, recently made Earl of Dunbar, succeeded at length, partly by intimidation, partly by corruption, in imposing silence upon the Scottish clergy. Two Courts of High Commission still more tyrannical than those of London, were sitting at St. Andrew's and at Glasgow when the king arrived in Scotland, in 1617. The Parliament presented for the royal sanction the bill which definitively constituted the Episcopal Church; but a remonstrance from the clergy arrested the king's arm as he extended the sceptre to give the authority of law to the project; the bill was withdrawn, Episcopacy was held to be established by the royal prerogative, and the refractory were cited before the High Commission. Calderwood went to swell the band of Scottish exiles upon the Continent, and the people, deprived of the religious form which pleased them and to which they were accustomed, allowed their resentment to slumber until the day when the Covenant was to protest against the work of the father as developed by the son.

King James had been much vexed in Scotland by the strict observance of the "Sabbath." When he set out to return to England, he composed a work to which he gave the authority of law, under the title of *The Book of Sports.* Under the pretext of regulating the pleasures permitted on Sunday, this new ordinance forbade the respectful observances which marked among the Puritans the return of the seventh day. The *Book of Sports* was ill received by the majority of the population. They refused to be merry by compulsion, and the new weapon, more dangerous to royalty than to the Puritans, lay in the arsenal of despotism, until Archbishop Laud subsequently drew it forth for his own injury as well as that of his master.

At the moment of setting out for Scotland, the king had raised Bacon to the dignity of Keeper of the Seals, and had intrusted extensive powers to him. This royal favor turned the brain of the illustrious lawyer; he played the king during the absence of the legitimate monarch. Upon the return of James, however, Bacon resumed his accustomed humility in presence of the great men of the land. After waiting for two days at the door of Villiers, who had become Duke of Buckingham, he at length obtained admission, and threw himself prostrate before the favorite, kissing his feet. He did not rise until he had obtained his pardon. "I was obliged to kneel myself before the king to make him revoke your disgrace," said the haughty favorite to the repentant magistrate. The disgrace had reference especially to the part which Bacon had played in a project of marriage for the brother of Villiers with the grand-daughter of Coke. The union was accomplished, but Coke, by the sacrifice of his grand-daughter, gained only a place in the Council, while Bacon, reconciled with Buckingham, became Chancellor and Lord Verulam, thus adding fresh riches to the treasures which he dissipated as quickly as he acquired them.

Bacon was not the only person who sold justice and favor. Buckingham, his family and his friends, were publicly trafficking in offices, posts, and titles, which were even imposed sometimes upon those who did not ask for them. The favorite had been created a marquis, and appointed high admiral, to the detriment of the aged Howard, formerly commander of the fleet that had vanquished the Armada. Trials, skilfully conducted by Bacon and Coke, added fines and confiscations to the revenue obtained by the malversations. All articles of primary necessity were the subject of monopolies. The people regretted Somerset, and still more the wise administration and the economy of Queen Elizabeth.

Amid the system of plunder which he tolerated, the king was still poor. He had for a moment hoped for a fresh source of wealth: Sir Walter Raleigh, still confined in the Tower, had succeeded in bringing to the knowledge of the king details of a gold-mine, formerly discovered by himself in Guiana. Raleigh was quite ready to direct an expedition, promising to pay all expenses, and asking from the king nothing but his liberty. A fifth of all the profits was to belong to the crown. James hesitated for a long time. He dreaded the valor of Raleigh, which might involve him in a war with Spain; but the skilful adventurer contrived to purchase the good will of the favorite. Raleigh came forth from the Tower, free but not pardoned. Protesting his pacific intentions with regard to the Spaniards, he set sail on the 28th of March, 1617, just as King James was preparing to start for Scotland.

From the moment of its departure misfortune attended Raleigh's expedition: sickness decimated his crews and stretched him upon a bed of suffering. He found the Spaniards warned of his approach, and disposed to oppose his progress. The little squadron which he commissioned to ascend the river Oronoco, in search of the gold-mine, was attacked by the Spaniards of the town of St. Thomas; in retaliation, the English captured and burned down the town. Raleigh's son was killed, the crews mutinied, and the expedition returned without gold and almost without soldiers. Sir Walter, distracted

PORTRAIT OF SIR WALTER RALEIGH.

with grief and anger, violently reproached Captain Kemyss who commanded the detachment; his old friend, in despair, killed himself. Other captains abandoned the unfortunate leader. The sailors were in revolt; those who remained urged Sir Walter to return to former methods, and to overrun the sea and the coasts with them, in order to seize and pillage the Spanish ships and settlements. Raleigh resisted, not without some efforts and relapses. Finally he set sail for England. When he landed in the month of June, 1618, he learned that a warrant of arrest had been issued against him. Spain had complained of the capture of St. Thomas. The governor, who had been killed, was a relative of Gondomar, the ambassador in England; the latter had raised the cry of piracy, and made threats of the royal vengeance. The moment was fatal to Raleigh. James was negotiating for the marriage of his son with the Infanta, Donna Anna, daughter of Philip III. He was resolved to please Spain at any price. Raleigh was soon lodged in the Tower once more. "The guilty man is in our hands," wrote Buckingham to Gondomar, "and we have seized his ships; if it please the king your lord, his Majesty will punctually fulfil his engagements, by sending the criminals to suffer their punishment in Spain, unless he should find it more satisfactory and exemplary that the chastisement should be inflicted upon them in England." Philip III. deigned to intrust this business to King James.

Raleigh was still under the weight of the old sentence of death pronounced against him fifteen years previously, without which it would have been difficult to convict him this time of a crime involving capital punishment. "Your recent offences have awakened the justice of his Majesty," declared the great judge Montague; "may God have mercy on your soul!" Weak and ill as he was, Raleigh defended himself with as much skill as coolness. He asked for a short delay, in order to put his affairs in order. "Not," he said, "that I desire to gain a minute of existence. Old, sick, and dishonored, and approaching my end, life has become wearisome to me." It was, indeed, the expression of supreme weariness in this man, who had always loved life more than he had dreaded death, even according to the statements of his enemies. The respite was refused. Lady Raleigh, on going to say farewell to her husband, announced to him that she had obtained the favor of receiving his body after the execution. The frightful punishment of traitors had been commuted. Raleigh was to be beheaded. "Well done, Bess," he said, smiling; "it is fortunate that you will be able to dispose in death of a husband whom you have not always had when alive at your disposal." He had cast aside, by an effort of his powerful will, all the ambitious projects, all the wild, romantic, adventurous ideas, which were crowding into his brain. The grandeur of his soul, often obscured during his lifetime by many faults and even vices, freed itself from clouds at the hour of death. On the 29th of October he was calm, grave, devout. He received the sacrament before walking to the scaffold, erected at Westminster. An immense crowd surrounded it. He addressed the people, and made a long speech, protesting his innocence. The morning was cold. It was proposed to the condemned man that he should warm himself for an instant before the fatal moment. "No," said Raleigh, "it is the day of my ague; if I were to tremble presently, my enemies will say I quake for fear. It were better to have done with it." He knelt, uttering aloud a beautiful prayer. He touched the axe. "'Tis a sharp medicine, but a sound cure for all diseases," he said, and he laid his head upon the block. The executioner delayed. "What do you fear?" exclaimed Raleigh; "strike." His

EXECUTION OF SIR WALTER RALEIGH.

THE NOVEL PETITION-BEARER.

head fell immediately. The great soldier, the illustrious sailor, the statesman, the man of letters, the incomparable adventurer, was not yet sixty-seven years of age. King James had truckled to Spain, and had added yet one more stain to his name.

One of the judges most eager for the ruin of Raleigh was already threatened in his exalted seat. At the beginning of 1621 the king was compelled to convoke a Parliament, to obtain the subsidies which he needed. His son-in-law, the Elector Palatine, called by the Protestant party to the throne of Bohemia, had imprudently accepted that offer without measuring the opposition which would be raised against him by the Catholics of the Empire. He was now in danger of being driven from Bohemia, and deprived at the same time of his hereditary states. The Lower Palatinate had been attacked by the Catholic armies. James hesitated, lamented, cursed the ambition of his son-in-law, which had brought this matter upon his hands; but he had already sent a small army corps to the assistance of the Elector, and promised larger reinforcements. Parliament alone could place him in a position to keep his promises.

Parliament had no objection to this war, popular in England as a Protestant crusade; but it desired to set a price upon its liberality, and demanded that prosecution should be made of several persons enjoying monopolies, who had shamefully abused their disgraceful privileges. From Sir Giles Mompesson and Sir Francis Mitchell, they soon came to the Attorney-General, Sir Henry Yelverton, and from him to one of the judges of the Court of Prerogatives, and to the Bishop of Llandaff, convicted of having sold or bought justice. The vengeance of the Commons aimed even higher still: the Chancellor Bacon had said that corruption was the vice of the time. He had been himself deeply tainted with it, and was to bear a signal punishment for his offences. On the 21st of March, 1621, the Parliamentary commission intrusted with the inquiry into abuses in the matter of justice accused the Lord Chancellor, Viscount of St. Alban's, upon twenty-two personal counts, at the same time reproaching him with his connivance at offences of the same nature among his subordinates.

Bacon had hitherto resolutely denied the charges which the public voice made against him; but the blow was too bold and the accusations too plainly specified for him to be able longer to resist the evidence. His eloquence, the marvellous resources of his mind, the brilliancy of his genius, all failed him with the loss of the court favor. He felt himself abandoned by the king, who had never had any liking for him, even Bacon's servility not being able to veil his intellectual superiority. The Duke of Buckingham coveted his offices for some of his own dependants. The great chancellor fell ill; he took to his bed, and asked for time to prepare his defence. It was not a defence, but a complete confession which he caused to be presented on the 24th of April to the House of Lords. Being pressed with questions, he avowed successively all the shameful acts of which he was accused, palliating them as best he could, and asking mercy of his judges. "The poor gentleman," wrote a contemporary, "elevated formerly above pity, has now fallen below it; his tongue, which was the glory of his time for eloquence, is like a forsaken harp hung upon the willow, while the waters of affliction flow over upon the banks." The abasement was complete. The Lords had spared this great criminal the humiliation of appearing at their bar, but a deputation repaired to his residence to be certified of the authenticity of the writing and of the circumstantial confession. "It is my act, my hand, my heart. O, my lords, spare a broken reed!" sobbed the great philosopher, the brilliant genius, the profound thinker, who is still one of the glories of England. Moral character was lacking to these intellectual gifts.

Bacon was condemned to lose all his offices, and to pay a fine of forty thousand pounds sterling, which was remitted by the king, for he was in no condition to discharge it. After two days' imprisonment in the Tower he was set at liberty, but it was forbidden him during his lifetime to approach the court, to sit in Parliament, or to serve his country in any capacity whatsoever.

No punishment could be more bitter to Bacon. Shut up in his country-seat, he revised his former works, his *Essays*, his *Novum Organum*, or New Philosophy, his two books on the *Progress of Science.* He caused them to be translated into Latin; he even wrote a *History of Henry VII.;* but his heart was still at court and in public life. He only asked to reappear upon that scene from which he had been so ignominiously expelled, and harassed with his petitions the king, Prince Charles, and the Duke of Buckingham. None gave ear to him, none replied to him; his temper became imbittered, his health gave way, and this great man, fallen so low, died, at the age of sixty-five, in 1626, five years after his disgrace.

The affairs of the Elector Palatine, the new King of Bohemia, went from bad to worse. The five thousand Englishmen sent by King James, ill-paid and poorly commanded, had rendered little service. The embassies with which he importuned all the powers interested were able to exert no influence. The throne of Bohemia, as well as the hereditary states of Prince Frederick, had been taken from him, and, driven from Germany, he had been compelled to take refuge at the Hague with his wife and children, there to live upon a pension allowed him by the Dutch; but his father-in-law, King James, had conceived a project which would, he thought, at least re-establish his son-in-law in the Palatinate. He counted in this affair upon the influence of Spain.

In spite of the national opposition to a Catholic marriage for the heir to the throne, in spite of the recent petitions of Parliament to this effect, King James, who had moreover quarrelled with the House of Commons, and had caused several of its members to be arrested, continued his negotiations with Philip IV. for the marriage of Prince Charles with the Infanta, Donna Maria. For nearly twenty years the King of England had, in common with Spain, dreamed of this alliance, which he at length regarded as on the point of being realized. The scheme had been proposed more than once in the shape of a union between Prince Henry with the Infanta Anne; the prince had died, and the Infanta had married the King of France. The King of Spain, Philip III., had at first appeared favorable to the marriage, but on his death-bed he had recommended his son Philip IV. to make his sister an empress by uniting her to her cousin the Emperor Ferdinand. King James did not know of the last wish of the dying king, and he hoped to find the new Spanish sovereign more accommodating than his father. After endless negotiations, and journeys to and fro, after Catholic pretensions on the part of Spain, and displays of pecuniary avidity on that of King James, that threatened to break off everything, an almost complete understanding had been arrived at in the month of January, 1623: the Infanta was to be undisturbed in the free exercise of her religion; the English Catholics were to enjoy a practical, if not a legal, toleration; the manner of payment of the dowry of two millions of crowns was settled, the dispensation from Rome was expected, and it was planned to celebrate the marriage by proxy through the ambassador forty days after the arrival of that important document. Everything appeared propitious. Lord Digby, Earl of Bristol, ambassador at Madrid, wrote to the king: "I do not wish to inspire by uncertain reasons a vain hope in your Majesty, but I can inform you that the court of Spain openly manifests its intention of giving you real and prompt satisfaction. If this is not really their design, they are more false than all the devils in hell, for they could not make more protestations of sincerity nor more ardent vows."

The Spaniards could scarcely, however, be absolved from the disgrace of double-dealing in this affair; for notwithstanding appearances, the two negotiations in favor of the Elector Palatine and the Prince of Wales did not make progress. The towns of the Palatinate, which still held out for their hereditary prince, were falling one after another into the hands of the Emperor without Spain intervening in any manner, and the dispensation from Rome did not arrive. A strange and chivalrous project suddenly arose in the mind of Prince Charles, suggested, it is said, by Buckingham, who had himself conceived it upon a proposal of the Duke Olivarez, first and all-powerful minister in Spain. Why not go himself to Madrid to conquer and bring back the Infanta? Why not put an end to this interminable negotiation by a stroke worthy of a prince and a lover? King James consented to the scheme after much hesitation, and even after tears. He had the matter at heart; his self-love was at stake. The prince set out secretly, accompanied by Buckingham.

The undertaking was hazardous, and appeared even more so than it was. When it was known in England that the prince had departed, and with what object, the excitement and anxiety were extreme. The public agitation communicated itself to the king. "Do you think," he said to his Keeper of the Seals, Bishop Williams, "that this knight-errant journey will succeed?" "Sire," said the bishop, "if my Lord Marquis of Buckingham treat the Duke Olivarez with great consideration, remembering that he is the favorite in Spain, and if the Duke of Olivarez is very polite and careful towards my Lord Marquis of Buckingham, remembering that he is the favorite in England, the prince your son may pay his addresses happily to the Infanta; but if the duke and the marquis mutually forget what they both are, it will be very dangerous for the design of your Majesty. God will that neither one nor the other fall into that error!"

The far-seeing good sense of the bishop had not deceived him. The whims and the vanity of Buckingham encountering the Spanish haughtiness, were to be the rock to this frail bark. The undertaking had succeeded well: the prince and the favorite had traversed Paris and France under an incognito, which was penetrated on several occasions, and they had arrived safe and sound at Madrid on the 17th of March, 1623, "more gay than they had ever been in their lives." The chivalrous freak, with all its frankness and imprudence, had appeared for a moment to fascinate the Spaniards. "It only remains for us to throw the Infanta into his arms," Duke Olivarez exclaimed, and the prince, laying aside all mystery, had been sumptuously received at the court of Spain, admitted to the presence of the Infanta, and entertained with hopes of a speedy triumph. Appearances were soon to give way to reality. Months elapsed, the Prince of Wales and Buckingham were still at Madrid. The demands of Pope Gregory XV. became every day more exacting, and the situation more treacherous. The three sovereigns reciprocally demanded an act of respect for religious liberty, which at heart and on principle no one of them recognized or intended to grant. The King of England wished his son to marry a Catholic princess, while he himself, his son, and his people remained exclusively Protestant. The King of Spain desired that his daughter and all the personal servants of his daughter should remain openly Catholics, while living in a Protestant family and among a Protestant people, and while himself strictly excluding all Protestants from his realm. The Pope claimed for the Catholics of England full liberty of conscience, while peremptorily refusing the same privilege to the Protestants throughout his own dominions, and while calling upon the King of England to return, together with his people, to the yoke of the sole and sovereign Church.*

So many conflicting and obstinate pretensions could not be reconciled. King James yielded as much as he could; he signed the articles which were demanded of him for toleration of the Catholics, publicly so far as public opinion in England grudgingly permitted; secretly in respect to that which concerned the influence to be exerted upon the Parliament on the subject of the penal laws. He even sent to his son and to Buckingham a blank signature, approving in advance of all that they might concede. Matters proceeded from bad to worse; the first surprise at the proceeding of the Prince of Wales had subsided. There was no longer any hope of seeing Charles become a Catholic. "I have come to Spain to seek a wife and not a religion," he said frankly. The views of the English and Spanish favorites had clashed upon several occasions. Buckingham, irritated at not having succeeded immediately in an undertaking which his foolish vanity had suggested to him, had, in reality, altered his mind, and no longer urged the completion of the project. Nothing had been broken off, but everything remained in suspense, and King James as well as England demanded the return of the Prince of Wales, who had now been absent more than six months. "I care neither for the marriage nor for aught

* M. Guizot, *Un Projet de Mariage royal.*

else, provided I fold you once more in my arms," wrote the king to his son and to his favorite. "God grant it! God grant it! God grant it! Amen! amen! amen!" A leave-taking, tender at least in appearance, took place between the royal persons. The two favorites were less friendly. "I remain forever," said Buckingham to Olivarez, "the servant of the King of Spain, the queen, the Infanta, and I will render to them all the good offices in my power. As to you, you have so often thwarted and disobliged me that I make you no declaration of friendship." "I accept your words," dryly replied the Count Duke. "If the prince had come here alone he would not have gone away alone," it was said in Madrid. He embarked at Santander on the 28th of September, and landed on the 5th of October at Portsmouth, amid the acclamations and transports of joy of all England. This time, Buckingham was of the same opinion as the people of England, and he henceforth exerted all his efforts towards preventing this marriage for which he had toiled so much, and which Spain at length appeared to seriously desire. In the month of January, 1624, the Earl of Bristol was recalled from Spain, where he had loyally served the king his master, and had made himself a mortal enemy in the Duke of Buckingham. The sumptuous preparations for the nuptials were suspended. The Infanta renounced the title of Princess of Wales, which she already bore, and war with Spain became imminent. King James, who detested war, and who had striven so many years for a union with Spain, was greatly dejected. "War," he said, "will not restore the Palatinate to my son-in-law." The Protestant enthusiasm of England and the ill-humor of Buckingham, helped on by the tardiness and the demands of the Pope and of Spain, had triumphed. Parliament, reluctantly convoked in 1624, immediately offered large subsidies, and the rigorous laws against the Catholics, suspended for a moment, were applied with more severity than ever. Alliances began to be formed against the House of Austria in Germany and in Spain. France, Savoy, Denmark, Sweden, united with England and Holland, which latter country had already resumed the war against her perpetual enemies. The object desired was now nothing less than completely to free the Low Countries from the presence of the Spaniards, and to retake the Palatinate. The English troops, placed under the orders of Prince Maurice of Nassau, had been defeated, and the prince had just died at the Hague. The Count of Mansfeldt, the great free-lance of those days, came to seek in England the reinforcements which had been promised to him. The soldiers were inexperienced, the quarters unhealthy; before arriving at the frontiers of the Palatinate half the troops were unfit for service. The Elector Palatine had not yet come very near the recovery of his domains.

While England was thus raising the standard of the Protestant war, King James was negotiating another Catholic marriage. He had long kept the court of Spain in suspense, pretending successively to seek for his two sons the hand of a French princess. When the affair evidently failed at Madrid, he turned again towards Paris. Cardinal Richelieu was more resolute, and his views were broader than those of Olivarez. "The marriage of the Princess Henrietta Maria with the King of England, and the league of the Protestant states under the protection of the King of France, were necessary to the greatness of France and to his own power."* He had formed the league against the House of Austria, and consolidated it by promising the sister of Louis XIII. to the Prince of Wales. A secret act, securing to the English

* M. Guizot, *Un Projet de Mariage royal.*

Catholics not only toleration, but more liberty and immunity, was signed on the 12th of December, 1624, by King James and the Prince of Wales. Preparations were already begun for receiving the French princess in London, when King James fell ill and died on the 6th of April, 1625, at the age of fifty-eight. He had been twenty-two years King of England. His foolish pretensions to absolute power, his religious tyranny, his bad and weak policy, had prepared the storm which was destined to burst upon the head of his son.

CHAPTER XXIII.

CHARLES I. AND HIS GOVERNMENT. 1625–1642.

KING JAMES I. had wearied his people, who had come at last to despise him. King Charles I. ascended the throne amidst popular enthusiasm. He was respected in advance, and his subjects were disposed to have confidence in him. Immediately upon his accession he convoked a Parliament, and when, on the 18th of June, 1625, the two Houses assembled at Westminster, the Parliament, as well as the king, was as yet ignorant of the profound hostility which separated a sovereign imbued with all the notions of absolute power which had been for half a century developing upon the Continent, and a people who, on their side, had made progress, and who now claimed to take a part in the affairs of the country and in their own government.

The struggle was not long in beginning. It was to the king that all the petitions and remonstrances of the House of Commons were addressed, but Parliament looked to everything and claimed to reform all abuses. The supplies necessary for carrying on the war against Spain were withheld during the examination of grievances. They had only been partially voted, when the king, young and impatient, wearied by delays and complaints, pronounced the dissolution of Parliament, and had recourse to a loan to procure himself money.

The loan succeeded ill, and the enterprise against Cadiz, which had rendered it necessary, having miscarried, the king found himself compelled to convoke another Parliament, which it was hoped would be found more docile; but at the court of Charles, and in the closest intimacy with him, lived a man, the favorite of the son as well as of the father, to whom the English people attributed the differences in sentiment and opinion which separated them from their sovereign. The Commons arrived in London, resolved to overthrow Buckingham. The king protected him, and angrily rejected the accusations which were presented. Two of the commissioners intrusted with the impeachment — Sir John Eliot and Sir Dudley Digges — were placed in the Tower for insolent words. On the 15th of June, 1626, the second Parliament of the reign of Charles I. was dissolved like the first, and the monarch felt himself king.

He was resolved to govern alone, but he had no money. The war with Spain and Austria weighed heavily upon his finances. Buckingham, animated by personal spite against Cardinal Richelieu, involved his master in a struggle with France, in the name of the interests of threatened Protestantism. It was thought that the heart of the English people would be regained, and its purse everywhere opened on announcing an expedition for the deliverance of La Rochelle, which was besieged. This expedition Buckingham himself was to command.

But distrust was felt towards the favorite and his zeal for the Protestant cause. The new loan supplied little money; the tax called ship-money, imposed for the first time upon the ports and sea-side districts, produced fewer vessels, armed and equipped, than had been hoped for, and the expedition sent to the assistance of La Rochelle failed miserably. Buckingham, who had effected a descent upon the island of Ré, was not able to take possession of it. He lost many men, and returned to England after this sanguinary blow, more hated and more despised than ever. "All the known or possible resources of tyranny had been exhausted." * The king and

* M. Guizot, *Histoire de la Révolution d'Angleterre.*

CHARLES I.

the favorite, haughty as they were, felt the necessity of becoming reconciled with the people. A new Parliament was convoked, and on the advice of Buckingham, as was everywhere announced.

This Parliament assembled on the 17th of March, 1628. There were numbered in it nearly all the men who, in their counties, had resisted the tyranny or exactions of the king. The language of Charles, on opening the session, was haughty and threatening. He had yielded, but he desired to raise himself in his own eyes as well as those of the world by an especially regal attitude. The Houses were not disturbed by his threats. They too were animated by a passionate and haughty resolve. Their purpose was openly to proclaim their liberties and have them recognized by the Government. The aged Coke, young Wentworth, destined shortly to serve the interests of absolute power under the name of Lord Strafford, Denzil Hollis, Pym, and many others, of different manners and different sentiments, but united in the same patriotic desire, were at the head of the Parliamentary coalition. Less than two months after its assembling, on the 8th of May, 1628, the House of Commons had voted the famous political declaration known under the name of the *Petition of Right.* After some hesitation, the Upper House accepted it also. The petition was immediately presented to the king, who, after struggling in vain for several weeks, ultimately promised his assent.

It was one of the misfortunes of Charles I., perhaps his greatest misfortune, to be unable to admit that a monarch owed to his subjects, however refractory, truth and fidelity. He evaded replying to the Petition of Right, contenting himself with protesting his attachment to Magna Charta, and he forbade the House to meddle in future with state affairs.

The exasperation was great. Charles and Buckingham

took alarm; they yielded. This Parliament, which had but lately been thought of no use but to vote subsidies, was already treated with upon a footing of equality; the Petition of Right was again presented to the king, and he replied with the usual formula, always uttered in French: *Soit droit fait comme il est désiré.* But the abuses were not reformed; it became a question of applying principles. The king collected the customs dues without the authority of Parliament. The conflict recommenced; the king wished to gain some respite without dissolving the Parliament. He prorogued the Houses until the month of January, 1629. Before that period, on the 23d of August, 1628, the Duke of Buckingham was assassinated by a disaffected officer named Felton, and in the hat of the latter was found some writing which recalled to mind the recent remonstrance of the House. The king, indignant and disconsolate, returned noiselessly into the path of despotism which he had, for a moment, appeared to forsake. He had lost a favorite odious to the Parliament; he detached from the coalition of the Commons one of its boldest and most esteemed chiefs. Sir Thomas Wentworth, soon afterwards Lord Strafford, entered the council of the king, notwithstanding the entreaties of his friends. When the House again assembled, on the 20th of January, 1629, it learned that the evasive reply of the king to the Petition of Right had alone been affixed at the bottom of the petition. The printer had received orders to modify the legal text in this manner. The commissioners of the Commons, intrusted to verify the matter, did not mention it,* as though ashamed to disclose such a breach of faith; but their silence did not promise oblivion.

All the attacks against still subsisting abuses recommenced. The king, on his part, endeavored to secure the concession of

* M. Guizot, *Histoire de la Révolution d'Angleterre.*

ASSASSINATION OF THE DUKE OF BUCKINGHAM.

the customs dues, which he claimed to obtain in advance and for all the duration of his reign, like the majority of his predecessors. The Commons remained immovable, the voting of subsidies being the sole efficacious weapon which remained to them wherewith to fight against absolute power. The king spoke of proroguing the Houses again. The Commons caused their doors to be closed in order to deliberate without restraint. As preparations were being made to open them by force, the Council were apprised that the members had retired, after having voted that the collecting of the customs duties was illegal, and that those who should raise them, or who should merely consent to pay them, were traitors to the country. On the 16th of March, 1629, the Parliament was dissolved. A few days afterwards the king published a declaration, which ended in these terms: "It is spread abroad, with evil design, that a Parliament will soon be assembled. His Majesty has well proved that he had no aversion to Parliaments, but their last excesses have determined him against his wish to change his conduct. He will in future account it presumption for any to prescribe a time to him for convoking a new Parliament."

The king was about to endeavor to govern alone, after having attempted in vain to govern with his Parliament.

The English people did not rise in revolt. They were exasperated and distrustful, their attention was occupied with the prosecutions which everywhere awaited the leaders of the parliamentary resistance; but there was nowhere any popular outbreak. At the beginning of his exercise of absolute power, Charles I. met no obstacle on the part of his subjects. It was his friends who soon caused embarrassment to his government. The capricious frivolity of Queen Henrietta Maria, her attachment to favorites ambitious and frivolous as herself, the court intrigues, and the division which was becoming greater and greater between these persons absorbed in pleasure and the nation, serious, zealous, passionately devoted to the affairs of this world and to those of eternal life, — such were the first obstacles encountered by King Charles and the two ministers to whom he had given his confidence, Lord Wentworth and Bishop Laud.

In forsaking the national party, to which he belonged rather through his hatred to Buckingham than from any fixed principles, Wentworth had embraced the royal cause with all his heart. "With an intellect too great to confine itself to domestic intrigues, and a pride too tyrannical to bow to the rules of court life, he gave himself up enthusiastically to business, braving all rivalry and breaking down all resistance, ardent in extending and strengthening the royal authority, which had become his own, but assiduous at the same time in re-establishing order, in repressing abuses, in subjugating private interests which he deemed illegitimate, in serving the general interests which he did not fear." * Laud, a friend of Wentworth, who was soon appointed archbishop of Canterbury, had, with passions less worldly and with sincere piety, carried to the Council the same dispositions and the same designs. He had less mental ability than his colleague, and "pursued incessantly, with an activity indefatigable but narrow, violent, and harsh, whatever fixed idea dominated him, with all the transport of passion and the authority of duty." *

Such counsellors would necessarily before long enter into contention with the court. Strafford (to give him the title under which he is known in history, although he did not yet bear it) went over to Ireland, where he re-established order in the country and in the finances, so that this kingdom, but lately a source of great expenditure, furnished, on the contrary, revenues to the king. Laud was commissioner of the treasury,

* M. Guizot, *Histoire de la Révolution d'Angleterre.*

and endeavored to apply the same rules in England; but the queen's prodigality, the somewhat disdainful generosity of the king, who readily granted pensions, and the sumptuous life of the court, exhausted the resources of the arbitrary but regular government of the two ministers. The central power was weak and inefficient, the foreign policy ill-directed, and the King of England was held in but little respect upon the Continent. The Barbary Corsairs ventured into the British Channel, and as far as St. George's Channel, landing, pillaging the houses along the coast, and making prisoners. The merchant navy in vain asked for protection; the royal fleet was unarmed and ill equipped. Everywhere money was wanted; recourse was had to ever-increasing exactions. Strafford had convoked the Irish Parliament, and had succeeded in chaining it at his feet like a docile slave. The king forbade him to assemble it again, for both he and the queen dreaded the very name of Parliament. There, as elsewhere, the able, skilful, and foreseeing minister suffered under the yoke of ignorant incompetence. Monopolies reappeared, affecting the trade in all the necessaries of life: justice was sold, and everything furnished matter for litigation, out of which there was no escape but in the payment of money. Absolutism continued without strength, while its contemptible tyranny and administrative abuses weighed upon all classes of the nation. The county gentlemen especially were always a mark for the rigors of authority, and saw grow up beside them, in every village, a new power. Laud had enrolled the Anglican Church in the service of his king; thus bringing to him a faithful and numerous militia. Charles, sincerely devout and an ardent Protestant, notwithstanding the weaknesses charged against him with regard to the Catholics, had the utmost confidence in this army which came to his assistance. The alliance between the king and the Church soon became close and irrevocable.

It was the Puritans, as the dissenting sects were then called, who bore the burden of this alliance. Laud insisted upon establishing everywhere an absolute conformity in rights and ceremonies, modifying them without scruple in a Roman Catholic direction. In all cases where the conscience of the Anglican ministers opposed these innovations they were dismissed from their livings. The churches which they went forth to found in France, Holland, and Germany, did not even secure to them the liberty of their faith. Laud claimed to extend his jurisdiction upon the Continent, and pursued them with his tyranny even on the foreign soil where they sought to find a home.

The numerous refugees who had been driven from their country by religious persecution, and who had obtained permission for the free exercise of their national worship in England, now found this permission recalled. Absolute conformity with the Anglican rite was required by the Archbishop, supported by the royal power. Imprisonment and exile overtook the delinquents on all hands.

The anger and terror of the English people were becoming great. The Reformation had been, in England, of a twofold character. Interested and worldly on the part of the king and the great noblemen, it had been earnest, sincere, profound, among the nation properly so called, and it had always leaned to the side of the Puritans. The novelties introduced by Laud into the forms of worship troubled minds and consciences alike. The Catholics rejoiced, and the Pope thought himself justified in offering to the Archbishop a cardinal's hat; but Laud wished only to secure the supremacy of the Anglican Church and of the bishops in the Anglican Church. When he caused the office of high treasurer to be given to Juxon, Bishop of London, Laud exclaimed in the excess of his joy, "Now that the Church subsists and supports itself unassisted, all is consummated; I can no more." He had done enough, for he had brought the Anglican Church to the brink of destruction, and had prepared for it the most serious disasters.

For some time discontent had been increasing among all classes of society. The weakness and incapacity of the general government, notwithstanding the efforts of Strafford and Laud, the pecuniary exactions and religious tyranny, threatened and exasperated all; numerous emigrations had begun; men passionately attached to their faith went to seek upon the Continent, and soon even in America, that liberty of worship which had been denied them in their own country. Obscure and unknown sectaries had been the first to adopt the refuge of exile; by degrees men of more importance followed their example. When an order of the royal council forbade emigration, a ship anchored in the Thames already had on board the future heroes of the revolution of England, about to expatriate themselves in order to escape an odious government. It was the king's own hand which retained in England Pym, Haslerig, Hampden, and Oliver Cromwell.

The popular indignation did not yet burst forth, but it began to be heard in suppressed tones; the assemblages of nonconformists increased everywhere under different names. The Independents, or Brownists, were the most numerous of those who separated themselves openly from the Anglican Church, and all the vigilance of Laud did not suffice to disperse these believers, nor his severity to punish them. Numerous pamphlets of a daring and vigorous kind circulated among the people. They were eagerly bought, and the rigors of the Star Chamber did not succeed in arresting the smugglers who brought them from Holland, and the peddlers who spread them throughout the country. It was resolved to make a great example: a lawyer, a clergyman, and a physician — Prynne, Burton, and Bastwick — were arrested at the same time, and, after an iniquitous trial, were condemned to the pillory, to lose their ears, to pay an enormous fine, and to be imprisoned for life.

The populace of London thronged around the pillory, when the three prisoners, pale and bleeding, were placed there. Their courage had not faltered for a moment, and their sufferings served their cause better than all their writings. A pamphleteer by profession, John Lilburne, condemned to a punishment of the same kind, received at the hands of the nation the same impassioned, albeit still silent sympathy. The whole country was moved, but it awaited a chief who should give the signal of legal resistance — a name around which the scattered forces might range themselves. It was John Hampden who had the honor to be this chief.

Hampden was a man of wealth, a serious and high-minded person. He lived quietly in Buckinghamshire, esteemed and honored by all. He was known to be adverse to the government, but not violently so, and when, in 1636, the king was desirous of collecting ship-money, which was illegal without the authorization of Parliament, Hampden was rated at twenty shillings only. He refused to pay, determining to bring the question before the courts. The trial was conducted with moderation on the part of the accused as well as on that of the prosecution and judges; there was no disrespect towards the royal government, there was no violence towards Hampden; but justice was not in the proceeding, and Hampden was condemned. The court congratulated themselves upon the decision which gave sanction to arbitrary power. They did not foresee that the name of Hampden was about to serve as a rallying-point to all discontents and all intrigues. The party of resistance was beginning to form in England.

The outburst came sooner and with more violence in Scotland. King James had succeeded in founding Episcopacy there against the wish and notwithstanding the traditional habits of a population ardently attached to the Presbyterian system; but the new bishops had been prudent and had attempted nothing, either against the clergy whom the people loved, or against the forms of worship to which they were accustomed. Charles I. and Laud were more bold. By degrees the bishops began to assert themselves; secure of being acknowledged and supported, they had become imbued with the doctrine of the divine right of Episcopacy, and had taken their place in political councils. The Archbishop of St. Andrews was chancellor of Scotland, the Bishop of Ross was about to become treasurer, nine bishops sat in the privy council. On the 23d of July, 1637, the Anglican liturgy was suddenly put in force in the cathedral at Edinburgh.

When the astonished people heard these accents, foreign to their ears and regarded by them as an approach to Popery, a profound and spontaneous emotion took possession of the whole assembly. An old woman threw her foot-stool at the head of the officiating clergyman; a popular tumult sprang up in the streets. Repression did not calm the excitement. From Edinburgh it spread into all the counties of Scotland. Every day the privy council, the municipal council, were besieged by a crowd, numerous, earnest, and ardent; by gentlemen, farmers, townsmen, artisans, peasants, who complained of the innovations introduced into their worship. Upon being ordered to retire, they gave way without violence, but the petitioners came back in greater numbers on the morrow. Everywhere resistance was organized, and when a royal order came finally, prohibiting any assemblage under pain of treason, following in the steps of the herald who read the royal proclamation, the Lords Hume and Lindsay, both peers of the realm, posted on the walls a protest which they had signed in the name of their fellow-citizens. The same thing was done in all places in which the king's proclamation was made public. Six weeks after the imprudent and arbitrary act of Charles, all Scotland was confederated under a solemn pledge called the "Covenant," at once a profession of religious faith, and a national protest against the new liturgy which the Government sought to impose upon them. The king and Laud had roused the whole Scottish nation to rebellion.

Charles was both astonished and indignant. Imbued with all the Continental principles respecting royal dignity and authority, he looked upon resistance as a crime of the lower classes, and marvelled to see the noblemen and gentlemen united in the same feeling to serve the same cause. He resolved immediately to have recourse to force in order to chastise the rebels, but he required time to raise an army. The Marquis of Hamilton, dispatched into Scotland to negotiate with the Covenanters, promised all that was desired, and authorized the assembling of a General Synod, wherein all controverted questions might be discussed. The assembly met at Glasgow; but the Scots, distrusting with good cause so much condescension, soon perceived that Hamilton sought only to delay matters. At the moment when the Synod was ready to accuse the bishops, the marquis suddenly pronounced its dissolution. At the same time it was learned that war was imminent, and that a body of troops raised in Ireland by Strafford would shortly disembark in Scotland. The king was preparing to chastise his rebellious subjects. Hamilton returned precipitately to London, while the Synod, without being disturbed at its dissolution, continued to deliberate, and abolished Episcopacy.

The Scottish Covenanters did not confine themselves to words, however serious and impassioned. They raised troops. The Scots who were serving upon the Continent, and one of their best officers, Alexander Lesley, formerly in the service of Gustavus Adolphus, were enjoined to return and defend their country.

The Scottish people addressed to the English, their brothers, a declaration intended to expound to them their grievances. Before the common beliefs and sentiments which now united the two peoples, the old national hatred between England and Scotland disappeared. When the king arrived at York with all his court, and his general, the Earl of Essex, entered Scotland, the two armies communicated with each other fraternally. The soldiers were more disposed to embrace than to fight. The royal troops did not begin the struggle. Lord Holland, who commanded the first corps, fell back without fighting. Negotiations were soon resorted to, and peace was concluded at Berwick on the 18th of June, 1639, without the firing of a shot. The disbanding of the two armies was resolved upon, as well as the convocation of a Synod and a Scottish Parliament; but the treaty did not affect the root of the difficulties, and the situation remained the same. It was a suspension of hostilities, not a peace.

Both parties felt this. The Scots disbanded their troops, but retained the officers. Charles summoned Lord Strafford from Ireland to his assistance; this was equivalent to announcing that he refused in advance all conciliation. "It is necessary," said the earl, "to bring back all these people to their senses with the lash." The conditions of peace with the Scots, ill-defined and scarcely reduced to writing, gave occasion to interminable discussions. The Parliament and the Synod assembled at Edinburgh raised every day fresh pretensions. War was resolved upon in the royal council, but a pretext was necessary. A letter, written by the Scottish chiefs to Louis XIII., with this simple address, *To the King*, fell into the hands of Strafford. The support of a foreign monarch was invoked. Charles I., indignant himself, thought that his indignation would be shared by all his people. He needed money wherewith to fight against the Scots; his coffers were empty, and he had exhausted every means, legal or otherwise, of obtaining resources. With a sudden resolution he convoked Parliament.

Great was the astonishment in England. Time had calmed the public excitement. The king, in his own person, had governed ill, but people remembered the impediments which the last Parliament had placed in the way of the royal administration; they desired more prudence and moderation in the newly-elected members. The former leaders of the liberal party re-entered the House; but they found themselves surrounded by a group of sensible, moderate men, resolved to abolish abuses without violence and without insult. They desired neither to alienate the king nor to disturb the peace of the country. Charles himself was animated by the same spirit towards the Parliament which he had been compelled to summon.

The power of circumstances easily triumphs over good intentions. Upon the reading of the letter of the Scots to the King of France the House remained cold; and thus the weapon upon which the king had reckoned failed him completely. Charles had decided for war, and demanded supplies, but the House was resolved that the public grievances should be redressed before the voting of the taxes. Negotiations were of no avail; the king began to grow angry; the Parliament was still calm, urging forward their discussion, but without departing from their pacific resolutions. At length the king caused the House to be informed that if they would vote twelve subsidies, payable in three years, he would abandon the system of demanding ship-money without the approbation of Parliament. The sum was enormous, they became alarmed and angry, but the House would not break with the king. They were about to proceed to the voting of some subsidies without fixing the amounts, when Sir Henry Vane, a favorite of Queen Henrietta Maria, who had been raised against the wish of Strafford to the post of Secretary of State, rose in his seat, and announced that, without adopting the entire message, the vote was useless; for the king would not accept a reduction of his demands. The anger and amazement of the Commons were at their height, when, on the morrow, at the moment of opening the sitting, the king caused them to be summoned to the Upper House, and announced the dissolution of Parliament; it was on the 5th of May, 1640; the Houses had assembled on the 13th of April.

Strafford had succeeded better than his master; he had obtained from the Irish Parliament all that he had asked, and the voluntary subscriptions which he instigated brought to the royal treasury nearly three hundred thousand pounds sterling. Vexations of all kinds resumed their course; the policy was to get money at all hazards. Strafford impelled the king towards despotism; it was necessary either to conquer or die. Twice the earl fell seriously ill; but he raised himself from his bed when scarcely recovered, and set out with the king for the army of Scotland, which he was to command.

The Scots did not wait for his arrival. They entered England, and defeated at Newburne the first English army which they encountered. It was an easy matter; the war was still less popular among the English people than it was with Parliament, and the secret dealings which existed between the Scottish generals and the chiefs of the malcontents in England were repeated among the soldiers. When Strafford assumed the command of the army, he found it undisciplined and disaffected. The two camps confronting each other were in reality animated by the same feelings as well as by the same beliefs. An action took place upon the banks of the Tyne, insignificant in itself, but the Scots crossed the river, and Strafford was compelled to fall back upon York, leaving the enemy masters of the north of England. The royal ardor had been vanquished by the popular ardor. All the authority and enthusiasm of the general could not make the soldiers fight against those whom they called their brothers, and Charles even had gone so far as to feel a dread of the energy of Strafford's policy. The negotiations between the two armies continued without regard to the king, notwithstanding the protestations of loyalty of the Scots. With the cry of *peace* began to be associated the word *Parliament.*

The king dreaded Parliaments. He endeavored to escape from the dilemma by convoking at York the great council of the peers of the realm, a feudal assembly, fallen into disuse for four centuries past. The peers had not yet assembled when two petitions, one from the City of London and the other signed by twelve of the most powerful noblemen, formally demanded the convocation of a real Parliament. The king no longer resisted. The great council of the peers appointed a commission who were to negotiate with the Scots. As a preliminary, it was decided that the two armies should remain on foot, both to be paid by the king. It was found necessary to provide for this expense by a loan, and the signatures of the sixteen commissioners were added to that of the king to guarantee the objects for which it was to be raised. Charles departed for London, weary and sad. The whole of England was ardently engaged in the elections, of which the importance was felt. Everywhere the candidates of the court were rejected. The assembling of the new Parliament was fixed for the 3d of November, a fatal date, it was said, for Laud. The Parliament assembled upon the same day under Henry VIII. had begun by overthrowing Wolsey, and had ended with the destruction of the abbeys. Laud refused to alter the date of the convocation. He was, like his master, weary of the struggle, and he abandoned himself, without further resistance, to the chances of a future as yet veiled in obscurity.

The session opened, and scarcely had the king quitted Westminster when his friends — few in number among the Commons — were compelled to realize that the public wrath was even greater than had been foreseen. The dissolution of the last Parliament had made the cup overflow. Charles, imbued with the haughty idea of absolute power, had desired to govern alone. In principle Parliament did not claim the sovereignty, but the Commons felt their strength, and were resolved to exert it. The monarch was foredoomed to defeat.

The session began with a long and complete enumeration of grievances. Tyrannical misdeeds were numerous, and all were brought to light. Monopolies, ship-money, arbitrary arrests, venality of justice, the bishops' exactions, the Star-Chamber proceedings, nothing was spared. Before considering the redress of wrongs, it was voted that complaints were legitimate; they rained down from all quarters, and more than forty committees spent their days in receiving the petitions which came from the counties. Everywhere were drawn up lists of "delinquents," a name given to the agents of the crown who had taken part in the execution of the measures reprobated. Without any definite action being taken against these numerous offenders, they found themselves suddenly in danger of being summoned before the House, and condemned to a fine, imprisonment, or confiscation. All the king's servants were thus placed at the mercy of their enemies. Once inscribed upon the list of "delinquents," no man could enjoy an instant's repose.

The explosion of the new power was sudden and terrible. Strafford had foreseen it. He begged the king to excuse him from appearing before the Parliament. "I cannot," Charles answered him, "do without your counsels here. As truly as I am King of England, you incur no danger; they shall not touch a hair of your head." Strafford was not reassured. He set out, however, bold as usual, and resolved to strike the first blow. He was not allowed time to do so: on the 9th of November he arrived in London ill; on the 11th, upon the motion of Pym, the House of Commons charged him with high-treason. "The least delay may ruin all," the latter said. "If the earl has communication but once with the king, the Parliament will be dissolved; besides, the House are not judges, but only accusers." At this moment Strafford arrived at the House of Lords, but his impeachment had preceded him. The door was closed; the earl caused it to be opened to him, and he was entering the House when his colleagues called out to him to withdraw. He stopped, looked round him, and obeyed after a few minutes' hesitation. Being recalled an hour afterwards, he was enjoined to kneel down at the bar. There he learned that the House had admitted the impeachment of the Commons. On the same evening he was conducted to the Tower, whither Laud was conveyed not many days afterwards.

Some other important personages were accused with Strafford; but it was upon the latter that vengeance concentrated itself. Scotland and Ireland united with England to overwhelm him with the proofs of his arbitrary rule. For nothing less than this league of three nations against the imprisoned minister could satisfy the feeling of hatred and apprehension among the people.

The House of Commons was henceforth master of the Government; commissioners taken from its midst alone had the right of administering the supplies which it voted, and the loans which it decreed in its own name. Political reforms, important and radical, succeeded each other almost without discussion, upon a simple exposition of grievances. The exceptional tribunals were all abolished, a law was passed requiring triennial Parliaments. If the king should fail in this duty, twelve peers of the kingdom assembled at Westminster were empowered to summon the Houses without his concurrence. Parliament could not be dissolved or adjourned without the approbation of the two Houses, at least for fifty days after its assembling. The king accepted the bill with ill-humor; but he attempted no resistance. He hoped, and he had some reason to hope, for divisions among his enemies.

Upon political questions there was agreement. Hampden, Pym, Hollis, Stapleton, moderate leaders of the Commons, were followed by Cromwell and Henry Martyn, more violent, but as yet obscure. The divergences of feeling were made manifest when the discussion turned upon matters of religion. The question of Episcopacy, passionately attacked by the numerous Presbyterians in the House, was not yet settled, and in the nation opinions were as various and conflicting as in the House. The friends of the king advised him to attach himself to the more moderate of the political chiefs, and to take advantage of the religious differences which were at work in the party. Secret negotiations were opened; but at the same time, through the intervention of the queen, Charles was receiving the proposals of a certain number of officers of the army, dissatisfied with the favor which Parliament manifested towards the Scots. Various schemes, all menacing for the House, were discussed without much result and without the proposal of any practicable measures. The king listened to all, and often accorded his approbation. He even consented to affix the initials of his name to the petition which the army was to lay before the Houses. This petition was never presented; but the chiefs of the popular party were apprised of it, and without a word, not even breaking off their negotiations with the king, they came to the decision to unite with the fanatical Presbyterians, and to ruin Strafford. The trial of the earl began.

The Commons of England were the prosecutors, supported by commissioners from Scotland and Ireland. Eighty peers were present as judges. The bishops were absent against their wish, yielding to the desire of the Commons. The king and queen were there, "in a closed gallery,* eager to see all, but concealing, the one his anguish, the other her curiosity." The crowd of spectators was immense.

The accused arrived without suffering any insult from the multitude. "As he passed, his frame prematurely bowed by illness, but with the proud and brilliant look that had distinguished his youth, the crowd gave way, all raised their hats, and he bowed courteously, looking upon this attitude of the people as of good augury." He was full of hope, not at all doubting the happy issue of his trial. He was soon undeceived.

For seventeen days he sustained his cause without aid against thirteen accusers. The most odious impediments embarrassed his defence; but the earl manifested neither bitterness nor anger.† He simply claimed his right, thanking his judges if they consented to recognize it, forbearing from complaint if they refused, and replying to his enemies, angered by the delay arising from his skilful resistance, "It is as much my business, I think, to defend my life, as for any other to attack it." The Commons trembled with rage, for Strafford was gaining the ascendancy. The examination into the facts cleared the earl from the charge of high-treason. The text of the law, and the steadfast ability of the accused, had triumphed over all the obstacles opposed to the defence. Sir Arthur Haslerig proposed to declare Strafford guilty by Act of Parliament, and to condemn him by a bill of attainder. This proceeding was more violent and arbitrary than most of the acts with which Strafford had been so loudly reproached; but passion easily blinds even the most sincere. The bill, resting upon certain notes of Strafford delivered

* M. Guizot, *Histoire de la Révolution d'Angleterre.*

† Ibid.

by the son of Sir Henry Vane, at once obtained a first reading. This time, Strafford was accused of having advised the king to employ the army of Ireland for the subjugation of England. "Some thought they sacrificed law to justice; others, justice to necessity." *

The trial meanwhile continued. Before his counsel began to speak to the question of law, Strafford himself summed up his defence with admirable eloquence. "My Lords," he said, in conclusion, "your ancestors have carefully bound with the chains of our statute law these terrible accusations of high-treason; do not be ambitious of being more learned in the art of killing than our forefathers. Let us not awaken those sleeping lions to our destruction, by raking up a few musty records that have lain by the walls so many ages forgotten or neglected. I have troubled you, my Lords, longer than I should have done; were it not for the interest of those pledges that a saint in heaven left me" — at these words he stopped, burst into tears, but immediately raising his head, continued — "I would not give myself so much trouble to defend this body already falling into decay, and burdened with so many infirmities, that of a truth I have little pleasure in bearing the burden of it any longer;" here he stopped, as if in search of an idea. "My Lords," he resumed, "you will pardon my infirmity of weeping. I should have added, but am not able, therefore let it pass. And so, my Lords, even so, with all tranquillity of mind, I freely submit myself to your judgment, and whether that judgment be of life or death, *Te Deum laudamus.*"

Compassion and admiration had moved the most implacable enemies of the earl. Pym, in agitation, sought in vain for the paper upon which he had written his reply. None gave ear to him, and the prosecuting officer hastened to con-

* M. Guizot, *Histoire de la Révolution d'Angleterre.*

clude his speech, vexed and confused by his involuntary emotion.

It was necessary at all cost to have done with an enemy so able, and even when a prisoner, so powerful by the mere force of his courage and eloquence. The second reading of the bill of attainder was hastened on; the most able and distinguished lawyers contended against it; the infuriated Commons sought to prevent the Lords from listening to Strafford's counsel. The Lords resisted, and heard the pleadings, but the Lower House were not present, and, four days later, on the 21st of April, 1641, the bill was definitively passed. Fifty-nine members alone voted against it.

The king was most unhappy and anxious. He had himself exposed Strafford to this danger. "Be assured," he wrote to him, "upon my word as a king, that you shall suffer nothing, either in your life, or your fortune, or your honor." Negotiations and conspiracies were tried by turns, or together. Attempts were made to mollify the chiefs of the Commons, or to obtain in the House of Lords a majority in favor of the earl. Enormous offers were made to the Governor of the Tower, Sir William Balfour, to allow the prisoner's escape. All attempts failed in the presence of official fidelity and popular passion. The king at length caused the two Houses to be summoned, and, admitting the faults of the earl, and promising that he would never employ him again, even in the humblest office, he at the same time declared to them also that no reason, nor any threat, would ever make him consent to his death.

Charles presumed too much upon his own courage. He did not yet know how skilful and bold was the hatred of the Commons for Strafford. Popular violence was added to the Parliamentary prosecution. The Upper House, before which the bill of attainder had been brought, was besieged daily by a furious multitude, crying, "Justice! justice!" The Lords were insulted and were summoned to declare themselves. Pym had held in reserve what he knew of the plot of the court and the officers to excite the army against the Parliament; he now made it public. Some of the accused who had received warning fled, and terror spread in the House as well as among the people. It was decreed that all ports should be closed, and that all letters coming from abroad should be examined. Calling to mind the conspiracy of Guy Fawkes, some circulated a rumor that the Houses were undermined, and the people hastened thither to ascertain or to share the danger. Meanwhile the two Houses united themselves by an oath for the defence of the Protestant religion and of the public liberties. An attempt was even made to impose the same pledge upon all the citizens. In vain the Lords strove against the rising tide; they endeavored to modify the bill of attainder. This the Commons refused; they were resolved to obtain their complete vengeance. The Upper House yielded; thirty-four of the Lords who had been present at the trial absented themselves; twenty-six voted for the bill, fourteen against it; nothing was now wanting but the acquiescence of the king.

Charles still resisted. His affection and his honor were equally shocked. Hollis, brother-in-law of Strafford, advised the king to go himself and present to the Houses the petition of the earl, asking a respite. He promised to induce his friends in the House to be content with banishment; but the queen beset her husband with her apprehensions. She did not like Strafford; she was terrified by the riots; she wished to fly, to embark, to return to France. The king listened to her, troubled and undecided. He convoked the privy council, then the bishops. Juxon alone advised him to follow his conscience; all the others persisted that

Charles should sacrifice an individual to a throne, his conscience as a man to his conscience as a king. The Earl of Essex had said shortly before: "The king is obliged to conform both in regard to his person and his conscience to the advice and conscience of the Parliament." His servants were repeating to him under another form this harsh truth, when Charles received a letter from Strafford himself. "Sir," wrote the earl, "with much sadness I am come to a resolution of that which I take to be best becoming me, and to look upon it as that which is most principal in itself, which doubtless is the prosperity of your sacred person and the commonwealth, — things infinitely before any man's private interest. And therefore in few words, as I put myself wholly upon the honor and justice of my peers, so clearly as to wish your Majesty might please to have spared that declaration of yours on Saturday last, and entirely to have left me to their lordships; so now, to set your Majesty's conscience at liberty, I do most humbly beseech your Majesty to remove this unfortunate thing forth of the way towards that blessed agreement which God I trust shall ever establish between you and your subjects. Sir, my consent shall more acquit you herein to God than all the world can do besides. To a willing man there is no injury done, and as by God's grace I forgive all the world with a calmness and meekness of infinite contentment to my dislodging soul, so, Sir, to you I can give the life of this world with all the cheerfulness imaginable, in the just acknowledgment of your exceeding favors; and only beg, that, in your goodness, you would vouchsafe to cast your gracious regard upon my poor son and his three sisters less or more, and no otherwise than as their (in present) unfortunate father may hereafter appear more or less guilty of this death."

On the morrow Strafford learned in his prison that the

king had given his assent to the fatal bill. He did not reply, but raising his hands towards heaven, he softly repeated this passage of the Psalm: "Put not your trust in princes nor in the sons of men, for in them there is no salvation."

This was on the 10th of May. On the morrow, the 11th, the Prince of Wales presented himself before Parliament with a letter from the king ending with these words: "If he must die, it were charity to reprieve him till Saturday." Without taking heed of this last and miserable effort of Charles in favor of his great servant, the House appointed the morrow for the execution.

Strafford came forth on foot from his prison, walking before his guards as though he were marching at the head of his army. He had declined the coach offered him by the Governor of the Tower, who feared the violence of the people. "No, Master Lieutenant," he said, "I dare look death in the face, and I hope the people too. I care not how I die, whether by the hand of the executioner or by the madness and fury of the people. If that may give them better content, it is all one to me." Passing under the window of Laud's prison, he stopped. The old archbishop, informed on the previous evening of what was about to happen, stretched out his arms to bless the condemned man; but, agitated and enfeebled, he swooned and fell. "Farewell, my lord," said Strafford, as he went away, "God protect your innocence." He knelt upon the scaffold; then, rising, he addressed the immense crowd which surrounded him. "I wish," he said, "to this kingdom all the prosperity on earth: alive, I have always done so; dying, it is my only wish. But I implore each of those who listen to me to consider earnestly, with his hand upon his heart, whether the beginning of the reformation of a kingdom should be written in characters of blood. Think of it in returning to your homes. God forbid that the least drop of my blood fall upon any of you! But I fear that you are in a bad way." He knelt again, then shook hands with the friends who accompanied him. "I have nigh done," he said; "one stroke will make my wife husbandless, my dear children fatherless, and my poor servants masterless. But let God be to them all in all." He prepared himself to receive the fatal blow. "I thank God," he continued, "I am no more afraid of death, nor daunted with any discouragement arising from any fears, but do as cheerfully put off my doublet at this time as ever I did when I went to bed." He called to the executioner, and himself gave the signal.

"God save the king!" exclaimed the executioner, as he held up the head to the people. Shouts of triumph answered him; but some were silent, and many people returned to their houses sad, uneasy, and almost doubting the justice of the act which they had so ardently desired.

The feeble policy of the king had missed its mark, as such a policy always does. Strafford's death had not removed the obstacle in the way of a reconciliation between the king and his subjects. In accepting the bill which struck down the most illustrious of his servants, Charles had at the same time, and almost without observing it, sanctioned a bill which prohibited any dissolution of Parliament without the consent of both Houses. But harmony, far from being re-established, became every day less possible between the king and the people. The power which the Commons had wrested piece by piece from the sovereign seemed to impel them more and more towards tyranny. The political reform was accomplished, but the religious reform remained to be effected. Notwithstanding the moral enfeeblement of the Anglican Church it retained its position. It was henceforth against this object that were directed the confused and often contradictory efforts of many of the leaders of the Commons and of the people; but on the

STRATFORD GOING TO EXECUTION.

religious question their unanimity was not so complete as on the political, and the bold innovators were uneasy in the very midst of their success.

Charles suddenly announced his intention of visiting Scotland, where his presence had, he said, become necessary for the execution of the treaty of peace. At the same time the queen prepared to make a journey to the Continent. The House took alarm; they dreaded the king's passing through the army, which was being disbanded and was known to be disaffected; they feared the secret manœuvres of the queen among the absolute sovereigns. They asked Charles to delay his departure; they implored the queen to remain in England: both consented. The disbanding of the army was in vain hurried on by promising the soldiers the arrears of their pay. Money was borrowed, plate was melted down to suffice for this enormous expenditure. The work was not completed when the king at length set out on the 10th of August. On the 27th the House adjourned, and a committee, with Hampden at its head, was sent to Scotland to remain with the king, in order to watch over the interests of Parliament.

The measure was prudent and effective. Charles passed through the English and Scottish armies without daring to stay long; but his attempts to influence the officers had meanwhile engaged the attention of Lord Holland, who was intrusted with the disbandment. He wrote on this matter with uneasiness to the Earl of Essex in London. On arriving in Edinburgh the king accorded to the Scottish Parliament and Church all the religious and political concessions which they asked. He attended the Presbyterian worship with a pious gravity which touched the Scots. He appeared to have again taken into favor and confidence that early kingdom of his fathers, which had once risen as one man against the tyranny that attempted to interfere with its faith. The chiefs of the

Covenanters themselves were received with eager kindness. Distrustful people in Scotland, anxious lookers-on in England, in vain endeavored to penetrate the mystery of this conduct.

Suddenly it became known that the two most influential of the great lords in the Scottish Parliament, Hamilton and Argyll, had left Edinburgh with their friends, and had retired into the country to escape the danger of arrest. The king loudly complained of the conjectures which were in circulation; the Parliament ordered an inquiry. The proceedings were in secret; the committee declared, without any particulars, that there was no claim on the side of the king for any reparation nor ground for any alarm on the part of the fugitives. The latter resumed their seats in the Parliament, and the public knew nothing of what had happened.

Nothing was known, but the object of the king's journey into Scotland had failed. It had been his expectation to collect upon the spot such proofs of the correspondence of the English malcontents with the Covenanter chiefs of Scotland that the judges could not help declaring guilty of high-treason those leaders of the Commons who had, by their intrigues, caused the invasion of their country. He intended to hurl against them the accusation which Strafford had not had time to prepare. The hopes of the king were sustained by his correspondence with a young and impetuous nobleman, the Earl of Montrose, formerly attached to the Covenant, but who had now given himself up body and soul to the royal cause. In Scotland the king had found Montrose in prison, suspected by Argyll; but the prison bolts were drawn now and then. Montrose had come by night to see Charles; he had led the king to be suspicious of Hamilton and Argyll, asserting that their papers would furnish the desired proofs. The arrest of the two noblemen was agreed upon, when the latter frustrated the scheme by publicly quitting the Parliament and the city. Far from ridding himself of his enemies, Charles was compelled to load them with favors: Hamilton was made a duke, Argyll a marquis, Lesley, the general of the Scottish troops, became Earl of Leven. But appearances did not deceive Hampden; he knew all, and informed his London friends of the facts. The recess of Parliament was nearly at an end.

Great was the terror among the Parliamentary leaders when they received proof of the vindictive rancor of the king. They consulted with one another anxiously upon the course to be pursued. The Scottish Parliament had wisely suppressed the affair. The English Parliament could not make use of it to agitate the people. Ireland undertook this task.

On the 1st of November, 1641, it was suddenly reported that a great insurrection had broken out in Ireland, threatening the most imminent danger to the Protestant religion and the Protestants of the country. The Catholics had everywhere risen, chiefs and people, claiming the liberty of their faith, vaunting the name of the queen and even of the king, setting up a commission signed, it was said, by the latter, and announcing the design of delivering Ireland and the throne from the tyranny of the English Puritans. On the very day before the conspiracy was to break out it had been accidentally discovered and quelled in Dublin. Throughout the country it had met with no obstacle. Murders, fires, horrible and nameless crimes, it is said, were rife throughout Ireland. Everywhere the Protestants were massacred without resistance. The Government, disarmed by hatred of Strafford and the crown, found itself powerless in the presence of a half savage people eager to avenge in one day centuries of outrage and misery. The Earl of Leicester, appointed viceroy in the place of Strafford, had not yet arrived. Against so terrible a storm the English Government had in Ireland only two judges, men of no ability, of no credit, whose Presbyterian zeal alone had caused them to be invested with that difficult employment.

England uttered a prolonged cry of terror and rage; every Protestant considered himself attacked in common with his Irish brethren. The king, who had no knowledge of the insurrection, hastened to communicate to Parliament the information which had reached him in Scotland, placing the affair in the hands of the Commons and intrusting them with the repression, partly to rid himself of all complicity, partly to avoid in the eyes of his Catholic subjects, whom he had not encouraged, but whom he was in no hurry to restrain, the responsibility for the severities to which they might be compelled to submit.

The leaders of the Commons were not much more eager than the king to stamp out the Irish insurrection. It furnished them with the popular agitation and general uneasiness of which they stood in need in order to continue their work. They had eagerly seized upon the power which the king offered them; but their efforts against the Irish insurgents were more ostentatious than sincere, and more noisy than efficacious. The Protestants of Ireland were left in the hands of their enemies. All speeches and all acts were directed towards England; the moment for striking the great blow had come.

Shortly after the opening of the session, in the month of November, 1640, a committee was chosen to prepare, together with an exposition of grievances, a solemn remonstrance to the king; but political reforms had been so rapid, and the king had so completely given way before the growing power of Parliament, that most of the grievances had in reality disappeared, when, on the morrow of the Irish insurrection, amid the popular excitement, the committee received orders to resume and complete its work without delay. The remonstrance but lately intended for the king became a sombre exposition addressed to the people, going over all past evils, and all which yet subsisted, the king's misdeeds, the virtues of Parliament, and the dangers which faith and liberty incurred so long as the nation was not unreservedly devoted to the House of Commons, the only power capable of saving them from Popery, the bishops, and the king.

So much violence, without fresh pretexts or any direct or apparent aim, raised numerous murmurs. The ever-growing pretensions of Parliament began to create, even in its midst, a party of resistance, favorable, in a certain measure, to the threatened royal power. The popular chiefs sought to quiet the distrust and exasperation, asserting that they only wished to intimidate the court and to thwart its intrigues, and that, the remonstrance being once adopted, it should not be promulgated. They asked for the vote towards the end of a sitting, at the moment when the House, being fatigued, was about to separate. Lord Falkland, Hyde, Colepepper — the friends of the king as they were called — desired that the question should be postponed till the morrow. "Why," said Cromwell to Falkland, "do you so greatly desire this delay?" "Because it is too late to-day, and sure it will take some debate." "A very sorry debate," replied Cromwell tranquilly. On the morrow the discussion began; sides were taken. For the first time two national parties were arrayed against each other. It was no longer the court and the country; the nation itself was divided, and both sides found support in public interests and opinions. There were discussions; there was vehement speaking. Hour after hour passed by; the sitting had opened at three o'clock; it was now midnight. Members in feeble health or advanced in years had all retired. "This," said Sir Benjamin Rudyard, "will be the verdict of a starved jury." When the vote was taken, a hundred and fifty-nine members adopted the remonstrance, a hundred and forty-eight rejected it.

The result had scarcely been announced when Hampden rose and demanded that the remonstrance should be printed. "We said so," it was exclaimed on the other side: "you wish to take from the Lords their legitimate share of authority; you desire to walk alone and arouse the people to insurrection." "I protest, I protest!" exclaimed Mr. Palmer, and his friends followed his example. Protests were usual in the House of Lords; they were not so in the Lower House. Indignation was felt at this new proceeding, and the disturbance increased; several members had their hands upon their swords. Hampden addressed the House, deploring this sad disorder, and proposing to adjourn the discussion to the morrow. This was agreed to. "Well," said Lord Falkland to Cromwell, on leaving, "has it been debated?" "I will take your word another time," replied Cromwell, and he added in a lower tone: "If the remonstrance had been rejected, I would have sold all I have the next morning, and never would have seen England more, and I know there are many honest men of the same resolution." The printing of the remonstrance was voted on the morrow without disturbance, almost without discussion, by a majority of twenty-three. To publish it they only awaited the return of the king, to whom it must first be presented.

He arrived and was magnificently received by the city of London, the new lord-mayor, Richard Gurney, being devoted to him. Already confiding in the movement which manifested itself in his favor, he at once allowed his new hopes to be revealed by withdrawing from the Commons the guard which the Earl of Essex had given to them for their safety in his absence.

The remonstrance was immediately presented to Charles;

he listened patiently to the reading of it. "Doth the House intend to publish this declaration?" he asked. "We are not authorized to answer the questions of your Majesty." "Well, then," continued his Majesty, "I suppose you do not expect a present answer to so long a petition; I will send it to you as soon as the importance of the affair will allow." The leaders of the Commons did not wait for the royal answer before proposing to the Houses what were no longer reforms, but innovations. A bill relating to the impressment of soldiers, another to the militia, a third excluding the clergy, of whatever grade they might be, from all civil offices, were presented and adopted in a few days by the Lower House. The remonstrance was published on the 14th of December. The popular ardor corresponded with the new attitude, from day to day more impassioned, of the leaders of the opposition.* The aspect of affairs was undergoing a change; to a unanimous national movement succeeded the strife of parties; to reform, revolution. Parliament asked to have their guard back again; but the multitude which thronged around Westminster, the committees formed in all places for the defence of liberty and the faith, represented a militia more formidable than any soldiery, on the watch to proclaim with loud outcries the common danger.

The king did not stand alone against this bold and persevering effort of the popular reformers. Among the most esteemed members of the House of Commons who had fought against tyranny, a certain number, and these of the best, had been brought back to the crown by the dread of innovations and excesses. Charles resolved to secure the attachment of the chiefs of this growing royalist party — Mr. Hyde, Sir John Colepepper, and Lord Falkland. The latter did not please him; on his part, Lord Falkland had little

* M. Guizot, *Histoire de la Révolution d'Angleterre.*

esteem for the king, and a great effort of his friends was necessary in order to induce him to enter publicly into the royal service. He allowed himself to be overcome by the solicitations of Charles himself, constrained, as it were, by necessity; but when he accepted the office of Secretary of State, it was with a profound sense of discouragement and as the victim* of a devotion without affection and without hope. The three friends undertook the difficult task of directing the king's affairs in the House, and the latter promised to attempt nothing without their advice.

Charles could no more keep his word with his friends than with his enemies. He drew courage from the adhesion of the gentlemen attached by tradition to the throne, who arrived with clamor from their counties to offer to the king their service. Every day struggles took place in the streets, and particularly around Westminster, between the partisans of the king, the "Cavaliers" as they were called, and the "Roundheads," a name which the Cavaliers themselves gave to the citizens on account of the contrast which the short hair of the Puritans presented to the long curls of the courtiers. The bill for the exclusion of the bishops, still in suspension in the Upper House, was the special cause of outbreaks. The bishops every day ran risk of their lives in attending the session, and they were obliged on leaving to shelter themselves in the carriages of some popular noblemen. The House of Commons made no reply to the complaints of the Lords against the disturbance excited at its doors. "We need all our friends," said the leaders; "God forbid that we should prevent the people obtaining thereby that which they are right in desiring." At the same time the Commons decreed, that as the king persisted in refusing their guard, each of the members was entitled to bring an armed servant and to

* M. Guizot, *Histoire de la Révolution d'Angleterre.*

keep him at the door. Blood was shed incessantly around Westminster Palace.

The bishops adopted their course, a course strange and somewhat frivolous in so grave a situation: they resolved to absent themselves, protesting in advance against all bills which might be adopted during their absence, as not invested with the assent of the necessary members of Parliament. This declaration, signed by twelve bishops, being communicated to the king, was approved by him; he seized it as a pretext which would one day permit him to annul the acts of this indomitable Parliament against which he was struggling without success. He did not speak of the matter to his new councillors; but, on the same day, the Keeper of the Great Seal carried, by his orders, the protest of the bishops to the Upper House, who sent it immediately to the Commons.

The surprise of the Lords and the anger of the Commons were great, and the popular leaders were able immediately to find therein a new weapon. The impeachment of the bishops was suddenly proposed and resolved upon; they had assumed to determine the fate of Parliament itself, and to destroy it by absenting themselves from its sessions; they were conducted to the Tower, upon the vote of the Upper House, which received the indictment of the Commons. The point was urged further. The king had taken the government of the Tower from Sir William Balfour, to intrust it to a Cavalier, Sir Thomas Lunsford, a man of ill repute and very violent. The appointment of a new governor was demanded. Lord Digby, formerly animated with a patriotic zeal, but now become the most intimate confidant of the king, was denounced for having said that the Parliament was not free. The Commons again claimed their right to have a guard.

Charles did not lose his temper at so many proofs of growing distrust; he named as governor of the Tower, Sir John Byron, a man esteemed by all, and to the request of the House he replied: "We do engage to you solemnly on the word of a king, that the security of all and every one of you from violence is and ever shall be as much our care as the preservation of ourselves and our children;" but he refused the guard. The House caused the militia of London to be mustered, and bodies of troops were posted in different parts of the city.

END OF VOL. II.

www.ingramcontent.com/pod-product-compliance
Lightning Source LLC
LaVergne TN
LVHW021241110826
845150LV00002B/379

* 9 7 8 1 4 2 5 5 6 1 4 7 5 *